Picture from 2002 FIA Championship

Bad news for Formula One drivers.
Next season he'll be racing on Bridgestone tyres again.

Sorry, there's no good news.

Bridgestone congratulates Ferrari and Michael Schumacher on the 2002 FIA World Championship title.

As we have achieved our fifth consecutive World Championship success, we'd like to congratulate Ferrari and Michael Schumacher on their own impressive run of victories. At the same time, we'd like to point out that Bridgestone's race-winning tyre technology is also available to you, even if you don't happen to drive a Ferrari.

A GRIP ON THE FUTURE

www.bridgestone.com

ISBN 0-75259-146-0

© November 2002, Chronosports S.A.

Lausanne: Jordils Park, Chemin des Jordils 40, CH-1025 St-Sulpice, Switzerland. Tel. : (+41 21) 694 24 44. Fax : (+41 21) 694 24 46.
Paris: Chronosports France, 53 rue Boissière, F-75116 Paris, France. Tel. : (+33) (0)1 47 20 46 22. Fax : (+33) (0)1 47 20 46 22.
Milan: Chronsports Italia, Via Razori 4, I-20145 Milan, Italy. Tel. : (+39) 02 4810 2477. Fax : (+39) 02 4853 1805.

This is a Parragon book

This edition published in 2002

Parragon
Queen Street House
4 Queen Street
Bath BA1 1HE, UK

Copyright © Parragon

FORMULA 1 YEARBOOK
2002-03

Pictures
LAT Photographic, Thierry Gromik, Steve Domenjoz, Mario Renzi

(LAT Photographic: Steven Tee, Clive Rose, Lorenzo Bellanca, Charles Coates, Michael Cooper, Martyn Elford, Steve Etherington, Chris Dixon)

Conception and Grands Prix reports
Luc Domenjoz

Page layout
Cyril Davillerd, Solange Amara, Sabrina Favre

Results and statistics
Sara Bochicchio, Désirée Ianovici, Aline Zwahlen, André Vinet

Drawings 2002
Pierre Ménard

Gaps charts
Michele Merlino

Technical summary
Giorgio Piola

Contents

Foreword

"With the 2002 season over, I am delighted to write the preface to "The Formula 1 Yearbook" at the end of a year which brought so much success for Scuderia Ferrari.

2002 was indeed a record year for Scuderia Ferrari. This season we managed to notch up a fourth consecutive Constructors' title, while Michael Schumacher took his third Drivers' crown with us, the fifth of his career.

We managed to do even better than in 2001, setting a new record for the number of points scored in a season, totalling the same number as all the other teams put together and winning fifteen races, including nine one-two finishes.

Our car proved to be extraordinarily reliable this season, with Michael Schumacher completing every single one of the 1090 laps on the 2002 world championship calendar. Unfortunately, we were not able to achieve the same level of reliability on Rubens Barrichello's car.

Our team tackled the championship with an even more united spirit than ever. Because these successes, far from lessening our thirst for victory, only served to sharpen it. The atmosphere within our squad is that of a "dream team", although we were aware that we could trip up at any moment.

Ferrari is now at the summit. It is considered as the ultimate reference point in Formula 1. Our motivation, as well as our passion for motor racing and for Ferrari is such that we will do all in our power to reach the same level of success in 2003. If for the only reason of pleasing all our "tifosi" around the world.

Enjoy the read, "

Jean Todt

In a world of their own
By Didier Braillon «L'Equipe»

Didier Braillon
48 years old, he first discovered F1 in 1979 working for French magazine Autohebdo, before taking hold of the reins at Grand Prix International magazine in 1982. When the publication folded in 1984, he became press officer for the Ram team, followed by a spell with the daily paper Le Sport, in 1987. A short time in charge of media relations for the Larrousse team led to a job with the France Soir paper in 1989. In 1991, he moved to Course Auto, a weekly from the Amaury stable, from where he was switched to the auto section of L' Equipe at the start of 1992 and he has been there ever since.

There are so many remarkable figures to pick on, but perhaps the most remarkable is this one: Ferrari scored 221 points this season, courtesy of its two sublime F2002s, which is exactly the same number as managed by all the other teams put together. From Williams to Arrows, via McLaren, Renault, Sauber, Jordan, Jaguar, BAR, Minardi and Toyota, the ten other players in the Formula 1 game needed twenty cars to amass half of the 442 points on offer, given there are 26 up for grabs at each of the 17 grands prix.

Let's take another statistic. Not only did Michael Schumacher set new records or establish a higher level for ones he held already; not only is he now a five times world champion, thus joining the legendary Juan Manuel Fangio in the pantheon of motor sport, but he also managed to finish every race on the podium. Not one retirement and always in the top three as he crossed the finish line! If the perfect score in a year is 170 points, consider this; Michael Schumacher scored 144.

The F2002 reached such a level of performance that there were times when the only thing it appeared to have in common with the opposition was the fact it was racing on the same circuits. It was even more reliable than the previous year's F2001, which was itself used by Schumacher, in modified form for the first two race. In his hands, it proved unbelievably robust, although Rubens Barrichello was hit with a few malfunctions at the start of the summer. Schumacher last posted a retirement on 29th July 2001 in Hockenheim, when he suffered a loss of fuel pressure. This year he averaged 8.47 points per grand prix. However, his score could have been even higher come Sunday night in Suzuka, because such was the backlash of the Spielberg "scandal" that team orders were immediately imposed to re-establish some sort of balance.

On 12th May, when Barrichello followed Jean Todt's orders and moved over for Michael within sight of the flag, Schumacher acquired a win he would not have taken on merit. But the sequel to this was that he paid back his team-mate not once, but four times over. On 23rd June at the Nurburgring, he was clearly quickest, as could be seen by the way he closed on Barrichello, having followed him from the start after losing ten seconds with a spin and then settled quietly for second place.

This took place three days before the World Council met to sit in judgement on the "incident" at the end of the Austrian Grand Prix. It was designed to appease the FIA and to a certain extent, reset the tripmeter to zero. In the end, Ferrari got away with a half million dollar fine and a further half million dollar fine, suspended for a year in case of a repeat performance. Note that this was not because of their on-track shenanigans, but because they did not follow the correct protocol on the podium after the race.

An embarrassed Schumacher settled for standing on the second step, pushing Barrichello up to the winner's position.

By mid-summer, with the Drivers' title already in his pocket after the Magny-Cours race, Schumacher had to accept his role of helping his team-mate secure the runner-up slot which had escaped him in 2001. This meant Ferrari could claim to have done even better than in the previous championship. It has to be admitted that this policy of going for total success made for some dull racing. On 18th August in Budapest, where Ferrari ran off with the Constructors' title, both drivers set off on a two stop strategy.

Once again nicely tucked in behind Barrichello, as they were under no threat from the opposition, Schumacher was the first to pit, despite the theoretical handicap of making the earlier refuelling stop. Twice he pretty much had to lift off, so that his team-mate maintained the lead coming out of pit lane. On 15th September in Monza, Ferrari did the same thing, except that this time, Barrichello was on a two stop strategy and Schumacher only one. "I was informed of the situation on the radio and we acted accordingly," said Ferrari's undoubted team leader. He lost two seconds on the lap when Barrichello emerged from the pits for the second time, to ensure he did not end up leading the race. Finally, on 29th September at Indianapolis, Schumacher tried to be too clever when it came to getting both Ferraris to finish as close to one

another as possible and he inadvertently handed victory to the Brazilian who, by then, no longer needed the win, as he had already secured second place in the championship.

Without any orders emanating from the pit wall, Schumacher had tried to get the cars to cross the line almost together, no doubt still conserving first place for himself, but again, without any word from the team, Barrichello did not know what was going on and thought he was being offered the win. This cock-up provoked a mixed response after the race. Having put himself in an embarrassing situation, Schumacher claimed he had been trying to orchestrate a dead heat, something which is virtually impossible when timing goes down to the nearest thousandth of a second. It was a better excuse than claiming his team-mate had been naïve.

He could have won 14

Let's get back to those figures. Spielberg first of all: Schumacher picked up four points which was judged scandalous. After that, at the Nurburgring, Budapest, Monza and Indianapolis he handed over sixteen, without it causing any fuss. Free to race, he would have ended the year winning 14 races instead of 11, giving him a career total of 67 instead of 64. He would have totalled 156 points instead of 144, which over the 17 races means an average of 9.18 per grand prix!

At this point, it is worth pointing out a few facts. Team orders which have caused ructions this year, have in fact been around since time immemorial. Indeed, driving for Ferrari almost half a century ago, Fangio owed the fourth of his five title to this strategy. Luigi Musso in Buenos Aires and then Peter Collins in Monaco and again in Monza, handed over their cars to the Argentinian. This practice was allowed up to 1957 and involved a sharing of the points gained. But for these noble gestures, Stirling Moss and his Maserati would have taken the title.

With hindsight, the only legitimate criticism of what happened in Spielberg is that it took place as early as the sixth race. What followed proved that it was a totally unnecessary ploy, but how was Jean Todt

expected to know that neither BMW-Williams nor McLaren-Mercedes would fight back. At the time, one imagined that if Michelin got their act together vis a vis Bridgestone, the picture could have been very different. A final word on the subject: Barrichello's performance was not without merit, as he never put a foot wrong when in the lead, thus playing a part in securing his own gifts.

With four constructors' titles since 1999 for Ferrari and three drivers' crowns for Schumacher, the Scuderia reigns supreme over the world of F1, having endured two barren decades. And don't forget that four years ago, Schumacher was out of the running, having broken his right leg. Thanks to the dream team put together by Jean Todt, with Ross Brawn and Rory Byrne on the chassis side and Paolo Martinelli and Gilles Simon looking after the engines, it is reaping the rewards of its diligence and determination.

If one can criticise its constant craving to play about with the race result and its affect on the accepted wisdom that motor racing should be all about the "glorious uncertainty of sport," one can but admire the work that went into producing this masterpiece. With a similar budget to BMW-Williams and McLaren-Mercedes, Ferrari in partnership with Bridgestone, whose exact role in this victory is hard to assess, created the perfect car.

A secret under the bodywork

With no chink in the armour, its two main opponents admitted they had "not done a good enough job" in an arena where the freeing up of rules regarding electronics in April 2001, meant that there could be no hint of cheating. Up to that point, as it began to show signs of supremacy, the Scuderia was suspected of interpreting the rules to its own benefit, without the governing body wanting or being able to do anything about it. Now that the Italian squad is even more dominant on a level playing field, the rest have nothing to say.

Apart from an exceptional driver who gets the best out of the car and the team, what is their secret? Leaving aside a transmission system shrouded in impenetrable secrecy and a highly developed engine management system, it must be tucked away somewhere under the bodywork.

With its wind tunnel working flat out, pointing the way as early as 1999, Ferrari has managed to eke out a substantial aerodynamic advantage, despite very restrictive regulations.

Rumour has it that the Maranello wind tunnel can "blow" on its car from all angles to simulate cornering forces rather than the more conventional straight on headwind approach. Difficult to achieve, this skill would fine tune the car's attitude through the corners, which is far more important than any aerodynamic effect down the straights. Indeed, other drivers who have followed the Ferraris always talk about their corner speed.

Other teams have enjoyed similar periods of dominance in the past, but in this record breaking year, Ferrari seems to have bored the pants off everyone including the tifosi. The technical achievement is admirable and so convincing that it

is hard to see an end to the current situation. The big danger is that the sporting spectacle is reduced and so is its audience. This has not gone unnoticed and since the last race of the season, FIA has instigated a major shake-up with the possibility of applying radical changes to the regulations with immediate effect. We must wait until 2003 to see if all this panic was justified or not.

The complicity established between Michael Schumacher and Ross Brawn dates back to the German's first world championship crowns in 1994 and 1995, when he drove for Benetton.
< v

David Coulthard finished the championship in fifth place, behind the two Ferraris and the two Williams-BMWs. It was a quiet year for the McLaren team, which never put a car on pole and only took one race win.
>

Williams: running out of steam

King of the Hill on Saturdays for qualifying, Williams lost the plot on Sundays. With seven poles on the end of "Zorro" Montoya's sword, Williams hoped in vain that first place would be a repeat option the next day.

Its aerodynamic package did not generate enough downforce, but it could be improved artificially and temporarily to deliver the goods over a single flying lap. It flattered to deceive, as the team faced the constant disappointment that came with the realisation they were still not on the right track in race trim.
They were in the same boat as McLaren, but

with less excuses, given they had been working with Michelin since the end of the 2000 season. Williams never managed to get their tyres to perform consistently in the two or three flat-out stints that make up a modern day grand prix.

"I know, I know," insisted Montoya. "Last time, even though I was on pole, everything went wrong in the race, but this time it will be different. Our performance in free practice makes me really optimistic. I think we can be competitive against the Ferraris." Excuse me? Right from the start of most grands prix, Williams could only watch as their apparent

rivals, whipped them to the tune of as much as two seconds a lap. However, it was hard to gauge what the total gap was over a race distance as the blue and white cars were not always running at the flag. Like McLaren, this team secured just the one victory, in Sepang, having taken four wins in 2001.

Engine performance could not be faulted, so the chassis and more precisely the aerodynamics had to shoulder the blame. A new wind tunnel is under construction, but it will be another two years until its contribution takes effect. What can they do in the meantime?

Juan Pablo Montoya was brilliant in racking up seven pole positions (as opposed to zero for his team-mate.) It was proof of the Colombian's immense talent.
v

Jaguar, The (Big) Cat is not yet out of the bag

In his no-nonsense version of English, Niki Lauda affirms he is a firm believer in Austrian work methods. "When I took control of Jaguar Racing, I said this to the staff: stop chatting, stop the bla-bla, get back to your desks, work!" Yes boss, okay boss. The last in the line of former world champions turned team boss, once Stewart sold out to Ford, so they could stick their Jaguar badge on the cars, and following the Prost saga, which ended in bankruptcy, Lauda spends his time sacking people. The car was a disaster at first and finally took a major leap forward at the end of the summer, the credit for which can certainly be laid at Lauda's door. But he will insist on giving his opinion on everything going on outside his own team. It seems he cannot resist the urge. He still has a rebellious streak as attests his strange dress code, with his ancient jeans and red cap; only a green shirt bearing allegiance to his team.
He even let it be known that he was looking for a new personal sponsor for his cap, now that Parmalat were not renewing their historic contract. He finally ended up with a heater manufacturer. How come he gets away with running a team at the same time as acting as a consultant to German TV station RTL. When Schumacher took the title in Magny-Cours, Lauda was actually there to stick the company microphone under the German's nose, before moving on to interview Jean Todt!
While he is famous for the one hat, he seems to

suffer from wearing too many. Boss of Ford's Premier Performance division and therefore of Jaguar Racing, Cosworth and PI Electronics, he doesn't really need to moonlight to swell his coffers. He wanders around talking too much. Is there anyone at Ford who dares tell him to "stop chatting and get back to work?" Maybe they could do something about his wardrobe at the same time.

Renault: a mountain to climb

It might only be symbolic, but a little plane flying through the clouds on its weekly journey from Enstone to Viry-Chatillon demonstrates that it is not easy running a team with two heads. The engine specialists, the "French" cross La Manche to go and soak up chassis culture with the "English" and vice versa.

Listen to Renault and you will be told that despite this geographical disparity, the team is already functioning with total efficiency, as a single entity. However, eavesdrop on conversations which seep through the motorhome walls when on-track performance has not been up to much and you will hear a different story.

The team took the courageous step of forming a "complete team" based on a Twin Towns approach. It also dared to come up with an innovative engine design which, in the short term, has created some major problems. But more than that, the French constructor has probably underestimated the qualities required, both human and financial, needed to succeed in F1 these days and allow it to build on all those world titles picked up in the Nineties as a simple engine supplier.

At the start of the season, up against McLaren, who were struggling to come to terms with new Michelin tyres, Renault appeared competitive. But appearances can be deceptive and in the heat of high summer it lost its footing and its reliability. Towards the end of the year, it picked up the pace again, sticking to its avowed intention of being fourth in the championship behind the established top three teams.

However, a glance at its points total and it is clear that the real fight for a world title will be a long drawn out affair. At the moment, it looks something of a lost cause, as Renault continues with this its third F1 era. Up to them to prove their doubters wrong.

McLaren off target

The silver arrows, once so sharp, continue to bounce off their target. Apart from an unexpected win in Monaco, they never scored a bullseye, having done so

four times the previous season. The transformation to rather blunt darts stemmed from a variety of factors, starting with the tyres.

McLaren abandoned Bridgestone for Michelin in the belief that they could sneak round Ferrari with different rubber. Instead, they encountered all sorts of difficulties, some of them down to underestimating the task in hand. While the French tyres might have had the better of their Japanese counterparts in terms of outright speed, they were only at their best in a very narrow operational range, which required a very specific car set-up. Set in their ways, unprepared to listen, the McLaren engineers either did not know how or did not want to adapt the rear end of their car in a way which they felt went against what was right. Concentrating on the Paragon project, its new headquarters which will have absolutely no connection with anything as vulgar as a factory, Ron Dennis the racer, would often delegate his race track duties to Martin Whitmarsh, whose competence owes more to administration.

Finally, in the design office, Adrian Newey seemed to have lost the spark which made his name in the past. He nearly slipped the leash in 2001 to go to Jaguar and apparently had his eye on other challenges to test his talent, such as the giant yachts which compete in the Americas Cup. His motivation was on the wane and in August, McLaren set about changing its technical family tree.

Newey and Neil Oatley adopted strange new job titles, making room for new blood in the shape of Mike Coughlan from Arrows and John Sutton, formerly a gearbox specialist with Ferrari. For such a conservative team, this represented a cultural revolution.

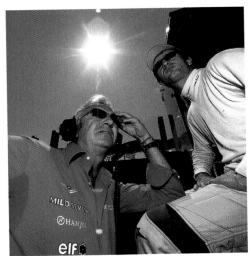

< and ∧
Jenson Button did better than Jarno Trulli at Renault, the Englishman scoring five more points than the Italian. Despite this, he was the one shown the door by Flavio Briatore at the end of the season. Interesting to note that the team boss also used to handle Jarno Trulli's business affairs!

The Arrows team missed six grands prix this year and is on the verge of bankruptcy, just as Prost Grand Prix was in 2001. And what about Minardi next season? One rule for the rich, another for the poor...
<

Drivers

1.	M. Schumacher	**144**
2.	R. Barrichello	77
3.	J.P. Montoya	50
4.	R. Schumacher	42
5.	D. Coulthard	41
6.	K. Räikkönen	24
7.	J. Button	14
8.	J. Trulli	9
9.	E. Irvine	8
10.	N. Heidfeld	7
11.	G. Fisichella	7
12.	J. Villeneuve	4
13.	F. Massa	4
14.	O. Panis	3
15.	T. Sato	2
16.	M. Webber	2
17.	M. Salo	2
18.	H-H. Frentzen	2
19.	A. McNish	0
20.	A. Yoong	0
21.	P. de la Rosa	0
22.	E. Bernoldi	0
23.	A. Davidson	0

Constructors

1.	Scuderia Ferrari Marlboro	**221**
2.	BMW WilliamsF1 Team	92
3.	West McLaren Mercedes	65
4.	Mild Seven Renault F1 Team	23
5.	Sauber Petronas	11
6.	DHL Jordan Honda	9
7.	Jaguar Racing	8
8.	Lucky Strike BAR Honda	7
9.	KL Minardi Asiatech	2
10.	Panasonic Toyota Racing	2
11.	Orange Arrows	2

Ferrari superstar

It is impossible to take a look at the technical side of the 2002 season, without dedicating a long paragraph to the Ferrari F2002. There is no doubt that it has to be regarded as the Italian team's best car of all time. "*The first time I saw it, I thought 'Wow,' it's the most beautiful F1 car I've ever seen*", confided Michael Schumacher. "*I did not think it was possible to produce a Formula 1 car in such a compact package.*" Beautiful inside and out, the F2002 had covered all the angles.

Draws: Giorgio Piola

From the outside, its overall shape borrowed much from its predecessor the F2001 in aerodynamic terms: its hooked nose, cut out front wing and enveloping barge boards. However, at the rear end there were many novelties, To start with, the exhaust outlets meant the team could produce several interesting and advantageous solutions. The lower profile of the side pods meant the engineers had to bring the exhausts out of the bodywork higher than usual. This meant they were shorter, allowing the 051 engine to develop more power. Finally, the chimney pots which covered in these elements also served as hot air vents. Further back, a brand new gearbox design, developed over the past two years, allowed for a more compact car which brought further aerodynamic advantages. In fact, progress on the aero front is most visible at the rear. The new transmission also allowed the engineers to save weight on a key area of the car, which was of the utmost importance to the Bridgestone engineers as it was the key to managing rear tyre wear. Indeed the F2002's new suspension was designed in collaboration with the Japanese engineers to optimise tyre performance. The other side of the coin was that this meant the tyres sometime took rather too long to reach the ideal operating temperature in qualifying. This explains why Ferrari's tally of poles this year is nowhere near as impressive as their list of wins. The Scuderia's chief designer, Rory Byrne, placed all the heavy parts of the car around its centre of gravity – situated approximately 23 cm off the ground, level with the fuel cell – in order to ensure the best possible handling. The driver's position had also changed, again to make the roll centre as low as possible. "*I was completely lying down in this car*", explained Schumacher. "*It would have been difficult to recline the seat any further!*" The other area to get the full treatment from the men of Maranello was the electronics. The traction control on the F2002 and its range of adjustment was quite simply a little piece of magic. Rubens Barrichello's best performances of the past season owed it a lot. Furthermore, Ferrari was one of the only teams to make full use of bi-directional telemetry. On the engine side, the 051 increased in power while losing weight and bulk. It lost none of the legendary Ferrari reliability. While it might have lagged a tiny bit behind the BMW, it did make up most of the difference and the 051 could push the Ferrari along at a top speed comparable to that of the Williams, mainly thanks to notably less aerodynamic drag from its chassis. To see how effective was the work of the Reds, just look at the figures: 15 wins, including 9 one-twos and over 200 points scored. Williams on the other hand was a bit disappointing. The technical team led by Patrick Head took a rather conventional route, to such an extent that, to the casual eye, it was hard to tell the difference between the FW23 and the FW24, when the new car was launched! The team paid dear for this timid approach, because not only was Williams off the pace

from the start of the season, but the gap to Ferrari grew bigger as the season progressed. The main defects with the 2002 car? The aerodynamic package did not produce enough downforce at the rear of the car and the overall concept was obsolete. New bodywork appeared at Silverstone, but although it improved the situation it was not a total cure. On top of that, the FW24 displayed very different characteristics in qualifying and the race. Very competitive on Saturday, it would struggle on Sunday. However, its BMW V10 had plenty to say for itself: it went past the 19,000 rpm mark at Monza and is clearly the best engine on the grid. Williams has learnt its lesson and the FW25 promises to be very innovative. It will need to be to catch up with the Ferrari.
McLaren finished up third in the championship, at the end of a difficult year. For starters, the Woking squad had to get to grips with the Michelin tyres. Then, the new 90 degree V10 from Mercedes did not give total satisfaction. Not enough power at the start of the year, the power unit designed by Mario Illien and his team evolved considerably all the way to Suzuka, but reliability was always a weak

point. On top of that, the twin keel system separating the two lower front wishbones did not deliver all its promises on the aero front. It made the steering heavy and the braking imprecise. Overall, the MP4/17 proved to be a very oversteering car, which is just what Coulthard hates.
Let us finish off with a look at interesting features on other cars. Renault's launch control is a little marvel: it meant the R92 could cover 92 metres in 4 seconds. On average, the Renault drivers overtook two cars before the first corner after the race start. The extreme twin keel system developed on the Arrows seemed very innovative. On the down side, we can turn to the aerodynamic disaster that was the Jaguar R3, which also suffered a lack of rigidity. The Sauber was inconsistent, the Honda engines unreliable and the Jordan chassis was too twitchy. Finally, a special mention for Toyota. It's TF102, although conventional, was on the pace. One of its strengths was the engine, designed by Norbert Kreyer. This V10 was definitely one of the top four engines on the grid. Pretty encouraging for a first year!

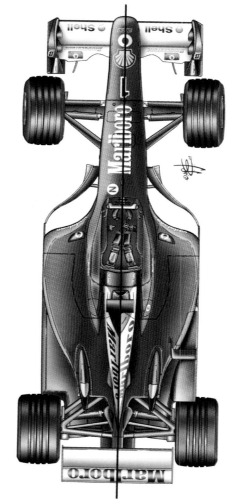

FERRARI SEEN FROM ABOVE

At its launch, the F2002 (at top of diagram was unveiled without the little winglets on the sides and the Williams-style fins ahead of the rear wheels, show in the lower diagram). The F2002 is shorter (3020 mm) compared with its two main rivals. The cockpit and the front edge of the sidepods are moved back from the front axle to clean up the airflow as it passes over the main bulk of the car. The car is also the smallest in terms of the distance between the rear axle and the rear centre of the tub (1585 mm).

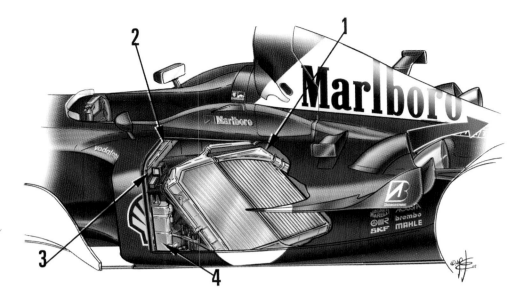

FERRARI RADIATORS

New position for the radiators on the F2002, which are inclined both vertically and longitudinally towards the front (**1**) so as to significantly reduce their height while providing a bigger cooling area. This layout also avoids the small area in the shadow of the monocoque and its mass is nearer to the car's roll centre. **2)** The safety elements on the side of the tub extend from the bodywork. **3)** Infrared sensors for the bi-directional telemetry. **4)** cooling liquid scavenge tank.

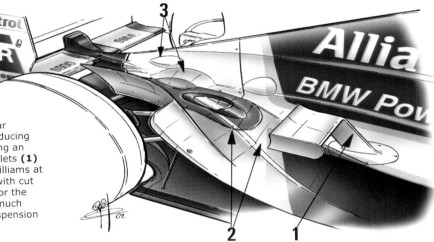

WILLIAMS

Williams sprung a surprise with a heavily modified version of the rear aerodynamics on the FW24. A great deal of work was invested in reducing the frontal area, as well as the space inside the rear wheels, following an idea first seen on the Ferrari F2002. Also similar to Ferrari, the winglets (**1**) above the side pods, although actually these were first seen on a Williams at Monaco in '99. Also worth noting, the tapering of the rear end (**2**) with cut out sides mounted obliquely which involved finding a new position for the exhausts. As well as being narrower, the revised FW 24 also had a much lower rear end (**3**), obvious because the bodywork covering the suspension is bigger.

FERRARI – BARGE BOARD

New barge boards mounted behind the front wheels on the Ferrari, with modifications to the lower part to which are added two small triangular sections (**1**), never seen before on any other cars. However, already seen before, the small winglets (**2**) positioned inside the barge boards in the area ahead of the sides. Seen from above, the shape and size of both elements is clearly visible.

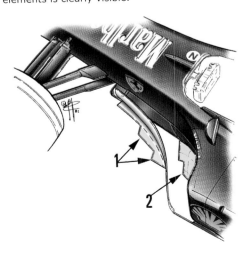

MP4-17 SIDEPODS

The McLarens had new fins similar to the Williams design (**1**) in the area ahead of the sidepods. Also new, the hot air vents on the sides, in three different sizes (**2**).

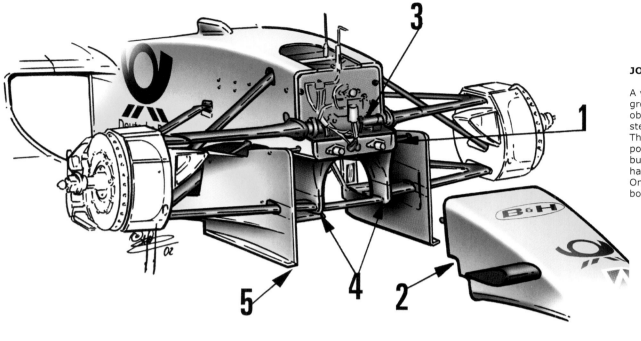

JORDAN

A very interesting stepped shape to the central groove on the front of the Jordan chassis, which obviously matches that on the nose (2). The steering column is fitted outside the chassis (3). The two vertical parts which serve as mounting points for the front suspension are very long, but not as long as those on the Arrows (4) and have a strengthening arm on the lower triangle. On the sides are the usual enormous barge boards (5) in the 50 cm central area.

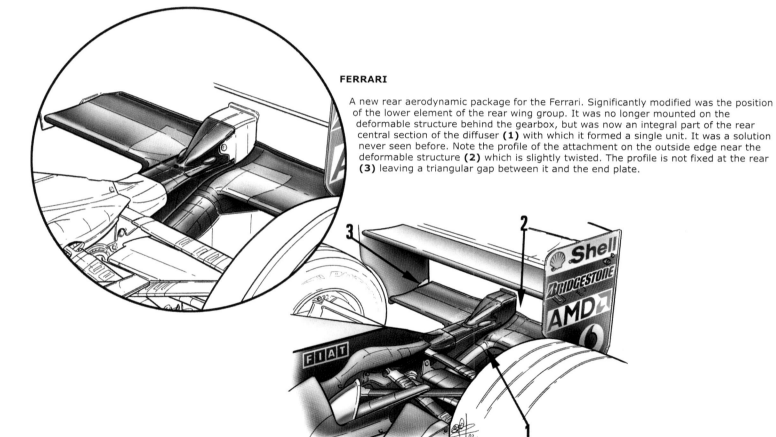

FERRARI

A new rear aerodynamic package for the Ferrari. Significantly modified was the position of the lower element of the rear wing group. It was no longer mounted on the deformable structure behind the gearbox, but was now an integral part of the rear central section of the diffuser (1) with which it formed a single unit. It was a solution never seen before. Note the profile of the attachment on the outside edge near the deformable structure (2) which is slightly twisted. The profile is not fixed at the rear (3) leaving a triangular gap between it and the end plate.

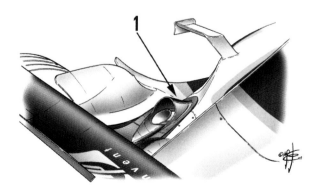

WILLIAMS EXHAUSTS REAR VIEW

Williams used a longer exit for its exhausts, a solution which was vaguely similar to that used by Ferrari on the F2002 when it was launched. In this view the extreme tapering of the rear of the Williams is visible, along with the new bodywork introduced at Silverstone.

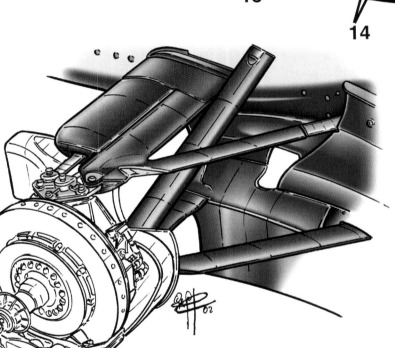

FERRARI STEERING WHEEL

1) Main display
2) LED to indicate correct revs for changing gear
3) start procedure button
4) pit lane speed restrictor
5) radio
6) engine settings
7) to go up the settings
8) engine
9) start preparation
10) data selection
11) engine
12) OK bi-directional
13) knob to change display info
14) secondary display
15) engine cut-out
16) oil tank
17) traction control
18) fuel flap
19) differential into corner
20) to go down the settings
21) differential out of corner
22) start
23) neutral

McLAREN

Many teams had to modify the front suspension wishbones as with an increase in the steering angle (22 degrees) these would end up touching the rims. The drawing shows the modifications to the upper wishbone on the McLaren.

McLAREN

The MP4-17 used a Ferrari-style front wing with two flaps (2) retaining the strange serrated gurney, seen last year from the Spanish GP onwards. The lower wishbone (3) has a small titanium strengthening ridge (4) on the inside of the two shaped pick-up points designed by Adrian Newey.

THE PLAYERS

Eleven teams and twenty three drivers, not forgetting dozens of engineers and hundreds of mechanics who beaver away supporting the stars.
Including security personnel, the marshals, medical crews, Paddock Club waiters, press officers, sponsors, photographers and journalists, there are over 6000 people working at each race. It is a huge pyramid with the drivers at the top.

Ferrari

1. Michael SCHUMACHER

DRIVER PROFILE

- Name: *SCHUMACHER*
- First name: *Michael*
- Nationality: *German*
- Date of birth: *January 3, 1969*
- Place of birth: *Hürth-Hermühlheim (D)*
- Lives in: *Vufflens-le-Château (CH)*
- Marital status: *married to Corinna*
- Kids: *one girl and one boy (Gina & Mick)*
- Hobbies: *karting, watches, movies, karaoke*
- Favorite music: *Tina Turner, rock and roll*
- Favorite meal: *italian food*
- Favorite drinks: *apple juice and mineral water*
- Height: *174 cm*
- Weight: *75 kg*

- Web: *www.michael-schumacher.rtl.de*

STATISTICS

		PRIOR TO F1
• Nber of Grand Prix:	*179*	*1984-85 : Karting:*
• Victories:	*64*	*Junior Champion (D)*
• Pole-positions:	*50*	*1986 : Karting: 3rd (D & EUR)*
• Best laps:	*51*	*1987 : Karting:*
• Accidents/off:	*22*	*Champion (D & EUR)*
• Not qualified:	*0*	*1988 : Champion F. Koenig,*
• Laps in the lead:	*3656*	*F. Ford 1600 (EUR) (2nd)/ F.*
• Kms in the lead:	*17082*	*Ford 1600 (D) (6th)*
• Points scored:	*945*	*1989 : F3 (D) (3rd)*
		1990 : Champion F3 (D)
		1990-91 : Sport-prototypes
		Mercedes (5th & 9th)

F1 CAREER

1991 : *Jordan-Ford, Benetton-Ford. 4 pts. 12th of championship.*
1992 : *Benetton-Ford. 53 pts. 3rd of championship.*
1993 : *Benetton-Ford. 52 pts. 4th of championship.*
1994 : *Benetton-Ford. 92 pts.* **World Champion.**
1995 : *Benetton-Renault. 102 pts.* **World Champion.**
1996 : *Ferrari. 49 pts. 3rd of championship.*
1997 : *Ferrari. 78 pts. Excluded from championship (2nd).*
1998 : *Ferrari. 86 pts. 2nd of championship.*
1999 : *Ferrari. 44 pts. 5th of championship.*
2000 : *Ferrari. 108 pts.* **World Champion.**
2001 : *Ferrari. 123 pts.* **World Champion.**
2002 : *Ferrari. 144 pts.* **World Champion.**

2. Rubens BARRICHELLO

DRIVER PROFILE

- Name: *BARRICHELLO*
- First name: *Rubens Gonçalves*
- Nationality: *Brazilian*
- Date of birth: *May 23, 1972*
- Place of birth: *São Paulo (BR)*
- Lives in: *Monte Carlo (MC)*
- Marital status: *married to Silvana*
- Kids: *one boy (Eduardo)*
- Hobbies: *jet-ski, golf*
- Favorite music: *pop, rock*
- Favorite meal: *pasta*
- Favorite drinks: *Pepsi light*
- Height: *172 cm*
- Weight: *77 kg*

- Web: *www.barrichello.com.br*

STATISTICS

		PRIOR TO F1
• Nber of Grand Prix:	*164*	*1981-88 : Karting (5 time*
• Victories:	*5*	*Brazilian Champion)*
• Pole-positions:	*6*	*1989 : F. Ford 1600 (3rd)*
• Best Lap:	*8*	*1990 : Opel Champion*
• Accidents/off:	*23*	*Lotus Euroseries,*
• Not qualified:	*0*	*F. Vauxhall (11th)*
• Laps in the lead:	*517*	*1991 : Champion F3 (GB)*
• Kms in the lead:	*2424*	*1992 : F3000 (3rd)*
• Points scored:	*272*	

F1 CAREER

1993 : *Jordan-Hart. 2 pts. 17th of championship.*
1994 : *Jordan-Hart. 19 pts. 6th of championship.*
1995 : *Jordan-Peugeot. 11 pts. 11th of championship.*
1996 : *Jordan-Peugeot. 14 pts. 8th of championship.*
1997 : *Stewart-Ford. 6 pts. 13th of championship.*
1998 : *Stewart-Ford. 4 pts. 12th of championship.*
1999 : *Stewart-Ford. 21 pts. 7th of championship.*
2000 : *Ferrari. 62 pts. 4th of championship.*
2001 : *Ferrari. 56 pts. 3rd of championship.*
2002 : *Ferrari. 77 pts. 2nd of championship.*

What can one say that has not been said already about this driver who has just blown the record book apart this season, equalling the legendary Fangio's record of titles? Maybe, one could point out that, having reached the pinnacle of his art, Ferrari's almost total supremacy allowed him to show off new forms of behaviour, as illustrated by those infamous race strategies. Because, after the Spielberg manoeuvre, which caused such an uproar, he clearly let his team-mate win at the Nurburgring and again in Budapest and Monza, before giving a further, if unscheduled present at Indianapolis! While displaying the selfishness which is a mark of all true champions, Michael Schumacher proved he could play the team game by making sacrifices. But for those, his list of successes would be even more impressive.

His success rate has increased, albeit artificially, but he can still be irritating. In Budapest and Monza, after his team-mate had throttled back and even braked, so as not to move ahead during the pit stops, he behaved in parc ferme, on the podium and later in the press conference as if he really believed he had won! Rubens Barrichello would have us believe, before listening to the more honest yet cautious words of his leader, that he had beaten the best driver in the world, fair and square. But on the probing Spa circuit, he was taught a monumental lesson and what a good thing that was. He might make the sign of the cross before stepping onto the top step of the podium, but this man is really not a racing god.

Jean Todt

Ross Brawn

Rory Byrne

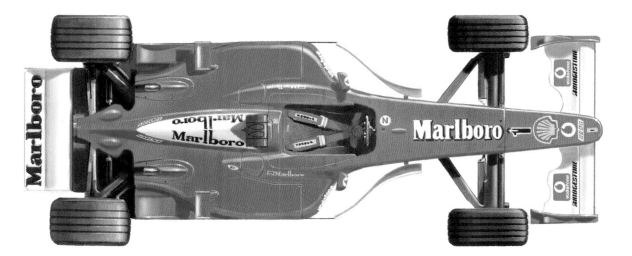

**FERRARI F2002
MICHAEL SCHUMACHER
GERMAN GRAND PRIX**

P.MÉNARD

Ferrari F2002

SPECIFICATIONS

- Chassis : *Ferrari F2002*
- Engine: *Ferrari 051- V10 (90°)*
- Displacement: *2997 cm³*
- Electronic ignition : *Magneti-Marelli*
- Tyres: *Bridgestone*
- Fuel / Oil : *Shell*
- Brakes (discs) : *Brembo*
- Brakes (calipers): *Brembo*
- Transmission : *Ferrari 7 gears, semi-automatic*
- Radiators: *not revealed*
- Plugs: *SKF*
- Shock absorbers: *not revealed*
- Wheels: *BBS*
- Suspensions : *push rods (ft/bk)*
- Dry weight: *600 kg, driver + on board camera*
- Wheelbase: *3050 mm*
- Total length : *4495 mm*
- Total height : *959 mm*
- Front track : *1470 mm*
- Rear track : *1405 mm*

TEAM PROFILE

- Adress : *Ferrari SpA*
  Via A. Ascari 55-57
  41053 Maranello (MO)
  Italia
- Telephone : *(00 39) 0536 94 91 11*
- Fax : *(00 39) 0536 94 64 88*
- Web : *www.ferrari.it*
- Established in: *1929*
- First Grand Prix : *Monaco 1950*
- General Director : *Luca Di Montezemolo*
- Technical director: *Ross Brawn*
  Paolo Martinelli (engines)
- Chief director : *Rory Byrne*
- General manager : *Jean Todt*
- Chief mechanic: *Nigel Stepney*
- Nber of employees: *681*
- Principal sponsors : *Marlboro, Fiat, Shell, Vodafone*

TEST DRIVERS 2002

- Luca BADOER (I)
- Luciano BURTI (BR)

SUCCESSION OF DRIVERS 2002

- Michael SCHUMACHER : *all Grand Prix*
- Rubens BARRICHELLO : *all Grand Prix*

STATISTICS

- Number of Grand Prix : 670
- Number of victories : 159
- Number of pole-positions : 158
- Number of best laps during the race : 159
- Number of driver's world titles : 12
- Number of constructor's titles : 12
- Total number of points scored : 2880,5
  (2924,5)

POSITIONS IN WORLD CHAMPIONSHIP

1958 : 2ⁿᵈ – 40 ⁽⁵⁷⁾ pts	1973 : 6ᵗʰ – 12 pts	1988 : 2ⁿᵈ – 65 pts
1959 : 2ⁿᵈ – 32 ⁽³⁸⁾ pts	1974 : 2ⁿᵈ – 65 pts	1989 : 3ʳᵈ – 59 pts
1960 : 3ʳᵈ – 24 ⁽²⁷⁾ pts	**1975 : 1ˢᵗ – 72,5 pts**	1990 : 2ⁿᵈ – 110 pts
1961 : 1ˢᵗ – 40 ⁽⁵²⁾ pts	**1976 : 1ˢᵗ – 83 pts**	1991 : 3ʳᵈ – 55,5 pts
1962 : 5ᵗʰ – 18 pts	**1977 : 1ˢᵗ – 95 pts**	1992 : 4ᵗʰ – 21 pts
1963 : 4ᵗʰ – 26 pts	1978 : 2ⁿᵈ – 58 pts	1993 : 4ᵗʰ – 28 pts
1964 : 1ˢᵗ – 45 ⁽⁴⁹⁾ pts	**1979 : 1ˢᵗ – 113 pts**	1994 : 3ʳᵈ – 71 pts
1965 : 4ᵗʰ – 26 ⁽²⁷⁾ pts	1980 : 10ᵗʰ – 8 pts	1995 : 3ʳᵈ – 73 pts
1966 : 2ᵗʰ – 31 ⁽³²⁾ pts	1981 : 5ᵗʰ – 34 pts	1996 : 2ⁿᵈ – 70 pts
1967 : 4ᵗʰ – 20 pts	**1982 : 1ˢᵗ – 74 pts**	1997 : 2ⁿᵈ – 102 pts
1968 : 4ᵗʰ – 32 pts	**1983 : 1ˢᵗ – 89 pts**	1998 : 2ⁿᵈ – 133 pts
1969 : 5ᵗʰ – 7 pts	1984 : 2ⁿᵈ – 57,5 pts	**1999 : 1ˢᵗ - 128 pts**
1970 : 2ⁿᵈ – 55 pts	1985 : 2ⁿᵈ – 82 pts	**2000 : 1ˢᵗ – 170 pts**
1971 : 4ᵗʰ – 33 pts	1986 : 4ᵗʰ – 37 pts	**2001 : 1ˢᵗ – 179 pts**
1972 : 4ᵗʰ – 33 pts	1987 : 4ᵗʰ – 53 pts	**2002 : 1ˢᵗ – 221 pts**

Implacable supremacy

Faster, higher and really stronger! And it was all done with the usual suspects; Montezemolo, Todt, Brawn, Byrne, Martinelli, Schumacher, Barrichello, Badoer, not forgetting new boy Burti. One doesn't change a winning team, when the absence of change is a source of strength. Ferrari wiped the floor with the opposition, making the most of a dream number one driver, foolproof organisation and perfect components making up a perfect car-chassis, engine, aerodynamics, transmission, electrical aids. However, as its war with Michelin came to nought, it was the Bridgestone tyres which were proposed as the single most effective weapon, perhaps artificially to detract attention from the car itself. The downside of this dominance is that the team did not have to wait long before starting to play games with the race results. At first and only for a short while, this was for Schumacher's benefit and then, for longer and rather labouring the point, the team did it for Barrichello, who needed pushing all the way to take the meaningless title of runner-up. The image of Formula 1 suffered, but whose fault was it? In fact it was down to the other teams.

McLaren-Mercedes

3. David COULTHARD

DRIVER PROFILE

- Name : *COULTHARD*
- First name : *David*
- Nationality : *British*
- Date of birth : *March 27, 1971*
- Place of birth : *Twynholm (Ecosse)*
- Lives in : *Monte Carlo (MC)*
- Marital status : *single*
- Kids : *-*
- Hobbies : *spending time with friends, movies*
- Favorite music : *pop music, Madonna, Oasis*
- Favorite meal : *pasta*
- Favorite drinks : *tea mineral water*
- Height : *182 cm*
- Weight : *72,5 kg*

- Web : *www.davidcoulthard.com*

STATISTICS | PRIOR TO F1

STATISTICS		PRIOR TO F1
• Nber of Grand Prix :	141	1983-88 : *Karting*
• Victories :	12	1989 : *Champion*
• Pole-positions :	12	*F. Ford 1600 (GB)*
• Best laps :	18	1990 : *F. Vauxhall-Lotus (4th),*
• Accidents/off :	15	*GM Lotus Euroseries (5th)*
• Not qualified :	0	1991 : *F3 (GB) (2nd)*
• Laps in the lead :	855	1992 : *F3000 (9th)*
• Kms in the lead :	4015	1993 : *F3000 (3rd)*
• Points scored :	400	1994 : *F3000 (9th)*

F1 CAREER

1994 : *Williams-Renault. 14 pts. 8th of championship.*
1995 : *Williams-Renault. 49 pts. 3rd of championship.*
1996 : *McLaren-Mercedes. 18 pts. 7th of championship.*
1997 : *McLaren-Mercedes. 36 pts. 3rd of championship.*
1998 : *McLaren-Mercedes. 56 pts. 3rd of championship.*
1999 : *McLaren-Mercedes. 48 pts. 4th of championship.*
2000 : *McLaren-Mercedes. 73 pts. 3rd of championship.*
2001 : *McLaren-Mercedes. 65 pts. 2nd of championship.*
2002 : *McLaren-Mercedes. 41 pts. 5th of championship.*

4. Kimi RÄIKKÖNEN

DRIVER PROFILE

- Name : *RÄIKKÖNEN*
- First name : *Kimi*
- Nationality : *Finnish*
- Date of birth : *October 17 , 1979*
- Place of birth : *Espoo (SF)*
- Lives in : *Espoo (SF), Chigwell (GB)*
- Marital status : *single*
- Kids : *-*
- Hobbies : *snowboard, skateboard, jogging*
- Favorite music : *U2, Darude*
- favorite meal : *pasta, finnish dish with reindeer*
- Favorite drinks : *pineapple juice, water and milk*
- Height : *175 cm*
- weight : *63 kg*

- Web : *www.racecar.co.uk/kimi*

STATISTICS | PRIOR TO F1

STATISTICS		PRIOR TO F1
• Nber of Grand Prix :	34	1987-99 : *Karting*
• Victories :	0	1998 : *Champion karting*
• Pole-positions :	0	*Formule A (SF & Nordic)*
• Best laps :	1	1999 : *Karting*
• Accidents/off :	5	*Formule A (SF) (2nd),*
• Not qualified :	0	*world championship*
• Laps in the lead :	21	*Formule Super A (10th)*
• Kms in the lead :	89	2000 : *Champion*
• Points scored :	33	*F. Renault (GB)*

F1 CAREER

2001 : *Sauber-Petronas. 9 pts. 9th of championship.*
2002 : *McLaren-Mercedes. 24 pts. 6th of championship.*

Damn it! Missed again. Every year he has methodically prepared his challenge, got over his disappointment, affirming proudly that he will have to wait for next year. Confronted by Ferrari's supremacy, David Coulthard was determined to go out on the attack this season and silence his critics. But, if he thought that with Hakkinen out of the way, he would automatically inherit the role of team leader, he was wrong, as he found himself up against another awkward Finn. The most important figures, those that relate to pure speed, do not make good reading for the Scot. Nevertheless, it was Coulthard not Raikkonen who picked up the team's solitary win in Monaco. Experience is a useful asset, as is courteous behaviour and a willing smile come sponsor promotion time.

Silence please, man at work! While there is no doubting his ability at the wheel, his conversational skills have earned him the nickname "The Iceman" which suits this cool customer well. By comparison, Hakkinen, his fellow countryman and predecessor, was a Chatty Cathy. But away from the paddock, Kimi Raikkonen is less shy. The head is held higher, the voice is more assured and his rudimentary press conference English expands its vocabulary. But for a slide on a patch of oil five laps from the end of the French Grand Prix, he would have taken his first win, slowing Schumacher's run to his fifth title. The Finn is still angry with himself over this mistake, but he has a very bright future...

Ron Dennis

Mario Illien

MCLAREN-MERCEDES MP4/17
DAVID COULTHARD
MONACO GRAND PRIX

McLaren-Mercedes MP4/17

SPECIFICATIONS

- Chassis : *McLaren MP4-17*
- Engine : *Mercedes-Benz V10 F0110M (90°)*
- Displacement: *2998 cm³*
- Electronic ignition : *TAG Electronic systems*
- Wheels : *Enkei*
- Tyres : *Michelin*
- Fuel / Oil : *Mobil unleaded / Mobil 1*
- Brakes (discs) : *Carbone Industrie*
- Brakes (calipers) : *AP Racing*
- Transmission : *McLaren 6 gears, semi-autom.*
- Radiators : *McLaren / Calsonic / Marston*
- Plugs / Battery : *NGK / GS*
- Shock absorbers : *Penske/McLaren*
- Suspensions : *torsion bar/push rod*
- Weight : *600 kg, driver + on board camera*
- Total length : *not revealed*
- Total height : *not revealed*
- Front track : *not revealed*
- Rear track : *not revealed*

TEAM PROFILE

- Adress : *McLaren International Ltd. Woking Business Park, Albert Drive, Sheerwater, Woking, Surrey GU21 5JY Great Britain*
- Telephone : *(44) 1483 711 311*
- Fax : *(44) 1483 711 448*
- Web : *www.mclaren.com*
- Established in : *1963*
- First Grand Prix : *Monaco 1966*
- General director : *Ron Dennis*
- Technical director : *Adrian Newey*
- Chief designer: *Neil Oatley*
- Nber of employees : *485*
- Principal sponsors : *Reemtsma (West), Exxon Mobil, Sun Microsystems, Hugo Boss, SAP, Schüco, Warsteiner, Catia solutions, Kenwood, Computer Associate International, Siemens Mobile, TAG Heuer, Canon, BAE Systems, Loctite*

TEST DRIVERS 2002

- Alexander WURZ (A)

SUCCESSION OF DRIVERS 2002

- David COULTHARD   *all Grand Prix*
- Kimi RÄIKKÖNEN   *all Grand Prix*

STATISTICS

- Number of Grand Prix :   *543*
- Number of victories :   *135*
- Number of pole-positions :   *112*
- Number of best laps during the race :   *109*
- Number of drivers world titles :   *11*
- Number of constructors titles: *8*
- Total number of points scored :   *2648,5*

Adrian Newey

POSITIONS IN WORLD CHAMPIONSHIP

1966 : *7ᵗʰ – 3 pts*	1979 : *7ᵗʰ – 15 pts*	1992 : *2ⁿᵈ – 99 pts*
1967 : *8ᵗʰ – 1 pt*	1980 : *7ᵗʰ – 11 pts*	1993 : *2ⁿᵈ – 84 pts*
1968 : *2ⁿᵈ – 51 pts*	1981 : *6ᵗʰ – 28 pts*	1994 : *4ᵗʰ – 42 pts*
1969 : *4ᵗʰ – 40 pts*	1982 : *2ⁿᵈ – 69 pts*	1995 : *4ᵗʰ – 30 pts*
1970 : *4ᵗʰ – 35 pts*	1983 : *5ᵗʰ – 34 pts*	1996 : *4ᵗʰ – 49 pts*
1971 : *6ᵗʰ – 10 pts*	1984 : *1ˢᵗ – 143,5 pts*	1997 : *4ᵗʰ – 63 pts*
1972 : *3ʳᵈ – 47 pts*	1985 : *1ˢᵗ – 90 pts*	1998 : *1ˢᵗ – 156 pts*
1973 : *3ʳᵈ – 58 pts*	1986 : *2ⁿᵈ – 96 pts*	1999 : *2ⁿᵈ – 124 pts*
1974 : *1ˢᵗ – 73 pts*	1987 : *2ⁿᵈ – 76 pts*	2000 : *2ⁿᵈ – 152 pts*
1975 : *3ʳᵈ – 53 pts*	1988 : *1ˢᵗ – 199 pts*	2001 : *2ⁿᵈ – 102 pts*
1976 : *2ⁿᵈ – 74 pts*	1989 : *1ˢᵗ – 141 pts*	2002 : *3ʳᵈ – 65 pts*
1977 : *3ʳᵈ – 60 pts*	1990 : *1ˢᵗ – 121 pts*	
1978 : *8ᵗʰ – 15 pts*	1991 : *1ˢᵗ – 139 pts*	

The empire needs rebuilding

For four years in a row now, this team has been given a thrashing in the constructors' championship by Ferrari. On the drivers' side the pain is only slightly less as Schumacher has taken a string of three championships after Hakkinen won it in 1998 and 1999. Ron Dennis admitted that McLaren has not done a good enough job, neither in terms of the chassis, where the creative talent and motivation of Adrian Newey, a man previously regarded as the leader of his generation of designers in terms of aerodynamics, seems to be called into question, nor on the engine front. It was not reliable enough and it was overtaken by the competition in every respect. The result was that, come the summer, DaimlerChrysler took a bigger share in Ilmor and is due to become its sole owner in 2005. While waiting to make the move to its futuristic new Paragon headquarters, which we are told is due to be a "domain of excellence," McLaren is working on its response, rather than licking its wounds. The question is when will its riposte be ready?

Williams-BMW

5. Ralf SCHUMACHER

DRIVER PROFILE

- Name : *SCHUMACHER*
- First name : *Ralf*
- Nationality : *German*
- Date of birth : *June 30, 1975*
- Place of birth : *Hürth-Hermühlheim (D)*
- Lives in : *Hallwang (Salzburg) (A)*
- Marital status : *maried to Cora*
- Kids : *one boy (David)*
- Hobbies : *karting, tennis, backgammon*
- Favorite music : *soft rock*
- Favorite meal : *pasta*
- Favorite drinks : *apple juice with mineral water*
- Heigth : *178 cm*
- Weigth : *73 kg*

- Web : *www.ralf-schumacher.net*

STATISTICS

		PRIOR TO F1
• Nber of Grand Prix :	100	1978-92 : *Karting*
• Victories :	4	1993 : *F3 ADAC Jr. (2nd)*
• Pole-positions :	1	1994 : *F3 (D) (3rd)*
• Best laps :	6	1995 : *F3 (D) (2nd),*
• Accidents/off :	22	*winner world final F3*
• Not qualified :	0	*Macao*
• Laps in the lead :	192	1996 : *Champion F3000 (J)*
• Kms in the lead :	984	
• Points scored :	177	

F1 CAREER

1997 : *Jordan-Peugeot. 13 pts. 11th of championship.*
1998 : *Jordan-Mugen-Honda. 14 pts. 10th of championship.*
1999 : *Williams-Supertec. 35 pts. 6th of championship.*
2000 : *Williams-BMW. 24 pts. 5th of championship.*
2001 : *Williams-BMW. 49 pts. 4th of championship.*
2002 : *Williams-BMW. 42 pts. 4th of championship.*

6. Juan Pablo MONTOYA

DRIVER PROFILE

- Name : *MONTOYA ROLDAN*
- First name : *Juan Pablo*
- Nationality : *Colombian*
- Date of birth : *September 20, 1975*
- Place of birth : *Bogota (COL)*
- Lives in : *Monte Carlo (MC)*
- Marital status : *married to Connie*
- Kids : *-*
- Hobbies : *computer and video games*
- Favorite music : *rock*
- Favorite meal : *pasta*
- Favorite drinks : *orange juice*
- Height : *168 cm*
- Weight : *72 kg*

- Web : *www.jpmontoya.com*

STATISTICS

		PRIOR TO F1
• Nber of Grand Prix :	34	1981-91 : *Karting (2 times*
• Victories :	1	*Junior World Champion)*
• Pole-positions :	10	1992 : *F. Renault (COL)*
• Best laps :	6	1993 : *Swift GTI (COL)*
• Accidents/off :	5	1994 : *Karting-Sudam 125*
• Not qualified :	0	*Champ. Barber Saab (3rd)*
• Laps in the lead :	187	1995 : *F. Vauxhall (GB)*
• Kms in the lead :	932	1996 : *F3 (GB)*
• Points scored :	81	1997 : *F3000 (2nd)*
		1998 : *Champion F3000*
		1999 : *Champion CART*
		2000 : *CART (9th)*

F1 CAREER

1997 : *Williams- Renault. Test driver*
2001 : *Williams- BMW. 31 pts. 6th of championship.*
2002 : *Williams- BMW. 50 pts. 3th of championship.*

Mein Gott, what a rubbish season! There was a ray of hope with a win in Sepang, giving his team their only success of the year. On the downside, having been pretty evenly matched last season, this time, he could not match his team-mate's qualifying pace. There was a definite rift, with Ralf being perceived as BMW's man and Juan Pablo as Williams'. Making life worse, they crashed into one another at Indianapolis! Indianapolis apart, Ralf Schumacher is a pragmatic and thinking driver. However, he seems to have lost that whiff of brio which makes a real champion and continues to demonstrate that when coming across his brother on the track, he is the first to throw in the towel. He needs to get back on track and quickly, because if he waits for Michael to hang up his helmet before making his move, it will be too late.

Only recently did we discover his nickname. Ever since he first started boarding Colombian airlines to head off to race in colder climes, his nearest and dearest called him Zorro. It was a sign of affection and admiration, but this year there was less of the foxy cunning of Don Diego about Montoya and more of the heavy spirit of Sergeant Garcia. The undoubted ace of the qualifying lap, he never has much to say about this other than the standard, ""okay, no problem with that." He needs to think more before launching another attack which often costs him dear. But a desperado can win the ultimate prize and Mansell is the proof of that.

Sir Frank Williams

Patrick Head

**WILLIAMS-BMW FW24
RALF SCHUMACHER
MALAYSIAN GRAND PRIX**

Williams-BMW FW24

SPECIFICATIONS

- Chassis : *Williams FW24*
- Engine : *BMW P82 V10 (90°)*
- Displacement : *2998 cm³*
- Electronic ignition : *BMW*
- Tyres : *Michelin*
- Wheels : *O.Z. Racing*
- Fuel / Oil : *Petrobras / Castrol*
- Brakes (discs) : *Carbone Industrie*
- Brakes (calipers) : *AP Racing*
- Transmission : *WilliamsF1 6 gears, semi-auto.*
- Radiators : *not revealed*
- Plugs : *Champion*
- Shock : *WilliamsF1*
- Suspensions : *WilliamsF1*
- Weight : *600 kg, driver + on board camera*
- Wheelbase : *3140 mm*
- Total length : *4540 mm*
- Front track : *1460 mm*
- Rear track : *1460 mm*

TEST DRIVERS 2002

- Marc GENÉ (E)
- Antonio PIZZONIA (BR)

TEAM PROFILE

- Adress : *Williams F1*
  Grove, Wantage, Oxfordshire,
  Great Britain - OX12 0DQ
- Telephone : *+44 (0) 1235 77 77 00*
- Fax : *+44 (0) 1235 76 47 05*
- Web : *www.bmw.williamsf1.com*
- Established in : *1969*
- First Grand Prix : *Argentina 1975 (Arg. 1973,under ISO)*
- Team principal : *Sir Frank Williams*
- Technical director : *Patrick Head*
- Team manager : *Dickie Stanford*
- Chief designer : *Gavin Fisher*
- Nbre of employees : *380*
- Principal sponsors : *HP, Accenture, Allianz, Castrol,*
  FedEx, BR Petrobras, Reuters,
  Veltins, Worldcom, Willy Bogner
  GmbH, Du Pont, OZ Racing, 7Up,
  Intel.

SUCCESSION OF DRIVERS 2002

- Ralf SCHUMACHER : *all Grand Prix*
- Juan Pablo MONTOYA : *all Grand Prix*

STATISTICS

- Number of Grand Prix : 462
- Number of victories : 108
- Number of pole positions : 119
- Number of best laps in the race : 121
- Number of drivers championship : 7
- Number of constructors championship : 9
- Total number of points scored : 2197,5

Gavin Fisher

POSITIONS IN WORLD CHAMPIONSHIP

1975 : 9th – 6 pts	1985 : 3rd – 71 pts	1995 : 2nd – 112 pts
1976 : not classified	1986 : 1st – 141 pts	1996 : 1st – 175 pts
1977 : not classified	1987 : 1st – 137 pts	1997 : 1st – 123 pts
1978 : 9th – 11 pts	1988 : 7th – 20 pts	1998 : 3rd – 38 pts
1979 : 2nd – 75 pts	1989 : 2nd – 77 pts	1999 : 5th – 35 pts
1980 : 1st – 120 pts	1990 : 4th – 57 pts	2000 : 3rd – 36 pts
1981 : 1st – 95 pts	1991 : 2nd – 125 pts	2001 : 3rd – 80 pts
1982 : 4th – 58 pts	1992 : 1st – 164 pts	2002 : 2nd – 92 pts
1983 : 4th – 38 pts	1993 : 1st – 168 pts	
1984 : 6th – 25.5 pts	1994 : 1st – 118 pts	

Not enough cavalry

In Monza, BMW flooded the media centre with press releases bragging that, having just taken the fastest ever pole position in F1 history, courtesy of Montoya, its engine had for the first time revved to 19,000 rpm. Technically, this was admirable, but it did not mean much come the race. Ralf Schumacher managed just four laps, his team-mate 33. All year long, a straight win was never on the cards. Its qualifying engine meant that Williams shone in terms of outright speed, helped by minor details like shutting down brake cooling ducts and indeed all the cooling vents to improve airflow over the bodywork. However, come race morning warm-up, when the cars were back in long distance configuration, it all went pear-shaped. The error was mainly one of design philosophy and not knowing how to chose the best compromise.

Sauber-Petronas

7. Nick HEIDFELD

DRIVE PROFILE

- Name : *HEIDFELD*
- First name : *Nick*
- Nationality : *German*
- Date of birth : *May 10, 1977*
- Place of birth : *Mönchengladbach (D)*
- Lives in : *Stäfa (CH)*
- Marital status: *engaged toPatricia*
- Kids : -
- Hobbies : *tennis, golf, cycling, moto, movies*
- Favorite music : *Kylie Minogue, Outkast, Zucchero, Texas*
- Favorite meal : *appetizers, japanese cuisine*
- Favorite drinks : *orange juice with mineral water*
- Height : *164 cm*
- Weight : *59 kg*

- Web : *www.nick-heidfeld.rtl.de*

STATISTICS

- Nber of Grand Prix : 50
- Victories : 0
- Pole-positions : 0
- Best laps : 0
- Accidents/off : 9
- Not qualified : 0
- Laps in the lead : 0
- Kms in the lead : 0
- Points scored : 19

PRIOR TO F1

1986-92: *Karting*
1993 : *Formule A Laval (F)*
1994 : *Champion*
    F. Ford 1600 (D)
1995 : *Champion F. Ford*
    1800 (D), F. Ford (D) (2ⁿᵈ)
1996 : *F3 (D) (3ʳᵈ)*
1997 : *Champion F3 (D)*
1998 : *F3000 (2ⁿᵈ)*
1999 : *Champion F3000*

F1 CAREER

1997-99 : *McLaren-Mercedes. Test driver*
2000 : *Prost-Peugeot. 0 pt.*
2001 : *Sauber-Petronas. 12 pts. 8ᵗʰ of championship.*
2002 : *Sauber-Petronas. 7 pts. 10ᵗʰ of championship.*

8. Felipe MASSA

DRIVER PROFILE

- Name : *MASSA*
- First name : *Felipe*
- Nationality : *Brazilian*
- Date of birth : *April 25, 1981*
- Place of birth : *São Paulo (BR)*
- Lives in : *Hinwill (CH)*
- Marital status: *single*
- Kids : -
- Hobbies : *water ski, football, movies, music*
- Favorite music : *all, from hip hop to techno*
- Favorite meal : *pasta, meat and brazilian cuisine*
- Favorite drinks : *podium's champagne*
- Height : *166 cm*
- Weight : *59 kg*

- Web : *www.felipemassa.com*

STATISTICS

- Nber of Grand Prix: 16
- Victories : 0
- Pole-positions : 0
- Best laps : 0
- Accidents/off : 5
- Not qualified : 0
- Laps in the lead : 0
- Kms in the lead : 0
- Points scored : 4

PRIOR TO F1

1990-97 : *Karting*
1998 : *F. Chevrolet (BR) (5ᵗʰ)*
1999 : *Champion*
    F. Chevrolet (BR)
2000 : *Champion F. Renault*
    (EUR & I)
2001 : *Champion F3000*
    Euroseries (I)

F1 CAREER

2002 : *Sauber-Petronas. 4 pts. 13ᵗʰ of championship.*

Image is everything! With his post-adolescent physique and his acned features, his attitude meant he was largely ignored by the media. He reinforced the image of the computer nerd, driving his engineers mad by spending hours studying telemetry read-outs, way past his bed time. Nick Heidfeld does not appear to have attracted the attention of the top teams, but his scholarly application pleases Peter Sauber, never one for glitz and glamour. He was a protégé of Mercedes who even built an F3000 team around him, but it might now be too late for him to build a high flying career. F1 has never been fair.

As a kid, he used to hang around the Sao Paulo paddock helping out the Benetton team and, just like Raikkonen, his rise to F1 was meteoric. This was the second time Peter Sauber had bet on youth, but this time it did not work out. While his Finnish baby-driver was pinched by McLaren, in this case, he got so fed up with all the broken cars that Felipe Massa was given his marching orders. He is very quick and a natural, but like many drivers from the lower formulae, he lacks a grasp of what the job involves, which often found him walking back from a crash. Visiting the factory ought to be a time for meeting engineers, not chatting up the secretaries. In short, he's a nice guy but the grey matter is lacking.

Peter Sauber

Willy Rampf

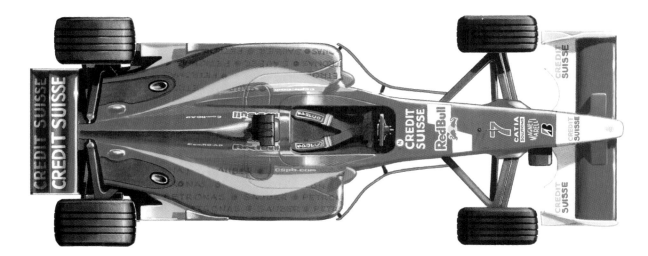

SAUBER-PETRONAS C21
NICK HEIDFELD
SPANISH GRAND PRIX

Sauber-Petronas C21

SPECIFICATIONS

- Chassis : *Sauber C21*
- Engine : *Petronas 02A V10 (90°)*
  (Ferrari 050 2001 version)
- Displacement : *2997 cm³*
- Electronic ignition : *Magneti-Marelli*
- Tyres : *Bridgestone*
- Wheels : *BBS*
- Fuel : *Petronas*
- Brakes (discs) : *Carbone Industrie / Brembo*
- Brakes (calipers) : *Brembo*
- Transmission : *semi-auto longitudin. 7 gears*
- Radiators : *Behr / Secan*
- Plugs : *Champion / SPE*
- Shock absorbers : *Sachs*
- Suspensions : *push rods (fr/abk)*
- Weight : *600 kg, driver + on board camera*
- Wheelbase : *3080 mm*
- Total length : *4450 mm*
- Total width : *1800 mm*
- Total height : *1000 mm*
- Front track : *1470 mm*
- Rear track : *1410 mm*

TEAM PROFILE

- Adress : *Sauber Motorsport AG*
  Wildbachstrasse 9
  CH - 8340 Hinwil
  Switzerland
- Telephone : *+ 41 1 937 90 00*
- Fax : *+ 41 1 937 90 01*
- Web : *www.sauber-petronas.com*
- Established in : *1970*
- First Grand Prix : *South Africa 1993*
- Team principle : *Peter Sauber*
- Technical director : *Willy Rampf*
- Team manager : *Beat Zehnder*
- Chief mechanic : *Urs Kuratle*
- Nber of employees : *240*
- Principal sponsors : *Petronas, Credit Suisse, Red Bull,*
  Temenos, Microsoft, In Motion...

TEST DRIVER 2002

- None

STATISTICS

- Number of Grand Prix : *163*
- Number of victories : *0*
- Number of pole positions : *0*
- Number of best laps during the race : *0*
- Number of drivers championship : *0*
- Number of constructors championship : *0*
- Total number of points scored : *122*

POSITIONS IN WORLD CHAMPIONSHIP

1993 : 6th – 12 pts	1998 : 6th – 10 pts
1994 : 8th – 12 pts	1999 : 8th – 5 pts
1995 : 7th – 18 pts	2000 : 8th – 6 pts
1996 : 7th – 11 pts	2001 : 4th – 21 pts
1997 : 7th – 16 pts	2002 : 5th – 11 pts

SUCCESSION OF DRIVERS 2002

- Nick HEIDFELD : *all Grand Prix*
- Felipe MASSA : *all Grand Prix except United States*
- Heinz-Harald FRENTZEN : *1 GP (EU)*

One step forward one step back

This team was in credit, "Credit Suisse" maybe, having worked wonders last year with a limited budget, spending much of it on a customer Ferrari engine, as there was no factory support in sight. It finished the year fourth. This year, it did not pay off. Trying to follow the Raikkonen route, having fished the Finn out of the European Formula Renault pond, Sauber came up with the prince of Italian Formula 3000, Felipe Massa. In Monza, the new-boy was the first driver to pick up the novel penalty of having to start ten places further back on the grid for the next race. But the team drove a tank through a loophole in the hastily concocted rules, replacing him in Indy by Frentzen. Apart from these on-track troubles, the team fell into the old trap of insufficient development. From the mid-point of the season, the team could do no more than tread water.

Jordan-Honda

If there was a remake of John Frankenheimer's film "Grand Prix," Giancarlo Fisichella would play the lead. Known as Fisico to the fans and Fisi to his team, Eddie Jordan will happily tell you he is one of the best three drivers in the paddock, apart from enjoying Boy Band good looks. Just like Trulli, he is always casting an eye towards the Ferrari camp, while Italy still waits for him to pick up the Patrese baton, the last Italian to win a grand prix. That is unlikely to happen as long as he stays with a mid-grid team, the blame for which can be laid partly at his door. Maybe a Fellini film would suit him better, given he comes from Rome, where La Dolce Vita was shot.

9. Giancarlo FISICHELLA

DRIVER PROFILE

- Name : *FISICHELLA*
- First name : *Giancarlo*
- Nationality : *Italian*
- Date of birth : *January 14, 1973*
- Place of birth : *Rome (I)*
- Lives in : *Rome and Monte Carlo (MC)*
- Marital status : *married to Luna*
- Kids : *one girl (Carlotta)*
- Hobbies : *river fishing, snookers*
- Favorite music : *E. John, italian singers, Madonna*
- Favorite meal : *bucatini alla matriciana (pasta)*
- Favorite drinks : *Coca-cola and orange juice*
- Height : *172 cm*
- Weight : *64 kg*

- Web : *www.giancarlofisichella.com*

STATISTICS

		PRIOR TO F1
• Nber of Grand Prix :	107	1984-88 : *Karting*
• Victories :	0	1989 : *karting world*
• Pole-positions :	1	*champion (4th)*
• Best laps :	1	1991 : *F. Alfa Boxer; kart*
• Accidents/off :	18	*(EUR) (2nd)*
• Not qualified :	0	1992 : *F3 (I) (8th)*
• Laps in the lead :	35	1993 : *F3 (I) (2nd)*
• Kms in the lead :	172	1994 : *Champion F3 (I)*
• Points scored :	82	1995 : *DTM/ITC Alfa Romeo*

F1 CAREER

1995 : *Minardi-Ford. Test driver.*
1996 : *Minardi-Ford. 0 pt.*
1997 : *Jordan-Peugeot. 20 pts. 8th of championship.*
1998 : *Benetton-Playlife. 16 pts. 9th of championship.*
1999 : *Benetton-Playlife. 13 pts. 9th of championship.*
2000 : *Benetton-Playlife. 18 pts. 6th of championship.*
2001 : *Benetton-Renault. 8 pts. 11th of championship.*
2002 : *Jordan-Honda. 7 pts. 11th of championship.*

10. Takuma SATO

DRIVER PROFILE

- Name : *SATO*
- First name : *Takuma*
- Nationality : *Japanese*
- Date of birth : *January 28, 1977*
- Place of birth : *Tokyo (J)*
- Lives in : *Marlow (GB)*
- Marital status : *single*
- kids : *-*
- Hobbies : *cycling and food*
- Favorite music : *pop and japanese groups*
- Favorite meal : *japanese cuisine*
- Favorite drinks : *fruit juice, beer from time to time*
- Height : *163 cm*
- Weight : *60 kg*

- Web : *www.takumasato.com*

STATISTICS

		PRIOR TO F1
• Nber of Grand Prix :	17	1996 : *Champion Karting (J)*
• Victories :	0	1997 : *Champion Karting (J)*
• Pole-positions :	0	*Honda driving school*
• Best laps :	0	1998 : *F. Vauxhall Jr (GB)*
• Accidents/off :	4	1999 : *F. Opel Euroseries*
• Not qualified :	0	*(GB) (6th), F3 (GB)*
• Laps in the lead :	0	2000 : *F3 (GB) (3th)*
• Kms in the lead :	0	2001 : *Champion F3 (GB)*
• Points scored :	2	

F1 CAREER

2001 : *BAR-Honda. Test driver.*
2002 : *Jordan-Honda. 2 pts. 15th of championship.*

Hard to know if Banger Racing is popular in Japan, but this knockabout sport does seem to have influenced Sato's driving style. He might have benefited from Honda's backing, but that did not stop him leaving bits of yellow car all over some of the most famous tracks in the world. That apart and erratic though he was, Takuma Sato was quick; quicker than any of his Japanese predecessors at any rate. But he started the season on the wrong foot. The way to find your limits is to work up to them, not overstep the mark and then try and go back. In fact, his worst accident was not his fault, when he was T-boned by Heidfeld in Spielberg. But it all came right, and how, at Suzuka!

Eddie Jordan

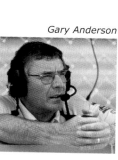

Gary Anderson

JORDAN-HONDA EJ12
GIANCARLO FISICHELLA
AUSTRIAN GRAND PRIX

Jordan-Honda EJ12

SPECIFICATIONS

- Chassis : *Jordan EJ12*
- Engine : *Honda RA002E V10 (96°)*
- Displacement : *3000 cm³*
- Electronic ignition : *Honda PGM IG*
- Tyres: *Bridgestone*
- Wheels : *OZ Racing*
- Fuel / Oil : *non révélé*
- Brakes (discs) : *Carbone Industrie / Brembo*
- Brakes (calipers) : *Brembo*
- Transmission : *Jordan longitudi. 7 gears*
- Radiators : *Secan / Jordan*
- Plugs / Battery : *NGK / Fiamm*
- Shock absorbers : *Penske*
- Suspensions : *push-pull carbone (ft/bk)*
- Weight : *600 kg, driver + on board camera*
- Wheelbase : *+ 3000 mm*
- Front track : *1500 mm*
- Rear track : *1418 mm*
- Total length : *4600 mm*
- Total height : *950 mm*

TEST DRIVER 2002

- None

TEAM PROFILE

- Adress : *Jordan Grand Prix Limited Dadford Road, Silverstone, Northamptonshire, NN12 8TJ Great Britain*
- Telephone : *+44 1327 850 800*
- Fax : *+44 1327 857 993*
- Web : *www.f1jordan.com*
- Established in : *1981*
- First Grand Prix: *USA 1991*
- General Director : *Eddie Jordan*
- Technical director : *Gary Anderson*
- Chief designer : *Henri Durand*
- Team manager : *Tim Edwards*
- Chief mechanic : *Andrew Stevenson*
- Nber of employees : *231*
- Principal sponsors : *Deutsche Post, Benson&Hedges, Damovo, Brother, Imation Corp., Hewlett-Packard, Virgin Mobile, Liqui Moly, MasterCard, Puma, Infineon...*

STATISTICS

- Number of Grand Prix : 197
- Number of victories : 3
- Number of pole positions : 2
- Number of best laps in the race : 2
- Number of drivers championship : 0
- Number of constructors championship : 0
- Total number of points scored : 261

POSITIONS IN WORLD CHAMPIONSHIP

1991 : *5ᵗʰ – 13 pts*	1995 : *6ᵗʰ – 21 pts*	1999 : *3ʳᵈ – 61 pts*
1992 : *11ᵗʰ – 1 pt*	1996 : *5ᵗʰ – 22 pts*	2000 : *6ᵗʰ – 17 pts*
1993 : *10ᵗʰ – 3 pts*	1997 : *5ᵗʰ – 33 pts*	2001 : *5ᵗʰ – 19 pts*
1994 : *5ᵗʰ – 28 pts*	1998 : *4ᵗʰ – 34 pts*	2002 : *6ᵗʰ – 9 pts*

SUCCESSION OF DRIVERS 2002

- Giancarlo FISICHELLA : *all Grand Prix except France*
- Takuma SATO : *all Grand Prix*

Oriental disorientation

Just over three years ago, as the 1999 was coming to a close, Michael Schumacher was out of action with a broken leg and this team was fighting Ferrari and McLaren to try and steal the championship crown for Frentzen. Different times, different results. As F1 costs spiralled, Jordan could do no more than pick up the odd point here and there. This team does not go through cycles, it tackles peaks and troughs. It still believes in itself. But this year, euphoria gave way to reality and the boss battened down the hatches, dumped some staff and tried to return to the old fashioned virtue of efficiency. It was saddled with a less than wonderful Honda engine; the last year it would share this power? unit with BAR, despite a contract which was due to expire at the end of 2003. Cutting out the dead wood staff-wise brought its own problems and for much of the year it was effectively running a one car team, because of the over-enthusiasm of Sato, although the Japanese driver metamorphosed from a caterpillar into a butterfly in Suzuka.

BAR-Honda

11. Jacques VILLENEUVE

DRIVER PROFILE

- Name : VILLENEUVE
- First name : Jacques
- Nationality : Canadian
- Date of birth : April 9, 1971
- Place of birth : St-Jean-sur-Richelieu, Québec, (CDN)
- Lives in : Monte Carlo (MC)
- Marital status : engaged à Ellen
- Kids : -
- Hobbies : ski, music, books, guitar, computers
- Favorite music : Roch Voisine, Lloyd, Train
- Favorite meal : pasta
- Favorite drinks : milk and "Root beer"
- Height : 171 cm
- Weight : 63 kg

- Web : www.jv-world.com

STATISTICS

		PRIOR TO F1	
• Nber of Grand Prix :	116	1986 :	Jim Russel school
• Victories :	11	1987 :	Spenard-David's
• Pole-positions :	13		driving school
• Best laps :	9	1988 :	Champ. ital. Alfa
• Accidents/off :	14	1989-91 :	F3 (I) (-, 14th, 6th)
• Not qualified :	0	1992 :	F3 (J) (2nd)
• Laps in the lead :	634	1993 :	Atlantic Formula (3rd)
• Kms in the lead :	2814	1994 :	IndyCar (6th)
• Points scored :	213	1995 :	IndyCar Champion

F1 CAREER

- 1996 : Williams-Renault. 78 pts. 2nd of championship.
- 1997 : Williams-Renault. 81 pts. **World Champion**.
- 1998 : Williams-Mecachrome. 21 pts. 5th of championship.
- 1999 : BAR-Supertec. 0 point.
- 2000 : BAR-Honda. 17 pts. 7th of championship.
- 2001 : BAR-Honda. 12 pts. 7th of championship.
- 2002 : BAR-Honda. 4 pts. 12th of championship.

12. Olivier PANIS

DRIVER PROFILE

- Name : PANIS
- First name : Olivier Denis
- Nationality : french
- Date of birth : september 2, 1966
- Place of birth : Lyon (F)
- Lives in : Varses (Grenoble) (F)
- Marital status : married à Anne
- kids : 2 girls one boy (Caroline, Lauren & Aurélien)
- Hobbies : family, ski, cycling, tennis, karting
- Favorite music : Florent Pagny, Garou
- Favorite meal : pasta
- Favorite drinks : Coca-cola and water
- Height : 173 cm
- Weight : 72 kg

- Web : www.olivier-panis.com

STATISTICS

		PRIOR TO F1	
• Nber of Grand Prix :	125	1981-87 :	Karting
• Victories :	1	1987 :	Champion Volant
• Pole-positions :	0		Elf Winfield Paul Ricard
• Best laps :	0	1988 :	F. Renault (F) (4th)
• Accidents/off :	17	1989 :	Champion
• Not qualified :	0		F. Renault (F)
• Laps in the lead :	16	1990 :	F3 (F) (4th)
• Kms in the lead :	53	1991 :	F3 (F) (2nd)
• Points scored :	64	1992 :	F3000 (10th)
		1993 :	F3000 Champion

F1 CAREER

- 1994 : Ligier-Renault. 9 points. 11th of championship.
- 1995 : Ligier-Mugen-Honda. 16 pts. 8th of championship.
- 1996 : Ligier- Mugen-Honda. 13 pts. 9th of championship.
- 1997 : Prost-Mugen-Honda. 16 pts. 9th of championship.
- 1998 : Prost-Peugeot. 0 point. 18th of championship.
- 1999 : Prost-Peugeot. 2 pts. 15th of championship.
- 2000 : McLaren-Mercedes. 3rd Driver
- 2001 : BAR-Honda. 5 pts. 14th of championship.
- 2002 : BAR-Honda. 3 pts. 14th of championship.

The alleged "free spirit" of the paddock wasted much of his energy in a psychological war with his new boss. In the Pollock days, Jacques Villeneuve ruled the roost and he was always forgiven his weaknesses – lack of interest in private testing, unwilling to play the media and public relations game. Once Richards was in control, he became an obvious target. A talented but incomplete driver, much of 2002 was dedicated to maintaining his ridiculously huge pay cheque. He even considered taking a crock of gold for a year off racing in the States, but in the end, he went for the Mastermind line of "I've started so I'll finish" in order to keep his boat afloat.

A stubborn fighter, Olivier Panis will never back away from any task, no matter how tedious, if it might improve his car. He is perseverance personified. The press reckon he is lukewarm, preferring to hide his true feelings, even when he is in a well justified stroppy mood. After numerous mechanical failures he insisted that "he never throws in the towel" and is still "positive" about the race, even adding that "we are making progress," when "we" are plainly doing nothing of the sort. He might have taken over the Hakkinen mantle when it comes to public speaking, but that obviously goes down well in Japan, given he is now leaving Honda for Toyota.

David Richards

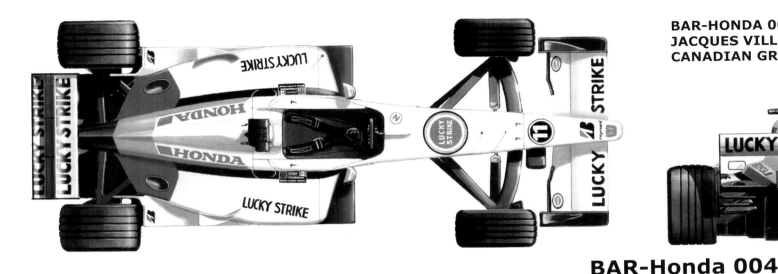

**BAR-HONDA 004
JACQUES VILLENEUVE
CANADIAN GRAND PRIX**

BAR-Honda 004

SPECIFICATIONS

- Chassis : BAR 004
- Engine : Honda RA002E V10 (94°)
- Displacement : 3000 cm³
- Electronic ignition : Honda PGM IG
- Tyres : Bridgestone
- Wheels : OZ
- Fuel / Oil : Elf / Nisseki
- Brakes (discs) : Hitco
- Brakes (calipers) : AP Racing
- Transmission : BAR Xtrac 7 gears, semi-auto.
- Radiators : Honda
- Plugs / Battery : Champion / Reynard
- Shock absorbers : Koni
- Suspensions : push rods (ft/bk)
- Weigth : 600 kg, driver + on board camera
- Wheelbase : 3050 mm
- Total length : 4550 mm
- Total width : 1800 mm
- Total height : 950 mm
- Front track : 1460 mm
- Rear track : 1420 mm

TEAM PROFILE

- Adress : British American Racing
  Brackley, Northamptonshire
  NN13 7BD
  Great Britain
- Telephone : +44 1280 84 40 00
- Fax : +44 1280 84 40 01
- Web : www.bar.net
- Established in : 1997
- First Grand Prix : Australia 1999
- General director : David Richards
- Technical director : Geoffrey Willis
- Chief engineer : James Robinson
- Managing engineers : Jock Clear, David Lloyd
- Chief mechanic : Alistair Gibson
- Nber of employees : 320
- Principal sponsors : British American Tabacco (BAT),
  Acer, Tiscali, Brunotti, Intercond, Sonax, SmugOne.com, EDS...

STATISTICS

- Number of Grand Prix : 67
- Number of victories : 0
- Number of pole-positions : 0
- Number of best laps during the race : 0
- Number of drivers world titles : 0
- Number of constructors titles: 0
- Total number of points scored : 47

David Richards, Jock
Clear & Jacques
Villeneuve

POSITIONS IN WORLD CHAMPIONSHIP

1999 : not classified	2001 : 6ᵗʰ – 17 pts
2000 : 5ᵗʰ – 20 pts	2002 : 8ᵗʰ – 7 pts

TEST DRIVERS 2002

- Darren MANNING (GB)
- Anthony DAVIDSON (GB)
- Patrick LEMARIÉ (F)
- Ryo Fuduka (J)

SUCCESSION OF DRIVERS 2002

- Olivier PANIS : all Grand Prix
- Jacques VILLENEUVE : all Grand Prix

Dirty washing in public

The name is unfortunate, given it is a play on words in several languages. When British American Racing threw up the shutters, the Bar was always open. Villeneuve was soldiering on and Panis never stopped trying to improve matters, but in the end, champagne was never served in this Bar. Heads rolled, including the boss' and engineers moved on. Pollock had always been more of a friend and mentor to his number one driver than a manager and in December 2001, British American Racing thanked him for his efforts, even though he remains a shareholder. In came David Richards. The boss of Prodrive, which runs Subarus in the World Rally Championship and the man who controls the sport's TV rights, he was not bothered about the controversy and set about cleaning out the dead wood. Honda was obviously impressed by all this laundering and not only continued to support the team, but also dumped Jordan to concentrate on BAR. That's all very well, but when is this team, which faces the threat of being renamed, ever going to get on an even keel?

Renault

14. Jarno TRULLI

DRIVER PROFILE

- Name : *TRULLI*
- First name : *Jarno*
- Nationality : *Italian*
- Date of birth : *July 13, 1974*
- Place of birth : *Pescara (I)*
- Lives in : *Monte Carlo (MC) and Pescara (I)*
- Marital status : *single*
- Kids : -
- Hobbies : *music, jogging, karting, computers*
- Favorite music : *Vasco Rossi, E. John, U2, Giovanotti*
- Favorite meal : *pizza*
- Favorite drink : *Coca-Cola*
- Height : *173 cm*
- weight : *60 kg*

- Web : *www.jarnotrulli.com*

STATISTICS

- Nber of Grand Prix : 97
- Victories : 0
- Pole-positions : 0
- Best laps : 0
- Accidents/off : 15
- Not qualified : 0
- Laps in the lead : 38
- Kms in the lead : 165
- Points scored: 38

PRIOR TO F1

- 1983-86 : *Karting*
- 1988-90 : *Kart 100 Champion (I)*
- 1991 : *Monde Kart 100 FK Champion*
- 1992 : *Kart 125 FC (2nd)*
- 1993 : *Kart 100 SA (2nd)*
- 1994 : *Monde Kart 125 FC Champion and Kart 100 FSA Champion (EUR & Nord USA)*
- 1995 : *Kart 100 Champion FA (I)*
- 1996 : *F3 Champion (D)*

F1 CAREER

- 1997 : *Minardi-Hart, Prost-Mugen Honda. 3 pts. 15th championship.*
- 1998 : *Prost-Peugeot. 1 pt. 15th of championship.*
- 1999 : *Prost-Peugeot. 7 pts. 11th of championship.*
- 2000 : *Jordan-Mugen-Honda. 6 pts. 10th of championship.*
- 2001 : *Jordan-Honda. 12 pts. 9th of championship.*
- 2002 : *Renault. 9 pts. 8th of championship.*

15. Jenson BUTTON

DRIVER PROFILE

- NAME : *BUTTON*
- First name : *Jenson*
- Nationality : *British*
- Date of birth : *January 19, 1980*
- Place of birth : *Frome, Somerset (GB)*
- Lives in : *Monaco (MC)*
- Marital status : *engaged to Louise*
- Kids : -
- Hobbies : *Internet surfing and partying*
- Favorite music : *Jamiroquaï, Kool And The Gang, the 70'*
- Favorite meal : *curry, fish and pasta*
- Favorite drinks : *orange juice, Redbull*
- Height : *181 cm*
- Weight : *72 kg*

- Web : *www.racecar.co.uk/jensonbutton*

STATISTICS

- Nbrer of Grand Prix : 51
- Victories : 0
- Pole-positions : 0
- Best laps : 0
- Accidents/off : 13
- Not qualified : 0
- Laps in the lead : 0
- Kms in the lead : 0
- Points scored : 28

PRIOR TO F1

- 1989-1996 : *Karting (3rd worl cup in 96)*
- 1997 : *Kart Champion Super A (EUR)*
- 1998 : *Formules Ford and Ford Festival Champion(GB)*
- 1999 : *F3 (GB) (3rd)*

F1 CAREER

- 2000 : *Williams-BMW. 12 pts. 8th of championship.*
- 2001 : *Benetton-Renault. 2 pts. 17th of championship.*
- 2002 : *Renault. 14 pts. 7th of championship.*

Just like his brilliant fellow countryman Ascari, Trulli could well become a superstitious sort. Being unluckier than the Italian would no doubt involve getting out from the wrong side of the car, adopting a family of black cats or carrying ladders on the car. Tipped to become the team leader, he was outpaced by Button in the early part of the year and certainly took longer than expected to build a good working relationship with his engineers. On top of that, he racked up a painful run of mechanically-induced retirements. And when the car held together, he flew off the road! The end of the season saw an improvement, but at the moment, Jarno Trulli is still the eternal hope in search of a goal.

Last year, he proved that the second season can be tougher than the first, especially when you use up precious reserves of energy partying the night away to the delight of the English tabloids, keen to report on your female conquests. It didn't help having a manager (now departed) whose sole concern was the sound of the cash register. This year, Jenson reinvented himself and changed his lifestyle completely. The first of the baby drivers, who opened the cot door for Raikkonen and Massa, he rebuilt his career, taking strength from his trials and tribulations. He wants to win and he's quick. Sadly, just as he was turning the corner, the door slammed in his face, as Briatore gave him his marching orders from Renault. His future now rests with BAR.

Jean-Jacques His

Mike Gascoyne

Denis Chevrier

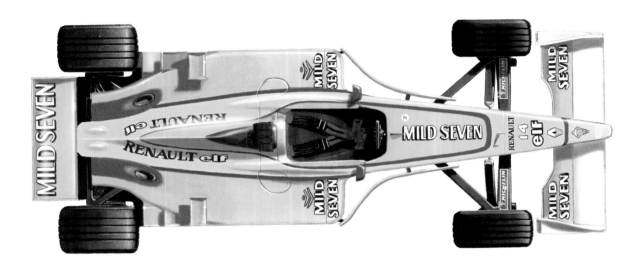

**RENAULT R202
JARNO TRULLI
ITALIAN GRAND PRIX**

Renault R202

SPECIFICATIONS

- Chassis : *Renault R202*
- Engine : *Renault RS22 V10 (110°)*
- Displacement : *3000 cm³*
- Electronic ignition : *Magnetti-Marelli*
- Tyres : *Michelin*
- Wheels : *BBS*
- Fuel / Oil : *Elf*
- Brakes (discs) : *Hitco*
- Brakes (calipers): *AP Racing*
- Transmission : *Renault F1 6 gears, automatic*
- Radiators : *Renault F1*
- Plugs / Battery : *Champion*
- Shock absorbers: *Dynamics*
- Suspensions : *triangles (ft/bk)*
- weight: *600 kg, driver and on board camera*
- wheelbasse: *3100 mm*
- Total length : *4600 mm*
- Total width : *1800 mm*
- Total height : *950 mm*
- Front track : *1450 mm*
- Rear track : *1400 mm*

TEST DRIVER 2002

- Fernando ALONSO (E)

TEAM PROFILE

- Adress : *Renault F1 UK*
  Whiteways Technical Centre
  Endstone
  Oxon OX7 4EE
  Great Britain
- Telephone : *+44 (0) 1608 67 80 00*
- Fax : *+44 (0) 1608 67 86 09*
- Web : *www.renaultf1.com*
- Established : *1973*
- First Grand Prix : *Great Britain 1977*
- General manager : *Patrick Faure*
- General director : *Flavio Briatore, Jean-Jacques His*
- Technical manager : *Mike Gascoyne*
- Engineering manager : *Pat Symonds*
- Nber of employees : *640*
- Principal sponsors : *Mild Seven, Elf, Michelin, Hanjin Group, 3D Systems, Alpinestars, Altran, Magnetti-Marelli, Catia, Charmilles Technologies, Novell, BMG, Lycos, Veritas...*

STATISTICS

- Number of Grand Prix : *140*
- Number of victories : *15*
- Number of pole positions : *31*
- Number of best laps during the race : *18*
- Number of drivers championship : *0*
- Number of constructors titles : *0*
- Number of points scored : *335*

POSITIONS IN WORLD CHAMPIONSHIP

1977 : *not classified*	1981 : *3rd – 54 pts*	1985 : *7th – 16 pts*
1978 : *12th – 3 pts*	1982 : *3rd – 62 pts*	2002 : *4th – 23 pts*
1979 : *6th – 26 pts*	1983 : *2nd – 79 pts*	
1980 : *4th – 38 pts*	1984 : *5th – 34 pts*	

SUCCESSION OF DRIVERS 2002

- Jarno TRULLI : *all Grand Prix*
- Jenson BUTTON : *all Grand Prix*

Out on its own

No one dared, no one followed. In 2001, running under the Benetton banner, before becoming 100% Renault this year, the team came up with an innovative engine architecture. This year, the engineers gambled on it producing a major step forward in terms of the car's overall performance. They improved its integration with the chassis, lowering the car's centre of gravity still further. It was a brave step, all built around the very wide 111 degree V10. Most of the opposition ran 90 degrees, having spent ages stuck on 72 and 73. Only Honda finally put one timid foot on the bandwagon, producing a 94 degree V10. But the engines in the BAR and Jordan did not do the trick and next year they return to the more acute angles of the past. Therefore, the French constructor which shone as an engine supplier to Williams and Benetton in the Nineties is ploughing its own furrow. Let's hope the crop is a good one.

THE ACTORS — **RENAULT**

Jaguar

16. Eddie IRVINE

17. Pedro DE LA ROSA

DRIVER PROFILE

- Name : *IRVINE*
- First name : *Edmund*
- Nationality : *Irish*
- Date of birth : *November 10, 1965*
- Place of birth : *Newtownards (IRL)*
- Lives in : *Dublin (IRL), Milan (I), Oxford (GB),*
- Marital status : *single*
- Kids : *one girl (Zoé)*
- Hobbies : *fishing, stock market, flying*
- Favorite music : *rock, Van Morrison, U2*
- Favorite meal : *chinese food*
- Favorite drinks : *Miller beer*
- Height : *178 cm*
- Weight : *70 kg*

- Web : *www.eddie365.com*

STATISTICS · PRIOR TO F1

STATISTICS		PRIOR TO F1
• Nber of Grand Prix :	147	1983 : *F. Ford 1600 (IRL)*
• Victories :	4	1984-86 : *F. Ford 1600 (GB)*
• Pole-positions :	0	1987 : *F. Ford 1600 (GB)*
• best laps :	1	*Champion*
• Accidents/off :	35	1988 : *F3 (GB) (5th)*
• Not qualified :	0	1989 : *F3000 (9th)*
• Laps in the lead :	156	1990 : *F3000 (3rd)*
• Kms in the lead :	838	1991 : *F3000 (J) (7th)*
• Points scored :	191	1992 : *F3000 (J) (8th)*
		1993 : *F3000 (J) (2nd)*

F1 CAREER

1993 : *Jordan-Hart. 1 pt. 20th of championship.*
1994 : *Jordan-Hart. 6 pts. 14th of championship.*
1995 : *Jordan-Peugeot. 10 pts. 12th of championship.*
1996 : *Ferrari. 11 pts. 10th of championship.*
1997 : *Ferrari. 24 pts. 7th of championship.*
1998 : *Ferrari. 47 pts. 4th of championship.*
1999 : *Ferrari. 74 pts. 2nd of championship.*
2000 : *Jaguar. 4 pts. 13th of championship.*
2001 : *Jaguar. 6 pts. 12th of championship.*
2002 : *Jaguar. 8 pts. 9th of championship.*

DRIVER PROFILE

- Name : *MARTÍNEZ DE LA ROSA*
- First name: *Pedro*
- Nationality : *Spanish*
- Date of birth : *February 24, 1971*
- Place of birth : *Barcelone (E)*
- Lives in : *Barcelone (E)*
- Marital status : *married to Maria*
- Kids : *-*
- Hobbies : *music, reading, squash, kart, sailing*
- Favorite music : *Mecano, Bruce Springsteen, K. Minogue*
- Favorite meal : *paëlla, pasta*
- Favorite drinks : *mineral water*
- Hight : *177 cm*
- weight : *74 kg*

- Web: *www.pedrodelarosa.com*

STATISTICS · PRIOR TO F1

STATISTICS		PRIOR TO F1
• Nber de Grand Prix :	63	1988 : *Karting*
• Victories :	0	1989 : *F. Fiat (E) Champion*
• Pole-positions :	0	1990 : *F. Ford 1600 (E)*
• Best laps :	0	*Champion*
• Accidents/off :	13	1991 : *F. Renault (E) (4th)*
• Not qualified :	0	1992 : *F. Renault (GB &*
• Laps in the lead :	0	*EUR) Champion*
• Kms in the lead :	0	1993 : *F3 (GB) (6th)*
• Points scored :	6	1994 : *F3 (GB)*
		1995 : *F3 (J) Champion*
		1996 : *F3000 & GT (J) (8th)*
		1997 : *F3000 & GT (J)*
		Champion

F1 CAREER

1998 : *Jordan-Mugen Honda. Test driver.*
1999 : *Arrows. 1 pt. 17th of championship.*
2000 : *Arrows-Supertec. 2 pts. 16th of championship.*
2001 : *Jaguar. 3 pts. 16th of championship.*
2002 : *Jaguar. 0 pt. 21st of championship.*

It would have been good fun to sit in on Jaguar's technical briefings this year, as Eddie and Lauda apparently fought like cat and dog. To the point where, on one occasion, the exasperated boss barked at his rebellious driver something along the lines of "listen, I was a three times world champion you know!" That is something Eddie Irvine will never be. He can be irritatingly laid-back and scathing and can fall asleep in his car, as though he has thrown the "off" switch in that crash helmet, which looks uncannily like brains. But, give him a good car, he wakes up and scores points. With good results in Melbourne, Spa and especially Monza, he singlehandedly saved Jaguar's season, proving there is life in the old dog yet, or is it a cat?

Aristocratic and awkward is our Pedro. He is keen on exchanging pleasantries with Carlos Sainz or the real King Juan Carlos and he is king of the excuses. Whenever he goes off the track, it's the strange handling of his car which caught him out. When he crashes into a colleague, no matter how hard it is to make the call, Pedro always blames the other driver. More than that, he tells tales, as it was the Spaniard's whinging to the Stewards in Monza which got Massa penalised a ten place slide on the grid for the following race. "Peter of the Roses" has airs and graces and would not talk to Irvine. It is unlikely that the Irishman was bothered.

Niki Lauda

Guenther Steiner

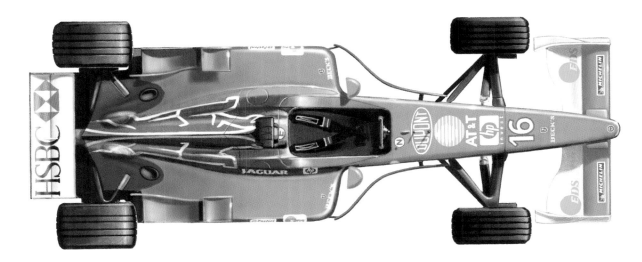

JAGUAR-FORD COSWORTH R3
EDDIE IRVINE
ITALIAN GRAND PRIX

Jaguar R3

SPECIFICATIONS

- Chassis : Jaguar R3
- Engine : Ford-Cosworth CR-3 V10 (72°)
- Displacement : 2998 cm³
- Electronic ignition : Pi "VCS"
- Tyres: Michelin
- wheels: BBS
- Fuel / Oil : Castrol
- Brakes (discs) : Carbone Industrie
- Brakes (calipers): AP Racing
- Transmission : Jaguar 7 gears, semi-automatic
- Radiators : IMI
- Plug / Battery : Champion / JRL
- Shock absorbers: Jaguar / Penske
- Suspensions : Upper / Bilstein,carbon fiber
- Weight: 600 kg, driver + on board camera
- Wheelbase: not revealed
- Total lenght : not revealed
- Total width : not revealed
- Total height : not revealed
- Front track : not revealed
- Rear track : not revealed

TEAM PROFILE

- Adress : Jaguar Racing Ltd
  Bradbourne Drive, Tilbrook,
  Milton Keynes, MK7 8BJ
  Great Britain
- Telephone : +44 (0) 1908 27 97 00
- Fax : +44 (0) 1908 27 97 11
- We: www.jaguar-racing.com
- Established in : 2000
- First Grand Prix : Australia 2000
- Chairman : Niki Lauda
- Managing director : Guenther Steiner
- Chief Engineer : Malcolm Oastler
- Chief aerodymicist : Ben Agathangelou
- Nber of employees : 345
- Principal sponsors : HSBC, Beck's, AT&T, EDS, DuPont,
  HP, Castrol, Lear, 3D Systems, Aqua-Pura, Rolex, S. Oliver...

TEST DRIVERS 2002

- André LOTTERER (D)
- James COURTNEY (AUS)

STATISTICS

- Number of Grand Prix : 51
- Number of victories : 0
- Number of pole positions : 0
- Number of best laps in the race : 0
- Number of drivers championship : 0
- Number of constructors championship : 0
- Total number of points scored : 21

POSITIONS IN WORLD CHAMPIONSHIP

2000 : 9th – 4 pts	2002 : 7th – 8 pts
2001 : 8th – 9 pts	

Vincent Gaillardot

SUCCESSION OF DRIVERS 2002

- Eddie IRVINE : all Grand Prix
- Pedro DE LA ROSA : all Grand Prix

Crop rotation

Three attempts, three failures. After 2000 and 2001, this year's car was another disaster, at least to start with. Stewart, Ressler, Rahal and Lauda at the helm, Anderson, Nichols, Russell, Handford and Steiner in front of the computer screens, the final outcome remains unchanged. We had to wait until the team finally gave up crossing the Pond to use the Swift wind tunnel in California, turning instead to a closer facility in Bicester, for the major errors to be slowly turned around. In the end, all it took was an anodyne change to the front suspension geometry which brought the biggest improvement, rocketing a Jaguar to third place in Monza. Just as Ford was thinking about restructuring (read canning) its involvement, because of a lack of meaningful results and going back to being a mere engine supplier, this result could not have come at a better time. But to become a "British Ferrari" its crazy stated aim at its launch, there is still a very long way to go.

Arrows-Cosworth

20. Heinz-Harald FRENTZEN

DRIVER PROFILE

- Name : *FRENTZEN*
- First name : *Heinz-Harald*
- Nationality : *German*
- Date of birth: *May 18, 1967*
- Place of birth: *Mönchengladbach (D)*
- Lives in : *Monte Carlo (MC)*
- Marital status : *married to Tanja*
- Kids : *one girl (Léa)*
- Hobbies : *aviation, VTT*
- Favorite music : *U2, Rolling Stones, Simple Minds, Elvis*
- Favorite meal: *paëlla, fish and pasta*
- Favorite drinks : *apple juice, mineral water*
- Height: *178 cm*
- Weight: *63 kg*

- Web: *www.frentzen.de*

STATISTICS | PRIOR TO F1

STATISTICS		PRIOR TO F1
• Nber of Grand Prix :	141	1980-85 : *Karting*
• Victories :	3	1986-87 : *F. Ford 2000*
• Pole-positions :	2	1988 : *F. Opel Lotus*
• Best laps :	6	*Champion (D), 6th Euroseries*
• Accidents/off :	25	1989 : *F3 (D) (2nd)*
• Not qualified :	0	1990 : *F3000 (7th)*
• Laps in the lead :	149	*Sport-prototypes (16th)*
• Kms in the lead :	746	1991 : *F3000 (14th)*
• Points scored:	161	1992 : *F3000 (J) (14th)*
		Sport-prototypes (13th)
		1993 : *F3000 (J) (9th)*

F1 CAREER

1994 : *Sauber-Mercedes. 7 pts. 13th of championship.*
1995 : *Sauber-Ford. 15 points. 9th of championship.*
1996 : *Sauber-Ford. 7 points. 12th of championship.*
1997 : *Williams-Renault. 42 pts. 2nd of championship.*
1998 : *Williams-Mécachrome. 17 pts. 7th of championship.*
1999 : *Jordan-Mugen Honda. 54 pts. 3rd of championship.*
2000 : *Jordan-Mugen Honda. 11 pts. 9th of championship.*
2001 : *Jordan-Honda, Prost-Acer. 6 pts. 13th of championship.*
2002 : *Arrows-Cos., Sauber-Petronas. 2 pts. 18th of champ.*

21. Enrique BERNOLDI

DRIVER PROFILE

- Name : *LANGUE DE SILVÉRIO E BERNOLDI*
- First name: *Enrique Antônio*
- Nationality : *Brazilian*
- Date of birth: *October 19, 1978*
- Place of birth: *Curitiba (BR)*
- Lives in : *Curitiba (BR), Monte Carlo (MC)*
- Marital status: *single*
- Kids : *one kid*
- Hobbies : *jet-ski, surf, Brazilian beaches*
- Favorite music : *Alanis Morisette, All Saints*
- Favorite dish : *italian cuisine*
- Favorite drinks : *Sprite*
- Height: *178 cm*
- Weight: *68 kg*

- Web: *www.enriquebernoldi.com.br*

STATISTICS | PRIOR TO F1

STATISTICS		PRIOR TO F1
• Nber of Grand Prix :	28	1987-93 : *karting.*
• Victories :	0	*Champion (BR) (1990 & 91)*
• Pole-positions :	0	1995 : *F. Alfa-Boxer (I) (4th)*
• Best laps :	0	1996 : *F. Renault*
• Accidents/off :	3	*Champion (EUR)*
• Not qualified :	0	1997 : *F3 (GB) (5th)*
• Laps in the lead :	0	1998 : *F3 (GB) (2nd)*
• Kms in the lead :	0	1999 : *F3000 (18th)*
• Points scored :	0	2000 : *F3000 (15th)*

F1 CAREER

1999 : *Sauber-Petronas. Test driver.*
2000 : *Sauber-Petronas. Test driver.*
2001 : *Arrows-Asiatech. 0 pt, 21st of championship.*
2002 : *Arrows-Cosworth. 0 pt, 22nd of championship.*

Just like Prost, who always needed to surround himself with problems to get motivated, Frentzen was often at his most convincing when facing adversity. Sacked by Williams, sublime at Jordan, before tailing off and being sacked again, on the grounds he was unfit, he slid down the order landing up at Prost. When that folded, he was pulled out of the water by Arrows. He has experience aplenty and is reckoned to know how to set up a car, although some criticise him for thinking he is an engineer. At the start of the year, he managed to pull some decent results out of the bag, in the face of financial adversity. Now, the prodigal son heads home to Sauber, where he started off his career a decade ago. In fact, he had a taster with his old team, deputising for Massa in Indianapolis.

He has the strength of a bull, but unfortunately for him, it only comes in the form of the unconditional and unexplained support of Red Bull. Last year, he made his mark, legitimately holding up David Coulthard who had started from the back of the grid in Monaco. Bernoldi is one of many current Brazilian drivers who, although talented, will never hold a candle to the likes of Fittipaldi, Piquet or Senna. While he looked reasonably convincing when pitted against team-mate Verstappen, any illusions were shattered when Frentzen was called in to the team, before it went to the wall. Just like Zonta, he is unlikely to be seen again.

Tom Walkinshaw

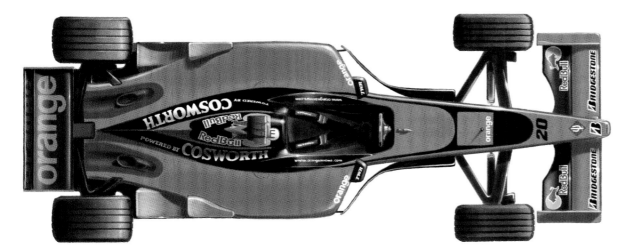

ARROWS-COSWORTH A23
HEINZ-HARALD FRENTZEN
SPANISH GRAND PRIX

P. MÉNARD

Arrows-Cosworth A23

SPECIFICATIONS

- Chassis : *Arrows A23*
- Engine : *Ford Cosworth CR-3 V10 (72°)*
- Displacement : *2998 cm³*
- Electronic ignition : *Cosworth Racing, Arrows/Pi VCS*
- Tyres : *Bridgestone*
- Wheels : *BBS*
- Fuel / Oil : *Total Fina Elf*
- Brakes (discs) : *Hitco*
- Brakes (calipers): *AP Racing / Arrows*
- Transmission : *Arrows 6 gears, semi-automatic*
- Radiators : *not revealed*
- Plugs : *Champion*
- Shock absorbers: *Dynamics*
- Suspensions : *push (ft/bk)*
- Weight: *600 kg, driver + on board camera*
- Wheelbase: *3080 mm*
- Total length : *4520 mm*
- Total width : *1830 mm*
- Total height : *1000 mm*
- Front track : *1465 mm*
- Rear track : *1410 mm*

TEAM PROFILE

- Adress : *OrangeArrows*
  Leafield Technical Centre
  Leafield, Witney, Oxon OX29 9PF
  Great Britain
- Telephone : *+44 (0) 1993 87 10 00*
- Fax : *+44 (0) 1993 87 10 87*
- Web: *www.arrows.com*
- Established in : *1977*
- First Grand Prix : *Brazil 1978*
- General director : *Tom Walkinshaw*
- Technical director : *Mike Coughlan*
- Chief designer : *Sergio Rinland*
- Chief aerodynamicist : *Nicolo Petrucci*
- Nber of employees : *200*
- Principal sponsors : *Orange, RedBull, Lost Boys, Paul Costelloe, Dell, Sgi, Fluent Europe, Catia, TWR, TCC...*

SUCCESSION OF DRIVERS 2002

- Heinz-Harald FRENTZEN : *11 GP (AUS, MAL, BR, SM, E, A, MC, CDN, EUR, GB, D)*
- Enrique BERNOLDI : *11 GP (AUS, MAL, BR, SM, E, A, MC, CDN, EUR, GB, D)*

STATISTICS

- Number of Grand Prix : 382
- Number of victories : 0
- Number of pole positions : 1
- Number of best laps during the race : 0
- Number of drivers championship : 0
- Number of constructors titles : 0
- Number of points scored : 167

POSITIONS IN WORLD CHAMPIONSHIP

1978 : 9th – 11 pts
1979 : 9th – 5 pts
1980 : 7th – 11 pts
1981 : 8th – 10 pts
1982 : 10th – 5 pts
1983 : 10th – 4 pts
1984 : 9th – 6 pts
1985 : 8th – 14 pts
1986 : 10th – 1 pt

1987 : 6th – 11 pts
1988 : 4th – 23 pts
1989 : 7th – 13 pts
1990 : 9th – 2 pts
1991 : not classified
1992 : 7th – 6 pts
1993 : 9th – 4 pts
1994 : 9th – 9 pts
1995 : 8th – 5 pts

1996 : 9th – 1 pt
1997 : 8th – 9 pts
1998 : 7th – 6 pts
1999 : 9th – 1 pt
2000 : 7th – 7 pts
2001 : 10th – 1 pt
2002 : 11th – 2 pts

TEST DRIVER 2002

- none

Broken arrow

Created in 1978, this team has never won a race and could not complete its 25th season in the sport. Bogged down with constant financial problems, it showed up in Magny-Cours but deliberately failed to qualify. Then, under pressure from the FIA, it was back in action at Hockenheim, failed to show in Budapest for reasons of force majeure, staged a comeback at Spa, only to leave on Friday night and then failed to show for the final three rounds at Monza, Indianapolis and Suzuka. This prompted an official enquiry from the governing body, while the team waits to see if it is declared bankrupt by the British courts. At the start of the year, Arrows owner Tom Walkinshaw was involved in the Phoenix fiasco, an attempt to relaunch the Prost team. On the sporting front, Arrows deserved better. The car had to make do with a customer Cosworth, once it had finally paid for them, carrying on where Supertec and Asiatech left off. Aerodynamically, it was pretty nifty and when it was competitive, Frentzen got the most out of it. He quit after Hockenheim and we will never know who might have replaced him if the team had gone the distance.

Minardi-Asiatech

22. Alex YOONG

DRIVER PROFILE

- Name : *LOONG YOONG*
- First name : *Alexander Charles*
- Nationality : *Malaysian*
- Date of birth: *July 20 1976*
- Place of birth: *Kuala Lumpur (MAL)*
- Lives in : *Kuala Lumpur (MAL) and Faenza (I)*
- Marital status : *single*
- Kids : *-*
- Hobbies : *water skiing, golf, reading, scuba*
- Favorite music: *Pearl Jam*
- Favorite meal : *curry laksa*
- Favorite drink: *sugar cane*
- Height : *178 cm*
- Weight : *68 kg*

- Web : *www.alexyoong.com*

STATISTICS | PRIOR TO F1

STATISTICS		PRIOR TO F1
• Nber of Grand Prix :	14	1984-91 : *Karting*
• Victories :	0	1982-94 : *Production cars*
• Pole-positions :	0	1994 : *F. Asia Inter. Series*
• Best laps :	0	1995 : *F. Asia Inter. Series (2nd)*
• Accidents/off :	3	1996-97 : *F. Renault (GB)*
• Not qualified :	0	1998-99 : *F3 (GB)*
• Laps in the lead:	0	1999 : *F3000, F3000 (J)*
• Km in the lead :	0	2000 : *F. Japanese (J)*
• Points scored :	0	2001 : *F. Japanese (J)*

F1 CAREER

2001 : *Minardi-European. (3 GP). 0 pt. 26th of championship*
2002 : *Minardi-Asiatech. 0 pt. 20th of championship*

23. Mark WEBBER

DRIVER PROFILE

- Name : *WEBBER*
- First name : *Mark Alan*
- Nationality : *Australian*
- Date of birth : *August 27 1976*
- Place of birth : *Queanbeyan (AUS)*
- Lives in : *Buckinghamshire (GB)*
- Marital status : *single*
- Kids : *-*
- Hobbies : *tennis, squash, VTT, Playstation 2*
- Favorite music: *Savage Garden, Madonna, Gabrielle, U2*
- Favorite dish: *pasta*
- Favorite drink: *apple juice*
- Height: *184 cm*
- weight: *74 kg*

- Web: *www.markwebber.com*

STATISTICS | PRIOR TO F1

STATISTICS		PRIOR TO F1
• Nber of Grand Prix :	16	1991-93 : *Karting*
• Victories :	0	1994 : *F. Ford (AUS) (14th)*
• Pole-positions :	0	1995 : *F. Ford (AUS) (4th)*
• Best laps :	0	1996 : *F. Ford (GB) (2nd)*
• Accidents/off :	1	1997 : *F3 (GB) (4th)*
• Not qualified :	0	1998 : *FIA-GT Series (2nd)*
• Laps in the lead :	0	2000 : *F3000 (3rd)*
• Km in the lead :	0	2001 : *F3000 (2nd)*
• Points scored:	2	

F1 CAREER

2000 : *Arrows-Supertec. Test driver.*
2001 : *Benetton-Renault. Test driver.*
2002 : *Minardi-Asiatech. 2 pts. 16th of championship.*

If one had to pick his strongest quality, it would be the fact he speaks very good English! Because, put him behind the wheel and it all goes pear-shaped! He joined Minardi at the end of last year, thanks to massive financial backing from Kuala Lumpur, but he only proved what everyone knew already: too slow, too unsafe, there was nothing doing. After three DNQs, in Imola, Silverstone and Hockenheim, he was replaced for two races by Davidson, to let him recharge his batteries. There was no visible difference when he returned to the cockpit. The image of the sport suffers from deals like this, but as was the case with Tuero, Mazzacane and Marques, Minardi needs the cash. Yoong would do better to become an impresario. After all, as Mr. 107% he would make a fortune!

How do you make your F1 debut and make a mark when you are driving for Minardi? By scoring points in your very first grand prix, which he did in his home race in Australia. It was a lucky result, given that it was only a mass of retirements at the front end that allowed him to join the ranks of Villeneuve, Prost, Stewart and Clark amongst others. He celebrated in front of his home crowd as though he had won the race, but that was to be the highpoint of the year. Happy to spend time with his mechanics, just like Panis, Webber cultivated the image of a real sportsman, totally confident in his own potential and determined to prove it. Given the calibre of his team-mates, it is impossible to say whether his confidence is justified or not.

22. Anthony DAVIDSON

DRIVER PROFILE

- Name : *DAVIDSON*
- First name : *Anthony*
- Nationality: *British*
- Date of birth: *April 18 1979*
- Place of birth: *Hemel Hempstead (GB)*
- Lives in : *Brackley (GB)*
- Marital status: *engaged to Johanna*
- Kids : *-*
- Hobbies : *electronics, photography, trips*
- Favorite music: *-*
- Favorite dish: *honey mustard chicken and rice*
- Favorite drink : *fruit juice*
- Height: *166 cm*
- Weight: *55 kg*
- Web: *www.anthonydavidson.info*
- Nber of Grand Prix : *2*

PRIOR TO F1

1987-98 : *Karting*	2000 : *F. Ford (GB)*
1999 : *F. Ford Zetec (GB)*	2001 : *F3 (GB)*

The diminutive red-headed BAR test driver stood in for Yoong on two occasions. He showed some promise but was inconsistent.

Paul Stoddart

Rupert Manwaring

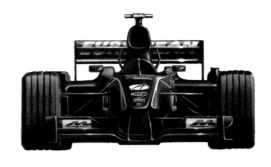

MINARDI-ASIATECH PS02
MARK WEBBER
AUSTRALIAN GRAND PRIX

Minardi-Asiatech PS02

SPECIFICATIONS

- Chassis : *Minardi PS02*
- Engine : *Asiatech AT02 V10 (72°)*
- Displacement: *2998 cm³*
- Electronic ignition : *TAG Electronics*
- Tyres: *Michelin*
- Wheels: *OZ Racing*
- Fuel / oil: *Elf*
- Brakes (discs): *Brembo / Hitco*
- Brakes (calipers): *Brembo*
- Transmission : *Minardi 6 gears, semi-automatic*
- Radiators : *Minardi*
- Plugs: *NGK*
- Shock absorbers: *Sachs*
- Suspensions : *Upper*
- Weight: *600 kg, driver + on board camera*
- Wheelbase : *3097 mm*
- Total length : *4572 mm*
- Total width : *1800 mm*
- Total height: *950 mm*
- Front track: *1480 mm*
- Rear track: *1410 mm*

TEAM PROFILE

- Adress : *Minardi Team SpA*
  Via Spallanzani, 21
  48018 Faenza (RA) - Italy
- Telephone : *+39 0546 696 111*
- Fax : *+39 0546 620 998*
- Web : *www.minardi.it*
- Established in : *1974*
- First Grand Prix : *Brazil 1985*
- President General Mg.: *Paul Stoddart*
- Technical director : *Gabriele Tredozi*
- Sports director : *John Walton*
- Commercial director : *Rupert Manwaring*
- Nber of employees : *155*
- Principaul sponsors : *GoKL, European Aviation, Magnum, Gazprom, PC Suria, BSA, Healthy Co, Quadriga, Telstra, PanGlobal, Allegrini, Pdp Box Doccia...*

TEST DRIVERS 2002

- Matteo BOBBI (I)
- Sergey ZLOBIN (RUS)
- Jirko MALCHÁREK (CZ)

STATISTICS

- Number of Grand Prix : 287
- Number of victories : 0
- Number of pole-positions : 0
- Number of best laps during the race : 0
- Number of drivers world titles : 0
- Number of constructors titles : 0
- Number of points scored : 30

POSITIONS IN WORLD CHAMPIONSHIP

1985 : *not classified*	1991 : *7th – 6 pts*	1997 : *not classified*
1986 : *not classified*	1992 : *11th – 1 pt*	1998 : *not classified*
1987 : *not classified*	1993 : *8th – 7 pts*	1999 : *10th – 1 pt*
1988 : *10th – 1 pt*	1994 : *10th – 5 pts*	2000 : *not classified*
1989 : *10th – 6 pts*	1995 : *10th – 1 pt*	2001 : *11th – 0 pt*
1990 : *not classified*	1996 : *not classified*	2002 : *9th – 2 pts*

SUCCESSION OF DRIVERS 2002

- Alex YOONG : *12 GP (AUS, MAL, BR, E, A, MC, CDN, EUR, F, I, USA, J)*
- Anthony DAVIDSON : *2 GP (HON, B)*
- Mark WEBBER : *All Grand Prix except Spain*

Engine handicap

You cannot hope to compete with the big boys if you are the smallest team, fighting for survival; a fight which was only won when the matter of television rights money left in the coffers after Prost folded, was sorted out towards the end of the year. It was hard enough arguing your case against the well-heeled teams. But changing engines all the time could only make matters worse. After the European power units and the Fondmetal lumps, based on the antediluvian 1998 Ford, this time it was Asiatech's turn and there was some merit in the deal. For starters it was free. What a relief! It hardly ever broke, which given how few revs it used is hardly surprising. Deprived of any technical development and forced to design its cars in a rush, it now has to find a replacement for the mysterious Asiatic group which is also cutting and running. The team always has to rely on pay drivers who only last a year or two. Minardi is in a state and has been since 1985. But it is still there and that in itself is admirable.

Toyota

24. Mika SALO

DRIVER PROFILE

- Name : *SALO*
- First name : *Mika*
- Nationality : *Finish*
- Date of birth: *November 30, 1966*
- Place of birth : *Helsinki (SF)*
- Lives in : *Castel San Pietro (CH)*
- Marital status: *married with Noriko*
- Kids : *one son (Max)*
- Hobbies : *musice, guitar, snowboard*
- Favorite music : *hard rock, Led Zeppelin, AC/DC*
- Favorite meal : *pasta*
- Favorite drink: *milk*
- Height: *175 cm*
- Weight: *69 kg*

- Web: *www.mikasalo.net*

STATISTICS

		PRIOR TO F1
Nber of Grand Prix :	110	1972 : *Karting*
Victories :	0	1978-83 : *Karting (SF) (4x 1st)*
Pole-positions :	0	1987 : *F. Ford 1600 (SF)(2nd),*
Best laps :	0	*(Scandinavian) (3rd)*
Accidents/off :	18	1988 : *Champion F. Ford*
Not qualified :	0	*1600 (EUR, SF, Scandinavian)*
Laps in the lead :	2	1989 : *F3 (GB) (13th)*
Kms in the lead :	13	1990 : *F3 (GB) (2nd)*
Points scored :	33	1991 : *F3 (D), F3000 (J)*
		1992 : *F3 (D), F3000(J) (14th)*
		1993 : *F3 (D), F3000 (J)*
		1994 : *F3000 (J)*

F1 CAREER

1994 : *Lotus-Mugen Honda. (2 GP). 0 pt.*
1995 : *Tyrrell-Yamaha. 5 pts. 14th of championship.*
1996 : *Tyrrell-Yamaha. 5 pts. 13th of championship..*
1997 : *Tyrrell-Yamaha. 2 pts. 16th of championship.*
1998 : *Arrows. 3 pts. 13th of championship.*
1999 : *BAR-Supertec, Ferrari. 10 pts. 10th of championship.*
2000 : *Sauber-Petronas. 6 pts. 11th of championship.*
2002 : *Toyota. 2 pts. 17th of championship.*

25. Allan McNISH

DRIVER PROFILE

- Name : *McNISH*
- First name : *Allan*
- Nationality : *British*
- Date of birth : *December 29, 1969*
- Place of birth : *Dumfries (Scotland)*
- Lives in : *Monaco (MC)*
- Married: *engaged to Kenny*
- Kids: *-*
- Hobbies : *relaxing, water skiing*
- Favorite music : *Lenny Kravitz, rock*
- Favorite dish: *food of the world*
- Favorite drink: *water tea, whisky*
- Height: *165 cm*
- Weight: *58 kg*

- Web: *www.allanmcnish.com*

STATISTICS

		PRIOR TO F1
Nber of Grand Prix :	16	1981-86 : *karting.*
Victories :	0	*Champion (Scotland)(1982, 83,*
Pole-positions :	0	*84 & 86), (GB) (1983 & 86)*
Best laps :	0	1987 : *F. Ford (GB) (3rd)*
Accidents/off :	4	1988 : *Champion F. Vauxhall*
Not qualified :	0	*Lotus (GB),GM Lotus Euroseries (3rd)*
Laps in the lead :	0	1989 : *F3 (GB) (2nd)*
Kms in the lead :	0	1990 : *F3000 (4th)*
Points scored :	0	1991 : *F3000 (16th)*
		1992 : *F3000 (11th)*
		1995 : *F3000 (7th)*
		1996 : *Porsche SuperCup*
		1997 : *GT (USA-N)*
		1998 : *FIA-GT (3rd),*
		winner 24 H. of le Mans
		1999 : *24 H. of le Mans*
		2000 : *Champion ALMS ,*
		24 H. of le Mans (2nd)

F1 CAREER

1990-91 : *McLaren-Honda. Test driver.*
1993-94, 96 : *Benetton. Test driver.*
2002 : *Toyota. 0 pt. 19th of championship.*

Tasked with developing the Toyota "laboratory" car in 2001, he was making his return to competition. He was keen to explain that his job was to "teach the team about F1, a new experience for most of them." Mika Salo might have had ideas above his station. His main motivation seemed to be a high salary. The man who, in 1999, managed to bring Ferrari down to the level of Arrows at Spa, when acting as stand-in for Schumacher, was not the charismatic leader Toyota was looking for in F1, nor the best adviser on technical matters. Despite having a contract for 2003, he was hoofed out, proving that his employers had rumbled him. Did he really think he could make a silk purse out of a sow's ear? Could a dissipated pupil become a diligent teacher?

He was seraglio man; the guide for the Toyota GT One's adventures in the Le Mans 24 Hours. Charged with handling development when this car was fitted with the engine which would eventually power the F1 car, Allan McNish eventually found himself alongside Mika Salo in the "laboratory" car before racing for real. He was making his F1 debut at the same time and age that Schumacher was heading for a fifth title. At last, a decade of testing for other F1 teams had reaped its reward. While his testing abilities were rated, he lacked speed and there seemed little hope that things would change on that front. He proved that making the switch from long distance runner to sprinter late in life does not really work. In his F3000 days, he topped the time sheets, but ten years later the magic had gone.

Gustav Brunner

Ange Pasquali

TOYOTA TF102
MIKA SALO
BRAZILIAN GRAND PRIX

Toyota TF102

SPECIFICATIONS

- Chassis : _Toyota TF102_
- Engine: _Toyota RVX-02 V10 (90°)_
- Displacement : _2998 cm³_
- Electronic ignition : _Magneti-Marelli_
- Tyres : _Michelin_
- Wheels : _BBS_
- Fuel / oil: _Esso_
- Brakes (discs) : _Brembo_
- Brakes (calipers): _Brembo_
- Transmission : _Toyota 6 gears, semi-automatic_
- Clutch : _Sachs_
- Radiators : _Toyota_
- Shock absorbers : _Sachs_
- Suspensions : _roll bar / push (fr/bk)_
- Weight: _600 kg, driver + on board camera_
- Wheelbase: _3090 mm_
- Total length : _4547 mm_
- Total width : _not revealed_
- Total height : _950 mm_
- Front track: _1424 mm_
- Rear track: _1411 mm_

TEAM PROFILE

- Adress : _Toyota Motorsport GmbH_
  Toyota-Allee 7
  50858 Koln
  Germany
- Telephone : _+49 (0) 2234 182 34 44_
- Fax : _+49 (0) 2234 182 337_
- Web: _www.toyota-f1.com_
- Established in : _1999_
- First Grand Prix : _Australia 2002_
- General manager : _Tsutomu Tomita_
- President : _Ove Andersson_
- Chief designer : _Gustav Brunner_
- Team manager : _Ange Pasquali_
- Nber of employees : _550_
- Principal sponsors : _Panasonic, AOL Time Warner, Avex,_
  Catia, EMC², Exxon Mobil Corporation, Magneti-Marelli, MAN,
  Meteo France, Ratiopharm, Sparco, St Georges, Travelex,
  Wella, X-lite, Yamaha...

STATISTIQUES

Number of Grand Prix:	_17_
Number of victories :	_0_
Number of pole-positions :	_0_
Number of best laps during the race :	_0_
Number of drivers world titles :	_0_
Number of constructors titles :	_0_
Number of points scored :	_2_

POSITION IN WORLD CHAMPIONSHIP

2002 : _10ᵗʰ – 2 pts_

TEST DRIVER 2002

- Ryan BRISCOE (AUS)
- Stéphane SARRAZIN (F)

SUCCESSION OF DRIVERS 2002

- Mika SALO : _all Grand Prix_
- Allan McNISH : _all Grand Prix except Japan_

Ove Andersson

A giant's first steps

The arrival of this automobile colossus was a major event for F1. Unlike Ford, which via Jaguar, bought Stewart in 2000, Toyota went for the start from scratch, do it all yourself option. Everything, chassis and engine, was designed on a clean sheet of paper after paying FIA a whopping 48 million dollars deposit, as laid out in the rules for new teams wishing to join the fun. Toyota had a very impressive budget, but much of its personnel had absolutely no experience of the discipline. It started off the year with some impressive and surprising performances, scoring two points even before the circus arrived in Europe. While not exactly quick, its car was pretty reliable, but that was not enough to maintain momentum. Kept on after thousands of miles of testing in 2001, Salo and McNish were not quick enough, nor were they adept enough at setting up the car. They also lacked the charisma which might have saved their careers. The team met its avowed target for the year. Hardly surprising, as all they aimed for was qualifying within the 107% margin at every race.

SPOTLIGHT

As with past editions of "The Formula 1 Yearbook" we look at the season from several angles. We turn the lens to five views of 2002, going on to spotlight tyres and a study of Juan Manuel Fangio's five world championships, a parallel with Michael Schumacher's five.

2002: a British point of view

Coulthard: "the next one will be mine"

"A reasonable year, in the circumstances, but obviously not a great one." David Coulthard finished fifth, behind the Ferrari and Williams drivers, in the World Championship, with 41 points, and a single victory.

Nigel Roebuck - Autosport, London

Nigel Roebuck
55 years old, decided to quit his industrial job and enter journalism at the age of 24. In 1971, he starts writing for the American magazine «Car & Driver», before joining the British weekly motor racing magazine «Autosport» in 1976. He is covering Formula One since 1977, while workingfor the «Sunday Tmes», for the «Auto Week» and the Japanese magazine «Racing On».

His season did not prove an easy one. He had felt sure that the MP4-17 would be competitive, but its Mercedes engine, although improving through the year, never had the power of Ferrari or BMW. As well as that, McLaren switched to Michelin, and in 2002 Bridgestone invariably had the last word.

Therefore, had it been difficult for David, at last the senior driver at McLaren, following the departure of Mika Häkkinen, to keep his motivation alive?

"Actually, no", he said. *"I've got a fixed goal in my mind: I want to win the championship - and I know my future is with McLaren, so it's a reality, rather than a fantasy. Most guys on the grid are never going to get the opportunity."*
When first he drove MP4-17, David found it much

better than its predecessor, although not comparable with the 1998 car, which was the class of the field. *"In '98 we had Bridgestones, when Ferrari had Goodyears, we had a good aero package, a good engine... we had everything. In '99, Ferrari went over to Bridgestone, and it was closer, but we still had a race-winning package. Then, in 2000 and 2001, everything became more competitive, and also we've had some performance drop-off in certain areas...but we're working on them.*

"Because we didn't do any winter testing alongside Ferrari, I went to Melbourne believing I had a car that could win. The penny dropped very quickly! It was difficult to accept that there was no championship potential, but I thought, 'OK, it's not about a championship, it's about developing a car

now that's going to suit me better in the future'."
It was said of Prost and Senna, just as of Schumacher, that, while much of their success came from genius, so also a great deal was the result of hard work. Coulthard says that he, too, is working harder than ever before.

"There's still so much I don't understand, and I'm trying to learn progressively from the engineers. In the past Mika and I rather relied on each other - I knew if he tested something, and it made him go quicker, it would make me quicker, and it was the same the other way round. So we probably got a bit lazy - and we also had a car that was competitive..."

If DC soon had to accept that he was not going to be a championship contender in 2002, so he had to remain in a positive frame of mind. *"In the past, I had never looked beyond the next race, but now I had to think in terms of the season - and the direction in which I wanted the car and tyres to go.*

"I'm developing as a driver, as well. I first tried left-foot braking, for example, when I joined McLaren, but at first it feels like trying to write with your left hand. So I said, 'No, I don't like this', and went back to right-foot braking. Then, when we got hand clutches, suddenly you could have a big brake pedal, and now, through choice, I right-foot brake for the big stops, and left-foot for the rest."

Rubens Barrichello is another right-foot braker, and one who has decided to stick with it. *"Yes, I know,"* said Coulthard. *"I've talked with him about it - there's nothing like getting a driver with a couple of drinks in him, you know!"*

Coulthard has sympathy with Barrichello's situation at Ferrari, perhaps because, although Ron Dennis has always allowed his drivers to race one another, in Häkkinen's era there was always the perception that it was 51:49 in Mika's favour.

"Well, there were times of frustration in the past, when I maybe thought, 'How do I beat the team of Mika and Ron?', and I concluded I had to work harder to achieve the same, because I was starting half a step back. Ron would probably disagree. As you say, he always let us race - and I know I wouldn't want to win a race the way Schumacher did in Austria.

Prior to this year, a perfect race would have been to have Michael and Mika each side of me on the podium. OK, a win is a win, but I'm old-fashioned and romantic in that I want it to be a (itals) race (end itals). Some people seem happy to take a victory any way it comes."
Although Coulthard drove superbly this season, the raw speed of Kimi Räikkönen caused some to speculate that DC's days at McLaren were numbered, but clearly David's commitment to the team is as strong as ever. If Mercedes people are perhaps more overt in their support of him, he perfectly understands what makes the whole

operation tick. "*It's true that Mercedes are more vocal, and obviously that's appreciated at times when... you might be getting criticism elsewhere.*

As you know, Ron's not one to waste time in small talk - he's not going to say something just to make you feel good. At first you think that's a bit strange, but once you know the system, Ron's very consistent.

"I'll admit that in the past a little bit more 'arm around the shoulder' would have taken away some insecurities, but if McLaren could have found someone better, they would have done it; I've been here all these years because I do a good job."

At the end of the season, Dennis paid tribute to Coulthard. "*There's no doubt*", he said, "*that Kimi is developing into an outstanding F1 driver - but David has responded to his presence in the team with precisely the balance we would have expected of him. In the circumstances it would have been easy for an experienced driver to lose his focus, but he hasn't been destabilised at all.*"

"*The thing is, I absolutely love what I do*", said Coulthard. "*I don't ever remember waking up on a race morning, and thinking, 'We're wasting our time...' There are moments when you get reminded not to moan, to say to yourself, 'You could be further down, with no chance'.*"

Other drivers have said that, while they envy much about a McLaren driver's lot, they hate the thought of all the promotion work required. David grinned.

"*Well, there are times when I think, 'Why am I doing all these things?' But Ron tries to control the number of requests from the sponsors. If I could be paid less to drive more, yes, I would do that - but it's not an option. A part of your contract is marketing, so I may as well be paid more, and do it!*"

Although Coulthard won only race in 2002, it came at Monaco, after a quite brilliant drive. Remarkably, though, David didn't consider it anything special - certainly not comparable, for example, with his win at Magny-Cours in 2000.
"*Well, I think the Monaco weekend was a mature one. I kept it off the barriers, found the right tyre,*

found the set-up, and kept clear of all the bullshit, in my apartment. We had all the ingredients for a perfect day, and we came out with a result."

Surely, though, there was a little more to it than that? For one thing, there was pressure all the way, from such as Schumacher and Montoya, and there was also the dread 'off' period, when the Michelins lost grip for several laps. "*If that had been me*", said Martin Brundle, DC's manager, "*I'd have stuck it in the barrier, trying to compensate...*"

"*Well,*" said Coulthard, "*for a few laps I was slower than the car would go, because I knew there were only two places where I could be passed - the chicane and Ste Devote. So the important thing was not to panic where they couldn't pass you, and really get it right where they could.*

That took the pressure off until the tyres came back - and then I had to push, because otherwise I was going to get passed at the pit stops.
I was able to use experience that day - but it wasn't like Magny-Cours in 2000. That really was one of my best races. I passed Rubens, I got angry at Michael for doing his weaving act, I passed him, and I won the race. For me, that was a classic race - and it involved overtaking for the lead."

Prior to 2002, Coulthard and Häkkinen were team mates for six seasons, and inevitably there was a different atmosphere now, with the arrival of the youthful Räikkönen.

"*Fundamentally, it's the same, but obviously there's an ingredient missing. I mean, Mika's a good guy, and so are the people he had round him - Keke Rosberg and so on - so you miss them.*

"For me it took away 'the Mika factor', in that I'd always been slightly behind - he had joined the team before me, and he won a couple of championships, and I hadn't. Kimi brings different challenges. If he's close to me on performance, people say, 'That's not unexpected'. If he's quicker, it's, 'Oh, what's happened to David?'
"Kimi and I get along fine. All right, he's 22, and I'm 31, but I haven't noticed any age difference, as such - maybe because Finns are known to drink socially, and I'm not teetotal, either! I think there's

a sort of levelling of mental ages when you're a bit drunk..."

Next season will be Coulthard's ninth as a fulltime F1 driver, and he has no idea how long he will continue. "*I don't have a plan about it. Maybe I'll wake up one morning without the motivation, who knows?*

"I remember seeing Damon (Hill) at Hockenheim in '99, literally with his head in his hands, saying, 'I can't do this any more'. I thought, 'Jesus, if you're really feeling that, why - when you've got a wife, kids, a few million pounds in the bank - are you going to do 215 mph this afternoon? Get out of here!'

"As and when I do stop, the thing I'll value most is not having to travel constantly. Mika didn't stop because he didn't know how to drive racing cars any more - I'm sure if he could have just raced, without the testing and promotion work, he'd never have stopped. But that wasn't an option. I get bored with the travel, too, but I like it when I get here - no, that's an understatement, I (itals) love (end itals) it when I get here..."

∧
Monaco was McLaren's only win of the season. Despite all his best intentions, Coulthard once again had to settle for the role of also-ran.

For most of the season, this was the view Coulthard faced during the races: the rear end of the Ferraris.
∨

Mercedes/BMW: strategies for a return to winning ways

2002 was something of a nightmare for the men of Mercedes and BMW, who had good cause to think the world championship was in their grasp. The harsh wake-up call came at the San Marino Grand Prix. From then on, the two German car giants put strategies and budgets in place which should see them get back on track

Anno Hecker – Frankfurter Allgemeine Zeitung

Imola 2002 will stick in the minds of those in charge at McLaren-Mercedes and BMW-Williams. Because that was the weekend when during and after the San Marino Grand Prix, their eyes must have been opened to the awful truth that the race for the title was pretty much over. After four of the seventeen races, Ralf Schumacher declared: "*In Imola it is already clear that we have no chance of winning the championship.*" This was hard to swallow for the ambitious young driver, who felt that above all, it was the cars which made the difference when it came to deciding who walked off with the Formula 1 crown. "*Montoya and me could also have been world champions, if we were driving a Ferrari.*"

That bad mood still lingered in the BMW office at Suzuka for the final race of the season. It was their third race on Japanese soil since coming back to Formula 1 in 2000. They had expected to do better. "*We were third in 2001 and wanted to be second this year, which we have done*", explained motor sport director, Mario Theissen. But truth be told, the Bavarians thought this year would be time for the big push. They believed they had the most powerful engine and with a few tweaks to the chassis, they should have been challenging Ferrari. After winter testing, Mercedes too were full of optimism. It seemed that a prediction made by board member Jurgen Hubbert, responsible for the Formula 1 programme, was about to come true a bit earlier than expected. Towards the end of the 2001 season, in Indianapolis, he had bragged that the team would soon be back where it should be- at the front.

After a crushing defeat at the hands of Michael Schumacher and Rubens Barrichello, Ralf Schumacher left the Imola circuit in a very bad mood, despite finishing third. "*I could do no better*", he cursed. As for Jurgen Hubbert, in the paddock, he completed blanked a group of journalists he knew well, evidently in high dudgeon over Kimi Räikkönen's retirement and even more embarrassing, the fact that David Coulthard was lapped. All he could bring himself to say was: "*There is nothing to say at the moment. We must just work.*"

Maybe in a couple of years time, if the battle to topple Ferrari from its perch has come to anything, we will be saying that the turning point came at Imola in 2001when DaimlerChrysler and BMW took a serious kicking. It was here that everyone realised that the red arrows would be quick on all types of circuit and therefore unbeatable throughout the year. Obeying orders from Hubbert, Mercedes motorsport boss Norbert Haug assembled the troops for a crisis meeting in the team's brand new motorhome,

a veritable palace in glass and steel. In the BMW camp, the war meeting took place behind closed doors. The two companies had different strategies with BMW happy to criticise the team in public, whereas Mercedes drew down the shutters and refused to accept any criticism aimed at its partner, McLaren, claiming that all was rosy in the garden. But come spring and McLaren blew away this cosy comfort blanket. Unless it was someone else who fed the British press about the weaknesses of the Mercedes engine. This new approach even drew a comment from Ilmor's Mario Illien, the man in charge of engine design. "*When things are not working, it is always the fault of others. They have always done that*", declared the Swiss, shrugging his shoulders in response to McLaren's salvo. He knew that these comments about his engine, which was by no means perfect, was a way of diverting attention from weaknesses on the chassis side. BMW however, did not stint when it came to dishing the dirt. Technical director, Burkhard Goschel accused Williams in public of adopting too conservative an approach and his views were actually endorsed by none other than Sir Frank Williams! "*You were right to criticise us,*" he said during an interview in Spa-Francorchamps. "*We were not good enough.*"

Even though their methods were different, Mercedes and BMW reacted in a similar way. Just like Hubbert, his opposite numbers in Munich rolled up their sleeves, concocted plans in the spring, set the ball rolling in

summer and struck in the autumn. It soon became clear that the Stuttgart men were taking more control of Formula 1 engine production and could therefore justify the name Mercedes appearing on the cam covers. They increased their share in Ilmor by 30% to reach a total of 55%, with the aim of buying it out completely next year.

A Mercedes production specialist, Hans-Ulrich Maik has now been appointed manager at Ilmor's Brixworth headquarters, while specialists and parts builders from the mother country will work on unleashing more power from their V10. Most significantly, Mercedes poached BMW project director Werner Laurenz to be Mario Illien's right hand man. His job is to show Illien how to apply industrial processes to his programme. Laurenz is considered a major catch. "*We will not be weaker without him*" claimed BMW motor sport boss Gerhard Berger, "*but he will strengthen Mercedes.*" It is easy to say, but hard to swallow. Formula 1 is not a game for the car manufacturers. It is a battlefield and a

Anno Hecker
38 years old, worked first as a physical education instructor befor turning to journalism in 1986. After working as a political correspondent for a Bonn news agency, he joined "Frankfurter Allgemeine Zeitung" in 1991 to cover motor sports. He specialised in stories combinig politics and sport.

showcase for their high technology. In the case of Mercedes, it involves hundreds of engineers and billions of dollars over the next five years, even if the company tried to deny it when the story broke cover. "*It is not correct that the Mercedes board has put aside a billion dollars for engine development,*" they said, adding that, "*DaimlerChrysler does its accounts in Euros and our budget for Formula 1 would not have been set out over the timescale mentioned.*" However, given

that the dollar and the Euro are pretty evenly matched and the timescale changes little, then one arrives at the same figure. DaimlerChrysler was not denying the investment of a billion, be it in dollars or Euros. The important point of the plan was to mount a campaign to topple the serial winning Ferrari and rework McLaren's planning programme. The first step of this plan was to start the first three races of the 2003 season with a revised version of this

year's car, before bringing a radically different car to Imola. The aim is to knock Ferrari off its perch in 2004, when Kimi Räikkönen will be sufficiently mature to fully exploit his talent. "*We are on the right road. We are turning the corner, even if Ferrari is the big favourite at the moment,*" commented Haug. "*Our team has never been more motivated about Formula 1 than it is at the moment.*"

BMW seems to want to get even more involved in the production of the Williams cars. The chassis had weaknesses which were only hidden during qualifying by the power and torque of the BMW engine and that puts the Germans in a strong position. They are asking for a total exchange of data, offering gently but firmly, their full support. The plan is for BMW engineers to be present or at least consulted when it comes to the build of the cars. This could put Williams in an even weaker position reckon some insiders, in the light of BMW's rumoured plans to go it alone after 2004. It is not by chance that the men from Munich have let this be known in public. This degree of honesty is designed, first and foremost, to put Williams under serious pressure. Because, given the current recession, what team can allow itself to lose what is currently the best engine builder? In fact, Frank Williams would like to see BMW more implicated in his team and that is why, next year's car will almost certainly be more adventurous. If the team's performance does not improve, it would be the first time since they returned to the sport that BMW would be seriously embarrassed. It will take a major step forward, as it involves getting ahead of Ferrari in the Constructors' Championship.

∧
A lack of power and reliability from the Mercedes engine meant Räikkönen could not show what he could do.

Gerhard Berger and Mario Theissen of BMW ask themselves what they can do to close the gap to Ferrari. Close collaboration with Williams will be vital if they are to succeed.
<

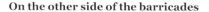

Inimitable Italian Style

The 2002 season can be summed up in a single word: Ferrari. The Maranello marque performed beyond even its own wildest dreams in this world championship, triumphing from the curtain raiser in Melbourne to the grand finale in Suzuka.

Barbara Premoli – F1 Racing Italia, Milan

The Scuderia covered all the angles, starting the season with an updated version of last year's F2001. It was only for round 3 in Brazil, that it brought out the 2002 car, running just one of them for four times world champion Michael Schumacher. Hardly surprising, it was a success straight out of the crate. It did cause something of a controversy as the German's team-mate Rubens Barrichello was still making do with the old "jalopy," even though it proved quick enough given that it was good enough to take pole in Australia with the Brazilian, while Schumi went on to win.

When the F2002 was launched, it was obvious that it would be successful. At Ferrari, nothing had been left to chance and the team was already regarded as having the championship in the bag before it turned a wheel. Main rivals McLaren had virtually been forced into switching to Michelin tyres in a bid to outwit the Italian squad, but that involved embarking on a whole new programme. The ace up the Scuderia's sleeve was the fact it was now the only top team running Bridgestones and immediately set up a test team exclusively dedicated to tyre development.
The F2002 was the definitive package, with all its elements combining to work towards a common goal. That stems from the fact that everything is made in-house, with every part linking and functioning with the next, with nothing left out of the core process. McLaren, feeling it was not getting first class service from the Japanese tyre manufacturer, chose to look elsewhere, while knowing it would have to share Michelin's attentions with BMW-Williams.

Records ad infinitum

You needed a pocket calculator to follow the 2002 season. Michael Schumacher and Ferrari were on a record breaking spree, as irresistible as a flooding river in full flow. The superiority of the machinery and the undoubted talent of the driver literally drove the tifosi wild. Faced with this onslaught, even the Scuderia's nearest rivals had to doff their caps and recognise the unique technical and human qualities of this team. Of the latter, one can highlight the importance of key figures within the squad: Michael Schumacher, not just for his evident talent on the track, but also his intelligence; the spirit of cooperation of Rubens Barrichello, the mastery and charisma of Jean Todt and the technical abilities of Ross Brawn, Rory Byrne and Paolo Martinelli.
This perfect synergy produced those much talked about figures: 15 wins from 17 races, a Formula 1 record 221 points scored in a season and 9 one-two finishes. Schumacher's achievements are enough to make one's head spin: 144 points (67 more than second placed Barrichello,) reaching a career total of 50 pole positions, a host of laps in the lead, totalling 1,090 km, 12 hat-tricks of pole, win and fastest race lap. In 2001, it seemed a miracle that he took the Driver's title in Budapest in August, but this year Schumacher did even

better, wrapping it up in France in July, to take his fifth title.

Insatiable Ferrari

Success always has its critics and Ferrari was accused of sucking the life blood out of the series, of reducing the global audience who switched off in their millions. However, the Scuderia came in for the harshest words over events in Zeltweg, when Barrichello slowed in the final metres of the race to hand victory to his team-mate. It was really the only low point in an impeccable season. The contrived result soon proved to have been unnecessary given the ease with which the titles were won, but it generated a wave of anger against the Scuderia, accused of bringing the sport into disrepute. Then there was the matter of the photo-finish in Indianapolis. The Italian team certainly knew how to get itself talked about, for better or for worse, whether the debate centred on their on-track performance or their off-track politics. But the team was always united which was its strength. The structure is unbeatable and grows in strength from year to year. Rubens Barrichello has become Michael Schumacher's perfect team-mate. Luca Badoer racks up thousands of kilometres in testing, improving and perfecting the car, while Luciano Burti concentrated on tyre development this year. The home crowd certainly appreciated this

solidarity and proved it at this year's Italian Grand Prix. Under the new futuristic podium at Monza, the crowds cheered Rubens, Michael and Eddie Irvine, as a sign of the passion they have for the red team and its drivers, both past and present. At that moment, the Zeltweg fiasco seemed to have been forgotten.

On the other side of the barricades

In contrast to this all-conquering view of Italy, with a virtually unlimited budget, its pursuit of the latest technology, there is another Italy, which is fighting hard just to survive. KL Minardi's season should in no way be seen as a negative one. The opening round in Melbourne was a shot in the arm for Gian Carlo Minardi, Paul Stoddart and the whole team. On home turf in Melbourne, Mark Webber took a very important fifth place and those two points would prove vital come the end of the year, which saw the Faenza based squad finish ninth. "The other Italian team" has a loyal following, as fans and not just in Italy, admire its determination and perseverance. In 2002, Minardi acquired backing from Russian company Gazprom just as the team looked like going under, in a year when an economic downturn saw the disappearance of Prost GP and, at least for the moment, Arrows. Gazprom money will allow the team to buy engines and next year, Cosworth will replace Asiatech which pulled out

Barbara Premoli Born in Milan (29/9/1963), Barbara has always been interested in cars, especially F1. She graduated in languages and intended becoming a teacher, a small Situations Vacant advertisement in "La Gazzetta dello Sport" changed her life. In the space of a few days, she found herself working for "Motociclismo" magazine, where she enjoyed working for ten years. Then, from January 1999, she accepted the challenge of launching the Italian version of "F1 Racing".

of the sport at the end of this season. The Minardi scenario is good for the sport and its popularity was proved with the staging of its Minardi Day event, which attracted a huge crowd at Imola, as the team welcomed its friends and Formula 1 fans. It was a fun day, where Minardi ran its two seater cars and the race car driven by Alex Yoong and test drivers Matteo Bobbi and Sergey Zlobin, its latest Russian acquisition. Those who love Formula 1 love Minardi, which has a long and worthy history and deserves credit for seeking out young talent. Gian Carlo Minardi has launched the career of many young drivers and continues to do so, with special programme devoted to the project. We lived through the German GP with this team, just as things seemed to be taking a turn for the worse. But the team are united, from mechanics to engineers, around their one true boss Gian Carlo Minardi, who does everything in his power to safeguard their future and in fact the lifesaving deal with the Russian oil giant was down to him. The team deserves its place in F1 simply for being there and surviving up against giants like Toyota with its huge manpower and budgets. Minardi is a living reminder of the golden age of the sport; the days when the great Senna would leave his own motorhome to go and join his Italian mates for a plate of pasta at the other end of the paddock.

Italy expects

There are two Italian hopes in Formula 1 who are constantly improving and deserve to pick up the rewards for all their sacrifice: Jarno Trulli and Giancarlo Fisichella swapped seats this year. Jarno has embarked on a big adventure with Renault, while Giancarlo has landed at Jordan. Both men endured a difficult 2002, full of hard work. But that was to be expected and they were ready for the fight, which involved difficulty, disappointment and too many retirements. Both

men are quick, very quick, determined and capable and they are under no illusions. Jarno is a real grafter and this year was a major turning point, given it was the first time he has worked with a major manufacturer. Renault is starting a new phase with all the difficulties that entails. It has a very successful past and when it decided to return to F1, it did so with clear and definite goals of winning races and then the title. Jarno Trulli is the right man for the job of taking the French company back to the top. It is only a question of time. Jarno knows this, as do his legion of fans who have stuck with him through a difficult season. For them the highlight of the year was cheering him all the way to his unforgettable fourth place finish at Monza, which at the time, was worth as much as a win. It injected a dose of optimism after so much sacrifice. Giancarlo can also rely on fervent support from the fans. In 2003, his Jordan could make a major step forward thanks to the team's deal to run Ford Cosworth engines. Farewell to Honda and thanks to a new engine, it is probable that our Fisico will enjoy a good season.

The Italian question

Italy loves Formula 1 and most Italians support Ferrari. However, despite all the success of the past few years, one element is still missing: an Italian driver in Italy's car. Why does the Scuderia never pick one of our youngsters? This is the most common question from the legions of faithful fans who would not dream of missing a grand prix on their televisions; those who got up in the middle of the night or at dawn to watch qualifying and the race from Suzuka, even when the titles had been wrapped up long ago. Modern F1 is all about high-technology and major budgets and so it is easy to forget the "end user," the spectators who turn up at the circuits or watch the races at home. The public needs more spectacle and cheaper tickets and changes to the regulations planned for 2003 will only answer some of these demands. The real fans are looking for excitement and one of their dreams is to see a young Italian at the wheel of a Ferrari. It would be their apotheosis! There are so many drivers doing well in all sorts of race series around the world and it would be great if one of them was to get the call from Maranello. When that day comes, the Scuderia will be even greater than today, receiving even more support than it does now, with Michael Schumacher a five times world champion breaking records aided by the talented Rubens Barrichello. When that day comes, Jean Todt and President Montezemolo will really be able to say they have done their utmost, because they will definitely be taken to heart by the tifosi.

∧
Despite money troubles, Minardi always managed to line up at the start. The result of the Australian Grand Prix was a big surprise, which delighted not only the fans but also people in the paddock.

A season of highs and lows. That was Jarno Trulli's year. His fans are still waiting impatiently for his first win.
<

Jacques Villeneuve's *annus horribilis*

Jacques Villeneuve may well have felt he had been banished to the wilderness in 1999, during his first season with BAR, but that was nothing compared with 2002, his worst year yet. The tale of a long and winding road

Stéphanie Morins – La Presse, Montreal

Like cattle

The shock wave hit the world of F1 in mid-December 2001: 24 hours before the launch of the new car, Craig Pollock announced he was leaving BAR, the team he had helped create. No one was taken in, as it was obvious the Scotsman had not chosen to leave the ship, but rather that the title sponsor, British American Tobacco, had shown him the door.

Change was definitely needed at BAR, which had been stagnating in the middle of the pack since its earliest days, despite its substantial budget. But Villeneuve found this particular pill hard to swallow. Along with Pollock, his friend and adviser, the Canadian had dreamed of success with the BAR team. He invested in it with his talent, his credibility and his energy. Without Pollock, there seemed little sense in the Canadian being there. Why linger with a team which was going backwards rather than forwards? The dream had been shattered.

As the BAR-Honda 004 was unveiled, the team confirmed what everyone knew already: BAR's destiny was now in the hands of Prodrive supremo, David Richards. During the launch, Villeneuve had a major sulk on. If he could he would have been out the door. But where could he go? No competitive team had a seat available. He might as well stay put and hope.

In Melbourne, for the first race of the season, he poured his heart out. He was upset at the way BAT had handled the Pollock situation. "*The fact Craig was fired is the sort of thing that happens in business. I can live with that. But I am angry with the way it was done. After everything we had done for the team, we were treated like cattle. If Craig hadn't told me, I'd have found about it at the launch*", fulminated the Canadian.

The question would arise several more times during 2002. Had the former champion's unwavering friendship with Craig Pollock ruined his career? After all, it was the Scotsman who advised Villeneuve to launch himself into the disastrous BAR project. It had been a risky gamble which had not paid off as, in four seasons, the Brackley based team had only picked up 44 points, 33 of them courtesy of Villeneuve, with two podium finishes in 2001.

"*I took what seemed to be the best decision at the time*", reckoned the driver in explaining why he had extended his contract with them in 2000, when he had been courted by other teams. "*I believed what I was promised, but unfortunately things did not go the way I wanted. The technical staff were not realistic, they were too optimistic and I got sucked into it all.*"

Back to square one?

David Richards knew that his first year in charge at BAR would not be a picnic, but no doubt he had hoped for better. At the start of the year, its performance rivalled that of a tortoise, but unlike the fairy tale, it did not finish ahead of the hare,

Stéphanie Morin
A journalist with La Presse, a Montreal daily paper for the past four years. She covered tennis, ice hockey and basketball before experiencing Formula 1 for the first time in 2002. "Rather than engines and chassis, F1 for me is first and foremost about the people."

winding up in a measly eighth place in the constructors' championship.

Villeneuve suffered a lot of mechanical bothers in a car that was supposed to be more reliable than its predecessors: a wing flew off in Melbourne, engines broke in Brazil, Austria, Monaco and Japan, there were transmission problems in Hungary, a gearbox let go in Germany and so on. Matters were even worse for team-mate Olivier Panis, who only saw the chequered flag at his eighth attempt.

Under the circumstances, scoring a point was a minor miracle and miracles are not a forte at BAR. After nine races, the team was plum last in the championship, with not a single point to its name.

The finger of blame was often pointed at Honda. The Japanese engine had lacked grunt all year and just when it looked liking picking up, it coughed and spluttered. The Honda crew spent the early part of the year promising heaven and earth for the Canadian Grand Prix, with the arrival of a redesigned more powerful V10 engine. The expected revolution never happened.

At the Nurburgring, Villeneuve recorded the worst qualifying performance of his career, with a disastrous 19th place. He finished the race twelfth. The Canadian could no longer hide his disappointment. "*This season is screwed. We were promised a lot for Montreal and now there is no*

^
A disastrous start to the season meant Villeneuve did not know where to turn and the in-fighting within the BAR team did not help matters.

reason why it should get any better for the rest of the year."

Jacques fired off again before the British Grand Prix. "*This is the worst season of my career. I didn't think it could be worse than 1999, but it looks set to be that way. In our first season, we had an excuse, but not anymore after four years. There is no excuse for being as uncompetitive as we are. Honestly, I don't know how we are going to get through the rest of the year. I just hope we have a bit of luck and that we can pick up a few points so that we don't end up last.*"

Lady Luck finally woke up in time to grant BAR five points at Silverstone, with a fourth place for Villeneuve and a fifth position for Panis. It was reason enough to break open the champagne in the garage! The team would not finish last after all. Honour was saved!

Worn out by broken promises and four seasons of torture, the Canadian chose to keep his feet on the ground and took the role of killjoy while the others celebrated. "*It will take more than one good day to sort this out. This was just a small ray of sunshine. We have to be realistic. If you get carried away, things can even get worse and that really hurts. I don't want to start dreaming and then wake up with a bump.*"

This long and painful season threw up one positive change. After the Brazilian Grand Prix, technical director Malcolm Oastler and his right hand man, Andy Green were sent packing. Between them, these two men had been responsible for bringing the first four BAR chassis into the world; four mistakes which never delivered on their promises.

In their place came Geoff Willis, former head of aerodynamics at Williams, who found himself with the task (an impossible one?) of turning a sow's ear into a silk purse. Villeneuve had a lot of faith in him. Progress towards the end of the season, particularly the two points picked up in Monza and Indianapolis, point to a brighter future in 2003.

A question of money

Off the track, things were not much better for the Canadian. His relationship with the new boss quickly turned sour and the subject of their fall out was cash. It has been written a thousand times before that Jacques Villeneuve pockets a handy salary of 18 million dollars, making him the second highest paid driver after Michael Schumacher. This salary had been agreed by BAR's old management, by which we mean Craig Pollock. David Richards balked at paying so much for a driver running in the middle of the pack. He reckoned the money would be better spent on research and development.

It did not take long for the two men to be at loggerheads, using the press as their mouthpiece, much to the delight of the news-hungry media. Richards set the ball rolling, telling journalists that Villeneuve should accept a lower salary for the good of the team.

The driver then fought his corner at the European Grand Prix. "*He's only been here six months, so it's easy for him to say things like this. Me, I've been*

fighting here for four years. I would like to see what would have become of this team without me. To be treated like this after slogging away for four years is very annoying. Especially as he has never spoken about it with me. I just read about it in the newspapers. It's not fair to put me in this situation. And David Richards gets a salary too doesn't he?"

Apparently, the BAR boss had suggested that the former world champion take a year off, for a sensible amount of money, to come back and find a more competitive car in 2004 and 2005. Villeneuve did not have to think for long before rejecting the proposal.
Digging in, Richards then suggested a CART drive in 2003, before returning the following year. This was the scenario the BAR boss liked best, as the Forsythe team, which would have welcomed Villeneuve with open arms, would have picked up the tab. But again, the Canadian rejected the notion. It seems he does not plan on spending eternity with BAR as, with Pollock gone, BAR is now a team like any other. The special link with the team no longer exists. He might as well look elsewhere. But where?

F1 or CART? Our hearts are torn between the two The Canadian crowd would not object to seeing Villeneuve switch to CART. In 2002, Montreal hosted its very first CART Grand Prix and it was an instant success: a crowd of 172,000 passed through the turnstiles at the Circuit Gilles Villeneuve over the three days of the event. Great racing fans, the people of Quebec were delighted to be able to get close to the cars and talk to the drivers, a pleasure denied them in F1.
In 2003, some spectators might well decide to trade in their Formula 1 tickets to attend a more convivial event, especially if F1 delivers another monochrome season!

An all too familiar picture. Villeneuve retires his car at the side of the track. The Canadian is hoping that his 5th year with BAR will be more competitive.
<

All's well that ends well?

Finally, the giant that is Toyota has arrived in Formula 1. And they did not do too badly for a first season (two sixth places and regularly in the top ten during qualifying.) The other major Japanese manufacturer, Honda, had a catastrophic start to the season, but made significant progress during the summer, at least on the engine side. Adding to Japanese achievement was the performance of Bridgestone, who along with Ferrari, dominated the season. However, it was not these great corporations which fired the enthusiasm of the Japanese GP crowd. It was the superb performance of a little Japanese driver. After a difficult start to the year, Takuma Sato waited to the very last race on the calendar to prove his talent.

Kunio Shibata – GP Xpress, Tokyo

Sato, a young Schumacher?

This year, no less than 155,000 spectators showed up on race day in Suzuka. This figure represents an absolute record for the track. Even at the end of the Eighties and the start of the Nineties, during the era of Ayrton Senna, Honda's darling, there had never been such a large crowd at their home track.

What can we read into this phenomenon? Especially as it occurred just as the popularity of Formula 1 was going through a major slump throughout Europe. On top of that, the current economic crisis means that teams are struggling to find sponsors.

Japan is not immune to this situation. Furthermore, the fact the championship was wrapped up two months before Suzuka meant the organisers were not over-optimistic. However, much to everyone's surprise, the Japanese GP was one of the few events on the calendar which saw an increase in spectators over the previous year.

Was it down to the presence of Toyota? Definitely, because they mounted a huge advertising campaign just before Suzuka – four full pages in every daily newspaper and sports paper – and the company bought over 10,000 tickets for its employees and dealers, not to mention the 350 VIP tickets at 4000 dollars a pop! But one should not ignore Ferrari's contribution. Its dominance might have bored the Europeans, but for the Japanese "tifosi" this was a unique opportunity to get close to the Prancing Horse. The locals were simply pleased to see the Ferraris racing.

In the end, the hero that day was neither Toyota nor Ferrari, but without any doubt, Takuma Sato. At the end of the race, the scene in the grandstands turned from red to the yellow of Jordan. 7th in qualifying, 5th in the race, he was a long way off Michael Schumacher over the course of the weekend, but given his situation, these were results that went beyond his expectations.

Sato is the seventh Japanese driver to make it into F1 and he is considered the best. But the fact he is the first Japanese to take the British F3 title carries little weight in F1. Once the 2002 season was underway, he was constantly out-paced by team-mate Giancarlo Fisichella and rarely made it to the chequered flag. Of course, in his defence, one could claim force majeure, including incessant mechanical woes or accidents which were not his fault, such as his collisions with Nick Heidfeld in Austria and Kimi Räikkönen in Monza. But he also made several mistakes, worst of all running his own team-mate off the road in Sepang as well as various other crashes.

The result was that after 16 races, Sato had failed to score a single point and even the most optimistic of his followers did not rate his chances of saving his Jordan seat for 2003.

Sato came to Japan therefore with a "*burnt all his boats*" attitude and it paid off as he put together his best race weekend. "*I took strength from the spectators,*" he said. "*And also, I was always convinced that, even in my deepest despair, there were some who believed in me and supported me. I fought for them.*"

In the space of a single day, Sato became a national hero. Thanks to the two points he picked up, Jordan made up two places to end up sixth in the Constructors' Championship. But despite his last minute exploit, Sato may yet lose his seat at Jordan next season.

The young lad is probably no Schumacher, but at the very least, he deserves his place in this the blue riband series of the sport. It would be a shame if Sato was to disappear without really having time to show his true potential.

Not satisfied, but not exactly disappointed

Unlike Sato, Toyota did pretty well right from the start. They picked up sixth places in the first and third races, but it was their qualifying performance which was the most impressive. Meticulous preparation over the past two years certainly helped their cause. The engine was both reliable and powerful. Indeed, come the mid-season and a Toyota engineer dared to suggest: "*our engine is already the second most powerful after BMW.*"

However, all was not well on the chassis side. The TF102 suffered a cruel lack of downforce and the engineers were unable to improve that element during the course of the season. Another trick the car hid up its chassis was that it could be perfectly balanced in the morning session, but the equilibrium would vanish come the afternoon's qualifying hour, with catastrophic results, even if the car had been left untouched.

Keizo Takahashi, the team's technical coordinator explained: "*The increase in track temperature, the wind, the dust...we knew there would be a lot of factors capable of changing the car's behaviour. However, knowing how to adapt the car to cope is a different matter. We did not have the ability to react quickly enough in the very short time available.*"

The organisational side was also chaotic. Two days before the Belgian Grand Prix weekend, the team terminated its contracts with both its current drivers; Mika Salo and Allan McNish. It was evident that not much thought had been given to the timing of this announcement as the Thursday night in Spa saw a huge Toyota media party attended by the world's press. The whole programme for the night had to be changed and of course the drivers were no longer required to be on duty. Why such a mess? Toyota was unable to furnish a reasonable explanation, but it is highly likely that there was some sort of conflict between Toyota Japan and TMG, run by Ove Andersson, who took all the major decisions, including the choice of drivers. Toyota

Kunio Shibata
45 years old, he left Japan, giving up his jov in journalism in 1982 to move to Paris and study Politocal Science. He became a freelance producer for Japanese television and havinf always been interested in motor racing, he began covering the Grand Prix for a press agency in 1987 when Satoru Nakajima arrived on the scene. He has written for the specialist Japanese magazine «Grand Prix Xpress» since 1991.

Japan simply rubber-stamped these decisions. But in this case, it appears there had been some conflict, with the Japanese arm trying to influence the decision and take the upper hand. Indeed, Andersson said he knew nothing about the decision until the previous day. That leads one to believe that Toyota's second year in F1 will see a greater influence emanating from Toyota Japan.

One positive aspect: since the summer, the team has introduced the famous Toyota production system (TPS,) a methodology which has been very successful on the production lines and has now been adopted by other car manufacturers. First and foremost, it is a system combining quality control and efficient work practices and it is now in place at the race team's Cologne HQ. It is applied to everything, including evaluating the shortest distance a mechanic must cover to do a tyre change during a pit stop?

Toyota emerged from its home race with an eighth place, which is a fair summing up of Year One for Toyota: no remarkable success, but hardly disgraceful. But they are well and truly ready to introduce know-how from the parent company and with Toyota's dynamic and daring approach, the Toyota F1 team is bound to make constant progress.

No sign of light

This was Honda's third year since returning to F1 and it was also the worst, at least in terms of results. Although supplying two teams (BAR and Jordan) the car manufacturer only picked up 16 points, or less than fourteen times the number Ferrari scored! And not once did one of its drivers make it to the podium.

Of course, given that Honda operates as an engine supplier, not all the blame for this debacle can be laid at its door. However, if chassis performance in both cases was lamentable, one has to bear in mind that in the case of BAR, Honda is supposed to be involved on the chassis development side. Furthermore, at the start of the season, the engine was well down on power compared with its rivals.

It was a brand new engine. Rumour had it that the V angle was 94 degrees, although of course the constructor never confirmed this. If it is true, then the engine boasts the biggest V angle after Renault. It is a reasonably innovative engine, but prone to mechanical problems and the Honda engineers came up against all sorts of difficulties right from the start. Since then, they made enormous efforts and ended up almost matching the power outputs of the top engines such as those in the back of the Ferraris and McLarens. At the Italian GP, Honda's race and test development engineer, Shuhei Nakamoto revealed: *"We have already gone past our performance aims for this season and we are continuing to develop the engine further."* Sure enough they launched a new evolution at the next race in the United States and

rounded off the year with a *"Suzuka Special,"* their most powerful engine of the year, sadly with disastrous consequences. Outright performance was evidently on tap given the results of qualifying – Sato 7th, Fisichella 8th, and Villeneuve 9th, with Sato recording the third highest top speed, after M. Schumacher and Coulthard. Reliability was the problem and on Saturday morning, Sato's engine exploded. On Sunday morning, it was Fisichella's turn to suffer a similar fate and in the race, two engines blew up and one suffered a management problem. Sato found himself the only Honda driver still in the race. So how does Honda sum up its year: *"The notable progress in terms of engine evolution is satisfactory"*, said Nakamoto. *"But of course the reliability is a problem. Apart from that, our collaboration with BAR is becoming closer and more productive."* The new gearbox launched at the United States GP is an example of that. It was designed by BAR and Honda engineers, with the Japanese side contributing to reducing its weight. On top of that, Nakamoto now takes part in the team's strategy meetings and it was Honda's decision to go for a two stop strategy in this race. There are suggestions that Honda will take this collaboration to a logical conclusion and buy the team. The management always sticks with the same answer on this subject. *"We are interested in the technical challenge and we have no desire to run a team."* Doubtless they are aware of the difficulties facing them in realising their goals if they are not fully implicated in the running of the team. Honda and Toyota are rivals on the track and in the marketplace and now the latter has gone the *"own-team"* route which Honda rejected a few years back. Toyota's image is likely to pick up from this policy and apparently they even have their eye on Takuma Sato as a Toyota driver. At the moment, I have the impression that Toyota is looking more dynamic and making up ground on the more prudent, or is it hesitant, Honda.

∧

"Banzai!" In Suzuka, Takuma Sato pulled off the Japanese coup of the year with his fifth place finish.

2002 was not easy for Honda, who decided to concentrate its efforts on BAR next season. For its part, Jordan is switching to Ford.

<

Bridgestone: 100 Grands Prix, 70 wins and ten world championship titles!

> The British Grand Prix: Michael Schumacher wins, partly thanks to his Bridgestone rain tyres.

2002 was a record breaking year for Bridgestone. Not only did the Japanese marque take its fifth consecutive Drivers' and Constructors' World Championships (in six seasons of Formula 1), it also won 15 out of the 17 Grands Prix while celebrating its 100th grand prix in Japan, with its seventieth victory in the top motor sport discipline. This 70% success rate is exceptional in the history of motor sport. On top of that, this year Bridgestone also won all the grands prix which had eluded it last year, when the Japanese company found itself up against Michelin for the first time. In 2002, in Imola, Montreal, Hockenheim and Monza, it was a Ferrari on Bridgestone tyres which took the top honours.

> Hirohide Hamashima reveals the secrets of Bridgestone's F1 rain tyres: a super-computer which acts like a wind tunnel for tyres.

Magic tyres in the rain

The most remarkable win of the season for the Japanese company has to be the one at Silverstone, at the only grand prix of the year which was run in the rain. The rain that fell on England that day proved Bridgestone's undeniable superiority in these conditions. Juan Pablo Montoya's Williams losing entire seconds every lap to Michael Schumacher's Ferrari.

Bridgestone F1's Technical Director, Hirohide Hamashima explained the complexities of developing tyres for use on a wet track:

Is the technology behind wet and intermediate tyres different to that used for dry tyres?

Hirohide Hamashima: Yes, there is very big difference, compound wise and also the working area is very different. A wet surface and dry surface are completely different. If you think about adhesive tape, it is very sticky in the dry but if it gets wet, it is not sticky at all. That is the same situation with tyres.

- How do you design the rain tyre pattern?

-Hirohide Hamashima: We introduced a new technology to develop tyre patterns, called Hydro Simulation using a super computer. It has been a great help to the engineers, because, before we had that technology, we made patterns based on intuition, however now it is computer aided rather than trial and error. The pattern is mainly designed to clear water, but it also has a separate effect on the grip level provided. It affects how the compound works with the track.

- How does hydro-simulation work?

- Hirohide Hamashima: It is like a wind tunnel for tyres. We can calculate how much resistance there is on the tyre coming from the water and how much we can clear using the pattern. When we give the basic pattern to the computer, it adjusts it for maximum effect of water flow. Sometimes it would come up with a result very similar to our original idea based on experience. But the computer gives us new ideas and might suggest a completely different direction for our experiments.

- Is this technology also used to produce intermediate tyres?

Hirohide Hamashima: We introduced a new intermediate pattern when Michelin arrived in F1. We only had a few minor problems with it, which is why we simply made a few modifications for this season. We now have an intermediate which works in a wide range of wet conditions.

- When it rains, there can be huge variations in the amount of water. How do you increase the operational range of your tyres?

Hirohide Hamashima: That comes from experience and testing. We can artificially water the track and we carry out a long run test on the track as it gradually dries out. We can try various compounds and see how well they run in drying conditions to find the one that gives us the biggest operational range.

- While dry tyres are different for almost every Grand Prix, the wet tyres are the same all season long. Why?

Hirohide Hamashima: In the dry, tyres vary according to the circuit surface. But when a track is wet the circuits all have similar characteristics with generally the same levels of grip, so it is not necessary to produce circuit-specific rain tyres.

A total complicity with Ferrari

Ever since McLaren returned to running on the rival tyre manufacturer's product, Bridgestone was able to concentrate on its relationship with Ferrari.

The Scuderia paid back handsomely for this attention as the Italian team set up a test team entirely dedicated to tyre testing and development. Behind the wheel was Luciano Burti who spent his 2002 season trying different compounds and constructions.

The Scuderia Technical Director Ross Brawn reckons that this year's championship titles owed a great deal to the relationship between Bridgestone and the Scuderia. *"Actually, the experience working with Goodyear taught us that we needed a very close relationship with our tyre supplier. Back then, we were very impressed with Bridgestone's effort and we had to do a lot of work with Goodyear to stay competitive. When we realised that Bridgestone's rival was working with a couple of top teams, we decided to strengthen our relationship with Bridgestone. Last season, we started planning how we could work more closely together, by putting more engineers to work with Bridgestone on present and future projects and by making more resources available to this task. The idea was to improve Bridgestone's understanding of how the car worked and our knowledge of the tyres. Bridgestone is an integral part of our success in the championships and our dominance this season."*

Ferrari engineers were thus sent to Japan to work alongside their Bridgestone colleagues, while the tyre company sent staff to Maranello to build a common approach. *"Instead of building the tyres and cars separately, we try and think of them as one single entity. We also spent more time in joint briefings after practice and the race to try and get a better understanding of what we should do in the future."*

One of the key figures in this relationship is of course, Luciano Burti. *"It's true that Bridgestone is dedicated to Ferrari, but the opposite is also true,"* confirms Brawn. *"We set up an extra test team, with a car and driver, either Luciano Burti or Luca Badoer, depending on the situation, entirely dedicated to tyre testing, which we tried to slot in between car tests."*

Ross Brawn reveals that these joint projects touch on all aspects of the car. *"We work on a lot of things. The tyre construction is close to the design of the car, whereas compound choice is more the work of the chemists. The construction of the tyre is structural and more in line with what we are doing on the car. But we also work on other areas, the benefits of which will not be seen for many years to come. In the past, tyre and car were developed independently and progress came either from the tyre or the car. Now we try and get both to progress together."*

Much progress during the course of the season

For Bridgestone's F1 Technical Manager, Hisao Suganuma, the 2002 season could not have gone better, even if the Japanese company had set itself the target of winning all the Grands Prix. *"Yes, it's true we wanted to win all the races,"* admitted the Japanese engineer. *"We worked very hard to improve on our 2001 tyres and we hoped for a 100% success rate. However, we did learn a great deal from our defeats in Sepang and Monaco. The data we gathered from these two races helped a great deal in our development from then on. This year, we made much progress in terms of traction. We also made a step forward in terms of heat durability, but there is still room for improvement in that area, as the cars are going quicker all the time, which means we have to constantly adjust the performance of our tyres."*

Suganuma reckons it is easy to explain what went wrong in Sepang and Monaco. *"We have reached the conclusion that our compound was a bit too soft in Malaysia and so were not good enough in terms of wear and heat resistance. We learnt our lesson. In Monaco, even though we did not win the race, we believe we had the best tyre on Sunday. Michael Schumacher was very quick and, but for the impossibility of overtaking in Monaco, he would have won the race by a comfortable margin. After his pit stop, he set several fastest laps, but he was stuck behind Juan Pablo Montoya, which meant he could not build a big enough gap to get ahead of David Coulthard during the pit stops."*

The Japanese engineer was quick to praise the F2002, which explains why it was so successful. *"It is an excellent car,"* he stated. *"It is very good at making the best use of its tyres, which is obviously a great help to the tyre supplier. Even more important was all the testing we did with Ferrari, which accelerated our rate of progress. Ferrari benefited from it, but so did our other teams. Essentially, there are no limits to tyre development. We made a lot of progress between 2000 and 2001, because we took a giant step to face up to our rivals. To do that again will not be easy, even though I feel we have made much progress this year. F1 is still a technical challenge which drives us forward and lap times continue to come down, although not at quite the same rate."*

Hisao
Suganuma

> The famous *"biggest tyre in the paddock,"* which provides Bridgestone with a venue to introduce its products to the general public, as well as affording them a close up of a Ferrari F1 car.

Marketing – the logical accompaniment to a racing programme

It's not easy to talk to Bridgestone/Firestone Motor Sport Marketing boss Nicolas Duquesne. He is always glued to a telephone and a walk across the paddock involves shaking dozens of hands, as one of the Japanese company's most charismatic employees appears to juggle several jobs at the same time.

A Grand Prix weekend for Duquesne involves many days of preparation and scrupulous organisation, as he is tasked with ensuring that company guests have a great weekend with no hitches. There are always problems of course, but it is Duquesne's job to sort them out behind the scenes, so that guests are unaware of what is going on.

Bridgestone's marketing operation in Formula 1 also features a presence in the public area, where the fans tend to congregate when the track action stops. Duquesne had the idea of catching their eye with a giant tyre, which he happily describes as *"the biggest tyre in the paddock."* It is essentially a huge inflatable tyre-shaped tent, which is eye catching and attracts racegoers to come inside, where, apart from a Ferrari F1 car, Bridgestone displays a full range of its products. The marketing push is also geared to underline the company's achievements to its major clients and suppliers. To this end, Bridgestone invites several hundred guests to its area in the Paddock Club. *"Starting with the San Marino Grand Prix in Imola, we bring a lot of people to the circuit; sometimes as many as 200,"* explains Nicolas Duquesne. *"The guests come from several different countries and we have to organise their transport and accommodation, as well as plan their day at the actual track."*

Most of the guests have Paddock Club tickets, the Holy of Holies in Formula 1 terms as it means they can watch qualifying or the race in great comfort, often from just above the pits. The Paddock Club also provides plenty of TV screens to follow the action, with a team of high quality caterers always on hand. Bridgestone ensures that every guest leaves with an excellent souvenir of the weekend. *"Nothing can be left to chance,"* continues Duquesne. *"In terms of organisation, we have fine tuned it over the past six years and Bridgestone has proved it is more than capable of doing the job. Transport, accommodation and transfers to the track have to be planned and we always have to expect the unexpected. Some guests have special dietary needs, while others do not show up when they are supposed to, which involves laying on extra transport from the hotels."* Duquesne's working day at the

track starts early and finishes late. He welcomes the guests, interviews the F1 drivers in the Paddock Club, sorts out the pass allocation and hunts for lost passes! All this takes up a good deal of time and getting the drivers to come and talk to guests at a certain time involves a perfectly synchronised schedule to be worked out with the teams.

The races themselves are not the only events on the calendar, as Bridgestone also invites guests to private test sessions, in a less formally regimented fashion. *"At tests in Barcelona, Valencia, Silverstone or Monza, we can get the*

fans even closer to the F1 action," explains Duquesne.

Bridgestone's F1 campaign goes a lot further than the classic advertising campaign. *"Of course, Formula 1 is a fantastic commercial shop window,"* concludes Duquesne. *"Most of the major manufacturers are there. Thanks to the world titles we have won, we are now seen in a different light. F1 has opened many doors for us and introduced us to new markets."* Nicolas Duquesne's phone is ringing again, as a guest has some questions. The day is far from over!

Bridgestone's Paddock Club suite is always packed. Sometimes, Michael Schumacher pays a visit, seen here in Barcelona.
>

(on right) Marketing Director for Bridgestone/Firestone Europe, Nicolas Duquesne hosts many of the drivers, who come to chat with the guests. Here we see Ferrari test driver, Luca Badoer.

(on left) The Japanese marque makes sure its suite is welcoming!
v

Bridgestone plays its part in Schumacher museum

The *"Michael Schumacher Karting Centre"* in the five times world champion's home town of Kerpen now has its very own museum dedicated to the Ferrari driver.

Situated just off the Cologne to Aix motorway, the outdoor track is 710 metres long and there is also a 600 metre indoor circuit for people of all ages to try their hand at karting.

The building is now home to *"The World of the Schumachers"* museum. Work started on it in 2000, organised by Michael Schumacher and his father Rolf, who runs the business to this day. The museum affords an insight into the life of the two Schumacher brothers, providing a snap-shot of where they come from and who they are, going behind the scenes of what the public usually sees on television.

A visit to the museum starts with a film about the career of the Schumacher brothers, before revealing their first karts. One very special item on display is the very first home-made kart built by Papa Schumacher

for a four year old Michael. It had no brakes and he crashed it into a lamppost.

The museum has over 200 exhibits, including several single seaters from the Schumachers' early days, such as Formula Ford, Formula Opel and Formula 3. Ralf Schumacher's F1 Jordan is also on show, as is Michael's first Benetton, along with various Ferraris and winner's trophies. You can even see the bicycle Michael Schumacher used on his first visit to the Spa circuit to learn the track, before tackling his debut grand prix in 1991; it's an amusing detail. Visitors are encouraged to handle various bits of carbon bodywork and to lift up F1 tyres to get an idea of their weight. *"People love lifting up these super-lightweight Bridgestone tyres,"* explains Gert Brandes, who is the museum curator, having previously run the karting club which saw the debut, not only of the Schumacher brothers, but also Heinz-Harald Frentzen and Nick Heidfeld. The site covers an area of 6000 sq. metres and a visit is certainly a worthwhile experience.

∧
The excellent relationship between Ferrari and Bridgestone has led the Japanese company to produce a tyre exclusively for the new *"Enzo Ferrari"* road car.

<
The *"Michael Schumacher"* karting circuit in Kerpen.

<
(on left)
The museum shop, with everything a Schumacher fan could dream of.

Rolf Schumacher, the brothers' father and founder of the museum.

<
Bridgestone supplies the kart tyres but also lent its support to the building of the museum.

Team tactics

Todt was not the first

Team tactics have existed pretty much ever since man invented the wheel. In Austria. Ferrari's Sporting Director simply added another chapter to the book. However, he picked the wrong moment, hence the general condemnation of his actions.

Formula 1 has not always enjoyed the popularity it does today. Twenty years ago, you could not watch the European races in their entirety on television. In days gone by, you were lucky to get a glimpse of a grand prix on a cinema newsreel. Champions went by the names of James Hunt, Jody Scheckter, Alan Jones and Keke Rosberg. Although undoubtedly talented, their exploits did not turn them into global stars and their bank accounts never matched those of the 2002 millionaire drivers. But since the early Nineties, the major manufacturers – Renault, Mercedes, Honda, Fiat and BMW – made the best possible use of this fantastic publicity opportunity. They fought tooth and nail for success and Formula 1 budgets went through the roof. The number of journalists coming to the circuits grew like Topsy and the slightest event made the news. These days, if a mechanic sprains a finger, column inches are devoted to the risks of the job. For several years, the players in the paddock have been complaining about the galloping costs and have warned that the sport would not survive if this went on much longer. From this point of view, the 2002 season might represent something of a turning point. On the one hand, the world economy is not enjoying the rude good health of just one year ago and the budgets which constructors and sponsors are prepared to pour into this shop window are going to decrease. On the other hand, the incredible domination over the rest of the field demonstrated by Ferrari killed all interest in the championship and a large number of fans got bored with the sport. This dominance naturally meant that Ferrari was constantly under the microscope. Anything any team member did was closely scrutinised and the moment Michael Schumacher opened his mouth, he came in for criticism. He says he feels vulnerable? He is accused of false modesty and of mocking his rivals. However, he says he is going to win the race no problem, then he is castigated for being arrogant.
That was pretty much the mood at the Austrian Grand Prix and it was this charged atmosphere which no doubt was at the root of the reaction to Ferrari's strategy.

Michael Schumacher adjusts his watch and fine tunes his strategy with Jean Todt. The two men get on famously, but it is still the team boss who gives the orders.

>

In fact, team tactics are nothing new. Within a team, one driver is often designated the Number 1, either contractually or by tacit hierarchical agreement as he is better paid than the other!
Jean Todt's decision in Austria, to ask Rubens Barrichello to move over for Michael Schumacher would have seemed completely natural in different circumstances and in a different age. However, as the German was clearly dominating the series and had already won four of five races, seeing him take an additional win through artificial means seemed excessive and pointless. Even the most fanatical tifosi took this view.

Courageously, despite the storm of protest, the Ferrari boss held firm and justified his decision, even if a few days later, he seemed surprised at the media frenzy he had created. He had definitely underestimated the reaction. "*Sometimes difficult decisions have to be taken when you run a team*", he explained on Sunday night in Austria. "*We are fighting for the world championship. It's hard. In 1997, 1998 and 1999, we lost it each time at the very last race and we are simply trying to avoid that situation. I am not saying we took the right decision, but it is the one we made. Sometimes, in life, you make the right decision and sometimes you take wrong ones.*"
The entire Ferrari team stood firm behind Todt. President Luca di Montezemolo even held a press conference from his kingdom in Maranello to justify the Frenchman's actions; actions which he had not been consulted about. Piero Lardi-Ferrari, son of Enzo Ferrari, the company founder, added that he thought his father would have taken the same decision. His position supported, the team boss moved on. "*Our image might seem to have been slightly damaged by what happened*", he concluded. "*But it would have been much worse if we lost the world championship.*"
Logically, FIA did not penalise the Scuderia for its strategy, but sanctioned it for inverting the drivers' positions on the podium at the end of the Austrian Grand Prix.
There were later repercussions and at the FIA World Council meeting at the end of the season, the governing body decided to ban team orders starting in 2003. It is a laughable measure, given that it is impossible to apply the new rule – in fact, how it will be done has not yet been specified. The last time such a rule was adopted it had to be overturned.

The finish to the Austrian Grand Prix, at the precise moment when Rubens Barrichello slows to let Michael Schumacher pass.

>

Team tactics - # A raft of previous incidents

The history of motor sport is peppered with examples of team orders and drivers who help their team-mates. Forbidden by the International Automobile Federation (the FIA) after the 1998 Australian Grand Prix, they have been made legal again since 1999. A few reminders:

(1) 1964 Mexican Grand Prix:
At the last race of the season, Lorenzo Bandini moved over to let through John Surtees, who therefore beat fellow Englishman Graham Hill to the world championship title by a single point.

(2) 1981 Brazilian Grand Prix
In the Williams team, reigning champion Alan Jones is the number one driver. In the rain in Brazil, the team asks Carlos Reutemann, who is leading, to move over for Jones, running second just behind him. The Argentinian refuses, bringing down on his shoulders the wrath of the entire team for the rest of the season.

(3) 1982 San Marino Grand Prix
After a stage-managed battle between the Ferraris and Renaults, put on to entertain the crowds and make up for the fact half the field had boycotted the race, Scuderia Ferrari puts out a pit board indicating that its two drivers, Gilles Villeneuve and Didier Pironi, should hold station. Pironi ignores the orders and passes Villeneuve no less than three times to win the race. Villeneuve was still furious at the next round in Belgian and attempting to lap quicker than his team-mate at all costs, was killed during practice.

(4) 1982 French Grand Prix:
The two Renault turbos of Rene Arnoux and Alain Prost are leading. Prost has a 15 point lead over Arnoux and it is decided that the latter should move over and his mechanics give him a pit board instruction to that effect over the last ten laps of the race. He refuses to obey and wins the race. The argument that ensued ends with Arnoux leaving the team to go to Ferrari.

(5) 1991 Japanese Grand Prix:
At the exit to the final corner, without having received any instructions to that effect, Ayrton Senna slowed to let McLaren team-mate Gerhard Berger take the win, *"to thank him for all his support during the season."* To this day, the Austrian refuses to consider this as a race he won.

1995 Portuguese Grand Prix:
Jean Alesi, on a three stop strategy is ordered to move over for his Ferrari team-mate Gerhard Berger, who is just behind him. "*Several times on the same lap, Jean Todt told me to let Gerhard pass*", recalled the Frenchman. "*Radio-Todt was getting boring, so I switched to another station!*" Alesi finished fifth, behind the Austrian.

(6) 1997 Japanese Grand Prix:
Lap 25: Eddie Irvine is leading from Michael Schumacher, who is in the running for the world championship. "*I was just waiting for my phone to ring*", joked the Irishman, who instantly moved over for the German.

(7) 1997 European Grand Prix:
This is the only known example of team orders between two different teams. The world championship was being decided that day between Jacques Villeneuve and Michael Schumacher. Williams had been assured by McLaren that its drivers would not hold up the Canadian. Once he had the title in the bag, Villeneuve said thank you by letting the McLarens through to take the top two places, settling for third place himself.

(8) 1998 Australian Grand Prix:
David Coulthard is in the lead and lets team-mate Mika Häkkinen pass him in the very first race of the season, out of respect for an agreement between the two drivers which decreed that whoever got to the

first corner first would win the race. Häkkinen had lost the lead because of a misunderstood radio message from the pit wall.

1998 Austrian Grand Prix:
Eddie Irvine is third, running ahead of Michael Schumacher. It was at a time when team orders were temporarily banned and so the Irishman made out he had brake problems to let the German through, as he was fighting Mika Häkkinen for the title.

(9) 1999 German Grand Prix:
Mika Salo replaces the injured Michael Schumacher, while Eddie Irvine is promoted to the role of number one driver. Salo is leading and moves over to let the Irishman take the win.

Mika Häkkinen passes David Coulthard at the 1998 Australian Grand Prix. The press did not make a meal of it.
>

(10) 1999 Malaysian Grand Prix:
Back at the wheel for the first time since his crash in the British Grand Prix, Michael Schumacher is out of the running for the title, so he helps Eddie Irvine, letting the Irishman through, having earlier led the race. In the end, Irvine lost out to Häkkinen in the title race by just two points.

2001 Austrian Grand Prix:
Same place, same players: coming out of the last corner, Rubens Barrichello slows and lets Michael Schumacher through into second place. The incident had the world of Formula 1 talking for several weeks. It led to the banning of team orders at the end of the season.

Formula 1 slumps in the face of destiny

The drop in Formula 1 TV audience figures pushed the sporting authority to hold an urgent meeting of the Formula 1 Commission on 28th October, after the season was over.

Two radically opposed schools of thought met across the table. On one side, those who wanted to reduce the costs of Formula 1, giving all teams the chance to win races. This was the group which approved an idea which came from Max Mosley himself, for drivers to rotate through the teams during the course of the season. They also wanted cars to take on a weight penalty of one kilo at races for each point scored. They also wanted to see private testing banned. The small teams, FIA President Max Mosley and F1's money man, Bernie Ecclestone were all in favour of these changes. Opposing them were the big teams; Ferrari,

Williams and McLaren, who were against any change, arguing that there would not be a repeat of the catastrophic 2002 season. For their part, McLaren and Williams were working on radically different cars for next year, in the hope of making a quantum leap forward in order to catch up with Ferrari.

It was therefore up to the Formula 1 Commission meeting in London to reach a decision. Made up of 26 members, it needed a majority of 18 to adopt these changes. After several hours of negotiation, much of it heated, the Commission settled for several minor changes. Most of it is down to how qualifying is run: on Friday cars will go out on track one at a time, to do just one flying lap, the order according to the driver's championship position. The result of this session then decides the running

order for Saturday's qualifying, when once again they will only be allowed one lap!

In terms of the championship, more points on offer; 10,8,6,5,4,3,2,1. Furthermore, team orders are banned, although, as yet there is no indication as to how this rule will be applied! Tyre manufacturers will be allowed to produce specific tyres for each team. For those who want to, private testing will be banned, to be replaced by an additional two hours during the grands prix weekends. Finally, the Belgian Grand Prix is off the calendar. The races themselves are unaffected by these changes. Therefore F1 voted against turning a sport into a show. Pressure from sponsors for the return of the good old days was not enough. So, contrary to what might be expected, it seems that money does not control every aspect of Formula 1...

Drivers according to the 2003 system

		2002 :	2003 :
1.	**M. Schumacher**	(144)	**156**
2.	R. Barrichello	(77)	93
3.	J.P. Montoya	(50)	74
4.	R. Schumacher	(42)	63
5.	D. Coulthard	(41)	63
6.	K. Räikkönen	(24)	36
7.	J. Button	(14)	31
8.	N. Heidfeld	(7)	22
9.	G. Fisichella	(7)	20
10.	J. Trulli	(9)	19
11.	E. Irvine	(8)	16
12.	F. Massa	(4)	15
13.	J. Villeneuve	(4)	14
14.	M. Salo	(2)	10
15.	O. Panis	(3)	8
16.	H-H. Frentzen	(2)	6
17.	T. Sato	(2)	5
18.	M. Webber	(2)	5
19.	A. McNish	(0)	3
20.	A. Yoong	(0)	2
21.	P. de la Rosa	(0)	2
22.	E. Bernoldi	(0)	0
23.	A. Davidson	(0)	0

Constructors (2003 system)

1.	**Scuderia Ferrari Marlboro**	(221)	**249**
2.	BMW WilliamsF1 Team	(92)	137
3.	West McLaren Mercedes	(65)	99
4.	Mild Seven Renault F1 Team	(23)	50
5.	Sauber Petronas	(11)	37
6.	DHL Jordan Honda	(9)	25
7.	Lucky Strike BAR Honda	(7)	22
8.	Jaguar Racing	(8)	18
9.	Panasonic Toyota Racing	(2)	13
10.	KL Minardi Asiatech	(2)	7
11.	Orange Arrows	(2)	6

Bernie Ecclestone and Max Mosley during their press conference in London on 28th October. When it seemed as though the FIA World Council was about to push through radical changes to the way F1 is run, they finally opted for a few cosmetic modifications.

<

Juan Manuel Fangio, the first five times Formula 1 champion

by Jacques Vassal
«Automobile historique»

> Juan Manuel Fangio in the mid-Fifties: Whether at the track or in town, he was always well turned out.

Silverstone, 13th May 1950: the European and British Grand Prix was the championship opener. Fangio retired his Alfetta 158 with failing oil pressure. He made up for it eight days later with a majestic win in Monaco, his first of 24 from just 51 grand prix starts.
v >

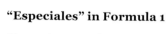

Jacques Vassal, Journalist, writer and translator, as well as being an expert in singing and popular music, Jacques Vassal has worked for "Auto Passion" magazine for over eleven years. Since 2000, he has worked as a freelance for various specialist magazines, especially the monthly magazine "Automobile Historique", writing tests, portraits, interviews, retrospectives and articles on cars and motor sport of today and yesteryear. Along with Pierre Menard, he is also the co-author of "Legendes de la Formule 1", a new Chronosports publication.

On 21st July 2002, Michael Schumacher scored enough points to put him out of reach of his challengers, thus taking his fifth world championship crown and equalling Juan Manuel Fangio's legendary record.

The record had withstood all assaults for the past forty five years. The 46 year old Argentinian clinched his fifth title on 4th August 1957 at the Germany Grand Prix, with two rounds to go in a seven round season. With 24 wins from 51 grands prix starts in the Drivers World Championship, he has a 47.6 success rate, an achievement which will prove hard to match. Since 1958, Fangio's career was the reference point for all F1 drivers. But how did he reach this peak?

Juan Manuel Fangio's European career only began in 1948, when he was already a national hero in Argentina, some of his notoriety down to participating in road races, before he switched to the circuits.

He was born on 24th June 1911 in Balcare, a small town 400 kilometres to the south of Buenos Aires, and was the last but one of six children. His father Don Loreto was a mason and his business grew with the town. The young Juan Manuel was a serious pupil at school and loved maths. He also played football and as a teenager was given the nickname "El Chueco," (bandy legs) by his team mates. Although he contracted pleurisy which kept him away from the classroom and the pitch for a year, "El Chueco" grew into a sturdy chap.

"Especiales" in Formula 1

He was interested in all things mechanical and aged 11, he took up an apprenticeship in a Balcare garage. He would go after school, at the end of the day, having got up at the crack of dawn to study. Then he switched to the local Studebaker dealer who prepared "especiales" for racing. Naturally enough, Juan was soon behind the wheel, on the road from Balcare to Buenos Aires, when his boss sent him to deliver or pick up cars. The roads were unsurfaced and turned into a bog when it rained. In the dry, the dust and gravel surface made a great driving school.

Once he had completed his Military Service, Juan Manuel set up his own garage, with his brother and a friend. He raced for the first time in 1936, at the wheel of a modified Model T Ford taxi! Then he switched to a Ford V8 specially prepared for circuit racing. In 1939, Fangio entered a Chevrolet coupe in the Touring Car "Gran Premios." These were very long, tough events which sometimes lasted up to a week with stages of over 1000 kilometres per day, on open roads. These events built his reputation as a resilient and quick driver. In 1940 and '41, with another

Chevrolet, he became Argentinian champion. His racing activities were then curtailed by the war as all racing stopped until 1946. Fangio kept going by selling trucks and tyres.

In 1947, his racing career took off again. He was to find success on the tracks at the wheel of a Chevrolet-powered Ford T, a Rickenbacker engined Volpi and eventually a Chevrolet. General Peron had just come into power in 1946. Realising he could make political capital out of promoting motor racing, the Argentine automobile club organised a series for single-seaters called the "Temporada" which ran in the southern hemisphere in summer. Large prize money and lavish hospitality attracted teams and drivers from Europe, who boosted the field and put on a show. At Peron's insistence, one car per team had to be driven by a local. Fangio thus took his chance in January 1948. In Buenos Aires and Mar del Plata, he was put behind the wheel of a Maserati 4CL; in Rosario and Buenos Aires he drove a

Simca-Gordini 1100 cc. French champion Jean-Pierre Wimille recommended him to the constructor Amedee Gordini and in July 1948, he was making his debut at Reims in the ACF Grand Prix in a works Simca-Gordini.

1949 saw Fangio's international career really take off. The Argentine automobile club bought two Formula 1 Maserati type 4 CLT, 1500 cc, four cylinder turbos for Fangio and Benedicto Campos, as well as acquiring two Simca-Gordini Formula 2 cars. He was a sensation and won three grands prix on the trot with the Maserati, in San Remo, Pau and Perpignan, and another in Marseille with the Simca. On 10th July, he won again at Albi in the Maserati, having previously taken a Formula 2 win at Monza in a 2 litre V12 Ferrari 166 F2. It was a brand new car bought by the Argentine auto club, much to the frustration of the works Ferraris.

1950: Second already

Spotted by Enzo Ferrari, welcomed as a hero on his return home, Fangio got an offer to drive for the Alfa Romeo team in the first season of the official Formula 1 World Championship in 1950. He was in a squad with Giuseppe "Nino" Farina and Luigi Fagioli, making up the "3 Fs" at the wheel of the Alfetta 158 which would be very competitive. Jean-Pierre Wimille was killed at the wheel of a Simca-Gordini in practice for the JD Peron GP in Buenos Aires in January 1949. Varzi was killed in Berne in summer 1948 before Alfa lost its best driver, Count Felice Trossi who died of cancer. Having pulled out of the sport in 1949, it was back in 1950. With Alberto Ascari and Luigi Villoresi snapped up by Ferrari, the Milan firm was therefore betting on this Argentinian to wake up their two Italian veterans. A fourth car was occasionally entrusted to local stars like Toulo de Graffenried in Switzerland and Reg Parnell in England. As a test and also to appease the partisan Italian press, Alfa Romeo boss Antonio Alessio put Fangio in a 158 for the non-championship San Remo GP. Despite the rain, he soon got to grips with the Alfetta and beat the field.

Francorchamps, which then measured 14.080 kilometres, Fangio once again took pole, ahead of Farina and Villoresi. In the early stages, the two Alfa men duelled with Farina leading until Fangio stormed past and set the fastest lap of the race. But when Fangio stopped on lap 14 to change tyres he lost no less than 14 minutes, as the mechanics struggled to remove one of his rear wheels. The Argentine maintained an olympian calm throughout and rejoined in 8th place, with victory going to Farina.

In Reims, on a baking hot 1st July, Fangio was yet again on pole and put himself back in contention for the title by winning the French Grand Prix, even though the race nearly escaped him. Ascari (Ferrari) and Farina fought it out for the lead. Fangio's Alfetta followed the example of Sanesi's similar mount and broke down with ignition

problems. Luckily, Fagioli's car was still a runner and as the rules allowed (with points being shared between the two drivers) the veteran Italian was called in to hand his car to Fangio. The Argentine drove like a man possessed, climbed through the field and making the most of Ferrari's problems, was up to second place. He then caught and passed Farina who had lost three minutes in the pits, which gave Fangio the win. As he also set the race fastest lap, he picked up 5 points, while Gonzalez and Ascari, who had shared a car, only got 3 each, with Farina scoring 2.

Fangio could tackle the rest of the season with no particular worries. At Silverstone on 14th July, it was his fellow countryman Jose "Froilan" Gonzalez who won the British Grand Prix; a historic first win for Ferrari, but Fangio 2nd ahead of Villoresi and Bonetto, increased his championship lead. However, in Germany, the Ferrari menace would strike again: on the Nurburgring on 29th July, this time it was Alberto Ascari who won. Fangio set the fastest lap on his way to second, to pick up valuable points, but behind him, three Ferrari drivers were in the points: Gonzalez 4, Villoresi 3 and Taruffi 2.

There were two grands prix remaining: Italy on 16th September and Spain on 28th October. The atmosphere was tense in Monza as the championship was being fought out between two drivers and two Italian marques who were very much rivals, with Italian and Argentine star drivers. That day, the Ferraris were unbeatable. Ascari won as he pleased from Gonzalez. Farina

He signed a contract with Alfa Romeo after taking the win, in an hotel in San Remo, saying to Alessio: "You can put as many noughts as you like." Other times, other customs!

That year, the world championship kicked off at Silverstone, on 13th May, with the British Grand Prix. Fangio retired after 8 laps with a loss of oil pressure, but from Monaco on 21st May he showed his mastery of racing. Starting from pole, he took the lead and built up a lead over his pursuers. On lap 2 there was a crash at the exit to Tabac, wiping out several cars which blocked the track. Fangio spotted the spectators had their heads turned and realised something was amiss. So he slowed for the corner, gently nudged one of the stranded cars out of the way and went on to take the first of his 24 wins in the world championship. He continued winning in style, in the Belgian and French Grands Prix and he was in the hunt for the title up to the final round, the Italian Grand Prix. Sadly, he was let down by his engine and "Nino" Farina took the win and the world championship on 30 points. Fangio was runner-up on 27. At the time a win was only worth 8 points, with the places 2 to 5 allocated as today, 6,4,3,2. There were no points for sixth, but a point was given to whoever set the fastest race lap.

1951: World Champion at 40

For 1951, it looked as though the 4.5 litre normally aspirated Ferrari 375 F1 would pose the biggest threat to the Alfetta. Its V12 engine developed "only" 380 horsepower,

but used a lot less fuel than the 1500 cc turbocharged cars. Over a 500 km grand prix distance, that gave it a distinct refuelling advantage. Alfa Romeo was developing the Tipo 159, with a de Dion rear axle and a power output of 425 ps. With the right gearing, the Alfetta 159 could hit 310 km/h, if given a long enough run up. But the big problem with this marvellous car was that it positively guzzled fuel; a clever mix of alcohol, acetone, benzol and petrol. It used 100 litres to cover 100 kilometres! It was therefore fitted with bigger tanks than the 158 (225 litres instead of 185) but its dry weight went up by more than 100 kilos (810 from 700.) At the start of a grand prix, on full tanks and with drivers who did not share the modern fashion for "jockey" sized pilots, the Alfetta 159 would weigh well over a tonne.

It makes Fangio's performance all the more remarkable in the Swiss Grand Prix which was the curtain raiser on the second world championship after Monaco had been cancelled. On Sunday 27th May, it was raining hard in the Berne park of Bremgarten when the cars took the start. Fangio started from pole, ahead of Farina (Alfetta) and Villoresi (Ferrari.) The reigning champion, usually not one to give up, appeared ill at ease in the wet with the Tipo 159 and only finished 3rd behind the Piero Taruffi Ferrari, himself 1'15" behind the winner, Fangio of course. He proved that he was totally dominant with a mix of speed and caution.

The championship moved to Belgium on 17th June. On the road course of Spa-

<

Spa-Francorchamps, 20th June 1954: waiting for the Mercedes to appear, Fangio raced the first two events in a Maserati 250 F, winning both. After Argentina, came Belgium. Here, the Argentine accelerates out of the Source hairpin.

Monza, 5th September 1954: Fangio and the Mercedes W196 takes fellow countryman Froilan Gonzalez and the Ferrari 555 Squalo in the Italian Grand Prix, the penultimate round. Fangio went on to win and take title number 2.
>

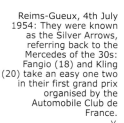

Reims-Gueux, 4th July 1954: They were known as the Silver Arrows, referring back to the Mercedes of the 30s: Fangio (18) and Kling (20) take an easy one two in their first grand prix organised by the Automobile Club de France.
v

all score points. Fangio had signed a contract with Maserati. On 18th May, the cars were not ready so the trident team did not attend the Swiss Grand Prix. More serious still, a serious accident at Monza in early June at the Autodrome Grand Prix, a non-championship event, put Juan Manuel Fangio out for the rest of the '52 season. Ferraris dominated, with Alberto Ascari taking a magnificent championship victory.

Ferrari and its drivers faced stiffer opposition in 1953, even if the 500 F2 had been improved: the Maserati A6 GCM had been replaced by the more powerful A6 SS/G. Fangio picked up several second places, notably at Reims, just beaten by Mike Hawthorn's Ferrari in a memorable ACF Grand Prix. He also won the Italian Grand Prix to give Maserati its only win in these two seasons in an equally exciting final.

(fastest lap) and Bonetto had shared an Alfetta to come home third. Fangio had led and stopped to change a puncture. Then, going flat out to make up time, his engine exploded.

The Barcelona-Pedralbes race would therefore decide the outcome of the 1951 World Championship. The two Italian marques had plenty of time to prepare their weapons. But unfortunately the Scuderia got their strategy wrong.

On the eve of the race, the Ferraris changed from 16 to 15 inch wheels to improve acceleration and traction. But in the race, the tyres were torn to shreds and Taruffi, Villoresi, Ascari and Gonzalez had to make innumerable stops to change them. This blew away the advantage the Ferraris had in

using less fuel. Fangio set the fastest lap and won from Gonzalez, Farina and Ascari. Thus, he took the first of his five world titles, with 31 points, ahead of Ascari (25,) Gonzalez (24) and Farina (19.)

1952-53: A long wait

In 1952, Alfa Romeo pulled out, BRM and OSCA only turned up occasionally and so the CSI was worried Formula 1 would become Formula Ferrari, so it switched the Drivers' World Championship to 2 litre Formula 2 cars. It boosted the grids in the short terms, while encouraging constructors to prepare the future 2.5 litre F1 cars, due to be introduced in 1954. This meant that the Ferrari 500 F2, Maserati A6 GCM, Gordinis, Cooper-Bristol, HWM and Connaught could

1954-55: Mercedes one-two

Mercedes staged its big comeback in 1954; a bit late but dominant. Legendary sporting director Alfred Neubauer, who had run the German team in the 30s, was back in charge, while the engineer from those days Rudolf Uhlenhaut teamed up with Fritz Nallinger and Hans Scherenberg to produce a remarkable car; the in-line 8 cylinder W 196 with desmodromic valves. Neubauer recruited Fangio as number one driver, with the Germans Karl Kling and Hans Herrmann. The Mercedes were not ready until early July and the ACF race, round three on the calendar. Fangio had been free to pursue his aspirations for the first two races in Argentina and Belgium, driving the new Maserati 250 F, 6 cylinder with 240 horsepower. He won both in style, beating the Ferraris of Gonzalez, Farina, Trintignant and Hawthord, setting the quickest lap in Spa.

The Mercedes therefore appeared in Reims with their streamlined body and 280 horsepower. Under Neubauer's impeccable management they got it right first time. Fangio took pole and won easily, ahead of Kling and Herrmann who set the fastest lap before retiring. But in Silverstone, the Mercedes were in trouble, even Fangio found his visibility was impaired by the enveloping wings and in the wet he suffered from lack of grip because of poor tyres. He

<
Aintree, 16th July 1955
Fangio (no.10) in the
Mercedes W 196 ahead of
that of Stirling Moss (no.
12.) In a matter of laps,
the order would change
and Moss would win his
first grand prix, the
British, ahead of Fangio,
his master and long time
friend.

finished fourth, behind two Ferraris and a Maserati. Mercedes reacted immediately, bringing out the W196 without the enclosed bodywork for the German GP at the Nurburgring. Fangio took a clear win, with Kling setting fastest lap on his way to 4th. Three weeks later in Berne, Fangio did it again, despite the attentions of Gonzalez in the Ferrari. The original W 196 was brought out again for Monza where Fangio took his fourth consecutive win and seventh of the season, ahead of Hawthorn. With the title already assured, Fangio finished 3rd in Spain, behind Hawthorn (Ferrari) and Musso (Maserati.) That day the Lancia D 50 had made its debut, proving in Ascari's hands that they could rival the Mercedes.

Mercedes brought in English rising star Stirling Moss to partner Fangio in 1955. The year got off to a wonderful start for the Argentine as he won his home grand prix in Buenos Aires in stifling heat. He and fellow countryman Roberto Mieres, 5th in a Maserati, drive the whole race of approximately three hours, without getting out of the car or handing over to a team-mate. He scored 9 points thanks to getting the fastest lap. In Monaco, on 22nd May, Mercedes suffered a rare reversal of fortune. Fangio and Moss, who had taken the lead at the start, retired one after the other, both with a broken distributor nut. The unexpected winner was Trintignant (Ferrari.) A chasing Ascari had missed the chicane and parked his Lancia in the

harbour. Three days later, having got over his minor Monaco injuries, he was killed in private testing of a Ferrari sports car at Monza. Racing lost one of its most worthy champions and Fangio and Mercedes lost a major rival. Ascari's death precipitated Lancia's withdrawal, as they were going through a financial crisis. In July, Lancia offered its six D50s and V8 engines, as well as spare parts to Ferrari, who would make good use of them in 1956. The first beneficiary was Fangio. But for the moment, the Argentine was back to his winning ways, along with Moss. The two Mercedes were stuck together so much they were known as "the train." They scored a one-two in Belgium and Holland and filled the first four places in England, for once with Moss the winner, from Fangio, Kling and Taruffi. As the French, German and Swiss races had been cancelled after the disaster at Le Mans, there was a final one-two in Italy; Fangio ahead of Taruffi. It was his third championship with 40 points ahead of Moss on 23. Fangio had won 4 of the 7 grands prix, with three fastest laps.

1956: a difficult fourth

Mercedes no longer had anything to prove having dominated Formula 1 for two years and taken the Constructors' Championship for Formula Sport cars in 1955. It therefore announced its retirement from racing. Fangio almost did the same: his Mercedes

and General Motors business in Buenos Aires was booming, he missed his family and, at 44, he had had enough of this dangerous sport. But the fall of the Peron regime in September 1955 and the new government's decision to freeze company and personal assets of wealthy people during the dictatorship bothered Fangio, even though he had come by his fortune honestly. At the same time, Enzo Ferrari summoned him to Maranello saying, "Fangio, I know you will be expensive, but I need you." Moss had just signed for Maserati. Fangio delayed his retirement and got a major pay cheque which previously, only Mercedes had been

Monza, 2nd September
1956: in the Italian Grand
Prix, Fangio (Lancia-
Ferrari no. 22) made a
steady start behind the
duelling Musso and
Castelloti. Here, he holds
off Harry Schell's Vanwall,
Stirling Moss in the
Maserati 250 F and the
Lancia-Ferrari of Peter
Collins, who would give
up his car for Fangio to
finish second behind Moss
and take his fourth world
championship.
∨

able to afford. His Ferrari team-mates were youngsters: the Italians Luigi Musso and Eugenio Castelloti, the Spaniard Alfonso de Portago and England's Peter Collins.

It was a difficult season for Fangio, who never felt comfortable with the Scuderia, run by Eraldo Sculati. The cause of the unease came from an Italian journalist and race organiser Marcello Giamberetone, self-proclaimed manager of Fangio. He was always creating intrigue and often complicated relationships between his driver and the team. In Monaco, the season got off to a bad start. Moss took the lead and Fangio, chased by all his young wolves and unusually tense, missed a braking point and went off at Ste. Devote at the start of the race. He set off again with a damaged car,

Silverstone, 14th July
1956: Fangio at work,
going through Stowe at
the wheel of the
magnificent Lancia-Ferrari
V8. He went on to record
yet another British Grand
Prix victory.
<

Rouen-les Essarts, 7th
July 1957: on the French
track for the ACF Grand
Prix, Fangio put on an
extraordinary display with
his Maserati 250 F,
seen here four wheel
sliding after the Nouveau
Monde hairpin. It was his
23rd win.

Nurburgring, 4th August
1957: the finish of the
German Grand Prix and
Fangio had pushed it to
the limit. It was his 24th
and final world
championship race win,
resulting in him taking a
fifth title in seven
seasons. No one has ever
done that!
∨

which he damaged further going over the
kerbs to make up the gap. He stopped at
third distance and, at half distance Sculati,
after a long discussion in the pits, brought
Collins in. Fangio took the young
Englishman's car and started an incredible
climb through the field, to finish second a
few seconds behind Moss. Collins won the
Belgian GP at Spa, his first victory, ahead of
Paul Frere, guesting for Ferrari. Fangio had
led from the start, but retired with
transmission failure. The atmosphere,
already tense in Monaco, got worse. In
Reims, Fangio was only fourth in the ACF
GP, won by Collins. However, it was one of
his best races, because he was delayed by a
stupid pit stop to repair a leaking fuel gauge
which was spraying petrol in his face! As he
charged back up the order, he broke the lap
record. After that, one mechanic was tasked
specifically with looking after his car. In
England, still suffering the after effects of
Reims, he won the British GP and did it
again at the Nurburgring to lead the
classification on 27 points, ahead of Collins
and Behra (22) and Moss (19) who were all
still in with a chance of taking the title.

down to circumstance and the machinery
available. The Argentine had only really
failed in Monaco and even then, only at the
start of the race. As for Collins gesture in
Monza, it was sincere, even if the
Englishman admitted later, he had not
really fancied being world champion!

1957: perfection

If any driver attained perfection in his era,
it had to be Fangio in 1957. Possibly a bit
embarrassed by the way he took the title in
Monza the previous year, he resolved to
give it one more shot and be remembered as
a great champion. Relations with Ferrari
had been, at best, cold, so he signed with his
old friends Maserati, Ferrari's eternal rival.
The new 250 F was lighter and more

powerful than the original which he had
driven in 1954. Moss had gone to Vanwall,
so Fangio was seconded by Frenchman
Jean Behra, the Paris-based American
Harry Schell and another Argentine, Carlos
Menditeguy.

Fangio was soon back in the groove,
winning the Argentine Grand Prix from
Behra and Menditeguy. Moss was on loan
to Maserati from Vanwall, who failed to
show and he took pole and fastest lap,
before retiring. In Monaco, Fangio did t
he lot; pole, the win and fastest lap. In the
French GP run that year at Rouen, a road
circuit which was almost as difficult and
dangerous as the Nurburgring, although
a third of the length, Fangio put on a
demonstration.

On the podium after the
1957 German Grand Prix.
Fangio is surrounded by
his friends and rivals,
Mike Hawthorn (right)
and Peter Collins (left,)
exhausted but happy.
"That day, I did things
I had never done before
and never want to
do again," admitted
Fangio later.
>

The situation would be resolved on 2nd
September in Monza at the Italian Grand
Prix. Starting carefully behind Musso and
Castelloti, overexcited to be at home. He
had warned them their tyres would not last
at this pace and both men had to stop early.
Moss (Maserati) made the most of it to lead.
Fangio had to stop on lap 19 with bent
steering. His car, once repaired would be
taken over by Castelloti. Fangio waited in
the pits, evidently waiting for a car. The one
used by the Marquis de Portago was out of
service with bent steering. Musso was asked
when he refuelled but he firmly refused and
held onto to his steering wheel. That just
left Collins: he got out of his car and offered
it to Fangio, for the second time this season.
In that moment, Collins gave up any hope
of taking the title. Fangio jumped into the
cockpit and finished second behind Moss.
The three points he picked up, sharing the 6
with Collins, were enough to make Fangio
world champion. This was definitely the
least glorious of his five titles, but that was

Monza, 8th September 1957: Fangio was second in the Italian Grand Prix behind Stirling Moss' Vanwall. The Argentine would win one more non-championship Grand Prix in 1958 in Buenos Aires.
<

<
Alfa Romeo 159
Spanish Grand Prix 1951

<
Mercedes W 196,
ACF Grand Prix 1954

<
Mercedes W 196,
Belgian Grand Prix 1955

Discover Juan Manuel Fangio; his life, his career, his races, his cars and a complete and detailed record of his racing, as well as exclusive eye-witness accounts, including those of the five times world champion himself, in "Juan Manuel Fangio – La course faite homme". The book features 150 photos (black and white and colour) and profiles of all the F1 cars he drove in the World Championship. This 160 page volume came out in 2002 and is the No. 1 book in the "Les Legendes de la Formule 1" written by Pierre Menard and Jacques Vassal, published by Chronosports. Also available: "Ayrton Senna – Au-dela de l'exigence", "Stirling Moss – Le champion sans couronne" and "Alain Prost- La science de la course."

<
Ferrari-Lancia D 50,
Italian Grand Prix 1956

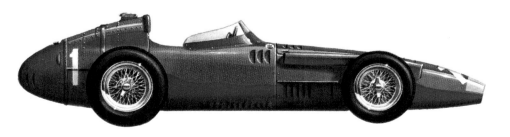

<
Maserati 250 F
German Grand Prix 1957

ATMOSPHERE

More girls than ever and more colourful images in the paddock. It is impossible to capture the atmosphere of a whole season in a couple of pages. We can only offer a glimpse. Fire it up!

And the prettiest is?

These photos prove it: there are plenty of pretty girls in Formula 1.

To many people in the paddock, more important than knowing who will win the next grand prix is the question, which is the prettiest girl.

Judge for yourself, but remember that the real beauties do not feel the need to show off in quite such an eye-catching fashion.

Bonus

Apparently, «The Formula 1 Yearbook» would not be the same without these two girl-filled pages. So this year, we are offering your four for the same price. One has to admit that the paddock was particularly well endowed this year. It was a hot summer.

Portraits of the stars

Complex though it is, Formula 1 is still centred on the drivers. They can be in turn happy, sad, worried, smiling, perplexed, jovial or mocking. Here's a selection.

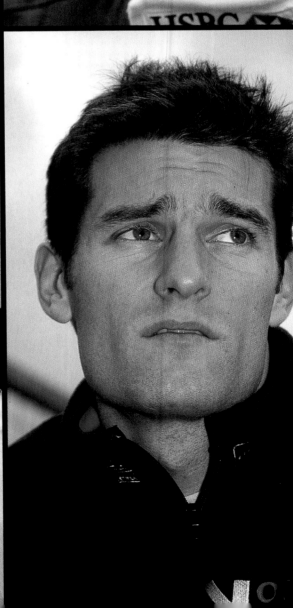

A transition year

In the end, Jordan finished sixth in the constructors' championship, thanks mainly to Takuma Sato's last minute effort for two points in Suzuka. The Irish team is now awaiting its new Ford engine for 2003.

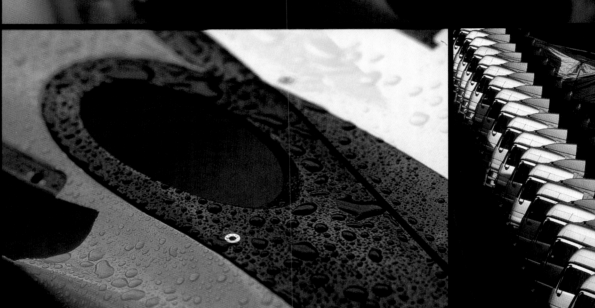

Abstract art

Formula 1 and art can go together as these photos prove.

Close-ups of bodywork and suspension detail, zoom in on gears: what could be better than F1 for techno-freaks?

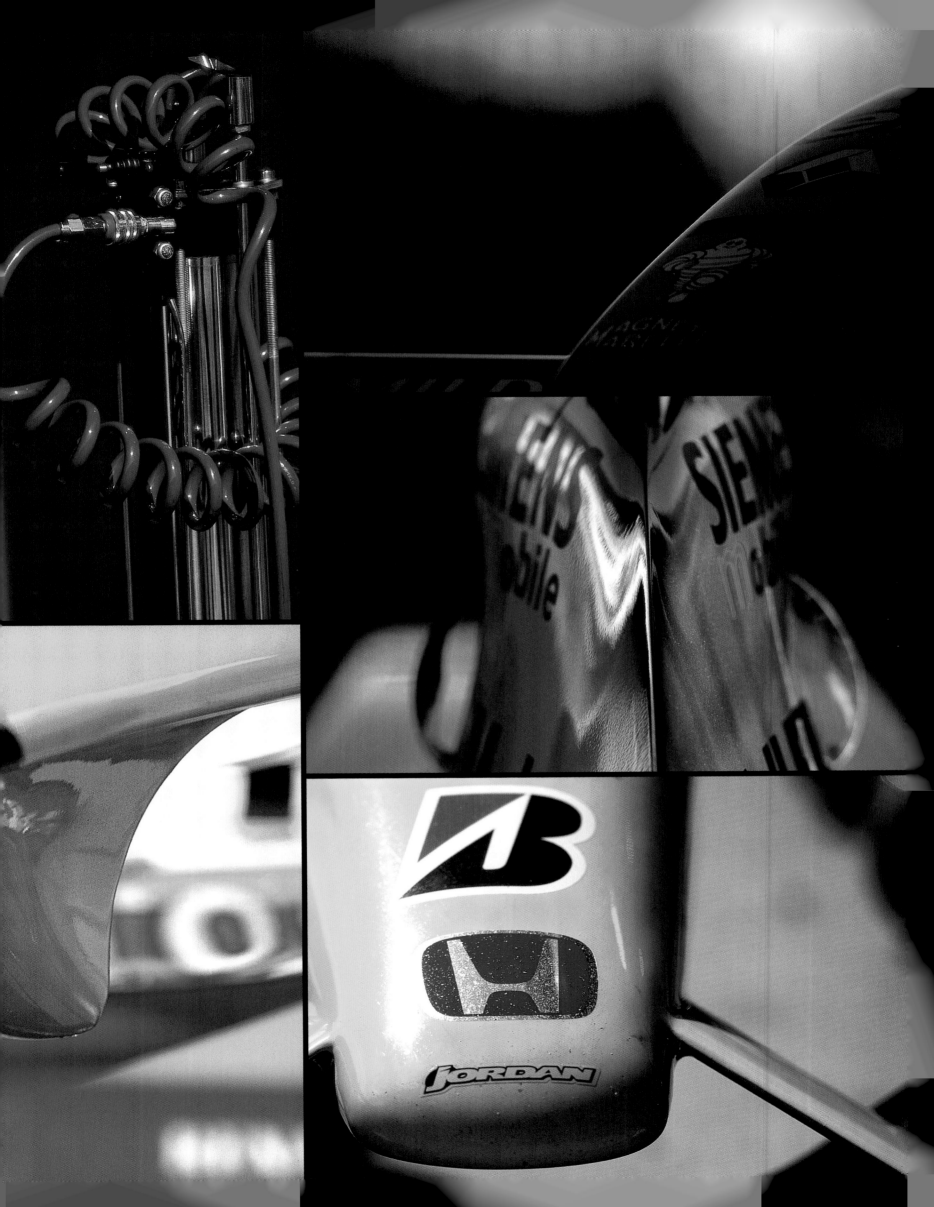

THE 17
GRAND PRIX

Once again, the 2002 season saw
the Formula 1 circus visit the four
corners of the earth.
But this year, whether the Grand
Prix was staged in Australia or
Japan, the dominant colour was
undoubtedly red. 2002 was a record
season for Scuderia Ferrari.

OFF WITH A BANG!

A fantastic start to the season! As the time came to draw a conclusion from the year just passed, one could almost hazard the opinion that, at the end of the day, the Australian Grand Prix was the most exciting of the 2002 season.

The event was marked by a mega crash at the first corner, caused when Ralf Schumacher appeared to forget to brake. Ten cars were involved and the majority were unable to continue.

From then on, Michael Schumacher, who had been fourth at the end of the first lap, had to use all his savvy to take the win. But above all, the Australian Grand Prix saw two "*new boys*" score points on their F1 debut. Mark Webber finished fifth for Minardi, while the Toyota team picked up a point for sixth, courtesy of Mika Salo. It was a fabulous weekend, crowned with the delight of the local crowd at seeing their own Aussie driver pick up his first F1 points.

> First grand prix and first row for Michael Schumacher, only out-qualified on the grid by his team-mate Rubens Barrichello.

After Kimi Räikkönen, Peter Sauber was once again playing the youth card. Felipe Massa kicked off his Formula 1 career in Melbourne, at just twenty years of age. He seemed unfazed by his new surroundings, out-qualifying Nick Heidfeld, his more experienced team-mate.

∨

Confusion: Ferrari starts the year with the 2001 car

Michael Schumacher did not seem to happy at the fact Scuderia Ferrari had opted to start the year running the 2001 car. He was far from delighted. "*Of course, I would have preferred to be running the F2002*", he complained, with tensions rippling through the microphone.

On Thursday, at the first press conference of the season, Michael Schumacher seemed to be sulking. "*I haven't got a clue where we are compared with the others*", he continued. "*We will see on Friday. I think we will be near the front of the grid, but it's not certain.*"

Had he been bluffing? Because come Friday morning, after the first hour of practice, Schumacher's name was already at the top of the time sheet, with around a four tenths of a second advantage over Rubens Barrichello. In third place, Giancarlo Fisichella was almost three seconds down (2.889 seconds to be precise). With just half a session completed it seemed as though the dice were already cast for the season! The gap to Ferrari meant the other teams could think about packing their bags and trying again next year. At the end of the day, after a further hour of free practice, the two Ferraris were "*only*" one and a half seconds quicker than the two Williams. The decision to use the previous year's car, rather than the F2002 was only taken shortly before all

the cars and equipment had to be shipped off to Australia. It was a hastily thrown together plan and not at all the Scuderia's style. "*I don't even know if we will have the new car in Malaysia in two weeks time*", added the world champion during a press conference. "*We still have a huge amount of work to do. So far, we have not had enough time to test the F2002. We were held up by the weather and then there were some small mechanical problems. It hasn't been easy. There came a time when we had to make a decision and we opted for the fallback situation of using the old car. And I'm not happy about it!*"

In theory, the Scuderia's lack of preparation should have allowed its rivals to make hay while the sun shone. "*That's clear*", agreed Schumacher. "*Especially as there a lot of teams which look promising and we don't know much about them, like Sauber and Renault.*"

However, come Friday night, after a day spent crushing the opposition, he had changed his tune. "*I am quite satisfied and to be honest, I feel more confident than when we arrived*", Schumacher was forced to admit. "*I am not over-confident, because a lot can change between now and tomorrow's qualifying. But I have to say I am quite surprised at the gap to the others.*"

Briefly

> Fine for Nick Heidfeld at the end of qualifying: the German was caught speeding in the pit lane at 64.9 km/h instead of 60! He was fined 1250 dollars.

> Takuma Sato, taking part in his first grand prix, had failed to qualify. An accident on Saturday morning meant he had to take the spare, which then broke down. When he finally got going, the track was wet.

However, the Stewards allowed him to start, given the extenuating circumstances.

> The Toyota team acquitted itself very well in its first ever qualifying session. However, Allan McNish was penalised because his team fitted his car with some of Friday's tyres on Saturday morning, which is forbidden in the regulations. He had to make do with one set less for qualifying.

< First grand prix with McLaren for Kimi Räikkönen, after the team paid Sauber a huge crock of gold for his services. It would seem to have been worthwhile given that the Finn was fifth on the grid.

The Ferraris on the front row, ahead of the Williams. Already.

The qualifying session started in the dry, before a shower soaked the track with 30 minutes remaining. Rubens Barrichello came out of this best, claiming pole position, just 5 thousandths of a second quicker than Michael Schumacher. Behind the two Ferraris, the two BMW-Williams were not as far back as the previous day. Ralf Schumacher was only giving away four tenths compared with the pole time. "*If the session had gone off normally, the Ferraris would have been quicker, but so would we*", commented the world champion's little brother. "*Our car still has a lot of room for improvement.*"

While sadly, Formula 1 is far too politically correct these days, at the Australian Grand Prix some drivers decided to fire a few destabilising salvos in the direction of their rivals. Or was it down to dislike, pure and simple? A few examples. Juan Pablo Montoya: "*Michael is not the best driver. In my opinion that was Ayrton Senna.*" Michael Schumacher: "*David Coulthard? I don't see why he would suddenly be capable of winning the world championship.*" David Coulthard: "*Michael (Schumacher) is getting too old. There are places where he is lifting, while I am flat out. That's why I can overtake him!*" Ralf Schumacher: "*Juan Pablo and me are not the best of friends. The important thing is that I beat him!*" Looks like being a fun year!

Melbourne, the biggest city in Australia. What better venue to kick off a new season than this southern hemisphere metropolis? With hordes of restaurants along the Yarra river, the bars on Flinders Street, the ocean and the busy city centre streets, everything about Melbourne is conducive to having a good time.

V

Starting grid

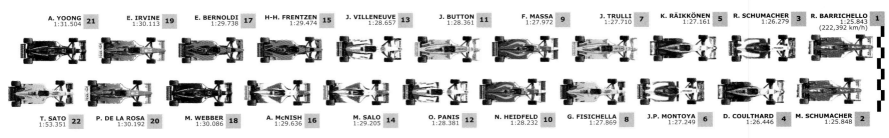

Pos	Driver	Time
21	A. YOONG	1:31.504
19	E. IRVINE	1:30.113
17	E. BERNOLDI	1:29.738
15	H-H. FRENTZEN	1:29.474
13	J. VILLENEUVE	1:28.657
11	J. BUTTON	1:28.361
9	F. MASSA	1:27.972
7	J. TRULLI	1:27.710
5	K. RÄIKKÖNEN	1:27.161
3	R. SCHUMACHER	1:26.279
1	R. BARRICHELLO	1:25.843 (222,392 km/h)
22	T. SATO	1:53.351
20	P. DE LA ROSA	1:30.192
18	M. WEBBER	1:30.086
16	A. McNISH	1:29.636
14	M. SALO	1:29.205
12	O. PANIS	1:28.381
10	N. HEIDFELD	1:28.232
8	G. FISICHELLA	1:27.869
6	J.P. MONTOYA	1:27.249
4	D. COULTHARD	1:26.446
2	M. SCHUMACHER	1:25.848

> *"Can I go over the top?"* Ralf Schumacher and, behind him, Nick Heidfeld, cause a memorable accident which involved ten cars. The top three photos show the aerial display which ended Ralf Schumacher's and Rubens Barrichello's chances. After the race, the Brazilian was showing off his crash helmet in the paddock, as it bore a five centimetre groove. Below is the accident caused by Heidfeld, which created mayhem in the pack.

Eight cars eliminated: carnage at the first corner of the season

Eight cars were beyond hope, while two more were in the pits changing front wings and other bits: a collision between Ralf Schumacher's Williams and Rubens Barrichello's Ferrari really caused chaos in the pack.

The cause of this, the most spectacular shunt in recent year, was a touch of late braking from Ralf Schumacher. He was unable to avoid ramming Rubens Barrichello, who according to the German, braked earlier than usual. The Brazilian reckoned he did it *"to avoid an accident!"* The Williams flew through the air, landing in the escape road. *"I felt like I was in a plane"*, recounted the Williams driver. *"I was really lucky not to roll and to have gone off where there was some room."*

Further back, it was total confusion. The two Saubers, Giancarlo Fisichella's Jordan, Jenson Button's Renault, Olivier Panis' BAR and Allan McNish's Toyota were all wiped out.

Naturally, these driver were hoping the race would be red flagged, but as there was not that much debris on the track, no such extreme measures were required. That certainly suited the cars left running.

> An incredible fourth place for Eddie Irvine's Jaguar. Thanks to a whiff of luck and experience, the Irishman avoided the mess at Turn 1. Having started from 19th on the grid, he came round at the end of the opening lap in fifth place!

Ferrari's secrets

Michelin's racing boss, Pierre Dupasquier seemed to be bouncing around on springs. He was watching Michael Schumacher's Ferrari. *"The way this car behaves reminds me of Colin Chapman's invention of ground effect in 1978"*, he commented. *"In the twisty parts of the track, it is taking a second off us and doing it easily. Ferrari has understood that you don't calibrate your downforce in a straight line."*

He had said it all. To maximise downforce, the force which sticks the cars to the road, the teams use very sophisticated wind tunnels, which usually work by simulating a straight line, even though downforce is not a prime requirement down the straights, its main purpose being to help the car through the corners. But, when the cars are cornering, they do not face the air current head on, but from an angle, which depends on the sharpness of the turn.

Since the day when it became possible to simulate these forces, the Ferraris have been unbeatable. One has to admit that the Scuderia has worked at it. In Maranello, the aero specialists work in three eight hour shifts, 24 hours a day, seven days a week, so as to gain every possible advantage.

The Scuderia's new aerodynamic package was given its first outing at Suzuka, for the last grand prix of the previous year. *"We are testing something fundamental for next season"*, the Scuderia's sporting director Jean Todt had warned at the time. It was in fact this new *"corner related"* aerodynamic set up which allowed Michael Schumacher to gain a full two seconds on the twisty opening section of the Melbourne track. All without losing out down the straights.

The 2002 season had only just begun and yet, it was hard to see who could trouble the Scuderia, given the combination of their almost perfect car and the best driver in field.

Weekend gossip

> Former BAR boss Craig Pollock was in Melbourne, in civvies, as Jacques Villeneuve's manager. Ever-smiling, the former ski instructor was returning to the role he occupied when he arrived in F1 in 1996, having been kicked out of his job as team boss, which he had held since 1997.

> Once again, Juan Pablo Montoya pulled out a daring passing move on Michael Schumacher. At the start of lap 12, as the Safety Car pulled in, the Colombian went round the outside of the German, overtaking him in the braking area at the first chicane. It was a brave manoeuvre. Five laps later, the Ferrari cruised easily back into the lead.

> David Coulthard led the first ten laps of the race behind the Safety Car. And when it pulled off the track… the Scotsman flew off the road. *"I began to have problems changing down"*, he explained afterwards. *"It meant I went off the track a few times, before the gearbox got stuck in sixth. It was all over."* His team-mate Kimi Räikkönen, in his first grand prix with McLaren, finished on the podium in third place.

> The two Saubers only completed 5000 metres in this first grand prix of the season, with both of them knocked out in the first corner carnage. Nick Heidfeld missed his braking point and embedded his C21 in Fisichella's Jordan…who rammed Felipe Massa.

> Comic relief at the start as both Arrows were left stranded on the grid. Heinz-Harald Frentzen and Enrique Bernoldi were victims of the same problem with their launch control. Once they got going, they were both black-flagged: Frentzen for having left the pit lane when the lights were red and Bernoldi for having switched to the spare car after the race had started.

> More misery for Jacques Villeneuve. The only BAR driver still in the race after the first corner had his rear wing fly off, just as it had done at this circuit three years earlier.

Minardi and Toyota in the points: everyone a winner at the Debutantes Ball

Misfortune for some can bring happiness for others. The main beneficiaries of the first corner crash were those who started from the back of the grid. As they picked their way through the wreckage, they found themselves promoted up the ranks.

Thus, having qualified 19th, Eddie Irvine ended the opening lap in...5th place! The Irishman then managed to go the distance, finishing the race in fourth spot. It was an unexpected result for the struggling Jaguar team.

But it was Minardi who pulled off the coup of the weekend. In Melbourne, it and Jaguar were the only two teams to see both their cars take the flag. Mark Webber even managed to finish his first ever grand prix in fifth place and in front of his home crowd to boot. The previous year, Minardi had

failed to score a single point and starting the season on such a high note was totally unexpected. Team owner Paul Stoddart was on Cloud Nine after the race. "*We had already enjoyed a fantastic week here in Melbourne, but scoring points in the first race of the season, with Mark doing it in his first grand prix is just surreal!*" In the second Minardi, Alex Yoong finished seventh, just outside the points.

With two laps remaining, Mika Salo nearly demoted Mark Webber to sixth, before spinning and recovering to pick up the final point on offer. It was an excellent result for the Toyota new boys and was way beyond their wildest hopes. Allan McNish was eliminated from his first grand prix in the first corner crash.

^
All quiet on the grid before the start of the Grand Prix, while two hours later it's all excitement for the podium ceremony.

Lap 14. "No room on the outside." Juan Pablo Montoya defends first place, having passed Michael Schumacher at the very same spot a few laps earlier.
V

Race summary

> **Start (1)**
Starting from pole position, Rubens Barrichello is hit by Ralf Schumacher at the first corner, causing general mayhem.

> **Lap 1 - Safety Car**
Race control wheels out the Safety Car to neutralise the race while debris is cleared away. David Coulthard leads, followed by the

incredible Jarno Trulli, Juan Pablo Montoya, Michael Schumacher and Eddie Irvine.

> **Lap 8 - Trulli**
Jarno Trulli goes off the track while lying second.

> **Lap 11 (2)**
David Coulthard, still in the lead, slides off the road and drops to fourth, immediately

after the Safety Car pulls in having come out while Trulli's car was towed away.

> In the other McLaren, Kimi Räikkönen had to spend a long time in the pits, having his front wing changed and debris removed from the back of the car. Rejoining last, thanks to the second appearance of the

Safety Car, the Finn manages to catch up with the pack and finish on the podium (**6**).

> After the Safety Car has completed its second tour of duty, the race is really underway. Juan Pablo Montoya manages to pass Michael Schumacher at the end of the straight.

> **Lap 28 (3)**
Watching from the BAR pit wall, Craig Pollock sees Jacques Villeneuve retire when his rear wing breaks.

> **Lap 38 (4)**
Michael Schumacher refuels, having re-passed Montoya on lap 17 and cruises to the finish. He does not even lose the lead during his pit stop on

his way to winning the first race of the season (**5**).

> Behind the Ferrari, Juan Pablo Montoya (**7**) has to work hard to maintain his second place and fend off the attentions of Kimi Räikkönen, third.

> Further back, Mark Webber brings the Minardi home in fifth

place, ahead of Mika Salo. Their duel in the closing stages has the crowd on its feet. The Finn manages to get past, but loses it with a spin, two laps from the flag and has to settle for sixth.

King of the world

If you drive for Minardi, fifth place is like winning. When it happens on your home turf it is a total triumph. The icing on the cake for Mark Webber was a snog from Aussie *"glamour model"* Sarah Jane.

The Prost team rises from the ashes

With his rugby player physique, Tom Walkinshaw is not exactly Mr. Popular in the Formula 1 paddock. The Scotsman runs his Arrows team with an iron fist, but he lacks the velvet glove. On top of that, his team is reckoned to be in debt to the tune of several million dollars. There was even talk of a hundred million dollars. This financial problem did not stop Walkinshaw from buying up the remains of the Prost team the Thursday before race week at the Commercial Court in St. Quentin en Yvelines, outside Paris. He made a last minute bid, before the deadline of midnight on 28th February. Minardi owner Paul Stoddart had also wanted to put in a bid, but his legal team got the time wrong and missed out by one hour!

Pressed on the matter in Melbourne, Walkinshaw was not giving much away. "*We will do all we can to run two cars in Malaysia in a fortnight*", he said. But with Ferrari refusing to supply engines, what would power the former Prosts? "*We will decide that on Monday*", replied the Scot. And what about mechanics and drivers? "*We will decide that on Monday*", he repeated.

Even if Walkinshaw reckoned he could get the team up and running in ten days, it seemed impossible in practical terms. Maybe he could use Asiatech engines left over from the previous year and maybe the drivers would be Gaston Mazzacane and Thomas Enge, Prost drivers in 2001. But it seemed impossible in the time available to modify the AP04 chassis (originally designed to take a Ferrari engine) to accept another V10.

Tom Walkinshaw concluded his Melbourne briefing by explaining that he had bought the team for "*a friend*", an English Real Estate millionaire. The news sent shock waves through the Albert Park paddock. "*I don't believe my ears*", admitted a shocked Frank Williams. "*This new team has missed the first grand prix of 2002, which means it ought to pay a huge penalty*", reckoned Jean Todt.

"*This matter isn't as straightforward as it sounds.*" With the threat of financial penalties hanging over it, the new team seemed to have lead in its wings and it was yet another unfortunate saga that Formula 1 could well do without.

For Minardi owner, the threat of the remnants of Prost Grand Prix being bought by Tom Walkinshaw represented a financial crisis. It meant the Italian team would slip one place down the team order, as Minardi had finished behind Prost in 2001 and would therefore pick up less television revenue. Although why Minardi should be entitled to move up a place in the previous year's standings just because one team had dropped out of this year's championship was none too clear.

Paul Stoddart was not about to let the matter rest. "*I need to be told why, one month ago, the Judge looking after the Prost business refused offers of between 30 and 50 million dollars, claiming they would not guarantee the team's future. And now, one month later, he is selling it for less than 10% of the worst offer (there was talk of 2.5 million dollars.) Why? According to my lawyers, the Judge did not have the right to sell the team and Tom Walkinshaw does not have the right to enter it in the championship. This matter will go to court.*"

Ron Dennis very angry with Paul Stoddart

On Sunday evening, the main talking point of the Melbourne weekend, Tom Walkinshaw's plans to buy the remains of the Prost team and run it to benefit from the TV rights monies, was still running its course. At the end of the weekend, Ron Dennis expressed his anger at the behaviour of the two main protagonists in this affair, Paul Stoddart and Tom Walkinshaw.

"*I cannot understand how two team owners can create such a scandal in public*", thundered Dennis. "*From my understanding of the Concorde Agreement (the document that contains all the financial agreements governing the sport) a team cannot be set up in this manner. It is impossible and I will do all in my power to make sure the rules are respected.*" Ron Dennis was clearly against the creation of this new team from the Prost ashes, which was due to appear in the Malaysian Grand Prix, running under the name of "*Phoenix*".

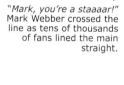

Michelin versus FIA

The season had barely started, but the tyre war was already underway. The Michelin engineers had come up with a tyre featuring asymmetric grooves.

The regulations state that tyres must have four grooves of a "*uniform*" design. The lads at Clermont-Ferrand evidently did not think that uniform meant symmetrical.

They therefore produced tyres with asymmetric grooves, which according to rumour would improve road holding and wear as the cars went round corners.

The International Automobile Federation (FIA) reckoned they were illegal. "*We do not agree with FIA*", explained the French company's spokesman Andy Pope on the Thursday. "*But being nice, we did not want to create a fuss by bringing these tyres here. We prefer to continue our dialogue with FIA and prove to them that we are obeying the rules.*"

In the end, the negotiations came to nought. Michelin gave up on the idea of running asymmetric tyres for 2002. Having lost the element of surprise, there was probably little point in the experiment.

Practice

All the time trials

N°	Driver	Car/Engine/Chassis	Practice Friday	Pos.	Practice Saturday	Pos.	Qualifying	Pos.	Warm-up	Pos.
1.	Michael Schumacher	Ferrari 2001/216	1'27''276	1°	1'26''177	1°	1'25''848	2°	1'41''509	1°
2.	Rubens Barrichello	Ferrari 2001/215	1'27''799	2°	1'26''331	2°	1'25''843	1°	1'42''891	2°
3.	David Coulthard	McLaren-Mercedes MP4/17/02	1'30''312	11°	1'27''505	5°	1'26''446	4°	1'43''537	3°
4.	Kimi Räikkönen	McLaren-Mercedes MP4/17/03	1'29''875	7°	1'27''635	6°	1'27''161	5°	1'44''027	5°
5.	Ralf Schumacher	Williams-BMW FW24/04	1'28''821	3°	1'27''424	4°	1'26''279	3°	1'43''580	4°
6.	Juan Pablo Montoya	Williams-BMW FW24/02	1'28''870	4°	1'27''394	3°	1'27''249	6°	1'46''929	15°
7.	Nick Heidfeld	Sauber-Petronas C21/02	1'29''572	5°	1'28''295	7°	1'28''232	10°	1'44''928	7°
8.	Felipe Massa	Sauber-Petronas C21/04	1'29''937	8°	1'28''700	11°	1'27''972	9°	1'44''389	6°
9.	Giancarlo Fisichella	Jordan-Honda EJ11/4	1'30''187	9°	1'28''605	10°	1'27''869	8°	1'45''159	8°
10.	Takuma Sato	Jordan-Honda EJ11/3	1'30''540	13°	1'30''914	19°	1'53''351		1'46''805	14°
11.	Jacques Villeneuve	BAR-Honda 004/03	1'30''352	12°	1'28''557	8°	1'28''657	13°	1'48''051	17°
12.	Olivier Panis	BAR-Honda 004/04	1'31''127	11°	1'28''570	9°	1'28''381	12°	1'46''499	13°
14.	Jarno Trulli	Renault R202/02	1'30''298	10°	1'28''773	12°	1'27''710	7°	1'45''625	9°
15.	Jenson Button	Renault R202/03	1'30''588	15°	1'28''881	13°	1'28''361	11°	1'48''169	18°
16.	Eddie Irvine	Jaguar R3/03	1'30''973	17°	1'29''737	17°	1'30''113	19°	1'45''808	10°
17.	Pedro de la Rosa	Jaguar R3/02	1'30''566	14°	1'31''286	21°	1'30''192	20°	2'03''262	22°
20.	Heinz-Harald Frentzen	Arrows-Cosworth A23/01	1'32''465	19°	1'29''174	14°	1'29''474	15°	1'46''006	11°
21.	Enrique Bernoldi	Arrows-Cosworth A23/02	1'32''912	21°	1'29''724	16°	1'29''738	17°	2'01''635	21°
22.	Alex Yoong	Minardi-Asiatech PS02/02	1'44''011	22°	1'33''425	22°	1'31''504	21°	1'49''490	20°
23.	Mark Webber	Minardi-Asiatech PS02/01	1'32''696	20°	1'31''203	20°	1'30''086	18°	1'48''198	19°
24.	Mika Salo	Toyota TF102/04	1'29''601	6°	1'30''100	18°	1'29''205	14°	1'47''524	16°
25.	Allan McNish	Toyota TF102/05	1'30''602	16°	1'29''663	15°	1'29''636	16°	1'46''412	12°

Maximum speeds

N°	Driver	P1 Qualifs	Pos.	P1 Race	Pos.	P2 Qualifs	Pos.	P2 Race	Pos.	Finish Qualifs	Pos.	Finish Race	Pos.	Trap Qualifs	Pos.	Trap Race	Pos.
1.	M. Schumacher	286,2	4°	282,5	3°	295,9	10°	294,5	4°	295,9	4°	295,6	3°	306,9	11°	307,7	4°
2.	R. Barrichello	286,3	3°			297,1	6°			295,8	5°			306,9	10°	236,8	19°
3.	D. Coulthard	285,7	5°	276,4	6°	297,6	5°	292,7	7°	295,7	6°	291,8	6°	307,6	6°	305,6	8°
4.	K. Räikkönen	284,1	6°	284,3	2°	297,1	7°	294,8	3°	294,1	9°	294,2	4°	308,9	5°	309,5	2°
5.	R. Schumacher	287,3	1°			299,9	1°			298,8	2°			310,6	2°	236,3	20°
6.	J.P. Montoya	286,4	2°	284,8	1°	297,7	4°	297,6	2°	298,9	1°	297,8	1°	309,5	3°	309,3	3°
7.	N. Heidfeld	278,7	16°			291,8	19°			292,3	15°			302,8	20°	250,1	16°
8.	F. Massa	282,6	8°			293,1	17°			292,8	12°			305,2	15°	251,8	15°
9.	G. Fisichella	283,3	7°			295,2	12°			294,0	10°			307,0	8°	233,7	21°
10.	T. Sato	257,6	22°	267,9	14°	266,0	22°	287,0	13°	279,6	22°	287,2	13°	259,6	22°	300,0	12°
11.	J. Villeneuve	281,3	10°	272,3	10°	293,3	15°	290,1	12°	292,2	16°	285,9	14°	307,0	9°	299,6	13°
12.	O. Panis	281,1	11°			295,0	13°			295,0	8°			306,7	12°	240,0	17°
14.	J. Trulli	281,6	9°	267,9	13°	296,9	9°	286,7	14°	295,2	7°	287,8	12°	307,3	7°	300,5	11°
15.	J. Button	279,9	13°			295,5	11°			292,7	13°			305,7	13°	229,1	22°
16.	E. Irvine	274,6	21°	275,1	8°	292,9	18°	291,7	10°	292,6	14°	292,2	5°	304,4	18°	307,7	5°
17.	P. de la Rosa	276,7	19°	276,4	7°	293,6	14°	291,8	8°	291,5	17°	291,5	8°	305,4	14°	306,9	6°
18.	H-H. Frentzen	277,0	17°	271,2	11°	290,1	21°	293,9	5°	289,9	20°	291,4	9°	298,9	21°	294,4	14°
19.	E. Bernoldi	276,8	18°	269,2	12°	299,4	2°	293,4	6°	291,3	18°	289,0	11°	304,9	16°	306,0	7°
22.	A. Yoong	276,0	20°	275,1	9°	293,2	16°	290,4	11°	290,7	19°	291,3	10°	304,3	19°	302,7	10°
23.	M. Webber	279,3	15°	275,9	5°	291,2	20°	291,8	9°	289,7	21°	291,8	7°	304,6	17°	305,3	9°
24.	M. Salo	280,5	12°	280,3	4°	298,4	3°	298,5	1°	296,1	3°	296,6	2°	311,3	1°	311,2	1°
25.	A. McNish	279,5	14°			297,0	8°			293,9	11°			308,9	4°	239,2	18°

Race

Classification & Retirements

Pos.	Driver	Team	Lap	Time	Average
1.	M. Schumacher	Ferrari	58	1:35:36.792	193,011 km/h
2.	J.P. Montoya	Williams BMW	58	18.628	192,386 km/h
3.	K. Räikkönen	McLaren Mercedes	58	25.067	192,171 km/h
4.	E. Irvine	Jaguar	57	1 lap	186,654 km/h
5.	M. Webber	Minardi Asiatech	56	2 laps	183,407 km/h
6.	M. Salo	Toyota	56	2 laps	183,323 km/h
7.	A. Yoong	Minardi Asiatech	55	3 laps	181,819 km/h
8.	P. de la Rosa	Jaguar	53	5 laps	175,141 km/h

	Driver	Team	Lap	Reason
	D. Coulthard	McLaren Mercedes	34	Jammed gearbox
	J. Villeneuve	BAR Honda	28	Loss of rear spoiler and goes off
	H-H. Frentzen	Arrows	17	Disqualified, red light at pit exit
	E. Bernoldi	Jaguar	16	Disqualified, used spare car after the start
	T. Sato	Jordan Honda	13	Transmission
	J. Trulli	Renault	9	Spin and hit the wall
	R. Barrichello	Ferrari	0	Hit by R. Schumacher
	R. Schumacher	Williams BMW	0	Hits R. Barrichello
	G. Fisichella	Jordan Honda	0	Accident at the start
	F. Massa	Sauber Petronas	0	Accident at the start
	N. Heidfeld	Sauber Petronas	0	Accident at the start
	J. Button	Renault	0	Accident at the start
	O. Panis	BAR Honda	0	Accident at the start
	A. McNish	Toyota	0	Accident at the start

Fastests Laps

	Driver	Time	Lap	Average
1.	K. Räikkönen	1'28''541	37	215,615 km/h
2.	M. Schumacher	1'28''628	32	215,403 km/h
3.	J.P. Montoya	1'29''143	35	214,159 km/h
4.	D. Coulthard	1'31''186	21	209,361 km/h
5.	P. de la Rosa	1'31''539	51	208,553 km/h
6.	M. Salo	1'32''225	53	207,002 km/h
7.	E. Irvine	1'32''548	36	206,279 km/h
8.	M. Webber	1'33''296	52	204,626 km/h
9.	H-H. Frentzen	1'33''534	16	204,105 km/h
10.	J. Villeneuve	1'33''540	25	204,092 km/h
11.	J. Trulli	1'34''233	7	202,591 km/h
12.	A. Yoong	1'34''653	31	201,692 km/h
13.	E. Bernoldi	1'35''052	8	200,845 km/h
14.	T. Sato	1'35''197	8	200,539 km/h

Pit stops

	Driver	Time	Lap	Stop n°		Driver	Time	Lap	Stop n°
1.	M. Salo	3'14''314	1	1	9.	M. Salo	30''069	32	2
2.	K. Räikkönen	1'10''122	2	1	10.	M. Webber	54''025	35	2
3.	H-H. Frentzen	27''124	7	1	11.	J.P. Montoya	27''999	37	1
4.	J. Villeneuve	26''883	10	1	12.	M. Schumacher	28''281	38	1
5.	E. Bernoldi	26''287	2	1	13.	E. Irvine	31''632	37	1
6.	T. Sato	1'09''258	11	1	14.	K. Räikkönen	28''290	38	2
7.	J. Villeneuve	17''257	13	2	15.	A. Yoong	32''838	37	1
8.	P. de la Rosa	4'30''135	21	1	16.	P. de la Rosa	27''246	40	2

Race leaders

Driver	Laps in the lead	Nbr of Laps	Kilometers	Driver	Nbr of Laps	Kilometers
D. Coulthard	1 > 10	10	53,030 km	M. Schumacher	43	228,029 km
M. Schumacher	11	1	5,303 km	D. Coulthard	10	53,030 km
J.P. Montoya	12 > 16	5	26,515 km	J.P. Montoya	5	26,515 km
M. Schumacher	17 > 58	42	222,726 km			

The table of « Leading gaps » is based on the lap by lap information, but only for some selected drivers (for ease of understanding). It adds in the gaps between these drivers. The line marked «0» represents the winner's average speed. In general, this starts at a slower speed than its eventual average speed, because of the weight of fuel carried on board the car. Then, it goes above the average, before dropping again during the refuelling pit stops. This graph therefore allows one to see at any given time the number of seconds (vertically) seperating the drivers on every lap (horizontally).

Lap chart

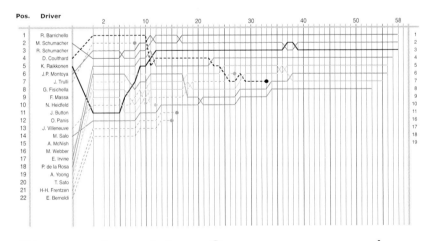

Gaps on the leader board

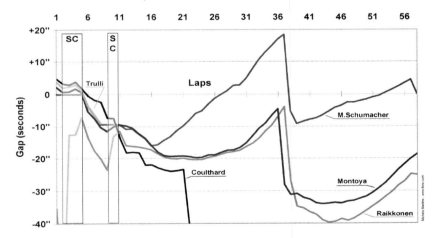

Championship after one round

Drivers

1.	M. Schumacher	10
2.	J.P. Montoya	6
3.	K. Räikkönen	4
4.	E. Irvine	3
5.	M. Webber	2
6.	M. Salo	1

Constructors

1.	Scuderia Ferrari Marlboro	10
2.	BMW WilliamsF1 Team	6
3.	West McLaren Mercedes	4
4.	Jaguar Racing	3
5.	KL Minardi Asiatech	2
6.	Panasonic Toyota Racing	1

The circuit

Name :	Albert Park, Melbourne
Date :	March 3, 2002
Length :	5303 meters
Distance :	58 laps, 307,574 km
Temperature :	overcast, 18°c
Track temperature :	21°c

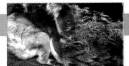

A WILLIAMS ONE-TWO? YOU'RE KIDDING!

Maybe the Ferraris were not as invincible as had been feared after the Australian Grand Prix. Because in Sepang, it was the Williams-BMWs which scored a one-two finish in the Malaysian Grand Prix, with Ralf Schumacher ahead of Juan Pablo Montoya.

The race turned into a stroll in the park for the world champion's little brother once his main rivals had put themselves out of contention.

Rubens Barrichello watched helpless as his engine went bang, while Michael Schumacher and Juan Pablo Montoya collided at the first corner. In any case, Ralf Schumacher might have been hard to beat in a straight fight at Sepang: on a one stop strategy, he had the advantage, as none of his rivals had been that brave, for fear of destroying their tyres.

So the Ferraris might be beatable then? The ray of hope did not shine for long as Sepang turned out to be the only win of the year for a Williams-BMW.

Spending millions to go slower

This was the home race for Alex Yoong. It had no effect on his performance, as he qualified 22nd and last.

Pole position for the Malaysian Grand Prix turned into a hard fought battle between Juan Pablo Montoya and Michael Schumacher. In the end, it went to the German with a lap time strangely slower than the one he had set at this track the previous year.

"*To be honest, spending millions to improve the cars and to end up going slower is ridiculous*", joked the world champion. In fact, the very high temperatures in Sepang that Saturday (track temperature above 40 degrees) caused the increase in lap times.

Nevertheless, Ferrari's advantage over its rivals seemed less than in Australia, as the German was only two tenths ahead of Juan Pablo Montoya's Williams. "*It's a bit frustrating to finish qualifying like this*", complained the Colombian. "*If you look at the split times, I would have been capable of taking pole. Unfortunately, I didn't manage to put together the perfect lap.*"

"*Everyone said this season would be boring*", added Michael Schumacher. "*But today it's obvious that we very nearly lost pole. I think it will be a very close race.*"

«*Whoops!*» Olivier Panis corrects a spectacular slide in his BAR during practice. The English team was really struggling in Sepang. The Frenchman eventually qualified 18th, his worst result of the season.

Second on the grid in Australia, Michael Schumacher took pole in Sepang. He would not make the most of it.

Briefly

> The Phoenix team (ex-Prost) which had been announced in Melbourne, was not present in Sepang, but maybe it was not as stillborn as a Friday FIA press release would have us believe. A representative of this ghost team was distributing its own press release in the paddock, indicating that its legal team in France was sure it had acquired the Prost team's rights to appear on the F1 grid. Phoenix Finance boss, Charles Nickerson added that FIA lawyers had made a mistake and that he would do all in his power to ensure his cars made it to the start in Brazil.

> It was only the second grand prix of the season, but McLaren boss Ron Dennis was already well aware that his team was lagging behind Ferrari. "*We are not quick enough, it's as simple as that*", he admitted. "*But we will have a completely revised car in Brazil and a further evolution in time for Imola. We are working very hard.*"

> The escalation of costs in F1 was frightening all the teams, including the biggest. On Friday in Sepang, all the team bosses got together in a four and half hour meeting to look at measures aimed at reducing costs. Among the ideas being bandied about, a total ban on private testing and a limit on the number of engines which could be used over a race weekend. "*Unfortunately, it is very difficult to reach unanimity on this sort of thing*", lamented Ron Dennis. "*There are always some who seek to gain an advantage from the changes and so you reach a point where agreement becomes impossible.*" Banning private testing for example, would have a major effect on

Scuderia Ferrari in particular, which has two of its own circuits on which to go testing: Fiorano and Mugello.

> The Scuderia was still running its old car in Malaysia and there was no guarantee that they would bring the new F2002 to Brazil. A major test session in Barcelona the week after Sepang would be decisive. "*Even if we go to Sao Paulo with the old car, we will still score points, that's for sure*", commented Schumacher. "*So there is no hurry.*"

> Staff from the defunct Prost team continue to find new employment after the French team went bankrupt. On Thursday, Jordan announced that Henri Durand, a first rate aerodynamicist who had joined Prost Grand Prix in 2001, had just signed a contract placing him in charge of development and design with the Anglo-Irish team. The 41 year old Frenchman would therefore be continuing a twenty year career in F1 which had seem him work for Ligier, Ferrari and McLaren.

> After the accident at the start of the Australian Grand Prix, the Sauber team, both of whose cars had been knocked out, had worked out the cost of the damage: bent suspension, broken bodywork and piping, wings and dampers rendered useless etc. It had been a race against the clock back at the factory, but no less than eight huge packing cases arrived in Sepang on Thursday. Supervising the operation, Technical Director Willy Rampf estimated the cost of the Melbourne mayhem at 600,000 Euros.

Starting grid

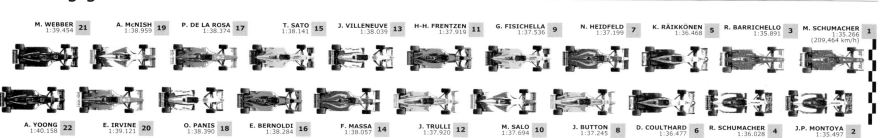

Pos	Driver	Time
21	M. WEBBER	1:39.454
19	A. McNISH	1:38.959
17	P. DE LA ROSA	1:38.374
15	T. SATO	1:38.141
13	J. VILLENEUVE	1:38.039
11	H-H. FRENTZEN	1:37.919
9	G. FISICHELLA	1:37.536
7	N. HEIDFELD	1:37.199
5	K. RÄIKKÖNEN	1:36.468
3	R. BARRICHELLO	1:35.891
1	M. SCHUMACHER	1:35.266 (209,464 km/h)
22	A. YOONG	1:40.158
20	E. IRVINE	1:39.121
18	O. PANIS	1:38.390
16	E. BERNOLDI	1:38.284
14	F. MASSA	1:38.057
12	J. TRULLI	1:37.920
10	M. SALO	1:37.694
8	J. BUTTON	1:37.245
6	D. COULTHARD	1:36.477
4	R. SCHUMACHER	1:36.028
2	J.P. MONTOYA	1:35.497

> The first corner accident which had everyone talking in Malaysia. Michael Schumacher reckoned Juan Pablo Montoya had not left him enough room, while the Colombian took the opposite view. Each to his own opinion.

Montoya –Schumacher: they're at it again

It was already very hot in Sepang, but with Michael Schumacher and Juan Pablo Montoya sharing the front row of the grid, temperatures were bound to go through the roof at the first corner.

And so it turned out: making a better start than the German, the Colombian got the outside line after the Ferrari had immediately swerved to the inside. They came charging into the first corner side by side. If Montoya could hold his line, he would have the right line for the hairpin and he would be away. But the Ferrari and the Williams touched, leaving the red car with a broken front wing and the blue and white one with no momentum.

Schumacher cruised (its all relative!) round to the pits for a new nose, while Montoya was able to continue, albeit down in eleventh place at the end of the opening lap. For both men, it was the start of a thrilling pursuit race which livened up the grand prix.

The Williams man had climbed as high as sixth before the Stewards penalised him for «having caused an avoidable collision». He thus had the honour of being the first grand prix driver to be sanctioned with the new "drive-through" penalty, which involves driving through the pit lane at the speed limit, without stopping before rejoining the track. "I am furious about this penalty", snapped

Montoya after the race. "I was on the outside of the corner and I left Michael enough room to get through, but his car understeered and he ran into me and that's it. Sure, I didn't leave him much room, because I didn't want to be on the dirty side of the track, but he could have got through. I didn't expect him to brake, he's a racing driver, but I didn't think he would drive into me. It was just an accident, that's all and I don't see why I should get a penalty."

Naturally enough, Michael Schumacher saw things differently. "He squeezed me and I really didn't have room to get by." However, on the subject of the penalty, the Ferrari driver agreed with his rival. "This penalty doesn't seem justified. We have seen people get away with worse without being penalised. There does not seem to be any consistency in the way these sanctions are applied. That should be changed."

Even Ralf Schumacher, team-mate but sworn enemy of Juan Pablo Montoya admitted the penalty was too severe.

The collision between the paddock's two tough guys was just another chapter in their on-going battle. Separated by just two points in the championship, it was unlikely that the situation would ease up.

> Hit and sinking: Michael Schumacher left his front wing buried in the side of Juan Pablo Montoya's Williams and the Colombian took a while to shake off this unwanted gift.

> Michael Schumacher had to complete the first lap without a front wing and came into the pits for a new one, before rejoining at the back of the pack.

42 degrees too many

Just before the start, the thermometer in the Ferrari garage indicated 42 degrees in the shade! On the grid, the driver trainers were rushing around with icy towels and anti-dehydration drinks to keep their charges from boiling over.

It was not just humans who were suffering in these conditions. The cars were struggling too. Both McLaren-Mercedes suffered from heat stroke. "Without any warning, my engine started running on nine cylinders and the team advised me to stop", explained David Coulthard. A few minutes later, on lap 25, his team-mate Kimi Räikkönen suffered a similar but more serious failure, as his engine exploded. Ferrari was not immune to the effects of the sun either and Rubens Barrichello's second place and his engine went up in smoke on lap 40.

> Takuma Sato spears his team-mate. At the finish, the Japanese driver looked sheepish, although finishing ninth was a decent result, even if his behaviour in the race was not. Having tangled with Giancarlo Fisichella, both men had to pit, one for a front wing, the other for a rear unit. "I am really very sorry for what happened. I apologise, it should not have happened. I missed my braking point", mumbled the distraught rookie.

Race summary

> **Start (1)**
> Michael Schumacher starts from pole position and immediately swerves over to the inside to block Juan Pablo Montoya. The two men collide and drop down the order: Michael Schumacher pits for a new front wing, while Juan Pablo Montoya comes round 11th at the end of the opening lap.

> **Lap 7 – Montoya**
> Juan Pablo Montoya is breathtaking as he stages an extraordinary comeback. He is already sixth.

> **Lap 9 – Montoya**
> The Stewards call the Colombian into the pit lane for having caused the accident at the start.

> **Lap 13 (2)**
> The McLarens are struggling, even though they use the same tyres as Williams. David Coulthard begins to drop down the order and retires in the pits on lap 16.

> **Lap 22 (3)**
> So far the Minardis had followed one another; Yoong ahead of Webber. They retired

on laps 30 and 35 respectively.

> **Lap 25**
> Kimi Räikkönen retires from fourth place. Ralf Schumacher leads with a 24 second advantage over Rubens Barrichello.

> **Lap 39 – McNish**
> For two brief laps, Allan McNish is in the points before refuelling and finishing seventh.

> **Lap 44**
> Ralf Schumacher has a fifty second lead over the duelling Jenson Button and Juan Pablo Montoya. The Williams manages to get past the Renault after two failed attempts.

> **Lap 55 – Button**
> Jenson Button's Renault is in trouble, losing seconds by the fistful and eventually he is

passed by Michael Schumacher, who finishes third.

> **Lap 56 – the finish**
> The two Saubers manage to pick up points (4), while out in front, Ralf Schumacher takes the win and congratulates his team-mate (5) before getting on the podium (6).

> The Malaysian Grand Prix was very tough on tyres (7), because of the very high temperatures at the Sepang circuit. At the finish, the tyres looked a mess, with blisters and very little sign of any grooves. Jacques Villeneuve's tyres were completely slick.

Renault just misses out on the podium

"We already had our heads in the champagne. We didn't see it coming!" Renault's Development Director Denis Chevrier was flabbergasted. In the team garage, everyone was shattered and it was wise to avoid bumping into Flavio Briatore. With two laps to go, Jenson Button was still solidly entrenched in third place. Against all expectation, Michael Schumacher seemed incapable of catching him and a podium finish, which would have symbolised Renault's return, was about to be celebrated in no uncertain terms.

Then, on the penultimate lap, the Englishman suddenly slowed by three seconds and lost a further eight seconds on the last lap. Michael Schumacher effortlessly swept by the Renault to scramble up to third place on the podium.

Logically, all it really meant was one less point for Renault and the result was still a worthy one, but the podium celebrations would have to wait, while the champagne stayed in the fridge. «Something suddenly broke in the suspension and I had to finish the race on three wheels,» explained Jenson Button, still managing a smile. He seemed decidedly less disappointed than his team.

> Refuelling stop for Jenson Button. The young Englishman almost finished third, but for a suspension problem which forced him to slow in the closing stages.

Kimi already a star

David Coulthard already had a furrowed brow. It seemed as though his young team-mate Kimi Räikkönen had not taken long to adopt the lead role within the McLaren team. In Melbourne, for his debut behind the wheel of a silver arrow, the Finn secured his first ever podium finish, even though he was involved in the first corner crash and had rejoined the race in last place.

In Sepang, he qualified fifth on the grid, ahead of his Scottish team-mate. It had not taken him long to find the measure of a team-mate with over 120 grand prix starts to his name.

For David Coulthard, the situation looked desperate. After Mika Häkkinen retired at the end of 2001, he became the Number 1 driver at McLaren, but that position was in danger if Kimi Räikkönen out-performed him.

The young Finn did not seem bothered. At only 22 years of age, he should have had a lot to learn. His team-mate? No problem. *"Of course I can beat him. In private testing, our lap times are very similar. But I expect to do better than him, every time."*

There is little point in asking him questions about his tyres or his chassis as he always replies that everything is fine. Not much point asking him to compare Sauber with McLaren either, as his standard reply is that he is happy to have made the change.

Kimi Räikkönen is not interested in questions. All he wants to do is race and win. It looks as though he has the talent to follow it through.

> Ralf Schumacher on his way to what turned out to be his only win of the season.

Sauber delivers for its sponsors

The intolerably hot conditions at the Sepang circuit had everyone worried about their cars' ability to cope over a race distance.

With a reputation for being tough and reliable, it looked like a good opportunity for the Saubers to shine: and so they did, with Nick Heidfeld fifth and Felipe Massa sixth, the young Brazilian picking up his first point in only his second grand prix.

At the flag, Peter Sauber was delighted. *"Scoring points with both cars at Sepang, the home circuit for our sponsors, is simply marvellous"*, enthused the man from Zurich as he enjoyed the icy air-conditioned comfort of his team office. *"We are going to celebrate, because it has not been easy to recover from our disaster in Melbourne."*

The two drivers had fought hard. *"You always hope for something better than you get, but it's not too bad"*, commented Nick Heidfeld after the race. *"I am optimistic for the future, because I could pretty much match Michael's (Schumacher) and Juan Pablo's (Montoya) pace when they caught up with me."*

While the German was phlegmatic as ever, Felipe Massa was in seventh heaven. *"Scoring a point in my second grand prix is fantastic. It's a fabulous feeling."*

> A daring one stop strategy resulted in Ralf Schumacher standing on the top step of the podium. «*I really was not expecting this victory. In qualifying, I was off the pace, but in the race my car was simply perfect, well balanced, powerful and stable. I can't believe it, it was almost easy. A dream.*»

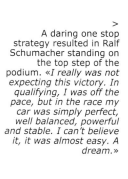

Practice

All the time trials

N°	Driver	Car/Engine/Chassis	Practice Friday	Pos.	Practice Saturday	Pos.	Qualifying	Pos.	Warm-up	Pos.
1.	Michael Schumacher	Ferrari 2001/215	1'38"490	3°	1'37"045	6°	1'35"266	1°	1'39"748	2°
2.	Rubens Barrichello	Ferrari 2001/216	1'39"279	7°	1'36"910	4°	1'35"891	3°	1'39"611	1°
3.	David Coulthard	McLaren-Mercedes MP4/17/02	1'38"038	2°	1'36"976	5°	1'36"477	6°	1'39"753	3°
4.	Kimi Räikkönen	McLaren-Mercedes MP4/17/03	1'37"399	1°	1'36"648	2°	1'36"468	5°	1'41"638	19°
5.	Ralf Schumacher	Williams-BMW FW24/04	1'38"650	4°	1'36"689	3°	1'36"028	4°	1'40"316	9°
6.	Juan Pablo Montoya	Williams-BMW FW24/02	1'39"158	6°	1'36"556	1°	1'35"497	2°	1'40"211	7°
7.	Nick Heidfeld	Sauber-Petronas C21/03	1'39"889	10°	1'38"320	10°	1'37"199	7°	1'39"935	5°
8.	Felipe Massa	Sauber-Petronas C21/04	1'41"917	21°	1'38"301	9°	1'38"057	14°	1'40"493	11°
9.	Giancarlo Fisichella	Jordan-Honda EJ11/4	1'40"815	14°	1'38"215	8°	1'37"536	9°	1'41"466	15°
10.	Takuma Sato	Jordan-Honda EJ11/3	1'41"111	16°	1'39"116	16°	1'38"141	15°	1'40"783	13°
11.	Jacques Villeneuve	BAR-Honda 004/03	1'41"461	17°	1'39"442	19°	1'38"039	13°	1'41"600	18°
12.	Olivier Panis	BAR-Honda 004/04	1'41"473	18°	1'39"490	20°	1'38"390	18°	1'42"101	20°
14.	Jarno Trulli	Renault R202/02	1'39"774	9°	1'38"796	15°	1'37"920	12°	1'39"791	4°
15.	Jenson Button	Renault R202/03	1'39"714	8°	1'37"609	7°	1'37"245	8°	1'40"192	6°
16.	Eddie Irvine	Jaguar R3/03	1'41"857	20°	1'39"319	17°	1'39"121	20°	1'41"521	17°
17.	Pedro de la Rosa	Jaguar R3/02	1'40"147	12°	1'38"734	14°	1'38"374	17°	1'40"266	8°
20.	Heinz-Harald Frentzen	Arrows-Cosworth A23/01	1'40"576	13°	1'38"613	13°	1'37"919	11°	1'40"436	10°
21.	Enrique Bernoldi	Arrows-Cosworth A23/02	1'41"095	15°	1'38"478	12°	1'38"284	16°	1'40"621	12°
22.	Alex Yoong	Minardi-Asiatech PS02/02	1'41"805	19°	1'40"656	22°	1'40"158	22°	1'43"719	22°
23.	Mark Webber	Minardi-Asiatech PS02/01	1'44"583	22°	1'40"060	21°	1'39"454	21°	1'43"058	21°
24.	Mika Salo	Toyota TF102/04	1'39"066	5°	1'38"366	11°	1'37"694	10°	1'41"093	14°
25.	Allan McNish	Toyota TF102/05	1'39"982	11°	1'39"349	18°	1'38"959	19°	1'41"510	16°

Maximum speeds

N°	Driver	P1 Qualifs	Pos.	P1 Race	Pos.	P2 Qualifs	Pos.	P2 Race	Pos.	Finish Qualifs	Pos.	Finish Race	Pos.	Trap Qualifs	Pos.	Trap Race	Pos.
1.	M. Schumacher	300,5	2°	291,3	3°	147,8	17°	149,7	7°	271,6	3°	269,7	4°	308,6	1°	311,1	3°
2.	R. Barrichello	295,4	7°	290,1	4°	151,1	5°	147,7	13°	270,2	6°	268,5	6°	305,5	6°	305,6	9°
3.	D. Coulthard	296,7	5°	275,0	20°	153,3	1°	149,0	8°	270,4	5°	263,3	18°	304,3	8°	300,1	19°
4.	K. Räikkönen	297,5	4°	286,7	10°	152,4	2°	148,9	9°	267,6	10°	264,5	17°	304,0	9°	299,9	20°
5.	R. Schumacher	301,1	1°	294,6	2°	147,2	19°	151,6	5°	273,8	1°	270,9	3°	307,6	3°	308,4	5°
6.	J.P. Montoya	299,4	3°	297,6	1°	148,4	14°	152,2	2°	273,4	2°	271,1	1°	308,6	2°	313,7	1°
7.	N. Heidfeld	295,4	8°	288,3	6°	145,3	22°	145,8	19°	266,1	17°	262,3	19°	302,0	12°	301,1	17°
8.	F. Massa	290,8	19°	284,8	15°	148,4	15°	147,6	15°	263,6	22°	261,3	20°	299,5	22°	296,8	22°
9.	G. Fisichella	292,4	15°	286,9	9°	149,8	7°	147,5	16°	266,3	15°	264,5	16°	301,6	16°	303,2	11°
10.	T. Sato	294,5	11°	287,6	7°	145,9	20°	148,1	11°	266,2	16°	265,0	15°	301,3	17°	302,4	14°
11.	J. Villeneuve	291,5	18°	285,4	13°	149,0	11°	146,8	17°	266,6	13°	267,8	7°	301,0	18°	302,6	13°
12.	O. Panis	289,5	21°	279,2	19°	149,4	10°	141,1	22°	265,6	18°	260,8	22°	302,0	13°	301,6	16°
14.	J. Trulli	295,1	9°	273,6	21°	145,8	21°	145,2	20°	267,4	11°	261,1	21°	301,8	15°	299,1	21°
15.	J. Button	292,2	16°	289,2	5°	149,6	8°	151,8	4°	267,9	9°	267,5	8°	303,4	10°	303,1	12°
16.	E. Irvine	293,0	14°	284,8	14°	148,2	16°	143,9	21°	265,5	19°	265,6	13°	299,8	21°	301,0	18°
17.	P. de la Rosa	293,8	12°	286,7	12°	152,3	3°	151,8	3°	268,6	8°	266,7	10°	306,6	4°	303,6	10°
18.	H-H. Frentzen	294,5	10°	287,3	8°	149,5	9°	149,9	6°	267,1	12°	266,4	11°	300,5	19°	308,4	6°
19.	Bernoldi	292,0	17°	282,5	17°	152,2	4°	148,2	10°	266,4	14°	266,7	9°	300,1	20°	308,6	4°
22.	Yoong	284,5	22°	282,3	18°	150,6	6°	153,0	1°	265,0	21°	265,2	14°	302,0	14°	302,2	15°
23.	Webber	293,3	13°	266,6	22°	148,5	12°	145,9	18°	265,4	20°	266,3	12°	303,2	11°	307,8	7°
24.	Salo	296,5	6°	286,7	11°	148,4	13°	147,9	12°	270,6	4°	271,0	2°	306,2	5°	311,1	2°
25.	McNish	290,4	20°	282,6	16°	147,7	18°	147,6	14°	268,7	7°	268,8	5°	304,5	7°	306,4	8°

Race

Classification & Retirements

Pos.	Driver	Team	Lap	Time	Average
1.	R. Schumacher	Williams BMW	56	1:34:12.912	197,680 km/h
2.	J.P. Montoya	Williams BMW	56	39.700	196,301 km/h
3.	M. Schumacher	Ferrari	56	1:01.795	195,542 km/h
4.	J. Button	Renault	56	1:09.767	195,270 km/h
5.	N. Heidfeld	Sauber Petronas	55	1 lap	194,126 km/h
6.	F. Massa	Sauber Petronas	55	1 lap	191,828 km/h
7.	A. McNish	Toyota	55	1 lap	191,268 km/h
8.	J. Villeneuve	BAR Honda	55	1 lap	190,797 km/h
9.	T. Sato	Jordan Honda	54	2 laps	189,753 km/h
10.	P. de la Rosa	Jordan Honda	54	2 laps	189,697 km/h
11.	H-H.Frentzen	Arrows Cosworth	54	2 laps	187,613 km/h
12.	M. Salo	Toyota	53	3 laps	184,280 km/h
13.	G. Fisichella	Jordan Honda	53	3 laps	183,844 km/h

Driver	Team		Reason
R. Barrichello	Ferrari	40	Broken engine
M. Webber	Minardi Asiatech	35	Electrical problem
E. Irvine	Jaguar	31	Hydraulic pressure
A. Yoong	Minardi Asiatech	30	Transmission
K. Räikkönen	McLaren Mercedes	25	Broken engine
E. Bernoldi	Arrows Cosworth	21	Fuel pump
D. Coulthard	McLaren Mercedes	16	Engine
O. Panis	BAR Honda	10	Clutch
J. Trulli	Renault	10	Overheating and loss of engine power

Fastest laps

	Driver	Time	Lap	Average
1.	J.P. Montoya	1'38"049	38	203,518 km/h
2.	R. Schumacher	1'38"369	29	202,856 km/h
3.	M. Schumacher	1'38"754	53	202,065 km/h
4.	R. Barrichello	1'38"931	20	201,704 km/h
5.	M. Salo	1'39"649	47	200,250 km/h
6.	K. Räikkönen	1'39"800	21	199,947 km/h
7.	J. Button	1'40"011	28	199,526 km/h
8.	H-H. Frentzen	1'40"267	54	199,016 km/h
9.	N. Heidfeld	1'40"575	18	198,407 km/h
10.	P. de la Rosa	1'40"675	52	198,210 km/h
11.	T. Sato	1'41"181	51	197,218 km/h
12.	A. McNish	1'41"321	38	196,946 km/h
13.	F. Massa	1'41"324	25	196,940 km/h
14.	G. Fisichella	1'41"410	49	196,773 km/h
15.	D. Coulthard	1'41"455	10	196,686 km/h
16.	E. Bernoldi	1'41"891	19	195,844 km/h
17.	E. Irvine	1'42"323	20	195,017 km/h
18.	J. Villeneuve	1'42"373	45	194,922 km/h
19.	M. Webber	1'43"125	20	193,501 km/h
20.	A. Yoong	1'43"190	18	193,379 km/h
21.	O. Panis	1'43"567	9	192,675 km/h
22.	J. Trulli	1'43"702	6	192,424 km/h

Pit stops

	Driver	Time	Lap	Stop n°
1.	M. Schumacher	39"638	1	1
2.	G. Fisichella	4'11"840	2	1
3.	T. Sato	49"885	2	1
4.	P. de la Rosa	58"778	7	1
5.	J. Trulli	33"482	8	1
6.	J.P. Montoya	24"366	9	1
7.	N. Heidfeld	37"149	19	1
8.	A. McNish	39"217	19	1
9.	M. Schumacher	35"788	19	2
10.	A. Yoong	43"155	19	1
11.	R. Barrichello	33"039	21	1
12.	J.P. Montoya	35"496	21	2
13.	M. Salo	36"118	21	1
14.	F. Massa	35"553	23	1
15.	H-H. Frentzen	38"500	22	1
16.	A. Yoong	41"787	23	2
17.	P. de la Rosa	26"745	24	2
18.	M. Salo	3'30"997	25	2
19.	J. Villeneuve	40"569	26	1
20.	E. Irvine	45"792	27	1
21.	M. Webber	41"989	29	1
22.	T. Sato	39"376	29	2
23.	R. Schumacher	37"880	31	1
24.	J. Button	38"561	31	1
25.	G. Fisichella	40"372	29	2
26.	R. Barrichello	37"041	35	2
27.	N. Heidfeld	36"475	36	2
28.	J.P. Montoya	34"417	39	3
29.	M. Schumacher	34"946	40	3
30.	M. Salo	38"337	38	3
31.	P. de la Rosa	36"860	39	3
32.	A. McNish	54"478	40	2
33.	H-H. Frentzen	36"487	39	2
34.	M. Salo	34"381	43	4

Race leaders

Driver	Laps in the lead	Nbr of Laps	Kilometers
R. Barrichello	1 > 21	21	116,403 km
R. Schumacher	22 > 31	10	55,430 km
R. Barrichello	32 > 35	4	22,172 km
R. Schumacher	36 > 56	21	116,403 km

Driver	Nbr of Laps	Kilometers
R. Schumacher	31	171,833 km
R. Barrichello	25	138,575 km

Lap chart

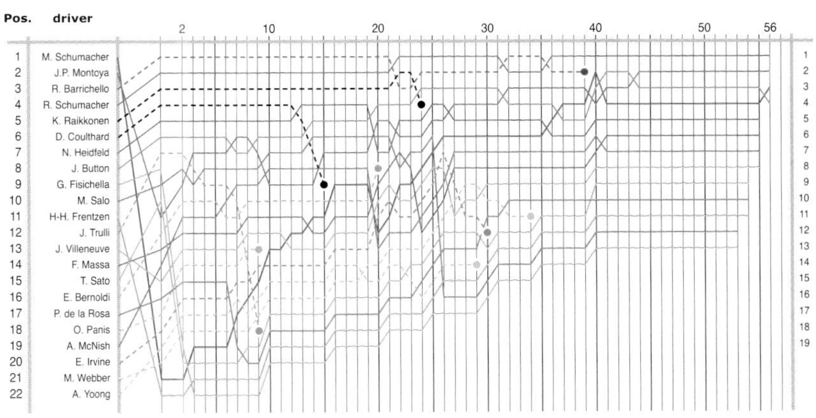

Gaps on the leader board

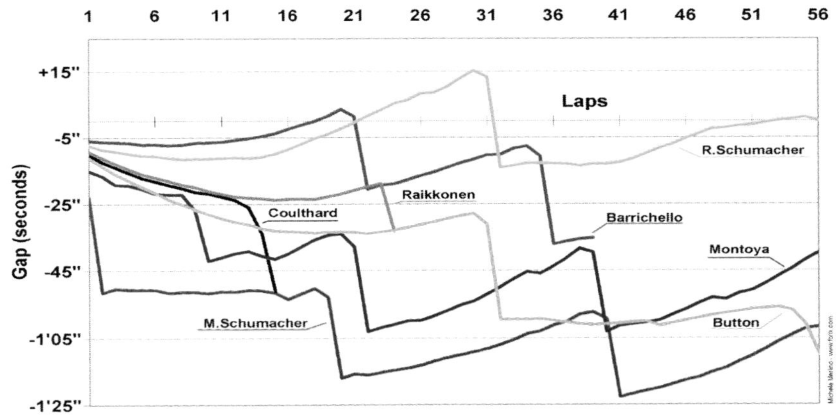

Championship after two rounds

Drivers

1. M. Schumacher 14
2. J.P. Montoya 12
3. R. Schumacher 10
4. K. Räikkönen 4
5. E. Irvine 3
6. J. Button 3
7. M. Webber 2
8. N. Heidfeld 2
9. M. Salo 1
10. F. Massa 1

Constructors

1. BMW WilliamsF1 Team 22
1. Scuderia Ferrari Marlboro 14
3. West McLaren Mercedes...............................4
4. Jaguar Racing..3
5. Mild Seven Renault F1 Team.........................3
6. Sauber Petronas 3
7. KL Minardi Asiatech....................................2
8. Panasonic Toyota Racing 1
9. Lucky Strike BAR Honda 0
10. DHL Jordan Honda 0
11. Orange Arrows 0

The circuit

Name :	Sepang, Kuala Lumpur
Date :	March 17, 2002
Length:	5543 meters
Distance :	56 laps, 310,408 km
Temperature :	warm and sunny, 35°c
Track temperature :	46°c

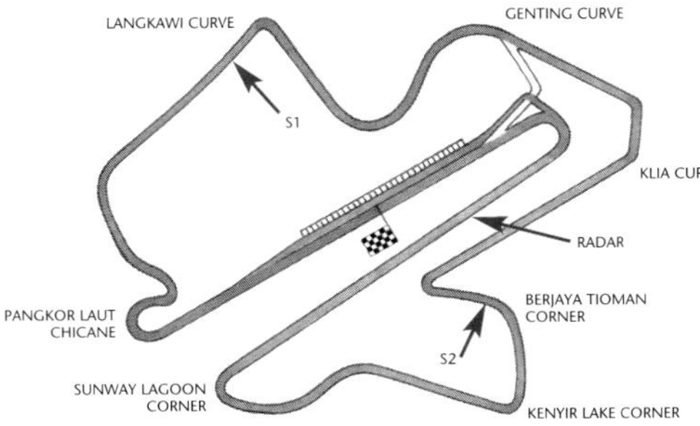

BRIDGESTONE

Best result for a driver running Bridgestone tyres:

Michael Schumacher, Ferrari, 3rd

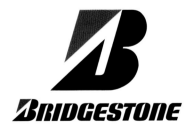

All results : © 2002 Fédération Internationale de l'Automobile, 2, Ch. Blandonnet, 1215 Geneva 15, Switzerland

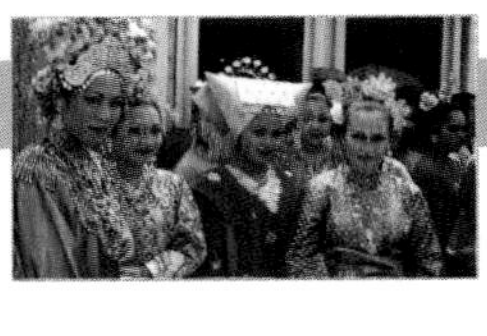

JUAN PABLO TRIED TOO HARD

Juan Pablo Montoya was starting from pole position for the first time this season. After his collision with Michael Schumacher in Malaysia, the Colombian was planning on taking his revenge and winning the race.

Unfortunately, he got too much wheelspin at the start and once again found himself on the outside of Michael Schumacher at the first corner. While any other driver would have chosen discretion as being the better part of valour, Juan Pablo was insistent. He braked late and was pushed to the outside. He fought back and came alongside the Ferrari, before losing out as he was on the dirty side of the track. He then got sucked into the Ferrari's air space down the straight....and drove into the back of it.

And all that in under a minute! Yet again, Juan Pablo had tried too hard and yet again a race was lost.

Juan Pablo Montoya's first pole of the season

In Brazil, Juan Pablo had embarked on what would be a string of seven pole positions this season. All his family had made the trip from nearby Colombia to cheer him on.

Enrique Bernoldi attacks the Interlagos toboggan run. For his home grand prix, the Arrows driver qualified 21st. Definitely not a prophet in his own land.

Gerhard Berger bumps into his old rival Nelson Piquet, who was a spectator at Interlagos.

It looked like being a hot start in Interlagos and once again we are not talking about the sticky weather which reigned over Sao Paulo. After a superb duel against the clock, Juan Pablo Montoya and Michael Schumacher were sharing the front row of the grid again.

That had been the case a fortnight earlier in Malaysia, but in the reverse order. "*Alongside Michael? Yes, so what?*" was all Montoya would say when quizzed about the explosive potential of their grid positions. "*I have already said that Michael does not scare me and that I am planning to beat him. This time, I hope to be ahead of him into the first corner and forget about the disappointment of last year.*" In 2001, the Colombian could have won the race, except that he was forced to retire after being hit from behind by Jos Verstappen. For his part, Michael Schumacher blamed his tyres and his car to explain the fact he was "*only*" second. "*With the tyre war, we knew that this year there would be circuits where we would have the advantage and others which would suit our competitors*", philosophised the world champion. "*On top of that, as it's the first time we have run the new car, we have had to work in a different way to usual and have not got the most out of it. But I am still happy we took this decision. I don't know where I would have qualified with the old car.*"

Ralf Schumacher had to settle for third place, which did not ruffle his feathers. "*The gaps are very small*", he commented after qualifying. "*There are only two tenths between me and*

Juan Pablo, which is really nothing. At least, starting from third place, I am on the clean side of the track for the start."

This Saturday in Interlagos, one had to have Michelin tyres or be called Michael Schumacher to have any hope of qualifying well. The French manufacturer shod six of the top seven cars. Behind the leading trio came the two McLaren-Mercedes of David Coulthard and Kimi Räikkönen. Following on, and an excellent surprise it was too, came the Renaults of Jarno Trulli and Jenson Button, sixth and seventh respectively.

Juan Pablo: "*Beating Michael does not scare me*"

At Interlagos, Ferrari finally showed up with one of its new cars, the F2002, for Michael Schumacher. Would the new red weapon make a difference? Juan Pablo Montoya, the only man who seemed capable of overtaking Michael Schumacher on the track did not think so. "*Michael is a good driver, but he does not impress me*", he said, throwing down the gauntlet. "*He is not unbeatable. I have already proved you can overtake him and beating him gives me a lot of pleasure. In fact, I am not the*

only one who can do it, as I reckon a few drivers are quicker than him." The war of words between the two rivals was well and truly underway and the Colombian had not finished yet.

"*Once again, Michael is pretty good, but he does have the best car after all. Do you think he would win grands prix in a Minardi? Obviously not!*" he added. Montoya reckoned Sunday's race was in the bag. "*Last year we were much quicker here than in Malaysia, so I hope everything goes well.*"

Starting grid

Pos	Driver	Time
1	J.P. MONTOYA	1:13.114
2	M. SCHUMACHER	1:13.241
3	R. SCHUMACHER	1:13.328
4	D. COULTHARD	1:13.565
5	K. RÄIKKÖNEN	1:13.595
6	J. TRULLI	1:13.611
7	J. BUTTON	1:13.665
8	R. BARRICHELLO	1:13.935
9	N. HEIDFELD	1:14.233
10	M. SALO	1:14.443
11	P. DE LA ROSA	1:14.464
12	F. MASSA	1:14.533
13	E. IRVINE	1:14.537
14	G. FISICHELLA	1:14.748
15	J. VILLENEUVE	1:14.760
16	A. McNISH	1:14.990
17	O. PANIS	1:14.996
18	H-H. FRENTZEN	1:15.112
19	T. SATO	1:15.296
20	M. WEBBER	1:15.340
21	E. BERNOLDI	1:15.355
22	A. YOONG	1:16.728

Michael v Juan Pablo: game on

It looked as though the first corner had "*accident*" written all over it. Tension between Juan Pablo Montoya and Michael Schumacher had been increasing race by race. Having collided two weeks earlier in Malaysia, it seemed plausible to think that the Colombian might be looking for a re-match. This time, he was starting from pole position, while his rival was alongside him on the front row. A merciless duel looked on the cards and we were not to be disappointed. Green light! The Williams did not get away as cleanly as the Ferrari and Montoya tried to squeeze Schumacher at the first corner. He braked too late and ran wide. "*I braked right on the limit at the end of the straight, but Juan Pablo braked even later! As far as I was concerned, there was no way he was making the corner*", recounted Schumacher after the race.

Getting back more or less on the line, the Colombian found himself alongside the German who now had the inside line and therefore the advantage. As they charged down the next straight, the Williams has another stab at it, but Montoya then ran into the back of the Ferrari. The result was that his front wing and his hopes of victory vanished into thin air (see the Colombian's version of events on page 104). "*I have to say Juan Pablo was very*

correct and left me enough room to get by", continued the German. "*When he drove into me, I didn't feel it and don't know what happened. My car wasn't damaged.*"

From then on, all Schumacher had to do was control his lead over brother Ralf. His Ferrari team-mate, Rubens Barrichello led briefly, but his two stop strategy meant he posed no threat to the German. In fact, the Brazilian would retire shortly after. In the final stages of the race, Ralf Schumacher made up some ground on the Ferrari, by tenths of a second per lap. But little brother could not pass big brother. "*I knew there was only one place where Ralf could pass, at the first corner*", explained Michael Schumacher after the race. "*So, all I had to do was make a clean exit from the previous corner to make sure I had enough of a lead going down the straight. In the slow section, I was not pushing too hard and was just trying not to make any mistakes, as it is impossible to overtake in that part of the track.*"

This second win of the year gave Michael Schumacher an eight point lead over his brother in the championship. Juan Pablo Montoya spent the race playing catch-up, finishing fifth, which put him ten points behind his sworn enemy.

Samba time

8h30 Sunday morning. There are still five hours to go before the start of the race, but the grandstands down the main straight are already overflowing with enthusiasm. The blinding sun is high in the sky and the temperature has already hit the 30 degree mark. It's going to be a hot day in all senses of the word. Five hours to go, but no sign of boredom amongst the crowd, as they roast in their open seating. They chat, sing and dance to the music blaring over the PA system. There are even a group of Malaysians proudly hoisting a banner which declares: "*The last shall be first – Go Alex Yoong!*" Young lads selling drinks are besieged by the crowd and the name of Felipe Massa is being chanted by fans of the young Brazilian Sauber driver. It is a good

humoured crowd and the atmosphere here is really unique. Half of Colombia seems to have flown into Sao Paulo to support Juan Pablo Montoya and their yellow, blue and red flags are everywhere, modified with words of encouragement for their hero, including "*One Pablo Montoya*" the moniker given him when he raced in the States two years ago, when he won the Indianapolis 500 Miles. Maybe his eagerness to please them was Montoya's undoing at the start.

∧
The two Schumacher brothers within sight of the flag. In the end, the younger never really attacked the elder.

∧
First corner: Juan Pablo Montoya runs wide and only just avoids going off.

David Coulthard does the best he can to come home third; his first visit to the podium this season.
<

Race summary

> At the start **(1)**, the entire crowd seems to be cheering for Rubens Barrichello. After the first chicane, Juan Pablo Montoya attacks

Michael Schumacher and breaks his front wing by ramming the Ferrari **(2)** which is having a trouble free run out on its own **(3)**.

> Giancarlo Fisichella retires on lap 7 with an engine failure **(4)**.

> David Coulthard finishes third to get

onto the podium for the first time this season. He spent much of the race fighting off the attentions of the Renaults of Jarno Trulli

and Jenson Button **(5)**. The Italian retired with a broken engine on lap 61 and the Englishman finished 4th.

> From lap 17 onwards, the two Schumacher brothers transformed the grand prix into a family affair **(6)**. But the younger of the two

seems loathe to attack the world champion and the drivers maintain position to the podium **(7)**.

A good start

The Renault F1 team had made a very good start to the season. Although Jarno Trulli posted his third retirement in Interlagos, his team-mate Jenson Button finished fourth, just as he did in Sepang. He does not know it yet, but that was the best it was going to get in 2002.

Juan Pablo is angry

Having qualified on pole, Juan Pablo Montoya had expected better than taking home a mere two points from the Brazilian Grand Prix. He reckoned Michael Schumacher had caused the collision which ended his chances. "*I was slipstreaming behind him when he lifted off in the middle of the straight*", boomed the Colombian after the race. "*We were doing over 300 km/h at that point and I had no way of avoiding the collision and he knew that. It's an intolerable attitude.*"

The Colombian's version, although difficult to prove, did stand up to further investigation. A glance at the replay showed that he did close very suddenly and quickly on the Ferrari, as if Schumacher's car had slowed.

On the other hand, slowing too much with another car right behind would have been a very risky move, as the ensuing collision could have ended Schumacher's race as well.

"*I don't know what Juan Pablo has against me*", said a surprised Michael Schumacher. "*I think I left him enough room to pass. I don't really see what he is complaining about.*"

Naturally, the German denied lifting off the throttle prematurely.

Montoya was now very angry with Schumacher and there was a risk he would see red every time a Ferrari was in his sights. It would be interesting to see how the rest of the season would pan out between them.

Lauda needs to get a move on

This year's Jaguar certainly took the award for the worst Formula 1 car produced in recent years. Basically, nothing seemed to work on the R3, from the rear suspension, which had to be changed, to the front wing, which was being modified during the course of the Brazilian Grand Prix, not forgetting the overall aero package, which did not generate enough downforce.

Oh, and the brakes were not too good either, as designer John Russell had placed the calipers on top of the discs. This goes against all received wisdom on the subject, as engineers usually try and lower the centre of gravity of the cars!

It looked like spoiling the entire season for Jaguar, especially as the similarly powered Arrows were out-pacing the green cars on one sixth of the budget. Jaguar boss Niki Lauda therefore decided to take immediate action. Usually, teams start looking at the following year's car around April and, at the time, Jaguar did not even have a technical director. It was also due to start using its new wind tunnel on the Tuesday following the race, which was another pressing reason to find a solution to the problems.

Weekend gossip

> There was much talk flying round the Brazilian paddock after several BAR top brass were shown the door the week before the Grand Prix. However, Jacques Villeneuve felt that the moves instigated by BAR's new boss David Richards were well founded. "*We needed to make changes*", admitted the Canadian. "*It will probably take several months before we see the benefits, so why not make the changes as quickly as possible.*" He also dropped a hint that he could well decide to stay on at BAR for one more season. Mind you, where else could he find a salary of 20 million dollars per year?

> Since the start of the season, there had been rumours that Renault's Director of Engineering would be kicked out at the end of the year. The Englishman had been with the team for 23 years and had even rejected an offer from Ferrari in 1996, as he did not fancy moving to Italy. However, in Interlagos, Renault put out a press release denying the rumours.

> The Williams team had succeeded in poaching one of the cornerstones of the Ferrari technical edifice. Antonia Terzi, a Doctor of Aeronautic Engineering had left the Italian squad for the English one with immediate effect.

> In Interlagos, the idea was being bandied about that Michael Schumacher would replace Jean Todt as Sporting Director at the end of the 2004 season, the date when contracts for all the Ferrari top brass were due to expire.

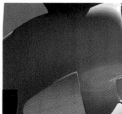

results

Practice

All the time trials

N°	Drive	Car/Engine/Chassis	Practice friday	Pos.	Practice saturday	Pos.	Qualifying	Pos.	Warm-up	Pos.
1.	Michael Schumacher	Ferrari 2002/220	1'15"627	5°	1'13"837	5°	1'13"241	2°	1'15"866	1°
2.	Rubens Barrichello	Ferrari 2001/216	1'15"933	7°	1'14"189	8°	1'13"935	8°	1'16"666	6°
3.	David Coulthard	McLaren-Mercedes MP4/17/02	1'15"075	1°	1'13"563	2°	1'13"565	4°	1'16"679	7°
4.	Kimi Räikkönen	McLaren-Mercedes MP4/17/04	1'15"883	6°	1'13"882	6°	1'13"595	5°	1'16"543	3°
5.	Ralf Schumacher	Williams-BMW FW24/04	1'15"477	4°	1'13"543	1°	1'13"328	3°	1'16"558	4°
6.	Juan Pablo Montoya	Williams-BMW FW24/02	1'15"345	2°	1'14"141	7°	1'13"114	1°	1'16"608	5°
7.	Nick Heidfeld	Sauber-Petronas C21/03	1'16"573	18°	1'14"508	10°	1'14"233	9°	1'17"412	13°
8.	Felipe Massa	Sauber-Petronas C21/04	1'16"548	17°	1'15"270	13°	1'14"533	12°	1'17"371	12°
9.	Giancarlo Fisichella	Jordan-Honda EJ12/4	1'16"539	16°	1'15"246	12°	1'14"748	14°	1'18"007	19°
10.	Takuma Sato	Jordan-Honda EJ12/3	1'17"432	19°	1'15"641	18°	1'15"296	19°	1'19"071	22°
11.	Jacques Villeneuve	BAR-Honda 004/03	1'16"183	9°	1'15"131	11°	1'14"760	15°	1'17"676	16°
12.	Olivier Panis	BAR-Honda 004/04	1'16"391	13°	1'15"298	14°	1'14"996	17°	1'17"482	14°
14.	Jarno Trulli	Renault R202/02	1'17"979	21°	1'13"714	4°	1'13"611	6°	1'17"676	17°
15.	Jenson Button	Renault R202/03	1'16"054	8°	1'13"686	3°	1'13"665	7°	1'17"361	11°
16.	Eddie Irvine	Jaguar R3/03	1'16"424	14°	1'15"534	17°	1'14"537	13°	1'17"496	15°
17.	Pedro de la Rosa	Jaguar R3/02	1'16"289	10°	1'15"305	15°	1'14"464	11°	1'16"391	2°
20.	Heinz-Harald Frentzen	Arrows-Cosworth A23/01	1'16"375	11°	1'15"933	20°	1'15"112	18°	1'17"007	8°
21.	Enrique Bernoldi	Arrows-Cosworth A23/02	1'16"379	12°	1'15"415	16°	1'15"355	21°	1'17"290	10°
22.	Alex Yoong	Minardi-Asiatech PS02/02	1'18"426	22°	1'16"727	22°	1'16"728	22°	1'18"569	20°
23.	Mark Webber	Minardi-Asiatech PS02/01	1'17"714	20°	1'16"294	21°	1'15"340	20°	1'19"034	21°
24.	Mika Salo	Toyota TF102/04	1'16"529	15°	1'14"484	9°	1'14"443	10°	1'17"994	18°
25.	Allan McNish	Toyota TF102/05	1'15"450	3°	1'15"892	19°	1'14"990	16°	1'17"222	9°

Maximum speeds

N°	Driver	P1 Qualifs	Pos.	P1 Race	Pos.	P2 Qualifs	Pos.	P2 Race	Pos.	Finish Qualifs	Pos.	Finish Race	Pos.	Trap Qualifs	Pos.	Trap Race	Pos.
1.	M. Schumacher	306,2	4°	308,3	5°	260,2	1°	251,1	1°	312,2	7°	319,3	8°	315,1	4°	311,4	3°
2.	R. Barrichello	305,4	6°	308,2	6°	253,6	14°	247,9	7°	310,3	12°	320,5	5°	310,3	13°	290,7	21°
3.	D. Coulthard	305,8	5°	306,6	12°	259,0	6°	248,6	5°	312,1	9°	318,5	9°	313,7	8°	304,8	12°
4.	K. Räikkönen	304,9	8°	307,6	10°	259,9	2°	248,3	6°	314,5	2°	324,8	1°	315,9	3°	306,3	10°
5.	R. Schumacher	307,4	2°	310,3	2°	258,8	4°	251,1	2°	313,5	3°	317,9	11°	316,1	1°	314,0	1°
6.	J.P. Montoya	308,2	1°	314,7	1°	258,8	5°	250,4	3°	313,4	4°	322,4	2°	315,9	2°	316,7	2°
7.	N. Heidfeld	300,3	19°	303,6	18°	255,7	8°	240,2	20°	308,4	17°	313,0	18°	310,2	14°	303,7	13°
8.	F. Massa	300,5	18°	299,0	22°	252,5	17°	239,3	21°	310,2	13°	309,3	21°	314,2	6°	301,8	17°
9.	G. Fisichella	301,7	15°	300,8	21°	252,8	16°	244,2	13°	308,3	19°	305,4	22°	308,4	17°	299,9	18°
10.	T. Sato	299,5	20°	307,7	9°	253,1	15°	243,9	14°	304,1	22°	315,1	14°	308,2	18°	307,4	9°
11.	J. Villeneuve	301,5	16°	305,2	14°	255,6	9°	245,9	9°	308,3	18°	317,0	13°	308,0	19°	305,1	11°
12.	O. Panis	301,3	17°	303,7	17°	254,4	12°	241,4	18°	308,5	16°	319,9	7°	310,5	12°	299,5	19°
14.	J. Trulli	304,7	9°	304,3	16°	256,9	7°	244,3	11°	312,0	10°	313,7	15°	314,9	5°	309,5	5°
15.	J. Button	301,8	14°	306,9	11°	257,6	6°	249,7	4°	309,8	15°	317,1	12°	309,6	16°	309,1	6°
16.	E. Irvine	302,9	11°	305,1	15°	252,0	18°	244,8	10°	310,9	11°	313,3	17°	313,9	7°	308,5	7°
17.	P. de la Rosa	303,0	10°	306,2	13°	255,5	10°	242,0	16°	312,2	6°	312,3	19°	313,4	9°	310,5	4°
18.	H-H. Frentzen	298,2	21°	308,0	7°	250,6	19°	246,2	8°	305,6	20°	320,6	4°	304,3	20°	302,6	15°
19.	E. Bernoldi	296,5	2°	308,6	3°	250,4	20°	241,7	17°	304,2	21°	318,4	10°	302,5	21°	289,4	22°
22.	A. Yoong	302,3	12°	301,9	20°	245,6	22°	239,0	22°	310,1	14°	313,5	16°	309,6	15°	308,4	8°
23.	M. Webber	302,2	13°	303,6	19°	249,5	21°	242,3	15°	312,2	8°	311,9	20°	301,0	22°	302,8	14
24.	M. Salo	307,1	3°	308,6	4°	255,5	11°	244,3	12°	315,0	1°	320,2	6°	313,3	10°	302,4	16°
25.	A. McNish	305,2	7°	307,8	8°	253,9	13°	240,7	19°	312,5	5°	320,7	3°	312,2	11°	299,1	20°

Race

Classification & Retirements

Pos.	Driver	Team	Laps	Time	Average	
1.	M. Schumacher	Ferrari	71	1:31:43.663	200,098 km/h	
2.	R. Schumacher	Williams BMW	71	0.588	200,076 km/h	
3.	D. Coulthard	McLaren Mercedes	71	59.109	197,971 km/h	
4.	J. Button	Renault	71	1:06.883	197,695 km/h	
5.	J.P. Montoya	Williams BMW	71	1:07.563	197,671 km/h	
6.	M. Salo	Toyota	70	1 lap	195,383 km/h	
7.	E. Irvine	Jaguar	70	1 lap	195,216 km/h	
8.	P. de la Rosa	Jaguar	70	1 lap	194,590 km/h	
9.	T. Sato	Jordan Honda	69	2 laps	194,161 km/h	
10.	J. Villeneuve	BAR Honda	68	3 laps	194,460 km/h	Cut engine
11.	M. Webber	Minardi Asiatech	68	3 laps	189,781 km/h	
12.	K. Räikkönen	McLaren Mercedes	67	4 laps	197,573 km/h	Broken right rear shaft
13.	A. Yoong	Minardi Asiatech	67	4 laps	187,787 km/h	

Driver	Team		Reason of abandon
N. Heidfeld	Sauber Petronas	62	Brake problems
J. Trulli	Renault	61	Broken engine
F. Massa	Sauber Petronas	42	Hit by M. Webber, spin
A. McNish	Toyota	41	Blocked rear wheel, spin
O. Panis	BAR Honda	26	Gear box
H-H. Frentzen	Arrows Cosworth	26	Broken rear suspension
E. Bernoldi	Arrows Cosworth	20	Broken rear suspension
R. Barrichello	Ferrari	17	Hydraulic problem
G. Fisichella	Jordan Honda	7	Broken engine

Fastest laps

	Driver	Time	Lap	Average
1.	J.P. Montoya	1'16"079	60	203,898 km/h
2.	R. Schumacher	1'16"224	55	203,510 km/h
3.	M. Schumacher	1'16"235	38	203,481 km/h
4.	J. Button	1'16"396	70	203,052 km/h
5.	R. Barrichello	1'16"511	16	202,747 km/h
6.	K. Räikkönen	1'16"529	54	202,699 km/h
7.	D. Coulthard	1'16"670	71	202,326 km/h
8.	J. Trulli	1'17"063	45	201,295 km/h
9.	J. Villeneuve	1'17"131	26	201,117 km/h
10.	T. Sato	1'17"320	51	200,625 km/h
11.	M. Salo	1'17"398	37	200,423 km/h
12.	G. Fisichella	1'17"511	3	200,131 km/h
13.	H-H. Frentzen	1'17"568	14	199,984 km/h
14.	E. Irvine	1'17"569	60	199,981 km/h
15.	P. de la Rosa	1'17"575	70	199,966 km/h
16.	N. Heidfeld	1'17"782	59	199,434 km/h
17.	A. McNish	1'17"868	26	199,214 km/h
18.	M. Webber	1'18"386	62	197,897 km/h
19.	O. Panis	1'18"705	23	197,095 km/h
20.	E. Bernoldi	1'18"814	14	196,822 km/h
21.	A. Yoong	1'18"837	54	196,765 km/h
22.	F. Massa	1'19"188	11	195,893 km/h

Pit stops

	Driver	Time	Lap	Stop n°
1.	J.P. Montoya	49"018	1	1
2.	G. Fisichella	59"077	1	1
3.	A. McNish	1'05"231	1	1
4.	E. Bernoldi	9'33"508	12	1
5.	A. Yoong	39"135	23	1
6.	J. Villeneuve	43"694	24	1
7.	A. McNish	38"082	24	2
8.	F. Massa	38"465	25	1
9.	T. Sato	39"446	27	1
10.	M. Webber	39"768	33	1
11.	M. Salo	44"237	38	1
12.	M. Schumacher	39"875	39	1
13.	N. Heidfeld	37"803	41	1
14.	J.P. Montoya	37"495	42	2
15.	P. de la Rosa	39"054	42	1
16.	J. Trulli	38"540	43	1
17.	R. Schumacher	37"183	44	1
18.	M. Webber	1'07"977	42	2
19.	J. Button	36"982	44	1
20.	E. Irvine	36"731	44	1
21.	D. Coulthard	37"619	45	1
22.	K. Räikkönen	37"004	46	1
23.	J. Villeneuve	37"303	46	2
24.	A. Yoong	37"735	45	2
25.	T. Sato	41"482	48	2
26.	N. Heidfeld	37"459	56	2
27.	M. Webber	33"866	63	3

Race leaders

Driver	Laps in the lead	Nber of Laps	Kilometers
M. Schumacher	1 > 13	13	55,987 km
R. Schumacher	14 > 16	3	12,927 km
M. Schumacher	17 > 39	23	99,107 km
R. Barrichello	40 > 44	5	21,545 km
M. Schumacher	45 > 71	27	116,343 km

Driver	Nber of Laps	Kilometers
M. Schumacher	63	271,437 km
R. Schumacher	5	21,545 km
R. Barrichello	3	12,927 km

Lap charts

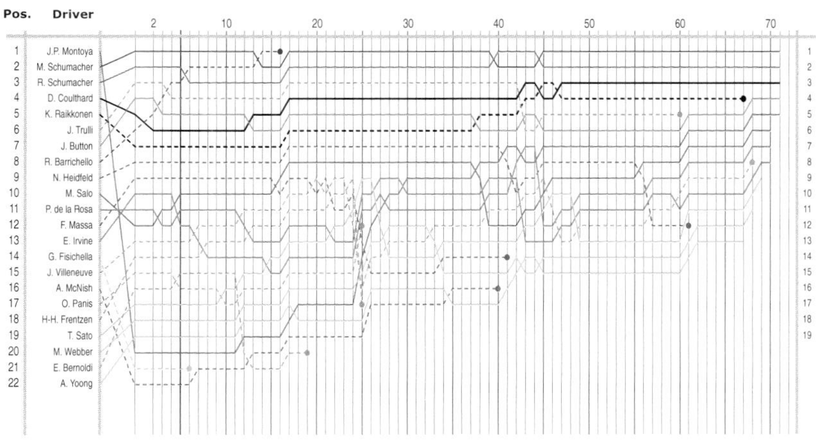

Gaps on the leader board

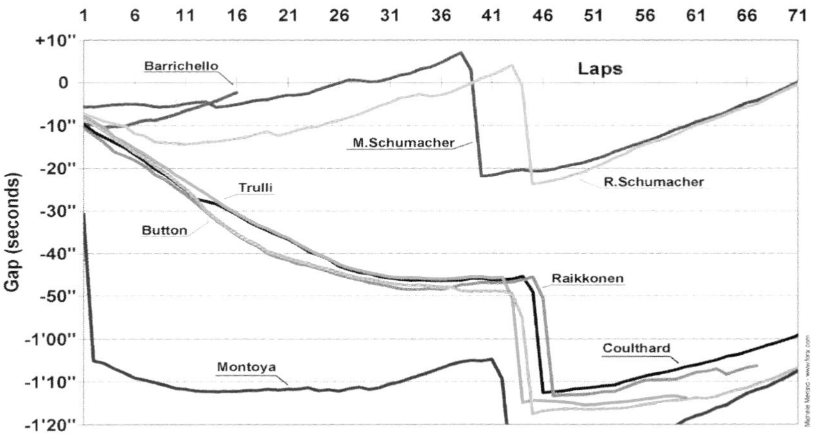

Championship after three rounds

Drivers

1. M. Schumacher 24
2. R. Schumacher 16
3. J.P. Montoya 14
4. J. Button 6
5. K. Räikkönen 4
6. D. Coulthard 4
7. E. Irvine 3
8. M. Webber 2
9. N. Heidfeld 2
10. M. Salo 2
11. F. Massa 1
12. A. Yoong 0
13. A. McNish 0
14. P. de la Rosa 0
15. J. Villeneuve 0
16. T. Sato 0
17. H-H. Frentzen 0
18. G. Fisichella 0

Constructors

1. BMW WilliamsF1 Team 30
2. Scuderia Ferrari Marlboro 24
3. West McLaren Mercedes............................8
4. Mild Seven Renault F1 Team......................6
5. Jaguar Racing...3
6. Sauber Petronas 3
7. KL Minardi Asiatech...................................2
8. Panasonic Toyota Racing 2
9. Lucky Strike BAR Honda 0
10. DHL Jordan Honda 0
11. Orange Arrows 0

All results : © 2002 Fédération Internationale de l'Automobile, 2, Ch. Blandonnet, 1215 Geneva 15, Switzerland

The circuit

Name :	Interlagos, Sao Paulo
Date :	March 31, 2002
Length :	4309 meters
Distance :	71 laps, 305,909 km
Temperature :	warm and sunny, 30°c
Track temperature :	40°c

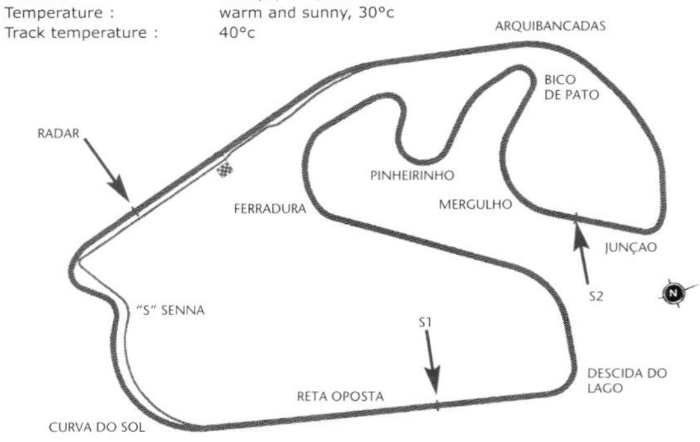

BRIDGESTONE

Best result for a driver running Bridgestone tyres:

Michael Schumacher, Ferrari, winner

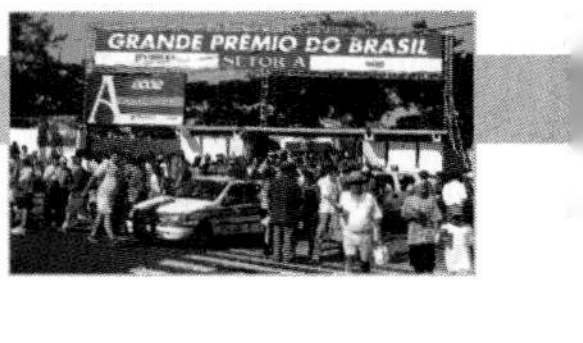

FIRST RED ONE-TWO

When they arrived in Imola, even Ferrari would not have dared dream of such a perfect weekend. With both cars on the front row of the grid, they simply crushed the opposition in the San Marino Grand Prix to record their first one-two finish of the season. It was to be by no means their last. The sparkling fight put up by the Williams-BMWs in the first few races simply evaporated in Imola. It was a bad sign for the rest of the season.

^
Michael Schumacher heads for his second pole position of the season at Imola.

Ferrari enters two F2002 for the first time and it's a whitewash

For the first time this season, Scuderia Ferrari showed up with two F2002 chassis and whitewashed the opposition. On Saturday, at the end of qualifying, Michael Schumacher had helped himself to pole position, ahead of team-mate Rubens Barrichello. For the previous three grands prix, the Brazilian had to make do with the F2001. At Imola, he was delighted to finally get his hands on the new car and was quick to praise it: "*The F2002 is better than the F2001 in every respect*", he explained. "*It is quicker in the dry, quicker in the wet. It has better braking and traction and everything is optimised.*" There was all sorts of speculation about the redoubtable F2002. Rival teams reckoned it hid several secrets, especially on the aerodynamic front. Secret or not, the main thing is it was the quickest in the pack.

The collapse of the Kirch group threatens the kingdom of Formula 1

In 1999, in one of those surprise moves which are his speciality, Bernie Ecclestone sold 50% of his holding company, SLEC Holding, to EM TV, a German group specialising in the negotiation of television rights. SLEC holds the commercial rights to Formula 1 up to 2099, so that selling half of it meant selling half the controlling interest in F1.

So far, this had not raised any eyebrows, or at least not in public. Matters turned sour however when EM TV saw its value on the Frankfurt stock market plummet by 50%. Bankrupt, the company was bought out by the Kirch group, which in February 2001 decided to exercise EM TV's option to acquire a further 25% of SLEC. Suddenly, Kirch owned 75% of F1, having coughed up 1.8 billion Euros. According to Leo Kirch, he had borrowed the money off his bankers. This sent a shiver through the major constructors involved in F1, who were worried that Kirch wanted to ensure F1 was only available to view through his pay-per-view channels, which would seriously limit its global audience.

In 2001, the constructors had threatened to form a breakaway group. But when the Kirch group announced it too was bankrupt, shortly before the San Marino Grand Prix, the major manufacturers met in Imola on the Saturday, to discuss buying the SLEC shares now held by Kirch's banks. While waiting to hear if their offer was accepted, they decided to continue with the GPWC (Grand Prix World Championship) and its original aim of creating a new championship, running parallel to Formula 1 as from the 2008 season, when the current Concorde Agreement governing Formula 1 will have expired.

It might seem a long way off, but in terms of how far forward car manufacturers usually plan their future, it is no time at all. The collapse of the Kirch group could yet have a profound influence on this threatened schism within the F1 ranks. Watch this space...

Juan Pablo believes in an eye for an eye

No way were they making plans to go on holiday together! With their last two encounters having ended in tears and collisions, feelings were running high between Juan Pablo Montoya and Michael Schumacher.

In Brazil, after the race, the Colombian was absolutely furious at the German's behaviour. On Thursday, when he arrived in Imola, he explained he was ready to give as good as he got from the Ferrari driver. "*I was behind Michael*", he reminded everyone. "*I was in his slipstream, I moved to the inside to pass him and that's when he moved over on me. It was very close and he touched my front wing and my race was over. As far as I understand the rules, he should first have looked in his mirrors before cutting in front of me. But we can talk about it as much as we like, it won't change anything. The damage is done.*" The Colombian reckoned Schumacher had behaved incorrectly. "*I've got my opinion, but apparently the Stewards reckon it was just a racing accident. It's good to know you can do something like this without getting a penalty. If Michael treats me like this, I will do the same to him.*" Warning! Danger!

Starting grid

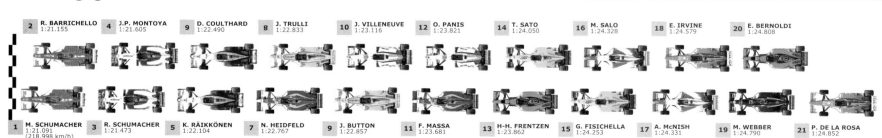

Pos	Driver	Time
2	R. BARRICHELLO	1:21.155
4	J.P. MONTOYA	1:21.605
9	D. COULTHARD	1:22.490
8	J. TRULLI	1:22.833
10	J. VILLENEUVE	1:23.116
12	O. PANIS	1:23.821
14	T. SATO	1:24.050
16	M. SALO	1:24.328
18	E. IRVINE	1:24.579
20	E. BERNOLDI	1:24.808
1	M. SCHUMACHER	1:21.091 (218,998 km/h)
3	R. SCHUMACHER	1:21.473
5	K. RÄIKKÖNEN	1:22.104
7	N. HEIDFELD	1:22.767
9	J. BUTTON	1:22.857
11	F. MASSA	1:23.681
13	H-H. FRENTZEN	1:23.862
15	G. FISICHELLA	1:24.253
17	A. McNISH	1:24.331
19	M. WEBBER	1:24.790
21	P. DE LA ROSA	1:24.852

First Ferrari one-two of the season. A total success for the Scuderia on home turf

Who or what can stop Michael Schumacher from taking his fifth world title? On the strength of his dominance at Imola, it seemed that no one was capable of contesting the supremacy of the Attila of the tracks.

At any rate, at Imola the world champion was never threatened. He led from the start and only dropped from the lead for two laps during the pit stops. As for the rest of the afternoon, his 62 laps of the Emilia Romagna track was more of Sunday drive than a motor race. *"I am very happy with this win"*, he commented as he stepped off the podium. *"Last year, we failed here and now we have made up for that in front of the tifosi. It is a very special grand prix for me."*

What was the secret of his insolent domination? The man himself reckoned it was all down to a new type of tyre brought to Italy by Bridgestone. *"I did not expect to have such an advantage today"*, he continued. *"Qualifying made it look as though the opposition was very close and I was expecting a tough fight. But Bridgestone produced a very consistent tyre. While the result is down to the whole package, I think it was due mainly to the quality of these new tyres."* Rubens Barrichello finished second, thus picking up his first points of the year. *"The car was just fantastic"*, enthused the Brazilian. *"It's the best I have ever driven."* Passed by Ralf Schumacher at the start, he had to wait for the first run of pit stops to get ahead of the German. *"I made a very good start, but I was on the*

dirty side of the track and Ralf got by. It is impossible to overtake on this track, but I had to wait until he pitted so that I could push harder and build a gap."* The Italian team had no intention of resting on its laurels. The very next Tuesday, the drivers were at Mugello,

testing in preparation for the Spanish Grand Prix. *"We will open a bottle of champagne, but nothing else"*, concluded Michael Schumacher. *"It is still much too early in the season to start celebrating. We are already thinking about the next race."*

Williams powerless against the Reds

Juan Pablo Montoya was hard to track down after the race. The Colombian was hidden away inside the Williams motorhome, unwilling to come out and relate his tale of woe to the world's media. He had just finished fourth and had never been on the pace. *"Juan Pablo had a major understeer problem on his first set of tyres"*, explained BMW motorsport boss Mario Theissen. *"We are not sure why, because he had no mechanical bothers."* Finally, the Colombian appeared to deliver his own version of events: *"Obviously, I had expected a lot more from this race"*, he admitted. *"I don't understand as the car was very good this morning in the warm-up, but it was badly*

balanced for the race. There was nothing I could do with it."*
Team-mate Ralf Schumacher was also puzzled. *"The strategy was good, the engine was good, the car was well set up and so there is nothing to add"*, he commented. *"We were simply not quick enough."*
Michelin competitions boss Pierre Dupasquier was equally confused in the Imola paddock. *"I cannot explain why we are so far behind the Ferraris"*, he sighed. *"Because our tyres worked exactly as we had expected them to. We will have to work hard to discover the cause of the problem."*

^
A happy atmosphere on the Imola podium. Jean Todt was given a good shower by his two drivers to celebrate the first of eight one-two finishes this season.

<
Ferrari one-two on the grid and a repeat performance at the end of the race. The Imola crowd saw red.

Race summary

> Start **(1)** Michael Schumacher maintains his pole position advantage. Behind him, Ralf Schumacher manages to get ahead

of Barrichello.
> In the pack, Jenson Button has made up a place and is eighth. He would finish 5th **(2)**
> While the two Saubers

are held up by the two Renaults, Nick Heidfeld thinks the team has called in him and he drives into the pits on lap 16, but the team

are not ready for him.
> The race was marked with several retirements. The last of them was Enrique Bernoldi on lap 51 **(3)**.

> Ralf Schumacher runs his own race **(4)** Starting 3rd, he finishes 3rd. He was second for a long time, but was passed by Barrichello

during the pit stops. Jenson Button passes Coulthard using the same method.
> Jacques Villeneuve finishes just outside the

points in 7th place **(5)**.
> A Ferrari one-two **(6)** and the crowd **(7)** goes wild.

Finger on the pulse

In Imola, Jenson Button managed to score points for the third race in a row, which put him in fourth place in the Drivers' classification.

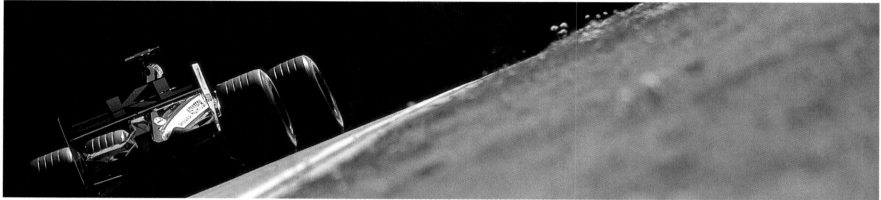

^
(top)
Ralf Schumacher qualified third and finished third. The San Marino Grand Prix was therefore particularly soporific as the top four qualifiers finished in grid order.

(above)
The Minardis had lost their Melbourne sparkle. In Imola, Alex Yoong failed to qualify for the first time this season. It would not be the last.

With an ultra-modern motorhome and factory, McLaren moves up a notch

Crisis? What crisis? While the world appears to be in recession and after McLaren boss Ron Dennis had issued several warnings over the winter that Formula 1 would not be spared, here was his very own McLaren team taking what appeared to be an extravagant step with a new motorhome.
Actually, one could hardly call it a motorhome as the team referred to it as the "*TCC*" (Team Communications Centre.) We had come a long way from the camping caravan as this was a structure built on two floors, with a reception desk, an interior atrium, several offices and no less than five meeting rooms, as well as driver rest areas. The whole was conceived in a superb glass and metal design, which kept some of the staff busy all day long keeping it clean! Rumour had it that this exotic creation had set McLaren back to the tune of 15 million dollars. The team was also working on a new factory called Paragon. Calling it a factory is way off beam, as it is a surrealist fantasy building with an elliptical shape, which juts out over a lake! Some crisis!

Weekend gossip

> Michael Schumacher headed for Paris the day after the grand prix, where he was honoured with the title *Champion of Sport* by UNESCO. He has been an ambassador for this organisation since 1997.

> Two Japanese top brass made the trip to Imola: Mr. Cho, the President of Toyota Motor Corporation and Mr. Watanabe, President of Bridgestone. The two men met in the Paddock Club above the pits, even though the former's team does not use the latter's tyres.

> The Sauber team was working flat out on a new wind tunnel near its factory, due to be ready in 2003. "*It will be the most up to date in Europe*", reckoned Peter Sauber.

> While he was chasing Ralf Schumacher, Rubens Barrichello was held up by Eddie Irvine when he came to lap the Jaguar. "*When I passed him, I gave him a sign which meant, 'go to hell'*" explained the Brazilian after the race. "*During the Drivers' Briefings, Eddie is always telling everyone what to do and this is how he acts. He's an idiot and on top of that, he's getting old!*" I think we get the point!

> No smiles from Olivier Panis after the race. The Frenchman had just posted his fourth retirement of the season from four starts. "*It's becoming a pain*", he muttered, as he left the circuit. "*The car is not well balanced and on top of that, the engine died when the clutch gave up.*"

>
In Imola, the Sauber team celebrated its 150th grand prix. On Friday, it organised a small party at its motorhome. It was not only the inside of the drinks glasses which were wet, as it rained all day on Friday. All the Swiss F1 folk turned out for the event.

Practice

All the time trials

N°	Driver	Car/Engine/Chassis	Practice friday	Pos.	Practice saturday	Pos.	Qualifying	Pos.	Warm-up	Pos.
1.	Michael Schumacher	Ferrari 2002/219	1'36"898	1°	1'23"046	1°	1'21"091	1°	1'25"906	2°
2.	Rubens Barrichello	Ferrari 2002/220	1'37"094	2°	1'23"675	3°	1'21"155	2°	1'25"483	1°
3.	David Coulthard	McLaren-Mercedes MP4/17/05	1'38"747	4°	1'23"550	2°	1'22"490	6°	1'26"443	7°
4.	Kimi Räikkönen	McLaren-Mercedes MP4/17/04	1'38"773	5°	1'24"651	7°	1'22"104	5°	1'26"412	6°
5.	Ralf Schumacher	Williams-BMW FW24/05	1'39"518	10°	1'23"900	5°	1'21"473	3°	1'27"106	12°
6.	Juan Pablo Montoya	Williams-BMW FW24/04	1'39"480	9°	1'24"078	6°	1'21"605	4°	1'26"116	3°
7.	Nick Heidfeld	Sauber-Petronas C21/06	1'39"971	12°	1'23"695	4°	1'22"767	7°	1'26"151	4°
8.	Felipe Massa	Sauber-Petronas C21/03	1'39"253	8°	1'27"282	21°	1'23"681	11°	1'26"179	5°
9.	Giancarlo Fisichella	Jordan-Honda EJ12/4	1'38"093	3°	1'25"542	13°	1'24"253	15°	1'27"861	16°
10.	Takuma Sato	Jordan-Honda EJ12/3	1'39"764	11°	1'25"576	14°	1'24"050	14°	1'27"400	14°
11.	Jacques Villeneuve	BAR-Honda 004/06	1'40"787	15°	1'24"965	9°	1'23"116	10°	1'26"694	8°
12.	Olivier Panis	BAR-Honda 004/04	1'41"565	17°	1'25"363	11°	1'23"821	12°	1'27"766	15°
14.	Jarno Trulli	Renault R202/02	1'39"204	7°	1'25"520	12°	1'22"833	8°	1'27"106	11°
15.	Jenson Button	Renault R202/03	1'40"601	14°	1'24"785	8°	1'22"857	9°	1'26"862	9°
16.	Eddie Irvine	Jaguar R3/01	1'40"551	13°	1'25"766	15°	1'24"579	18°	1'28"015	17°
17.	Pedro de la Rosa	Jaguar R3/02	1'40"809	18°	1'26"399	18°	1'24"852	21°	1'28"599	19°
20.	Heinz-Harald Frentzen	Arrows-Cosworth A23/01	1'39"558	6°	1'25"178	10°	1'23"862	13°	1'27"231	13°
21.	Enrique Bernoldi	Arrows-Cosworth A23/03	1'41"730	16°	1'25"781	16°	1'24"808	20°	1'26"913	10°
22.	Alex Yoong	Minardi-Asiatech PS02/03	1'43"986	21°	1'28"993	22°	1'27"241			
23.	Mark Webber	Minardi-Asiatech PS02/04	1'41"969	19°	1'27"022	19°	1'24"790	19°	1'28"992	20°
24.	Mika Salo	Toyota TF102/04	1'42"261	20°	1'25"951	17°	1'24"328	16°	1'28"478	18°
25.	Allan McNish	Toyota TF102/05	1'43"986	22°	1'27"138	20°	1'24"331	17°	1'28"998	21°

Maximum speeds

N°	Driver	P1 Qualifs	Pos.	P1 Race	Pos.	P2 Qualifs	Pos.	P2 Race	Pos.	Finish Qualifs	Pos.	Finish Race	Pos.	Trap Qualifs	Pos.	Trap Race	Pos.
1.	M. Schumacher	232,1	1°	222,0	2°	268,0	3°	263,2	4°	188,8	1°	178,0	2°	308,1	4°	305,3	7°
2.	R. Barrichello	231,1	3°	221,9	3°	267,8	4°	266,1	1°	187,9	2°	178,7	1°	307,6	5°	306,0	2°
3.	D. Coulthard	228,5	5°	218,3	9°	263,4	10°	262,8	6°	183,6	4°	175,4	5°	303,2	17°	305,3	8°
4.	K. Räikkönen	227,8	6°	219,6	7°	264,0	8°	260,9	10°	185,6	3°	176,2	3°	302,3	20°	305,3	13°
5.	R. Schumacher	231,2	2°	222,9	1°	268,7	1°	264,3	2°	182,5	7°	174,6	6°	309,0	2°	306,0	3°
6.	J.P. Montoya	230,8	4°	221,1	4°	268,3	2°	264,1	3°	183,2	6°	172,8	11°	309,0	1°	305,8	6°
7.	N. Heidfeld	224,4	11°	217,3	12°	265,1	6°	260,6	12°	181,5	11°	172,1	13°	308,2	3°	305,8	4°
8.	F. Massa	223,6	13°	218,0	10°	263,4	11°	261,1	9°	176,3	21°	169,9	17°	305,2	8°	305,9	4°
9.	G. Fisichella	222,5	18°	211,0	19°	261,8	19°	254,9	19°	177,1	20°	163,1	20°	302,4	19°	298,0	19°
10.	T. Sato	220,9	22°	205,4	20°	264,4	7°	252,3	20°	181,8	9°	168,1	19°	302,5	18°	291,7	20°
11.	J. Villeneuve	222,2	19°	219,0	8°	263,4	12°	262,7	7°	180,2	15°	172,4	12°	305,5	7°	307,9	1°
12.	O. Panis	223,5	15°	214,1	18°	262,3	17°	258,9	16°	180,4	14°	172,9	10°	305,1	9°	303,7	9°
14.	J. Trulli	223,4	16°	215,4	16°	263,4	13°	258,8	17°	181,4	12°	176,0	4°	306,3	6°	298,1	18°
15.	J. Button	227,4	7°	220,4	5°	263,2	15°	260,1	13°	181,9	8°	173,5	7°	303,3	14°	303,3	11°
16.	E. Irvine	225,1	10°	216,1	15°	263,2	14°	258,1	18°	179,9	17°	173,1	8°	303,2	15°	298,7	16°
17.	P. de la Rosa	225,7	8°	217,1	13°	262,7	16°	261,3	8°	180,1	16°	171,4	14°	303,2	16°	303,2	12°
18.	H.-H. Frentzen	223,6	14°	217,9	11°	261,8	18°	258,9	15°	181,7	10°	170,8	15°	302,1	21°	300,9	15°
19.	E. Bernoldi	224,2	12°	219,6	6°	261,5	20°	263,2	5°	183,4	5°	173,0	9°	301,2	22°	302,0	14°
22.	A. Yoong	222,7	17°			261,3	22°			176,1	22°			303,7	11°		
23.	M. Webber	221,9	20°	216,7	14°	261,5	21°	260,6	11°	177,9	19°	168,2	18°	303,6	13°	303,5	10°
24.	M. Salo	221,4	21°	215,4	17°	263,9	9°	259,6	14°	178,4	18°	170,7	16°	303,6	12°	298,5	17°
25.	A. McNish	225,6	9°			265,6	5°			181,3	13°			304,3	10°		

Race

Classification & Retirements

Pos.	Driver	Team	laps	Time	Average
1.	M. Schumacher	Ferrari	62	1:29:10.789	205,613 km/h
2.	R. Barrichello	Ferrari	62	17.907	204,927 km/h
3.	R. Schumacher	Williams BMW	62	19.755	204,856 km/h
4.	J.P. Montoya	Williams BMW	62	44.725	203,908 km/h
5.	J. Button	Renault	62	1:23.395	202,457 km/h
6.	D. Coulthard	McLaren Mercedes	61	1 Lap	202,259 km/h
7.	J. Villeneuve	BAR Honda	61	1 Lap	201,160 km/h
8.	F. Massa	Sauber Petronas	61	1 Lap	200,928 km/h
9.	J. Trulli	Renault	61	1 Lap	200,541 km/h
10.	N. Heidfeld	Sauber Petronas	61	1 Lap	200,317 km/h
11.	M. Webber	Minardi Asiatech	60	2 Laps	195,961 km/h

Driver	Team		Reason
E. Bernoldi	Arrows Cosworth	51	Fuel pressure, loss of engine power
E. Irvine	Jaguar	46	Broken drive shaft
K. Räikkönen	McLaren Mercedes	45	Broken exhaust pipe
O. Panis	BAR Honda	45	Throttle linkage
P. de la Rosa	Jaguar	31	Broken transmission shaft
M. Salo	Toyota	27	Broken 4th gear
H.-H. Frentzen	Arrows Cosworth	26	Fuel pressure, loss of engine power
G. Fisichella	Jordan Honda	20	Hydraulic pressure
T. Sato	Jordan Honda	6	Gear box stuck in first gear
A. McNish	Toyota	1	Broken transmission at the start

Fastest laps

	Driver	Time	Lap	Average
1.	R. Barrichello	1'24"170	38	210,987 km/h
2.	M. Schumacher	1'24"281	45	210,709 km/h
3.	R. Schumacher	1'24"718	62	209,622 km/h
4.	J.P. Montoya	1'25"040	31	208,828 km/h
5.	N. Heidfeld	1'25"301	61	208,189 km/h
6.	K. Räikkönen	1'25"483	38	207,746 km/h
7.	J. Button	1'25"761	43	207,073 km/h
8.	D. Coulthard	1'25"896	48	206,747 km/h
9.	J. Villeneuve	1'25"959	46	206,596 km/h
10.	O. Panis	1'26"189	25	206,044 km/h
11.	F. Massa	1'26"279	34	205,829 km/h
12.	J. Trulli	1'26"354	30	205,651 km/h
13.	H.-H. Frentzen	1'26"537	25	205,216 km/h
14.	E. Bernoldi	1'26"783	20	204,634 km/h
15.	P. de la Rosa	1'27"104	30	203,880 km/h
16.	E. Irvine	1'27"461	24	203,048 km/h
17.	M. Webber	1'27"914	24	202,001 km/h
18.	M. Salo	1'28"460	14	200,755 km/h
19.	G. Fisichella	1'28"741	12	200,119 km/h
20.	T. Sato	1'30"158	4	196,974 km/h

Pit stops

	Driver	Time	Lap	Stop n°
1.	T. Sato	2'05"019	5	1
2.	N. Heidfeld	34"805	16	1
3.	F. Massa	26"094	17	1
4.	N. Heidfeld	25"216	19	2
5.	J. Trulli	25"027	22	1
6.	E. Bernoldi	27"485	22	1
7.	J. Button	24"627	23	1
8.	M. Salo	27"942	23	1
9.	N. Heidfeld	14"187	24	3
10.	M. Webber	26"564	25	1
11.	O. Panis	25"602	26	1
12.	J. Villeneuve	25"743	27	1
13.	E. Irvine	25"501	29	1
14.	K. Räikkönen	27"555	30	1
15.	M. Schumacher	24"309	31	1
16.	R. Schumacher	23"886	31	1
17.	P. de la Rosa	32"222	30	1
18.	R. Barrichello	23"926	32	1
19.	J. P. Montoya	23"475	32	1
20.	D. Coulthard	23"888	34	1
21.	F. Massa	28"305	37	2
22.	N. Heidfeld	26"061	39	4
23.	J. Trulli	26"945	40	2
24.	J. Button	26"050	41	2
25.	M. Webber	26"862	42	2
26.	E. Bernoldi	26"483	43	2
27.	M. Schumacher	24"232	46	2
28.	R. Schumacher	24"004	46	2
29.	E. Irvine	27"012	45	2
30.	R. Barrichello	30"247	47	2
31.	J.P. Montoya	23"725	48	2
32.	J. Villeneuve	23"566	48	2
33.	D. Coulthard	23"105	49	2

Race leaders

Driver	Laps in the lead	Nber of Laps	Kilometers	Driver	Nber of Laps	Kilometers
M. Schumacher	1 > 31	31	152,686 km	M. Schumacher	60	295,743 km
R. Barrichello	32	1	4,933 km	R. Barrichello	2	9,866 km
M. Schumacher	33 > 46	14	69,062 km			
R. Barrichello	47	1	4,933 km			
M. Schumacher	48 > 62	15	73,995 km			

Lap chart

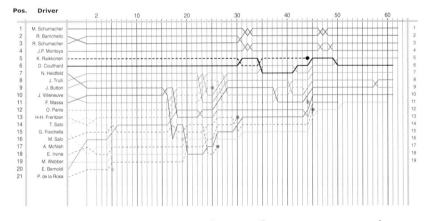

Gaps on the leader board

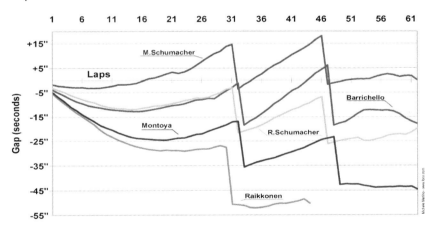

Championship after four rounds

Driver

Constructors

The circuit

Name :	Autodromo Enzo & Dino Ferrari, Imola
Date :	April 14, 2002
Length :	4933 meters
Distance :	62 laps, 305,609 km
Temperature :	Cloudy with sunny breaks 19°c
Track temperature :	23°c

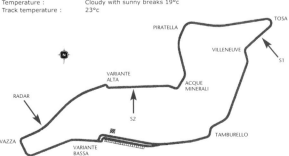

Best result for a driver running Bridgestone tyres:

Michael Schumacher, Ferrari, winner

All results : © 2002 Fédération Internationale de l'Automobile, 2, Ch. Blandonnet, 1215 Geneva 15, Switzerland

PICKING UP CRUMBS

There is nothing new under the sun in Barcelona. Once again the two Ferraris monopolised the front row of the grid and yet again Michael Schumacher was quickest. Rubens Barrichello was unlucky – his car got stuck on the grid at the start. The others had to make do with crumbs. Juan Pablo Montoya finished second and David Coulthard third. No way of doing better, given the strength of the Ferraris.

100% Ferrari front row. No problem for the Reds

The Barcelona track layout could have been drawn by the Scuderia Ferrari designers. Its long corners seem tailor-made for the F2002 chassis and under these circumstances, it is hardly surprising that the red cars dominated every practice session over the weekend.

On Saturday, the two Ferraris therefore monopolised the front row of the grid, with Michael Schumacher taking another pole position, although he waited until the dying moments of the session to snatch it away from Rubens Barrichello. As usual, the Ferraris put a second between themselves and their rivals, starting with the two Williams, who lined up together on the second row. At the other end of the scale, Eddie Irvine found himself demoted to the back row by the Barcelona stewards, after it was found that his fuel sample did not comply with the regulations.

A thoughtful Olivier Panis. Qualified 13th, the Frenchman was going through a disastrous start to the season and had yet to see a chequered flag.
>v

Recognise him? Alain Prost made a furtive appearance in the Barcelona paddock on the Friday, with a pass provided by Jean Todt. The Frenchman (here with Juan Pablo Montoya's manager, Julian Jakobi) reckoned he had plans for an early return to Formula 1.
v

Flexible deflectors: Ferrari accused

Bathed in the warm Catalan sun, on Thursday the Barcelona paddock appeared to be dozing as if enjoying a Spanish siesta.
It was a false impression. In the motorhomes, frenzied talks were taking place to discuss what stance to adopt vis a vis the "*Ferrari situation*". McLaren boss Ron Dennis paid a visit to Williams, while Arrows owner Tom Walkinshaw was in discussion with Renault's Flavio Briatore. Both men then headed for Williams. At Imola, for the San Marino Grand Prix, several engineers noticed that the digital television pictures showed that the flat bottom on the Ferraris appeared to be rather more flexible than the rules allowed. "*We noticed that the side deflectors move about 4 centimetres*", said one technical director, who wished to remain anonymous. The regulations state that aerodynamic devices must be fixed, so that they cannot flatten out down the straights and return to their usual shape through the corners. It seemed that Ferrari had found a way round this rule, so that the deflectors would bend under speed. That meant they would appear rigid when the cars were scrutineered, becoming moveable when the car is running. Had they been unmasked?
Apparently, Ferrari had introduced this subtle new element at Imola and it had immediately been spotted by engineers from other teams. They flagged their concern on the spot to the Federation Internationale Automobile. But the governing body deemed there was no infringement of the regulations and the Scuderia was allowed to run its deflectors.
At the end of the grand prix at Imola, there were rumours of a protest made by McLaren and Williams against Ferrari. In the end, it came to nothing as these two teams decided not to act. On Thursday in Barcelona, it now seemed that Ferrari's rivals had simply decided to copy the system, by fitting the same sort of flexible deflectors. No doubt the afternoon meetings were all about confirming the decision to run with them.

Starting grid

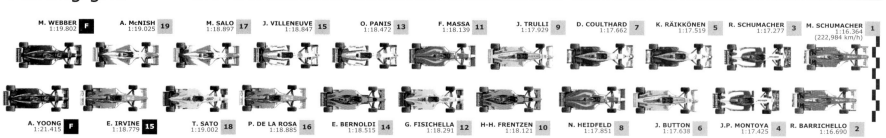

	M. WEBBER (F)	1:19.802
	A. McNISH 19	1:19.025
	M. SALO 17	1:18.897
	J. VILLENEUVE 15	1:18.847
	O. PANIS 13	1:18.472
	F. MASSA 11	1:18.139
	J. TRULLI 9	1:17.929
	D. COULTHARD 7	1:17.662
	K. RÄIKKÖNEN 5	1:17.519
	R. SCHUMACHER 3	1:17.277
	M. SCHUMACHER 1	1:16.364 (222,984 km/h)
	A. YOONG (F)	1:21.415
	E. IRVINE 15	1:18.779
	T. SATO 18	1:19.002
	P. DE LA ROSA 16	1:18.885
	E. BERNOLDI 14	1:18.515
	G. FISICHELLA 12	1:18.291
	H-H. FRENTZEN 10	1:18.121
	N. HEIDFELD 8	1:17.851
	J. BUTTON 6	1:17.638
	J.P. MONTOYA 4	1:17.425
	R. BARRICHELLO 2	1:16.690

Webber, Yoong: forfeit for security reasons concerning the multiple front and back wing failures

Irvine: Classified in last place for use of illegal fuel.

Schumi's Spanish Stroll

Ferrari's number 1 driver had only just taken the chequered flag, when the televisions in the press room linked up the sound to the Scuderia's pit-to-car radio. "*Well done Michael, a fantastic race*", said technical director Ross Brawn. "*And well done to you*", replied the driver, as he waved to crowd on his slowing down lap. "*You have given me a great car. It's a joy to drive.*" That summed it up pretty neatly. From start to finish, the Spanish Grand Prix was a long lonely trouble-free stroll for Michael Schumacher.

Once again, all the problems with the car landed at Rubens Barrichello's feet, who did not even complete the parade lap, because of a gear selection problem. As some press room wag put it: "*if a plane is going to land on the grid, it will be on Barrichello's car.*"
The Williams and McLarens could only reflect on the futility of it all, as they picked up the podium places left them by Michael Schumacher. "*The Ferraris are better than us and deserve to win*", admitted Gerhard Berger. "*We also have a good car, but we need to make a lot of progress with it. We will get there.*" When? That was the question on the lips of those waiting to see a motor race rather than a parade.

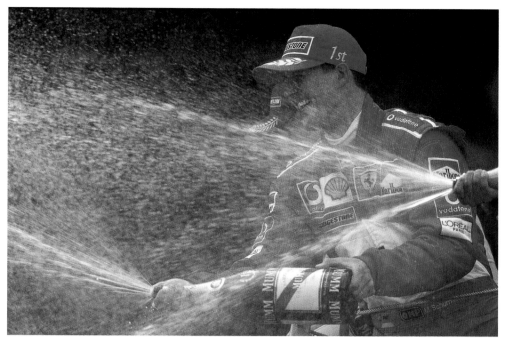

> Champagne for Michael Schumacher, who celebrated his third consecutive win in Barcelona.

Peter Sauber brings out the big cigars

In his third Formula 1 season, Nick Heidfeld was becoming a regular when it came to picking up points. Finishing fourth in Barcelona, the little German had to face a horde of journalists, with English television jostling Italian radio and the German TV stations trying to get the jump on the digital ones. It would take more than that to fluster the phlegmatic Sauber driver, calm as ever, as yet again he delivered the same post-race speech: "*It was really a super weekend*", he assured the press. "*We managed to improve the car and we finished on the same lap as the Ferrari. It's super.*" Heidfeld made the most of the retirement of those ahead of him, but he also profited from the efficiency of his team. Because, it was when he came into the pits on lap 43, that his crew got him refuelled quickly, allowing him to get ahead of Jenson Button's Renault. "*I knew it would be tight*", he explained. "*As I left, I floored the throttle to go quicker, but with the pit lane speed limiter it made no*

difference. *When Jenson got going, we were side by side. I just had a metre headstart, but I had the racing line and I had no intention of letting it go.*" While Nick Heidfeld handled the questions like a pro, alongside him, Felipe Massa was finding it hard to hide his excitement. Fifth at the end of his fifth grand prix, it was a result he had not dared hope for. As soon as he got back to the motorhome, he fell into the arms of his sister Fernanda and his parents, before a microphone was stuck under his nose and he was live on air with Radio Bandeirantes in Sao Paulo. Sitting under the motorhome awning, Peter Sauber had just lit the biggest cigar in his humidor. He is not the sort to get over-emotional and in public, he settled for a polite handshake and smile with Nick Heidfeld. But this reserve was too much for Felipe Massa, who gave his boss a big hug, who returned the gesture with a polite thank you. Taking on this young driver was a gamble and the Swiss team boss had just won his bet.

Only 15th in qualifying, Jacques Villeneuve is comforted by his girlfriend Elie Green on the grid. Yet again he would finish seventh, still looking for his first point of the season.
<

Two Saubers in the points was an achievement which would not be repeated in 2002. Fourth and fifth place in Barcelona meant the Swiss team moved up to fourth place in the Constructors' classification, which was its stated goal for the year.
∨

Race summary

> **Start (1)**
A fright for Ferrari on the formation lap: Rubens Barrichello's car refuses to start and has to be pushed back to

the pits.

> **Lap 1 (2)**
Michael Schumacher leads from his brother.

> **Lap 4 (3)**
Kimi Räikkönen leads Jenson Button and David Coulthard, before his rear wing flies off.

> On lap 30, Ralf Schumacher loses second place in the gravel. His front wing is broken and he has to pit to change it.

> **Lap 34 (4)**
Jenson Button is in trouble. Having been third, he is passed by David Coulthard, slips down the order and

> Juan Pablo Montoya **(5)** takes the chequered

retires near the finish with hydraulic problems.

flag to finish second.

> Out in front, it's another triumph for Michael Schumacher (6 and 7).

They're off

The start is always impressive as 22 cars, each with around 800 horsepower, charge off the line together. Especially when the 22 cars in question are all rushing at a chicane. That's F1 for you.

David Coulthard finished third in the Spanish Grand Prix. It was not enough to silence the team's critics.

Juan Pablo Montoya relaxes reading the papers, alongside his father Pablo. The Colombian went on to finish second in the Spanish Grand Prix, but he never posed a threat to Michael Schumacher.

Ron Dennis pulls a face

Insiders refer to Formula 1 as the "*Piranha Club*". Behind the air-conditioned luxury of the motorhomes, it's dog eat dog and survival of the fittest.

Therefore, as the 2002 season got underway, McLaren was constantly coming under fire from critics, happy to spread rumours. There were those who claimed that Jurgen Hubbert, a DaimlerChrysler board member, was angry with the lack of results from the team and was considering pulling Mercedes out of F1.

Others suggested that the team's principal sponsor, cigarette brand West, was outraged at the profligate expense of the new McLaren motorhome (around 10 million Euros) and the new Paragon factory (around 400 million Euros.)

Faced with these stories doing the rounds, team boss Ron Dennis held a press conference in Barcelona to put the record straight. "*I am fed up with reading and hearing these stories,*" he snapped on Saturday. "*People are always trying to find one single factor on which to pin the blame for our lack of results, whether it's the tyres, the engine or the chassis. It's ridiculous. Our car is one entity and it is impossible to separate one or more elements. We are in fact a very united team. There are no problems between us and our partners.*"

Having got that off his chest, Ron Dennis ended by admitting that the MP4-17 was struggling a bit with the changeover to Michelin tyres. "*We decided on this change around one month after finalising the design of the car. The Michelins are a bit wider than the Bridgestone and we should have made the suspension differently to accommodate that. That's it.*"

A first win? The boss still believed it was possible and admitted he always felt sick after every race when the team got beaten. "*But we are aiming at a moving target, because the others are also making progress. Having said that, there will be times when a victory is on the cards when a circuit suits our car or tyres better.*"

Weekend gossip

> The English monthly "*F1 Magazine*", owned by Bernie Ecclestone, took the risk of publishing a list of the 100 most important people in F1. Michael Schumacher was top of the pops, ahead of Bernie Ecclestone, Luca di Montezemolo and Max Mosley. It was a very subjective list and caused quite a stir in the paddock.

> 4.5 tenths: that's how much time a car loses over a lap of Barcelona for every 10 litres of fuel it carries. The track definitely suits a light car, which means that a two stop race strategy is almost compulsory.

> War of words in Barcelona: asked what he thought about his former team, Jordan,

making a large part of the workforce redundant, Heinz-Harald Frentzen replied that: "*if Eddie (Jordan) keeps sacking people, he will end up having to do some work himself!*"

> Over the weekend, McLaren announced it had renewed its agreement with Canon and signed a new one with Bloomberg.

Magnificent Barcelona. The Catalan city is one of the favourite stop-offs for the Formula 1 circus. It has a charming old town and in contrast, there is all the excitement of the Olympic Port, with its restaurants and countless discotheques.

Practice

All the time trials

N°	Driver	Car/Engine/Chassis	Practice friday	Pos.	Practice saturday	Pos.	Qualifying	Pos.	Warm-up	Pos.
1.	Michael Schumacher	Ferrari 2002/220	1'20"380	1°	1'18"226	3°	1'16"364	1°	1'20"884	3°
2.	Rubens Barrichello	Ferrari 2002/221	1'20"742	4°	1'18"048	1°	1'16"690	2°	1'20"229	1°
3.	David Coulthard	McLaren-Mercedes MP4/17/03	1'21"298	12°	1'18"386	4°	1'17"662	5°	1'23"082	16°
4.	Kimi Räikkönen	McLaren-Mercedes MP4/17/04	1'20"996	7°	1'18"993	7°	1'17"519	7°	1'22"642	14°
5.	Ralf Schumacher	Williams-BMW FW24/04	1'21"409	15°	1'19"367	12°	1'17"277	3°	1'21"846	6°
6.	Juan Pablo Montoya	Williams-BMW FW24/05	1'21"623	17°	1'19"574	14°	1'17"425	4°	1'22"397	12°
7.	Nick Heidfeld	Sauber-Petronas C21/06	1'21"301	13°	1'18"144	2°	1'17"851	8°	1'20"857	2°
8.	Felipe Massa	Sauber-Petronas C21/03	1'21"197	9°	1'19"043	8°	1'18"139	11°	1'21"068	4°
9.	Giancarlo Fisichella	Jordan-Honda EJ12/5	1'21"169	8°	1'19"319	11°	1'18"291	12°	1'22"207	11°
10.	Takuma Sato	Jordan-Honda EJ12/3	1'21"351	14°	1'20"168	15°	1'19"002	18°	1'22"072	9°
11.	Jacques Villeneuve	BAR-Honda 004/06	1'21"413	16°	1'19"468	13°	1'18"847	15°	1'22"461	13°
12.	Olivier Panis	BAR-Honda 004/04	1'20"758	5°	1'19"144	9°	1'18"472	13°	1'21"996	8°
14.	Jarno Trulli	Renault R202/01	1'21"278	10°	1'20"484	17°	1'17"929	9°	1'23"149	18°
15.	Jenson Button	Renault R202/03	1'20"693	3°	1'18"499	5°	1'17"638	6°	1'22"155	10°
16.	Eddie Irvine	Jaguar R3/05	1'21"294	11°	1'20"799	18°			1'23"284	19°
17.	Pedro de la Rosa	Jaguar R3/02	1'22"094	19°	1'20"198	16°	1'18"885	16°	1'23"099	17°
20.	Heinz-Harald Frentzen	Arrows-Cosworth A23/01	1'20"450	2°	1'18"900	6°	1'18"121	10°	1'21"729	5°
21.	Enrique Bernoldi	Arrows-Cosworth A23/03	1'20"834	6°	1'19"266	10°	1'18"515	14°	1'21"872	7°
22.	Alex Yoong	Minardi-Asiatech PS02/03	1'23"269	22°	1'21"700	22°	1'21"415	21°	1'24"596	22°
23.	Mark Webber	Minardi-Asiatech PS02/04	1'22"459	20°	1'20"963	19°	1'19"802	20°	1'23"517	20°
24.	Mika Salo	Toyota TF102/04	1'22"082	18°	1'21"133	20°	1'18"897	17°	1'23"002	15°
25.	Allan McNish	Toyota TF102/05	1'22"564	21°	1'21"219	21°	1'19"025	19°	1'23"849	21°

Maximum speeds

N°	Driver	P1 Qualifs	Pos.	P1 Race	Pos.	P2 Qualifs	Pos.	P2 Race	Pos.	Finish Qualifs	Pos.	Finish Race	Pos.	Trap Qualifs	Pos.	Trap Race	Pos.
1.	M. Schumacher	296,6	2°	284,7	1°	306,6	2°	300,1	3°	289,7	2°	280,5	1°	313,0	7°	312,5	9°
2.	R. Barrichello	297,6	1°			306,8	1°			290,0	1°			315,1	2°		
3.	D. Coulthard	294,4	3°	277,7	8°	301,2	11°	301,4	1°	286,5	4°	279,7	5°	313,9	4°	319,8	2°
4.	K. Räikkönen	292,2	6°	262,5	17°	301,7	9°	296,9	12°	286,3	6°	276,9	11°	312,7	9°	324,1	1°
5.	R. Schumacher	293,1	5°	279,3	5°	304,1	3°	298,0	8°	288,1	3°	279,3	6°	313,4	6°	308,0	16°
6.	J.P. Montoya	290,1	10°	281,2	2°	303,7	4°	299,5	4°	286,4	5°	280,3	2°	313,0	8°	308,0	15°
7.	N. Heidfeld	293,2	4°	275,8	9°	302,6	7°	297,2	10°	283,1	16°	275,8	14°	308,7	18°	312,7	8°
8.	F. Massa	290,4	9°	277,8	7°	302,4	8°	297,1	11°	282,3	18°	276,9	12°	310,8	14°	311,4	10°
9.	G. Fisichella	288,5	14°	243,8	19°	300,1	13°	287,0	19°	283,4	13°	273,9	18°	311,2	13°	307,2	18°
10.	T. Sato	285,1	20°	271,9	11°	297,1	20°	293,0	18°	280,5	20°	274,4	17°	305,7	20°	306,0	19°
11.	J. Villeneuve	287,5	17°	271,6	14°	302,9	5°	298,9	5°	283,3	14°	280,2	3°	312,4	10°	315,9	5°
12.	O. Panis	288,1	15°	271,8	12°	301,5	10°	296,6	13°	285,0	7°	278,8	7°	316,0	1°	317,6	3°
14.	J. Trulli	289,9	11°	280,0	4°	299,0	18°	295,3	15°	281,9	19°	274,7	16°	314,2	3°	307,3	17°
15.	J. Button	288,9	13°	278,2	6°	302,7	6°	299,4	14°	284,1	9°	277,2	10°	313,4	5°	308,7	13°
16.	E. Irvine	289,7	12°	274,9	10°	299,6	17°	297,8	9°	283,9	10°	276,2	13°	309,6	17°	308,1	14°
17.	P. de la Rosa	291,9	7°	256,8	18°	299,9	15°	293,0	17°	282,7	17°	272,5	19°	307,8	19°	310,1	11°
18.	H.-H. Frentzen	286,7	19°	271,6	13°	300,5	12°	300,6	2°	284,6	8°	280,0	4°	311,9	11°	316,6	4°
19.	E. Bernoldi	287,7	16°	271,0	16°	297,9	16°	295,0	16°	283,6	11°	275,5	15°	312,2	12°	309,6	12°
22.	A. Yoong	277,8	21°			294,5	22°			276,8	22°			302,6	22°		
23.	M. Webber	274,2	22°			296,0	21°			280,0	21°			305,3	21°		
24.	M. Salo	291,8	8°	280,3	3°	300,0	14°	298,1	6°	283,6	12°	278,0	9°	309,8	16°	313,2	7°
25.	A. McNish	287,3	18°	265,8	16°	299,0	19°	298,0	7°	283,1	15°	278,4	8°	310,8	15°	313,9	6°

Race

Classification & Retirements

Pos.	Driver	Team	Lap	Time	Average
1.	M. Schumacher	Ferrari	65	1:30:29.981	203,753 km/h
2.	J.P. Montoya	Williams BMW	65	35.630	202,425 km/h
3.	D. Coulthard	McLaren Mercedes	65	42.623	202,166 km/h
4.	N. Heidfeld	Sauber Petronas	65	1:06.697	201,281 km/h
5.	F. Massa	Sauber Petronas	65	1:18.973	200,832 km/h
6.	H-H. Frentzen	Arrows Cosworth	65	1:20.430	200,779 km/h
7.	J. Villeneuve	BAR Honda	64	1 lap	200,454 km/h
8.	A. McNish	Toyota	64	1 lap	199,474 km/h
9.	M. Salo	Toyota	64	1 lap	197,934 km/h
10.	J. Trulli	Renault	63	2 laps	199,601 km/h	Broken engine
11.	R. Schumacher	Williams BMW	63	2 laps	197,916 km/h	Broken engine
12.	J. Button	Renault	60	5 laps	199,346 km/h	Hydraulic problems

Driver	Team	Lap	Reason
O. Panis	BAR Honda	44	Broken exhaust pipe
E. Irvine	Jaguar	42	Hydraulic problem
E. Bernoldi	Arrows Cosworth	41	Hydraulic fluid leak
T. Sato	Jordan Honda	11	Off
G. Fisichella	Jordan Honda	6	Drop in the hydraulic pressure affecting the gear box
K. Räikkönen	McLaren Mercedes	5	Broken rear wing mast
P. de la Rosa	Jaguar	3	Off
R. Barrichello	Ferrari	1	Electrical problem affecting the gear selection (parade lap)

Fastest lap

	Driver	Time	Lap	Average
1.	M. Schumacher	1'20"355	49	211,909 km/h
2.	J.P. Montoya	1'21"740	47	208,319 km/h
3.	D. Coulthard	1'21"931	45	207,833 km/h
4.	J. Trulli	1'22"155	25	207,266 km/h
5.	F. Massa	1'22"186	28	207,188 km/h
6.	H-H. Frentzen	1'22"320	43	206,851 km/h
7.	M. Salo	1'22"524	44	206,339 km/h
8.	J. Button	1'22"607	26	206,132 km/h
9.	R. Schumacher	1'22"697	27	205,908 km/h
10.	J. Villeneuve	1'22"827	47	205,585 km/h
11.	N. Heidfeld	1'22"860	25	205,503 km/h
12.	O. Panis	1'22"872	26	205,473 km/h
13.	A. McNish	1'23"160	46	204,761 km/h
14.	E. Bernoldi	1'23"507	16	203,911 km/h
15.	K. Räikkönen	1'23"524	3	203,869 km/h
16.	E. Irvine	1'24"187	38	202,264 km/h
17.	T. Sato	1'24"198	10	202,237 km/h
18.	G. Fisichella	1'24"493	3	201,531 km/h
19.	P. de la Rosa	1'25"944	19	198,129 km/h

Pit stops

Driver	Time	Lap	Stop n°		Driver	Time	Lap	Stop n°
1. M. Salo	33"495	3	1		17. D. Coulthard	31"074	29	1
2. J. Trulli	30"828	23	1		18. R. Schumacher	50"504	29	2
3. J. Villeneuve	31"926	23	1		19. E. Bernoldi	1'11"372	38	2
4. A. McNish	32"957	23	1		20. R. Schumacher	33"460	40	3
5. R. Schumacher	30"461	24	1		21. J. Button	31"405	42	2
6. E. Bernoldi	32"060	24	1		22. N. Heidfeld	30"613	42	2
7. J. Button	30"252	24	1		23. J. Trulli	30"853	43	2
8. O. Panis	31"119	24	1		24. O. Panis	33"738	43	2
9. E. Bernoldi	32"060	24	1		25. F. Massa	30"894	44	2
10. M. Salo	31"302	24	2		26. H-H. Frentzen	32"155	44	2
11. J.P. Montoya	32"519	25	1		27. A. McNish	32"936	44	2
12. M. Schumacher	32"434	26	1		28. J.P. Montoya	37"001	45	2
13. F. Massa	31"016	26	1		29. J. Villeneuve	31"229	45	2
14. H-H. Frentzen	31"756	26	1		30. D. Coulthard	29"584	46	2
15. E. Irvine	30"759	26	1		31. M. Salo	31"718	45	3
16. N. Heidfeld	30"496	27	1		32. M. Schumacher	31"357	47	2

Race leaders

Driver	Laps in the lead	Nber of Laps	Kilometers	Driver	Nber of Laps	Kilometers
M. Schumacher	1 > 65	65	307,327 km	M. Schumacher	65	307,327 km

Lap chart

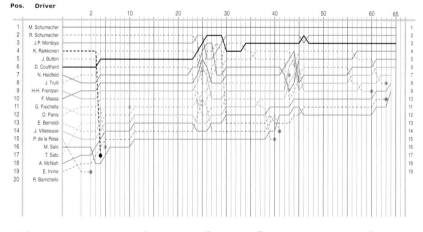

Gaps on the leader board

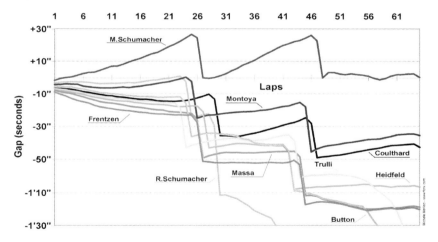

Championship after five rounds

Drivers

Constructors

The circuit

Name :	Circuit de Catalunya, Barcelone
Date :	April 28, 2002
Length :	4730 meters
Distance :	65 laps, 307,327 km
Temperature :	cloudy but warm, 20°c
Track temperature :	22°c

All results : © 2002 Fédération Internationale de l'Automobile, 2, Ch. Blandonnet, 1215 Geneva 15, Switzerland

BRIDGESTONE

Best result for a driver running Bridgestone Tyres :

Michael Schumacher, Ferrari, winner

SAINT RUBENS HANDS MICHAEL THE WIN. SCANDAL ENSUES

All brotherly love on the podium, the two Ferrari boys have no clue about the scandal they have just triggered. As the two men approached the finish line, Barrichello had just handed a win he truly deserved to Michael Schumacher. He was only obeying orders.

As a gesture of thanks, Michael Schumacher, the official winner, let him stand on the top step of the podium.

It was not enough to undo the damage caused. The public greeted them with boos and catcalls, but this was just a foretaste of the storm about to erupt in the media. The Ferrari management acted in accordance with its own logic, but it made it for an even speedier end to a championship, the outcome of which was already beyond doubt. Ferrari never really recovered from this scandal and 2002 could be divided into *"before"* and *"after"* Zeltweg.

"Rubinho" grows wings

> The magnificent setting of the A1-Ring, near Zeltweg, in the heart of Austria. With mountains in the background and wild flowers in the foreground, the Styrian circuit could have been a haven of peace in the middle of the season. It turned out to be nothing of the sort.

Against all expectation and contrary to the forecasts, the weather was absolutely superb in Styria for the Austrian Grand Prix qualifying session.

Despite the perfect conditions, plenty of cars flew off the track and generally slid around the place, throwing sand over the track. Add traffic problems to this scenario and qualifying turned into something of a game of roulette. It was Rubens Barrichello who put his money on the **right** number, despite going off the track twice. After four pole positions set in wet or changeable conditions, this was the Brazilian's first ever "*conventional*" pole. "*I was a bit lucky*", he admitted later that day. "*I had to change line a lot to avoid patches of oil and cars on the track, but I was always out on the circuit at the right time.*"

In the other Ferrari, Michael Schumacher was "*only*" third; his worst grid position of the year. "*I am not really sure what happened, because I was slower this afternoon than in this morning's free practice, which is strange. In the end, I had to take the spare. We will have to check out the car to find out why.*"

Ralf Schumacher and his Williams wedged himself between the two Ferraris, qualifying on the front row, a bit surprised to find himself there.

Barrichello sticks with Ferrari until the end of 2004

> Rubens Barrichello was really the man of the weekend in Zeltweg: with a renewed Ferrari contract in his pocket, he took pole position on Saturday, his second of the season after Australia

The press release could not have been shorter. "*Ferrari announces that it has extended its agreement with the driver Rubens Barrichello to cover the 2003 and 2004 seasons.*"

Short and surprising, given that all sorts of rumours about the Brazilian driver were doing the rounds since the start of the season. There were suggestions he might be replaced next year at the Scuderia, by Juan Pablo Montoya, Felipe Massa or Jenson Button.

Finally, no doubt under some pressure from Michael Schumacher, who likes the fact his team-mate does not make waves, Rubens Barrichello stayed put.

2004 will really represent the end of the world for the Reds: Jean Todt, Ross Brawn, Rory Byrne, Michael Schumacher and now Rubens Barrichello, Ferrari's key people, all held contracts due to expire at the end of 2004.

Did this mean "*Rubinho*" was in with a chance of being number one driver for the Scuderia in 2005? "*I am not prepared to look that far ahead*", commented the Brazilian in Zeltweg. "*I do my best, that's all. I think I am making progress, but on the other hand, I can't imagine Michael easing off and retiring. In any case, I can tell you he is certainly*

not getting any slower! Extending my contract was not a problem and I think I am as devoted to Ferrari as Ferrari is to me. We are one big family."

When he was a Ferrari driver, Eddie Irvine once said that being Michael Schumacher's team-mate was like waking up every morning and being hit on the head with a cricket bat, so hard was it to match his performance.

Nevertheless, Rubens Barrichello continues to dream his dream: "*I think I can become world champion with Ferrari*", he said, no trace of a smile on his lips. "*It's a dream, but you have to have one to achieve it.*" There's honesty for you.

Starting grid

Pos	Driver	Time	No
	M. WEBBER	1:11.388	21
	P. DE LA ROSA	1:10.533	19
	J. VILLENEUVE	1:10.051	17
	G. FISICHELLA	1:09.901	15
	J. BUTTON	1:09.780	13
	H-H. FRENTZEN	1:09.671	11
	O. PANIS	1:09.561	9
	F. MASSA	1:09.228	7
	N. HEIDFELD	1:09.129	5
	M. SCHUMACHER	1:08.704	3
	R. BARRICHELLO	1:08.082 (228,747 km/h)	1
	A. YOONG	1:12.336	22
	E. IRVINE	1:10.741	20
	T. SATO	1:10.058	18
	J. TRULLI	1:09.980	16
	A. McNISH	1:09.818	14
	E. BERNOLDI	1:09.723	12
	M. SALO	1:09.661	10
	D. COULTHARD	1:09.335	8
	K. RÄIKKÖNEN	1:09.154	6
	J.P. MONTOYA	1:09.118	4
	R. SCHUMACHER	1:08.364	2

A crazy Grand Prix

With hindsight, the Austrian Grand Prix was the most memorable race of the year. Not only did its outcome created a huge debate, but there was also a terrible accident which silenced the paddock.

On lap 28, Nick Heidfeld's Sauber was flying down the grass completely out of control and when it rejoined the track, it T-boned the side of Takuma Sato's Jordan-Honda at full speed. The two cars were completely destroyed, but the German climbed out of the Sauber uninjured.

However, trapped in the cockpit, the Japanese driver had to be released by the marshals and was taken to the circuit medical centre. He was then helicoptered to the University Hospital in Graz, where he spent the night under observation. Given the force of the impact, it was something of a miracle that no bones were broken.

Out in front, Rubens Barrichello handed the race to Michael Schumacher in sight of the flag. The entire paddock was up in arms, claiming Ferrari had brought the sport into disrepute.

<
Rubens Barrichello had finished second, but Michael Schumacher pushed him onto the top step of the podium. It was this breach of FIA protocol which saw him censured by the authorities in June.

(below)
A somewhat chaotic first corner, with several cars flying off into the sand.

(bottom)
There was plenty of action down the order, with Toyota, Minardi and Arrows all fighting for the minor placings.
V

Race summary

> **Start (1)**
No problems for the two Ferraris

> During the first third of the race, the Ferraris

run away from the field at a rate of two seconds per lap **(2)**

> After the first corner collision, Jacques

Villeneuve stages a remarkable climb through the field **(3)**

> **Lap 23 (4)**
In 13th place, Olivier

Panis spins like a top because of a transmission problem. Race Control brings out the Safety Car. The Ferraris refuel.

> The race restarts and Heidfeld and Sato collide. Another Safety Car period.

> The final part of the

race sees several retirements including Mark Webber **(5)**

> At the finish, the two Williams follow the

Ferraris home. Ralf Schumacher has gone blonde **(7)** Giancarlo Fisichella scores two points **(6)**

Miracle on lap 28

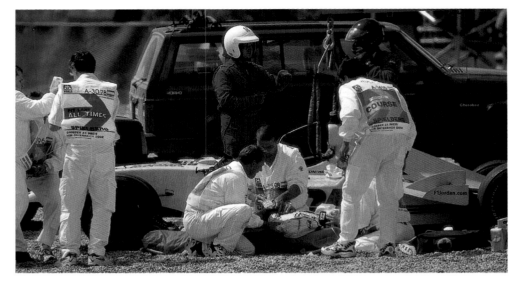

The Japanese reckon he is the best driver to emerge from the Land of the Rising Sun. But so far, Takuma Sato had hardly set the world on fire for his first Formula 1 season. In five grands prix, he accumulated a string of accidents and off-track excursions, as a result of over exuberance. In Malaysia, he had even managed to knock out his own team-mate.

However, in Austria, he was absolutely blameless. On lap 28, the Safety Car had just pulled in, having neutralised the race for four laps (see below.)

Out in front, Rubens Barrichello charged off into the lead ahead of the two Schumacher brothers. Juan Pablo Montoya was trying to stick with them, but he was held up by Takuma Sato, who was one lap down.

That was when it happened. At the Remus corner, Nick Heidfeld lost control of his Sauber, crossed the grass at around 280 km/h before slamming into the side of the Japanese driver's Jordan. The impact was terrible, like an explosion. The rear end of the Sauber was in bits and the side of the Jordan cockpit was punched in, level with the driver's hips. Several bits of the Sauber were embedded in the yellow car's tub. The two wrecks came to rest in the gravel trap and while Nick Heidfeld climbed unaided from his car, it took the rescue teams a long time to get Takuma Sato out of the car, as his legs were apparently trapped by bits of the Sauber.

The driver was conscious throughout the rescue. Back in the medical centre, F1's chief medical man, Sid Watkins, discovered that Sato was uninjured apart from some bruising on his right thigh. "*I was really worried about the accident until Sid told me it was alright and there was nothing broken*", said Eddie Jordan, boss of the team which bears his name. Once helicoptered to

the University Hospital in Graz, the doctors decided to keep Sato in overnight for observation. "*They said it was a real miracle*", revealed the driver's manager, Andrew Gilbert-Scott, once he was back at the circuit. "*They just want to keep him in, in case there are any secondary side effects from such a big impact. But the side protection structure did its job really well.*"

Heidfeld: cold brakes

Nick Heidfelt had been holding a solid fifth place, until cold brakes from following the Safety Car saw him lose control and spin like a top on the way down to the Remus corner. "*I was running side by side with David Coulthard on the straight, when we saw Yoong lock up his brakes in front of us*", he explained. "*I braked a bit too hard, given that the carbon discs were still cold. The car went sideways and the next thing I know, I'm sliding backwards on the grass and after that I don't know anything.*"

The German walked away from the shunt with a slight limp, but there were no real injuries.

Montoya misses by a whisker

Juan Pablo Montoya had a front row seat for the Nick Heidfeld-Takuma Sato accident, as he was trying to overtake the Jordan moments before it was hit by the Sauber. "*I was really lucky*", admitted the Colombian. "*If I'd been in front, I would have been hit. But my car was still in one piece. Actually, I saw the Sauber coming past me on the right, going like a rocket. I couldn't tell you if it was pointing forwards or backwards. It was going much too quickly. I only understood what happened a bit later, when I saw it on the giant TV screens around the track.*"

Panis in flames

In a way, it was Olivier Panis who was the unwitting cause of the crash. The engine in his BAR had seized at the start of lap 23, forcing the Frenchman to abandon his car in the middle of the track. "*I felt something strange on the car on lap 3 and then the engine just locked up on the 23rd lap. I had to leave it where it was.*"

That was when the race director called out the Safety Car, so that the marshals could tow away the BAR. It was those four slow laps behind the SC which caused Nick Heidfeld's brakes to go off the boil, resulting in his tangle with Takuma.

Ferrari in the dock

Whistles and boos greeted Rubens Barrichello and Michael Schumacher as they entered the press room for the traditional post-race press conference. It was an unheard of reception, the like of which had never been witnessed by any of the journalists present!

It was anything but pleasant for Schumacher, who had to face a barrage of questions, some of them phrased very aggressively, about his so-called win. *"Obviously, I am not happy with the way things went"*, admitted the World Champion. *"I take no satisfaction from this win, especially seeing the way the season has gone so far. Last year, we had an identical situation, but the championship fight was definitely much closer. Today, I didn't think it was necessary. This morning, a journalist asked me if there would be any team orders and I answered that I did not think so. And suddenly, the team came on the radio and told me Rubens was going to let me pass him. It was a team decision, which comes from Ferrari, from Mr. Montezemolo and Mr. Todt. You have to understand that the sponsors and the team spend a colossal fortune with just one aim, to win the championship. We have to do that as quickly as possible, because you never know what might happen. If, at the end of the year, we missed out on the title by just a few points, imagine how ridiculous we would look?"* Naturally, the German thanked his team-mate for the gift. *"Rubens drove a fantastic race. He was quicker than me all weekend and his gesture shows how close we are as a team. I thank him for the*

points, but I take no pleasure from the win."* Questioned as to the credibility of his forthcoming championship title, Schumacher had to defend himself tooth and nail. *"Team tactics like this are an integral part of motor racing. We have seen in often before in the past, with McLaren, Williams and Sauber. Some people understand, others do not. In general, I agree with team tactics, but not particularly with today's. I could do nothing about it. After I was told, I even considered disobeying and letting Rubens win. When he slowed down, I did the same, but he braked and I was past him before I could even think about it. It all happened very fast. Now, we are sitting down quietly and there is time to think, but that was not the case when I was in the car. If I could, I would turn back the clock and reverse the result. But it's too late. We have to move on now and turn the page."*

Ferrari had already been heavily criticised in several quarters for its outrageous dominance of the series. The Zeltweg decision did not improve matters.

FIA decided to bring the matter before the World Council on 26th June, taking the view that Ferrari had mocked the spectators over the matter of the podium ceremony. The story would just not go away. Jean Todt might well have regretted not delaying Barrichello during his pit stop, or thought of telling Rubens to drop a second a lap, which would have been more discrete. The damage would have been limited. In the end, honesty did not pay and that's a shame.

Rubens still believes, or is he faking it?

Qualified on pole position, in front at the first corner, Rubens Barrichello led the whole race except for one lap when he made is second pit stop. As he set off for the final lap, he still had a lead of just over a second on his team-mate. It was only as he came out of the final turn that Rubens braked and allowed Michael Schumacher to take a win that should have been the Brazilian's.

In fact, the German insisted that Barrichello stood on the top step of the podium, before seating him in the middle chair for the press conference. He also handed him the winner's trophy. The podium was certainly a strange sight, what with a Brazilian driver in tears, as he listened to the German National Anthem!

Indeed, it was this simple violation of podium procedure which got Ferrari in trouble with the FIA a few weeks later. The sporting power was powerless against anything to do with race strategy, as there is nothing in the regulations which forbids it. Team orders have been part of racing since its earliest days.

Once he got off the podium, Rubens Barrichello set about justifying his actions. *"For me, letting Michael through was not at all difficult"*, he

insisted. *"I was asked to do it. I didn't say anything and I did it. It was a team decision and I will not criticise it. I have just re-signed for a further two years with Ferrari. Everyday I am becoming a better driver and I think my determination means I will definitely win a lot more races in the future."*

Up to that point, *"Rubinho"* had only won one grand prix. *"I will win others, I know it. I only need to be in the right place at the right time and to seize the opportunity. Of course I would have preferred it if the team had sad nothing today, but at least I have the trophy. I will offer it to my wife,*

as it's her birthday. And it's also for my mother as it is "Mother's Day" in Brazil. What a nice lad!"* In fact, as he explained later, he never realised that the incident would cause such ructions. *"It was only when I came into the press office and heard the journalists that I realised this could become a really big deal."*

Juan Pablo understands Ferrari

In the post-race press conference, while the two Ferrari drivers were getting a grilling over their game of pass-the-trophy, sitting alongside them, Juan Pablo Montoya was laughing quietly to himself.

But he did admit that he could quite easily understand the Scuderia's decision. *"It's a shame for Rubens, as I think he really deserved the win, but team tactics are part of this sport and that's*

how they work. Having said that, thinking about it, Michael is not really facing a challenge for the world championship. I am second and Michael already had a twenty point lead over me before this race and the Ferraris are running rings around us, at least one second a lap quicker than us. I cannot see what the Ferrari management is worried about. But, once again, it is a team decision and I respect it. They are allowed to do this sort of thing."*

∧
(top)
The two Ferrari drivers hug one another in parc ferme.

(above)
Podium: at the insistence of Michael Schumacher, it is Rubens Barrichello who accepts the winner's trophy. But he is greeted with the German National Anthem, already prepared by the organisers.

Third, Juan Pablo Montoya's only consolation was finishing ahead of his team-mate.
∨

Hitting the target

The Toyota team was competing this season with a modest goal in mind; that of finishing races. With two points scored at the start of the year, they had more than hit this target, but after picking up points in Brazil, they would not do so again in the course of the championship. At least they were reliable and both red and white cars finished in Zeltweg.

> A dark look from Felipe Massa. In Austria, the Brazilian was forced to retire with suspension problems, while his team-mate had an accident on lap 28. It was a shame for the Saubers, which had qualified in 5th and 7th places, their best showing of the year.

Calm returns to F1

On Friday evening, Bernie Ecclestone convened a meeting of all the team owners to assess the current Formula 1 situation. It's findings were secret, but Minardi boss Paul Stoddart allowed himself to reveal that it was *"extremely positive."* *"We still have problems to solve, but Rome wasn't built in a day"*, he explained.

McLaren boss Ron Dennis added that, for once, the meeting was very calm. *"Usually during these meetings, everyone is shouting and talking at the same time. This time, everyone discussed things quietly which was much appreciated. The world is going through a crisis, with major companies experiencing economic difficulties and the Formula 1 championship is dominated by just one driver. In short, it looks as though F1 is facing serious problems. However, the latest TV viewing figures which Bernie showed us proves the opposite. So everything is fine, which is a minor miracle."*

A miracle which would not last the course of the summer, as the end of season viewing figures would prove.

Weekend gossip

> Peter Sauber came up with his own unique way of supporting the Austro-Swiss bid to host the 2008 Euro soccer championships: on Thursday, his team staged a game of giant table soccer near the circuit. A team made up of drivers Nick Heidfeld, Felipe Massa and team members faced up to a squad made up of managers and players from the Swiss and Austrian teams. There were plenty of laughs and a surprise result as the Sauber team emerged victorious at the end of this strange contest, by 6 goals to 4.

> The Jaguar team was showing no signs of improvement. On Saturday, a demotivated Eddie Irvine qualified 20th. Even team-mate Pedro De La Rosa did better. *"We knew this weekend would be difficult, but not this bad"*, commented Niki Lauda.

> 12 million. That was the pay cut facing Jacques Villeneuve for 2003 if he decided to stay put with the BAR team. In other words he would be on half his 2002 salary. New team boss, David Richards explained that the first priority for his budget was on the technical side. *"It would be stupid to run Michael Schumacher in a Minardi"*, he quipped. *"First you have to make the car work and then employ Michael!"* In Zeltweg, Olivier Panis was once again quicker than Jacques Villeneuve in qualifying, which did little to support the Canadian's cause.

Having picked up a point in Spain a fortnight earlier, the Arrows team had less cause to celebrate in Austria: Heinz-Harald Frentzen finished 11th, while Enrique Bernoldi had suspension problems.
v >

"So you think Honda will fall for it just because you've got a Japanese driver? No kidding?" David Richards and Eddie Jordan in deep discussion. Not difficult to guess they are talking about the future of Honda, the engine supplier which they share and fight over.
v

> It now seemed certain that Honda was preparing to drop Jordan, in order to concentrate its efforts on the BAR team. Long discussions were the order of the day.

Practice

All the time trials

N°	Driver	Car/Engine/Chassis	Practice friday	Pos.	Practice saturday	Pos.	Qualifying	Pos.	Warm-up	Pos.
1.	Michael Schumacher	Ferrari 2002/219	1'10"579	2°	1'08"433	1°	1'08"704	3°	1'10"895	2°
2.	Rubens Barrichello	Ferrari 2002/220	1'10"549	1°	1'09"146	2°	1'08"082	1°	1'10"876	1°
3.	David Coulthard	McLaren-Mercedes MP4/17/03	1'11"416	9°	1'10"044	13°	1'09"335	8°	1'12"123	7°
4.	Kimi Räikkönen	McLaren-Mercedes MP4/17/04	1'10"657	4°	1'09"752	8°	1'09"154	6°	1'12"369	9°
5.	Ralf Schumacher	Williams-BMW FW24/04	1'11"652	12°	1'09"216	3°	1'08"364	2°	1'13"325	14°
6.	Juan Pablo Montoya	Williams-BMW FW24/05	1'10"613	3°	1'09"288	4°	1'09"118	4°	1'13"568	18°
7.	Nick Heidfeld	Sauber-Petronas C21/06	1'12"023	16°	1'09"592	7°	1'09"129	5°	1'11"797	5°
8.	Felipe Massa	Sauber-Petronas C21/03	1'12"013	15°	1'09"526	6°	1'09"228	7°	1'11"512	3°
9.	Giancarlo Fisichella	Jordan-Honda EJ12/5	1'12"193	18°	1'10"470	17°	1'09"901	15°	1'12"907	12°
10.	Takuma Sato	Jordan-Honda EJ12/3	1'11"537	10°	1'11"016	18°	1'10"058	18°	1'13"362	15°
11.	Jacques Villeneuve	BAR-Honda 004/07	1'12"574	21°	1'09"873	10°	1'10"051	17°	1'12"157	8°
12.	Olivier Panis	BAR-Honda 004/04	1'11"382	8°	1'09"780	9°	1'09"561	9°	1'12"595	11°
14.	Jarno Trulli	Renault R202/01	1'12"155	17°	1'10"143	15°	1'09"980	16°	1'13"485	17°
15.	Jenson Button	Renault R202/03	1'11"770	14°	1'10"229	16°	1'09"780	13°	1'13"007	13°
16.	Eddie Irvine	Jaguar R3/05	1'11"608	11°	1'11"308	20°	1'10"741	20°	1'12"452	10°
17.	Pedro de la Rosa	Jaguar R3/04	1'11"336	7°	1'11"057	19°	1'10"533	19°	1'13"390	16°
20.	Heinz-Harald Frentzen	Arrows-Cosworth A23/01	1'11"743	13°	1'09"426	5°	1'09"671	11°	1'11"752	4°
21.	Enrique Bernoldi	Arrows-Cosworth A23/03	1'11"244	6°	1'10"090	14°	1'09"723	12°	1'11"958	6°
22.	Alex Yoong	Minardi-Asiatech PS02/03	1'12"564	20°	1'12"334	22°	1'12"336	22°	1'15"221	22°
23.	Mark Webber	Minardi-Asiatech PS02/04	1'13"219	22°	1'11"991	21°	1'11"388	21°	1'13"684	19°
24.	Mika Salo	Toyota TF102/04	1'12"375	19°	1'10"004	12°	1'09"661	10°	1'13"720	20°
25.	Allan McNish	Toyota TF102/02	1'11"140	5°	1'09"972	11°	1'09"818	14°	1'13"728	21°

Maximum speeds

N°	Driver	P1 Qualifs	Pos.	P1 Race	Pos.	P2 Qualifs	Pos.	P2 Race	Pos.	Finish Qualifs	Pos.	Finish Race	Pos.	Trap Qualifs	Pos.	Trap Race	Pos.
1.	M. Schumacher	310,7	3°	314,8	1°	213,9	4°	213,4	1°	277,7	6°	279,9	2°	307,5	3°	310,8	1°
2.	R. Barrichello	313,4	1°	312,7	2°	215,8	1°	209,7	2°	280,9	2°	279,6	3°	309,2	1°	308,6	2°
3.	D. Coulthard	304,8	16°	303,5	13°	209,8	15°	207,2	3°	275,5	10°	275,4	7°	300,4	21°	303,7	8°
4.	K. Räikkönen	304,8	15°	307,3	7°	212,7	9°	188,2	20°	274,9	13°	267,5	19°	301,0	19°	295,2	18°
5.	R. Schumacher	310,8	2°	307,8	5°	214,5	3°	205,9	6°	281,1	1°	280,3	1°	307,6	2°	307,9	3°
6.	J.P. Montoya	308,9	5°	307,3	8°	209,7	16°	207,1	4°	280,9	3°	278,9	4°	306,5	6°	306,7	4°
7.	N. Heidfeld	307,6	8°	302,4	17°	212,5	10°	196,6	16°	275,3	11°	269,1	15°	307,0	5°	298,7	14°
8.	F. Massa	309,3	4°	305,4	11°	212,0	11°	190,1	19°	276,2	9°	268,3	17°	306,1	7°	296,3	17°
9.	G. Fisichella	303,2	22°	302,4	18°	211,3	13°	204,0	9°	272,5	19°	270,7	13°	302,1	17°	298,6	15°
10.	T. Sato	303,7	20°	299,0	21°	208,3	19°	195,7	17°	274,0	16°	264,7	21°	305,1	8°	293,0	19°
11.	J. Villeneuve	304,9	14°	309,6	4°	212,8	8°	206,1	5°	271,9	20°	274,5	8°	303,6	12°	305,0	6°
12.	O. Panis	305,4	13°	299,5	20°	210,6	14°	198,6	14°	274,1	15°	267,3	20°	303,2	13°	292,9	20°
14.	J. Trulli	305,6	11°	305,6	10°	211,3	12°	200,9	11°	273,1	17°	271,3	12°	302,0	18°	301,9	10°
15.	J. Button	306,9	9°	306,4	9°	215,3	2°	205,5	7°	274,9	14°	274,5	9°	303,2	14°	304,8	7°
16.	E. Irvine	304,4	17°	306,6	12°	206,7	19°	196,9	15°	272,9	18°	271,6	11°	302,6	16°	299,7	13°
17.	P. de la Rosa	304,0	19°	137,1	22°	202,5	22°			275,2	12°			302,7	15°	51,0	22°
18.	H-H. Frentzen	308,7	6°	310,7	3°	213,0	7°	198,1	13°	278,9	4°	275,8	6°	303,9	10°	305,3	5°
19.	E. Bernoldi	307,9	7°	302,0	19°	213,7	5°	180,0	21°	278,7	5°	268,3	16°	307,2	4°	287,8	21°
22.	A. Yoong	303,4	21°	303,3	14°	205,8	20°	193,8	18°	270,8	21°	268,2	18°	300,6	20°	297,8	16°
23.	M. Webber	304,1	18°	302,6	16°	205,0	21°	200,7	12°	270,6	22°	270,0	14°	300,0	22°	300,5	11°
24.	M. Salo	305,5	12°	302,8	15°	213,2	6°	203,5	10°	276,9	7°	273,5	10°	303,7	11°	300,0	12°
25.	A. McNish	306,8	10°	307,7	6°	208,5	17°	205,0	8°	276,6	8°	276,3	5°	304,9	9°	303,0	7°

Race

Classification & Retirements

Pos.	Driver	Team	Lap	Time	Average
1.	M. Schumacher	Ferrari	71	1:33:51.562	196,344 km/h
2.	R. Barrichello	Ferrari	71	0.182	196,338 km/h
3.	J.P. Montoya	Williams BMW	71	17.730	195,728 km/h
4.	R. Schumacher	Williams BMW	71	18.448	195,703 km/h
5.	G. Fisichella	Jordan Honda	71	49.965	194,617 km/h
6.	D. Coulthard	McLaren Mercedes	71	50.672	194,593 km/h
7.	J. Button	Renault	71	51.229	194,574 km/h
8.	M. Salo	Toyota	71	1:09.425	193,953 km/h
9.	A. McNish	Toyota	71	1:09.718	193,943 km/h
10.	J. Villeneuve	BAR Honda	70	1 lap	194,244 km/h	Broken engine
11.	H-H. Frentzen	Arrows Cosworth	69	2 laps	190,415 km/h
12.	M. Webber	Minardi Asiatech	69	2 laps	189,704 km/h

Driver	Team		Reason
J. Trulli	Renault	45	Drop of fuel pressure
A. Yoong	Minardi Asiatech	43	Engine trouble
E. Irvine	Jaguar	39	Hydraulic problem
N. Heidfeld	Sauber Petronas	28	Spin and violently hits Sato
T. Sato	Jordan Honda	27	Hit by Heidfeld
O. Panis	BAR Honda	23	Exploded engine, spin
F. Massa	Sauber Petronas	8	Rear left suspension problem
K. Räikkönen	McLaren Mercedes	6	Loss of engine power
E. Bernoldi	Arrows Cosworth	3	Broken suspension pull-rod after a hit with Frentzen
P. de la Rosa	Jaguar	1	Accelerator problem

Fastest laps

	Driver	Time	Lap	Average
1.	M. Schumacher	1'09"298	68	224,733 km/h
2.	R. Barrichello	1'09"320	57	224,662 km/h
3.	J.P. Montoya	1'09"853	70	222,948 km/h
4.	R. Schumacher	1'09"862	66	222,919 km/h
5.	J. Villeneuve	1'10"823	52	219,894 km/h
6.	H-H. Frentzen	1'11"201	67	218,727 km/h
7.	J. Button	1'11"209	68	218,702 km/h
8.	D. Coulthard	1'11"223	69	218,659 km/h
9.	G. Fisichella	1'11"284	66	218,472 km/h
10.	A. McNish	1'11"456	67	217,946 km/h
11.	M. Salo	1'11"591	64	217,535 km/h
12.	M. Webber	1'11"819	67	216,845 km/h
13.	N. Heidfeld	1'12"180	20	215,760 km/h
14.	O. Panis	1'12"594	22	214,530 km/h
15.	E. Irvine	1'12"602	22	214,506 km/h
16.	J. Trulli	1'12"626	40	214,435 km/h
17.	T. Sato	1'13"119	20	212,989 km/h
18.	K. Räikkönen	1'14"028	5	210,374 km/h
19.	F. Massa	1'14"052	14	210,306 km/h
20.	A. Yoong	1'14"441	22	209,207 km/h
21.	E. Bernoldi	1'21"891	2	190,174 km/h

Pit stops

Driver	Time	Lap	Stop n°	Driver	Time	Lap	Stop n°
J. Villeneuve	29"458	23	1	J. Button	29"750	30	1
R. Barrichello	31"309	24	1	M. Salo	34"164	32	1
M. Schumacher	43"141	24	1	E. Irvine	27"230	32	2
T. Sato	32"265	23	1	H-H. Frentzen	33"313	32	1
D. Coulthard	28"628	28	1	A. McNish	46"962	33	1
G. Fisichella	30"635	28	1	M. Webber	18"730	45	2
A. Yoong	36"064	28	1	R. Schumacher	29"036	47	1
J. Trulli	30"531	29	1	J.P. Montoya	27"132	51	1
J. Villeneuve	22"289	29	2	J.P. Montoya	28"669	53	3
E. Irvine	29"260	29	1	R. Barrichello	26"782	61	2
M. Webber	35"709	29	1	M. Schumacher	26"492	62	2

Race leaders

Driver	Laps in the lead	Nber of laps	Kilometers	Driver	Nber of Laps	Kilometers
R. Barrichello	1 > 61	61	263,886 km	R. Barrichello	69	298,494 km
M. Schumacher	62	1	4,326 km	M. Schumacher	2	8,652 km
R. Barrichello	63 > 70	8	34,608 km			
M. Schumacher	71	1	4,326 km			

Lap chart

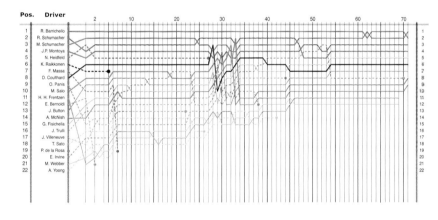

Gaps on the leader board

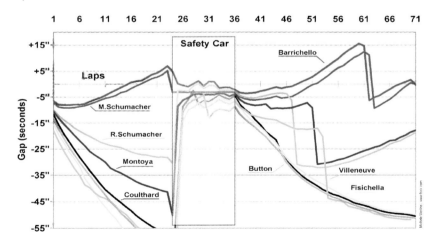

Championship after six rounds

Drivers

Constructors

The circuit

Name :	A1 Ring, Spielberg
Date :	May 12, 2002
Length :	4326 meters
Distance :	71 laps, 307,146 km
Temperature :	cloudy with sunny breaks, warm, 21°c
Track temperature :	29°c

BRIDGESTONE

Best result for a driver running Bridgestone tyres:

Michael Schumacher, Ferrari, winner

ONLY ONE, BUT THE BEST ONE

David Coulthard and the McLaren team recorded only one win in 2002, but it was the best one, given that victory came their way in the sumptuous setting of Monaco. It's the race every driver and team wants to win.

At the time, no one knew this would the last time this season that any other car than a Ferrari would take the top spot.

For David Coulthard, this Monegasque victory would go some way to wiping out the memory of last year's race, when he ignominiously spent most of the grand prix stuck behind an Arrows. Michael Schumacher came home second, ahead of Ralf Schumacher. Once again, Juan Pablo Montoya started from pole, before seeing hopes of glory vanish in a puff of smoke from his engine.

^
The unique setting of the Monaco Grand Prix. Racing F1 cars here verges on a mad anachronism, but there is a touch of genius involved.

Montoya-Coulthard: A first for the front row at Monaco

Michelin tyres were on the pace right from Thursday's practice, but the French marque's competitions boss, Pierre Dupasquier was not attaching any significance to it. "*It's just an illusion*", he suggested. "*The Ferraris are running heavy to give the impression they are not competitive, to tempt fans to come to the race. Wait and see. In qualifying, they will be at the front!*"
Wrong! Even if the Michelin Man refused to believe it, his tyres were definitely the ones to beat during the qualifying hour: eight of the top ten on the grid were using the Clermont-Ferrand product, with the two Ferraris the only interlopers. Michael Schumacher was third and Rubens Barrichello

fifth. Michelin had brought a tyre specifically developed for Monaco and it was this "*B*" compound which helped Montoya trounce the opposition. "*We studied the unique track surface here in Monaco, which includes different types of tarmac*", explained Pascal Vasselon, in charge of Michelin's Formula 1 programme.
"*It's true, the tyres are fantastic*", confirmed Montoya. "*The whole car is working brilliantly. We modified it a lot during practice and every time we moved forward in the right direction.*"
Even the McLaren men recognised the superiority of the Michelins, although they had accused these very same tyres of partly contributing to their lack of pace so far this year. It was therefore the first

time this season that there had not been a Ferrari on the front row. "*It proves our car is not perfect and there is still work to do*", said a clipped Jean Todt, the Scuderia's Sporting Director.
For his part, Michael Schumacher did not seem too bothered, even though it is virtually impossible to overtake on this tortuous Monegasque track. "*We were not quick enough today. You needed Michelins here. That's the way it goes.*"
Even though he was not starting from the front, the German knew it would be a tough race, with not many cars bothering the timekeepers come the end of it. Patience is the key to success at Monaco.

> On Wednesday, as has become a tradition, a friendly soccer match was organised, pitting the Formula 1 drivers, led by Captain Michael Schumacher, against a group of sports stars from various disciplines, led by Prince Albert. It is always a good humoured affair.

Bernie blames Ferrari

The T-shirt sellers were quick off the mark. On Wednesday, in the packed streets of Monte Carlo, they were selling the latest fashionable joke: a T-shirt bearing the legend, "*Formula One Farce-Ross Brawn, Jean Todt, Michael Schumacher-from hero to zero.*" The end to the Austrian Grand Prix ten days ago was still uppermost in people's thoughts.
For his part, Bernie Ecclestone, the boss of SLEC (the company which owns the commercial rights to Formula 1,) evidently did not appreciate the

contrived end to the race. "*I did not like what I saw*", he declared in Monaco. "*Team orders are only acceptable if the championship is in the balance at the end of the year. I was angry with the way Ferrari handled the situation. They could have come up with something more elegant or more discrete. What happened is not good for Formula 1 and I don't see why our sport should be punished because of the actions of one team. The spectators were tricked. If Ferrari did it again, it would be unacceptable in my view.*"

Starting grid

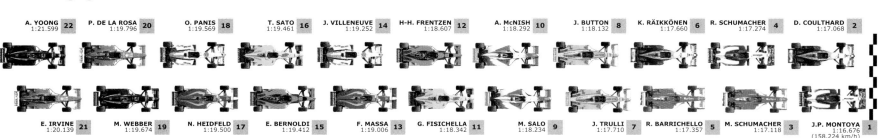

A. YOONG 22 1:21.599	P. DE LA ROSA 20 1:19.796	O. PANIS 18 1:19.569	T. SATO 16 1:19.461	J. VILLENEUVE 14 1:19.252	H-H. FRENTZEN 12 1:18.607	A. McNISH 10 1:18.292	J. BUTTON 8 1:18.132	K. RÄIKKÖNEN 6 1:17.660	R. SCHUMACHER 4 1:17.274	D. COULTHARD 2 1:17.068
E. IRVINE 21 1:20.139	M. WEBBER 19 1:19.674	N. HEIDFELD 17 1:19.500	E. BERNOLDI 15 1:19.412	F. MASSA 13 1:19.006	G. FISICHELLA 11 1:18.342	M. SALO 9 1:18.234	J. TRULLI 7 1:17.710	R. BARRICHELLO 5 1:17.357	M. SCHUMACHER 3 1:17.118	J.P. MONTOYA 1 1:16.676 (158,224 km/h)

David, the Prince of Monaco

A perfect start, a brilliant race, not a single mistake, one brief pit stop on lap 51 and it was in the bag: David Coulthard led the Monaco Grand Prix from start to finish, from the first corner to the last. It was a godsend for a driver whom many said was finished and on the point of getting the boot from the McLaren team. *"It was one of those races where you only realise how hard it's been once you get out of the car. I saw a pool of sweat at the bottom of my seat"*, said the Scotsman. *"It's the sign of a very tough race. I had not realised until then, as I was concentrating so much. I have to say, this win could not have come at a better time."*

A Monte Carlo resident, David Coulthard, as tradition demands, was a guest of the Prince's on Sunday night. Then, it was party time at Jimmyz, the trendy beachside nightclub. Coulthard had not won a race since the previous year's Brazilian Grand Prix. He was therefore over the moon with his Monaco victory. *"Yes, it's incredible, especially as we have had a dreadful start to the season"*, he agreed. *"We soon realised it would be very difficult for us to win a grand prix and that was a serious blow to my morale. Certainly more so than for my team-mate. We also realised that Monaco was one of our only chances of winning and we did all we could to make it happen. It seems to have worked."* Helping him to victory was a new traction control system developed by McLaren. It was only a year ago that the same system had seen him stranded on the grid, after he had qualified on pole. *"We have struggled to make good starts this season and our engineers worked flat out to sort the problem. It worked pretty well. It worked very well in Austria two weeks ago. Looking at my start times compared with Montoya's, we knew we had a good chance of beating him into the first corner. When the red lights went out, I let go of the button, I prayed it would do the job and it did."* Leading from the first corner, the Scotsman managed to eke out a small lead over Juan Pablo Montoya, who was

next in line. Apart from a scare at the halfway mark, victory was in the bag. *"Around lap 30, I felt something, as though the engine was tightening up"*, he continued. *"Then I saw puffs of smoke coming out of the car at Casino Square and I got on the radio to tell the pits. They said everything seemed fine, so I kept going."*
David Coulthard thus took his twelfth career win. *"I think everyone is happy"*, he concluded. *"Today, I proved that the Ferraris are beatable. So far, all the grands prix have been won by a Schumacher and I guess another name makes life more interesting."*

Ron Dennis savours the moment

This win came at just the right time for the McLaren boss. Over the past few weeks, Ron Dennis had strongly criticised the owners of the smaller teams for complaining about the costs of Formula 1, while swanning around in private jets and luxury yachts. *"If I was them, I would sell all that to invest the money in my team and help my cars to win."*
The fault in this argument, according to some, was that this very same Ron Dennis had just sunk 10 million Euros into a new motorhome and 400 million into a new factory, even though his cars were not winning. The entire paddock was having trouble not laughing.
Luckily for him, in Monaco, he was a winner once more. And he was more than a bit proud of the achievement. The man who reckons he is physically in pain whenever he loses, was able to savour Sunday in Monaco. *"We managed to solve a small problem on David's car by using the telemetry,"* he declared with pride after the race. *"This win is an extraordinary result for the team."*

<
The start. Thanks to his new launch control, David Coulthard makes the cleanest getaway, passing Juan Pablo Montoya. The Scotsman would not be seen again. It was a great result for the McLaren-Mercedes engineers.

<
"DC" punches the air as he takes the flag. He had been waiting over a year for this win.

<<
Heinz-Harald Frentzen finished sixth in Monaco, picking up another point for the Arrows team to add to the one he scored in Spain, one month earlier.

Schumi's damage limitation

In second place, Michael Schumacher was not unhappy with his weekend's work in the Principality. He had increased his lead in the championship, which now stood at 33 points and was enough to give him plenty to look forward to. *"I think we proved that if we had started at the front we would have clearly been quickest"*, he commented. *"But that's racing and this is Monaco. I tried to pass David during the pit stops, but I came up behind some traffic and there was nothing I could do. Having said that, I think he deserved to win today. I saw the smoke coming from his car and I continued to push hard. You never know what can happen."*

Race summary

> David Coulthard puts on a masterclass from start to finish, to win the most difficult grand prix of the season **(1)**.

> Qualified third, Michael Schumacher is unable to pass Juan Pablo Montoya **(2)**. Williams hopes of victory expire in a puff of smoke as Juan Pablo

Montoya's engine dies on lap 47 **(3)**.

> Having qualified poorly, Rubens Barrichello finishes outside the

points after a chaotic race, marred by two penalties and a collision with Kimi Räkkönen **(4)**.

> Running just behind his

brother for much of the race, Ralf Schumacher finishes third, to equal Montoya's points in the championship.

> Takuma Sato hits the barrier at the exit to the tunnel **(5)**.

> Jarno Trulli **(6)**, in the Renault, finishes fourth

after spending the latter stages of the race fending off Giancarlo Fisichella, who finishes fifth.

> **Podium (7)**

Go Alex go!

It is not an easy life being a racing driver when, as is the case for Alex Yoong, you owe your seat to a sponsor and the whole paddock knows it. It's an even tougher life when you have to make do with a Minardi and you have to overdrive simply to qualify. In Monaco, he managed it, in his favourite spot, 22nd and last.

paddock

In Monaco, even during the grand prix, thousands of tourists flock to visit the Prince's Palace on top of the Rock.

>∧
Mika Häkkinen did not have to come far to explain to the F1 press how his sabbatical year was going. He lives in Fontvieille, at least 300 metres from the paddock.

Giancarlo Fisichella at speed between the barriers on the Monaco track. After finishing fifth in Austria, the Italian repeated the feat with another fifth place in the Principality.
∨

Juan Pablo out of luck

Juan Pablo is often touted as a future world champion. But before he can turn that hope into reality, he needs to shake off his bad luck. In Monaco, he started from pole, only to retire on lap 47 when his BMW engine expired.
Things had started to go wrong several laps beforehand. Still holding off Michael Schumacher, the Colombian was losing ground

Mika on holiday

Mika Häkkinen turned up as a visitor in the Monaco paddock and the Finn brought wife and child with him. A creature of habit, he hardly left the McLaren motorhome on the Thursday and he was certainly no chattier than in the past. "*I still don't know what my future holds*", he admitted. "*I am still on a sabbatical year and I could always come back to racing next year. I still have some time before I have to make a decision. I don't miss Formula 1 at all. It's even fun to watch the races on television. Yes, I've put on a bit of weight, but I can get back to my "race" weight whenever I want to…*"

to David Coulthard. He then let team-mate Ralf Schumacher past before pulling over in a big cloud of white smoke. "*It is really disappointing to see the day end like this*", he commented once back in the pits. "*It's a shame, as the car was going really well, as it had done all weekend. Yes, maybe I made a bad start, but after that it was just a question of keeping cool and staying with David, which I was doing. I think I could have stayed ahead of Michael to the finish and make up some of the points gap, but then that's racing! I felt the engine gradually lose power and not long after that it broke.*"

A black day for Barrichello

After his moment of glory in Austria, it was not really Barrichello's day in Monaco on Sunday. The Brazilian started from fifth on the grid and had dropped two places by the time he got to the first corner. He was stuck behind Kimi Räikkönen and got impatient, which resulted in him colliding with the Finn on lap 40.
The Stewards did not appreciate his actions, and

Up to that moment, along with Michael Schumacher, Juan Pablo Montoya had been the only driver to score points in every race since the start of the season. Sometimes however, those points only came after a flamboyant fight back through the field. In Australia, Malaysia and Brazil, he could have done considerably better, but for a series of accidents which cost him dear.
The Colombian was now 33 points behind the world champion. He would not take the title this year, but the Colombian still had his whole career ahead of him.

they brought him into the pits for a 10 second penalty. To add to his woes, he speeded in the pit lane, exceeding the 60 km/h limit, as he came in for the first penalty. So in he came a second time. Now down in twelfth spot, Barrichello picked up places one at a time, ending up just outside the points, behind sixth placed Heinz-Harald Frentzen. It was the end of a messy race.

Practice

All the time trials

N°	Driver	Car/Engine/Chassis	Practice friday	Pos.	Practice saturday	Pos.	Qualifying	Pos.	Warm-up	Pos.
1.	Michael Schumacher	Ferrari 2002/219	1'20"404	11°	1'18"471	6°	1'17"118	3°	1'20"972	2°
2.	Rubens Barrichello	Ferrari 2002/220	1'19"945	7°	1'18"309	5°	1'17"357	5°	1'22"076	6°
3.	David Coulthard	McLaren-Mercedes MP4/17/02	1'19"597	3°	1'17"506	2°	1'17"068	2°	1'21"547	3°
4.	Kimi Räikkönen	McLaren-Mercedes MP4/17/03	1'22"904	19°	1'19"988	15°	1'17"660	6°	1'22"052	5°
5.	Ralf Schumacher	Williams-BMW FW24/04	1'19"937	6°	1'17"713	4°	1'17"274	4°	1'22"196	7°
6.	Juan Pablo Montoya	Williams-BMW FW24/02	1'20"264	9°	1'17"665	3°	1'16"676	1°	1'24"309	20°
7.	Nick Heidfeld	Sauber-Petronas C21/02	1'21"638	15°	1'19"185	11°	1'19"500	17°	1'23"929	17°
8.	Felipe Massa	Sauber-Petronas C21/04	1'21"683	16°	1'19"146	10°	1'19"006	13°	1'23"868	16°
9.	Giancarlo Fisichella	Jordan-Honda EJ12/4	1'19"680	4°	1'18"895	8°	1'18"342	11°	1'22"390	9°
10.	Takuma Sato	Jordan-Honda EJ12/3	1'21"868	17°	1'20"853	19°	1'19"461	16°	1'24"169	19°
11.	Jacques Villeneuve	BAR-Honda 004/03	1'21"086	14°	1'20"577	18°	1'19"252	14°	1'23"400	14°
12.	Olivier Panis	BAR-Honda 004/04	1'20"887	12°	1'19"384	12°	1'19"569	18°	1'22"388	8°
14.	Jarno Trulli	Renault R202/02	1'18"915	1°	1'17"429	1°	1'17"710	7°	1'21"952	4°
15.	Jenson Button	Renault R202/03	1'20"375	10°	1'18"693	7°	1'18"132	8°	1'23"227	11°
16.	Eddie Irvine	Jaguar R3/03	1'22"917	20°	1'21"739	22°	1'20"139	21°	1'24"972	21°
17.	Pedro de la Rosa	Jaguar R3/02	1'21"876	18°	1'20"306	16°	1'19"796	20°	1'24"071	18°
20.	Heinz-Harald Frentzen	Arrows-Cosworth A23/01	1'21"005	13°	1'19"133	9°	1'18"607	12°	1'20"875	1°
21.	Enrique Bernoldi	Arrows-Cosworth A23/02	1'23"150	21°	1'19"627	14°	1'19"412	15°	1'23"642	15°
22.	Alex Yoong	Minardi-Asiatech PS02/02	1'26"518	22°	1'21"603	21°	1'21"599	22°	1'25"366	22°
23.	Mark Webber	Minardi-Asiatech PS02/01	1'20"028	8°	1'20"983	20°	1'19"674	19°	1'23"374	13°
24.	Mika Salo	Toyota TF102/04	1'19"815	5°	1'19"430	13°	1'18"234	9°	1'22"842	10°
25.	Allan McNish	Toyota TF102/05	1'19"361	2°	1'20"374	17°	1'18"292	10°	1'23"345	12°

Maximum speeds

N°	Driver	P1 Qualifs	Pos.	P1 Race	Pos.	P2 Qualifs	Pos.	P2 Race	Pos.	Finish Qualifs	Pos.	Finish Race	Pos.	Trap Qualifs	Pos.	Trap Race	Pos.
1.	M. Schumacher	214,6	11°	203,6	11°	199,6	6°	196,9	1°	269,1	2°	267,5	2°	294,2	3°	295,4	1°
2.	R. Barrichello	217,0	4°	209,1	3°	203,3	3°	192,8	7°	267,9	4°	268,9	1°	295,3	2°	294,9	2°
3.	D. Coulthard	212,2	14°	206,5	8°	199,4	7°	187,4	15°	263,1	15°	260,4	16°	289,8	15°	290,5	13°
4.	K. Räikkönen	218,5	3°	206,8	7°	197,4	10°	190,0	10°	260,1	21°	258,8	18°	288,3	18°	288,2	16°
5.	R. Schumacher	217,0	5°	208,6	4°	201,0	4°	194,6	4°	267,9	3°	266,4	4°	292,7	6°	293,7	4°
6.	J.P. Montoya	219,0	2°	208,4	5°	208,0	1°	196,8	2°	269,8	1°	265,0	7°	295,4	1°	293,3	5°
7.	N. Heidfeld	215,1	10°	202,9	13°	191,3	19°	188,8	13°	264,8	8°	261,5	13°	292,6	8°	291,9	8°
8.	F. Massa	207,8	18°	203,3	12°	196,4	13°	189,6	12°	263,0	16°	258,4	19°	290,7	13°	286,5	18°
9.	G. Fisichella	214,5	12°	202,3	17°	199,9	5°	191,1	9°	261,4	20°	262,1	11°	288,0	19°	288,4	15°
10.	T. Sato	212,6	13°	197,0	21°	196,1	14°	186,0	17°	263,4	12°	256,7	22°	289,5	16°	285,1	21°
11.	J. Villeneuve	208,5	16°	197,5	20°	197,5	9°	182,6	18°	262,1	18°	258,1	21°	291,2	12°	285,7	20°
12.	O. Panis	205,4	20°	194,8	22°	197,3	11°	181,4	21°	263,2	14°	260,4	15°	286,0	22°	278,3	22°
14.	J. Trulli	216,3	7°	204,6	10°	199,1	8°	193,1	6°	262,3	17°	261,5	12°	292,1	11°	291,1	10°
15.	J. Button	215,7	8°	200,5	18°	204,3	2°	193,5	5°	263,4	11°	260,6	14°	292,7	7°	288,9	14°
16.	E. Irvine	203,7	21°	205,2	9°	194,4	16°	189,7	11°	264,8	7°	263,8	9°	292,5	9°	292,6	7°
17.	P. de la Rosa	208,0	17°	202,8	15°	194,2	17°	188,4	14°	263,8	9°	264,3	8°	292,2	10°	294,4	3°
18.	H-H. Frentzen	215,3	9°	207,8	6°	196,0	15°	192,2	8°	263,3	13°	265,0	6°	288,6	17°	291,1	11°
19.	E. Bernoldi	210,1	15°	210,5	2°	190,6	20°	186,4	16°	263,6	10°	265,6	5°	290,0	14°	291,4	9°
22.	A. Yoong	197,5	22°	202,5	16°	178,2	22°	181,2	22°	260,0	22°	258,3	20°	286,9	21°	286,0	19°
23.	M. Webber	205,7	19°	202,8	14°	186,9	21°	181,5	20°	261,6	19°	259,5	17°	287,7	20°	287,0	17°
24.	M. Salo	220,1	1°	210,5	1°	192,6	18°	195,3	3°	265,9	5°	266,6	3°	293,1	4°	293,3	6°
25.	A. McNish	216,3	6°	199,8	19°	196,9	12°	182,1	19°	265,6	6°	262,9	10°	293,1	5°	290,6	12°

Race

Classification & Retirements

Pos.	Driver	Team	Lap	Time	Average
1.	D.Coulthard	McLaren Mercedes	78	1:45:39.055	149,280 km/h
2.	M. Schumacher	Ferrari	78	1.050	149,255 km/h
3.	R. Schumacher	Williams BMW	78	1:17.450	147,478 km/h
4.	J. Trulli	Renault	77	1 lap	147,209 km/h
5.	G. Fisichella	Jordan Honda	77	1 lap	147,196 km/h
6.	H-H. Frentzen	Arrows Cosworth	77	1 lap	146,961 km/h
7.	R. Barrichello	Ferrari	77	1 lap	146,951 km/h
8.	N. Heidfeld	Sauber Petronas	76	2 laps	145,199 km/h
9.	E. Irvine	Jaguar	76	2 laps	144,912 km/h
10.	P. de la Rosa	Jaguar	76	2 laps	144,895 km/h
11.	M. Webber	Minardi Asiatech	76	2 laps	144,363 km/h
12.	E. Bernoldi	Arrows Cosworth	76	2 laps	143,671 km/h

Driver	Team		Reason
M. Salo	Toyota	70	Brake problems, throws his F1 in the guard-rail
F. Massa	Sauber Petronas	64	Brake problems, goes straight at St-Devote
O. Panis	BAR Honda	52	Hit by Button
J. Button	Renault	52	Hits Panis
J.P. Montoya	Williams BMW	47	Broken engine
J. Villeneuve	BAR Honda	45	Engine problems
K. Räikkönen	McLaren Mercedes	42	Handling problems after hit with Barrichello
A. Yoong	Minardi Asiatech	30	Off
T. Sato	Jordan Honda	23	Off
A. McNish	Toyota	16	Off

Fastest laps

	Driver	Time	Lap	Average
1.	R. Barrichello	1'18"023	68	155'492 km/h
2.	M. Schumacher	1'18"652	51	154'249 km/h
3.	G. Fisichella	1'19"120	70	153'336 km/h
4.	D. Coulthard	1'19"360	74	152'872 km/h
5.	M. Salo	1'19"479	62	152'644 km/h
6.	R. Schumacher	1'19"489	61	152'624 km/h
7.	H-H. Frentzen	1'19"601	76	152'410 km/h
8.	M. Webber	1'19"968	69	151'710 km/h
9.	E. Bernoldi	1'20"117	73	151'428 km/h
10.	J.P. Montoya	1'20"346	36	150'996 km/h
11.	K. Räikkönen	1'20"426	39	150'846 km/h
12.	J. Trulli	1'20"445	46	150'811 km/h
13.	J. Button	1'20"720	41	150'297 km/h
14.	N. Heidfeld	1'20"927	64	149'912 km/h
15.	P. de la Rosa	1'20"953	62	149'864 km/h
16.	F. Massa	1'21"057	55	149'672 km/h
17.	E. Irvine	1'21"059	63	149'668 km/h
18.	O. Panis	1'21"916	32	148'102 km/h
19.	J. Villeneuve	1'22"037	34	147'884 km/h
20.	T. Sato	1'22"148	18	147'684 km/h
21.	A. McNish	1'22"250	15	147'501 km/h
22.	A. Yoong	1'22"784	25	146'550 km/h

Pit stops

	Driver	Time	Lap	Stop n°
1.	J. Button	18"410	6	1
2.	M. Salo	31"217	21	1
3.	A. Yoong	32"514	26	1
4.	F. Massa	34"606	28	1
5.	M. Webber	36"471	29	1
6.	F. Massa	31"397	32	2
7.	J. Button	28"486	37	2
8.	K. Räikkönen	3'16"687	40	1
9.	R. Barrichello	37"583	40	1
10.	E. Bernoldi	47"296	41	1
11.	R. Barrichello	31"521	42	2
12.	E. Irvine	286"553	42	1
13.	J. Trulli	27"967	43	1
14.	M. Schumacher	28"874	44	1
15.	N. Heidfeld	28"042	44	1
16.	R. Barrichello	18"303	44	3
17.	H-H. Frentzen	28"743	46	1
18.	H-H. Frentzen	28"780	47	2
19.	P. de la Rosa	28"088	48	1
20.	R. Schumacher	28"221	50	1
21.	D. Coulthard	27"481	51	1
22.	G. Fisichella	30"514	52	1
23.	M. Salo	27"920	60	2
24.	E. Bernoldi	18"939	62	2
25.	M. Webber	43"792	63	2
26.	R. Schumacher	26"441	65	2

Race leaders

Driver	Laps in the lead	Nber of Laps	Kilometers
D. Coulthard	1 > 78	78	262,860 km

Driver	Nber of Laps	Kilometers
D. Coulthard	78	262,860 km

Lap chart

Pos. Driver

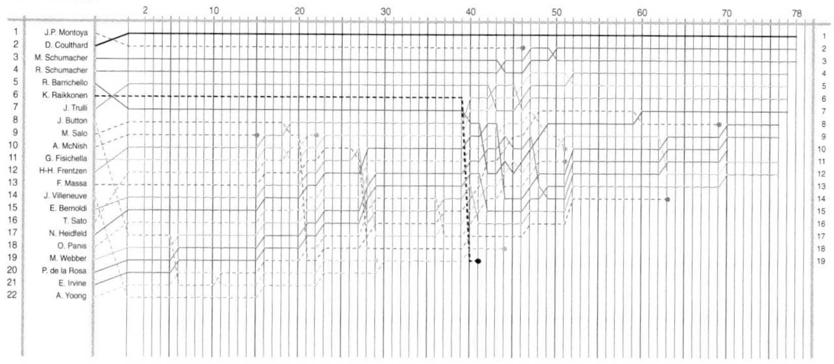

Gaps on the leader board

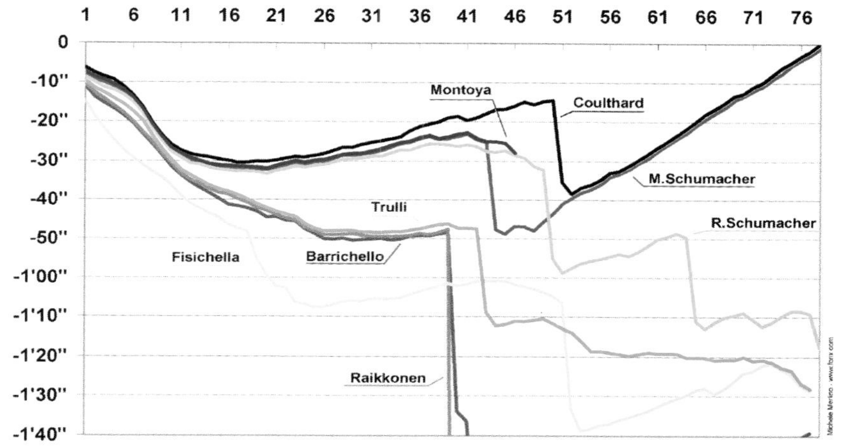

Championship after seven rounds

Drivers

	Driver	Points
1.	M. Schumacher	60
2.	R. Schumacher	27
3.	J.P. Montoya	27
4.	D. Coulthard	20
5.	R. Barrichello	12
6.	J. Button	8
7.	N. Heidfeld	5
8.	K. Räikkönen	4
9.	G. Fisichella	4
10.	E. Irvine	3
11.	J. Trulli	3
12.	F. Massa	3
13.	M. Webber	2
14.	M. Salo	2
15.	H-H. Frentzen	2
16.	J. Villeneuve	0
17.	A. McNish	0
18.	A. Yoong	0
19.	P. de la Rosa	0
20.	T. Sato	0
21.	E. Bernoldi	0
22.	O. Panis	0

Constructors

	Constructor	Points
1.	Scuderia Ferrari Marlboro	72
2.	BMW WilliamsF1 Team	54
3.	West McLaren Mercedes	24
4.	Mild Seven Renault F1 Team	11
5.	Sauber Petronas	8
6.	DHL Jordan Honda	4
7.	Jaguar Racing	3
8.	KL Minardi Asiatech	2
9.	Panasonic Toyota Racing	2
10.	Orange Arrows	2
11.	Lucky Strike BAR Honda	0

The circuit

Name : Monaco, Monte Carlo
Date : May 26, 2002
Length : 3370 meters
Distance : 78 laps, 262,860 km
Temperature : sunny and warm, 24°c
Track température : 30°c

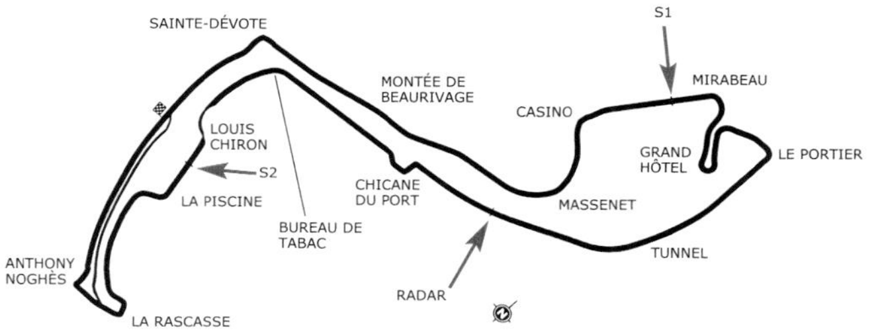

BRIDGESTONE

Best result for a driver running Bridgestone tyres:

Michael Schumacher, Ferrari, 2nd

All results : © 2002 Fédération Internationale de l'Automobile, 2, Ch. Blandonnet, 1215 Geneva 15, Switzerland

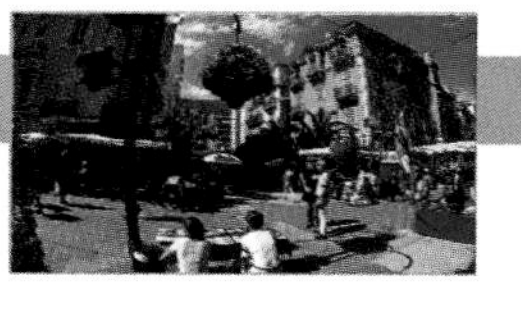

A WILLIAMS FAUX-PAS

Juan Pablo Montoya was making ground on Michael Schumacher hand over fist and maybe he could have overtaken him. However, we will never know, as the BMW engine in his Williams gave up the ghost. Out on his own at the head of the field, Michael Schumacher won as he pleased, without any bother. It was his sixth victory from eight starts...

Another pole position: viva Juan Pablo

(below)
The notorious Crescent Street is more than lively over the grand prix weekend. It is the place to see and be seen.

(right)
Pedro de La Rosa qualified 16th. It had been a difficult first half of the season for the Jaguar man.

∨

Ever since Michelin put an end to Bridgestone's Formula 1 monopoly, the perceived wisdom was that the French tyres did not work too well in cool weather and were at their best in a heatwave. In Montreal, qualifying took place in overcast conditions with temperatures no higher than 19 degrees on the Ile Notre Dame, with a cool breeze blowing. It even began to rain towards the end of the session.

However, during the press conference after qualifying, a local journalist, confused about who was running which tyres, asked Juan Pablo Montoya if he felt that, as usual, this chilly weather had helped his cause. "*I though the cold suited the Bridgestones better*", replied the Colombian with a glint in his eye. "*It's clear that is no longer the case.*" Although the Williams

man went on to admit that the warmer conditions predicted for the race would be more to his liking.
Contrary to the norm, Montoya set his best time in the first half of the session. After a

Circuit modifications

The first corner at the Circuit Gilles Villeneuve has often come in for criticism, as it has been the scene of several accidents at the start of the race. All it took was for one car to go off onto the grass at the outside of the first righthander and a serious accident would ensue.
Paradoxically, it was not this turn which was modified this year, but the hairpin at the back of the track, which had been brought forward by

conservative lap to get a time in the bag, he then set the pole time. "*As qualifying started, we knew there was a risk of rain and I wanted to get out early to be sure of setting a time. I knew there was still room for improvement.*"

80 metres to increase the run-off area. The much criticised pit lane exit had also been completely revised. In the past, drivers got back on track in the braking area for the notorious Turn 1 and those hurtling full pelt down the straight would often be in the slower drivers' blind spot. Now, the pit lane exit had been extended by several hundred metres and drivers got back on track after the Senna corner.

Starting grid

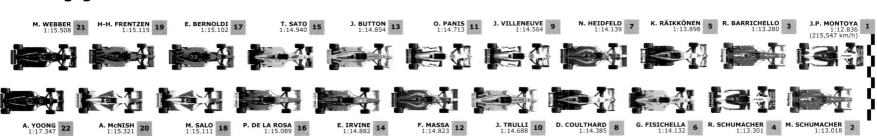

Position	Driver	Time
21	M. WEBBER	1:15.508
19	H-H. FRENTZEN	1:15.115
17	E. BERNOLDI	1:15.102
15	T. SATO	1:14.940
13	J. BUTTON	1:14.854
11	O. PANIS	1:14.713
9	J. VILLENEUVE	1:14.564
7	N. HEIDFELD	1:14.139
5	K. RÄIKKÖNEN	1:13.898
3	R. BARRICHELLO	1:13.280
1	J.P. MONTOYA	1:12.836 (215,547 km/h)
22	A. YOONG	1:17.347
20	A. McNISH	1:15.321
18	M. SALO	1:15.111
16	P. DE LA ROSA	1:15.089
14	E. IRVINE	1:14.882
12	F. MASSA	1:14.823
10	J. TRULLI	1:14.688
8	D. COULTHARD	1:14.385
6	G. FISICHELLA	1:14.132
4	R. SCHUMACHER	1:13.301
2	M. SCHUMACHER	1:13.018

Schumi takes six from eight

Did you say lucky? In Montreal, Michael Schumacher suffered an engine failure... at the end of the warm-up! If his engine had lasted four more laps, it would have blown up during the grand prix! His main rival, Juan Pablo Montoya was not so lucky. Towards the end of the grand prix, as the Colombian was making ground on the German at the rate of over one second per lap, the BMW engine in his Williams went up in a cloud of smoke on lap 56. It was the same scenario as Monaco two weeks earlier.

Luck and bad luck have always been part of motor racing, but when fate favours Michael Schumacher and hobbles his rivals, interest in the championship is the big loser.

In Montreal, Juan Pablo Montoya at least proved that the Williams were capable of posing an occasional threat. Before the start, the Colombian camp was far from confident: his warm-up times had been lamentable and the boffins could not work out why.

In the race, he opted for a two stop strategy, which should have seen him take off into the distance at the start. The tactic did not work. Towards the end of the opening lap, Rubens Barrichello overtook the Williams.

On lap 14, the Safety Car came out so that Jacques Villeneuve's car could be removed to a place of safety, as it had broken down alongside the rowing basin. The Williams team reacted quickly, calling Montoya in for his first refuelling while the race was neutralised. He rejoined in fifth place.

Weighed down by a full fuel load, he was unable to lap as quickly as before and he lost a lot of ground before Michael Schumacher pitted. From then on though, the Colombian began to pick up a second per lap and he got to within 6.1 seconds of the world champion, with victory now a distinct possibility...until his engine blew.

That left Michael Schumacher with a straightforward run to the flag to record the 59th win of his career. "I *was flat out for most of the race, until the final laps*", said the German. "*I have to admit that the arrival of the Safety Car played into my hands. But if Juan Pablo's car had not stopped, I think we would have had a close fight to the finish.*"

Barrichello is angry

There was no quarter given in the battle for second place between David Coulthard and Rubens Barrichello.

As he came up to lap Takuma Sato, the Brazilian pulled alongside the McLaren, while Coulthard also made a move on the Jordan. This meant they were three abreast charging down the main straight at over 300 km/h and both the McLaren and the Ferrari missed the braking point and cut the chicane! "*There is no point talking about it now, it's too late*", snapped the Ferrari man. "*But I think I could have braked later and still made the corner. But when you see someone coming up the outside very quickly, your natural reaction is to come off the brakes. That's what I did and then I went off the road as well!*" In total, the chicane was cut dozens of times during the race.

Rubens Barrichello was definitely in a huff after the race. "*I don't understand why the Safety Car was called out to move Villeneuve's car*", he snapped. "*It was at the side of the track and there was no problem and it was not in a dangerous place. I lost the race at that moment. I was on a two stop strategy and the Safety Car ruined it for me. On top of that, Villeneuve should have thought about where he stopped his car.*"

Michael Schumacher agreed with his team-mate on the subject of the Safety Car. "*We have to think about how the Safety Car is used*", he commented. "*In the circumstances, it is hard to justify its appearance. The situations have to be studied more carefully, but as it stands, I don't think it was the right decision.*"

∧
Michael Schumacher punches the air, having taken an easy win in the Canadian Grand Prix

(below)
All smiles on the podium, especially from second placed David Coulthard.

(left)
The two Williams and Räkkönen's McLaren tussle on the track.
∨

Race summary

> At the start, the cars run in grid order. Juan Pablo Montoya makes it through the first corner safely (**1**).
> Following Villeneuve's

retirement, the Safety Car is called out and ruins Barrichello's race (**2**).
> Something of a Montreal specialist, Fisichella

starts from the third row and scores points for the third consecutive time (**3**).
> Trulli tussles with Ralf Schumacher for sixth

place (**4**).
> To the great disappointment of the crowd, Juan Pablo Montoya retires. After his final pit stop, the

Colombian had staged an exciting climb through the field and had caught up with Schumacher's Ferrari (**5**).

> After the pit stops, Barrichello and Coulthard are engaged in a thrilling duel, which sees both men cut the final chicane (**6**).

> Michael Schumacher steps up to the top of the podium. By mid-season, he already looks unstoppable in the championship (**7**).

^
"*Hi guys!*" Olivier Panis waves at our photographers. Still looking for his first point of the season, the Frenchman finished eighth in Montreal.

>
"*Whoops!*" Heinz-Harald Frentzen slides extravagantly in the Arrows during qualifying.

>
Having started fourth, Ralf Schumacher finished seventh and out of the points: no wonder he has a headache...

>
5th position and two points for Giancarlo Fisichella

Jacques Villeneuve no longer the main attraction

As he has done every year since starting his F1 career, Jacques Villeneuve held a press conference in downtown Montreal on the Tuesday leading up to the Canadian Grand Prix.

This time, it was staged in his own restaurant, "*Newtown*". It was one way of getting people to come to a venue which, rumour had it, was not doing much business during the rest of the year.

Unlike past years, there was not much of a crowd hanging around outside, hoping to catch a glimpse of their hero, nor were there that many journalists inside. In the evening, the former champion's press conference failed to get even the briefest of mentions on the Radio Canada main news bulletin. In the good old days, it would have been the headline story. This lack of interest was primarily down to the BAR team's pathetic lack of results: after seven grands prix, it was the only squad not have scored a single point. Despite his impressive track record, Jacques Villeneuve had managed only two seventh places, at Imola and in Spain, while team-mate Olivier Panis had not yet finished a single race!

Bearing this in mind, the journalists who had bothered to turn up were less than impressed when Villeneuve opened proceedings by reeling off the names of his sponsors, including Remus, a brand of exhaust silencers. The following day, Montreal's biggest daily paper, "*La Presse*", began its report on proceedings with the observation: "*how apposite that a brand of silencers has chosen as its spokesman, a driver who makes less and less noise!*"

Outside, the streets of Montreal seemed as busy as ever for this Grand Prix. Sainte Catherine Street, one of the main shopping and restaurant areas was jam-packed all weekend long. Indeed, the ticket offices were proud to announce that the very last tickets had been sold on the Monday and that, as usual, the Grand Prix was a ticket-only sell-out. They did not point out that in past years, all tickets had been sold much earlier in the year.

The Canadian Grand Prix was in existence long before Jacques Villeneuve and it will no doubt continue long after the man from Montreal has hung up his helmet. Judging by the lack of interest shown in him this year, one could suggest that "*long after*" has already begun.

results

Practice

All the time trials

N°	Driver	Car/Engine/Chassis	Practice friday	Pos.	Practice saturday	Pos.	Qualifying	Pos.	Warm-up	Pos.
1.	Michael Schumacher	Ferrari 2002/221	1'15"788	3°	1'13"395	1°	1'13"018	2°	1'16"780	1°
2.	Rubens Barrichello	Ferrari 2002/222	1'16"440	8°	1'14"243	3°	1'13"280	3°	1'16"837	2°
3.	David Coulthard	McLaren-Mercedes MP4/17/03	1'15"407	1°	1'14"720	6°	1'14"385	8°	1'17"941	4°
4.	Kimi Räikkönen	McLaren-Mercedes MP4/17/06	1'15"946	4°	1'14"354	4°	1'13"898	5°	1'18"657	14°
5.	Ralf Schumacher	Williams-BMW FW24/06	1'16"018	5°	1'14"399	5°	1'13"301	4°	1'17"487	3°
6.	Juan Pablo Montoya	Williams-BMW FW24/05	1'15"543	2°	1'13"646	2°	1'12"836	1°	1'18"304	9°
7.	Nick Heidfeld	Sauber-Petronas C21/06	1'17"250	14°	1'14"791	8°	1'14"139	7°	1'18"666	15°
8.	Felipe Massa	Sauber-Petronas C21/07	1'17"489	16°	1'14"777	7°	1'14"823	12°	1'18"478	10°
9.	Giancarlo Fisichella	Jordan-Honda EJ12/5	1'16"989	12°	1'14"973	10°	1'14"132	6°	1'18"597	13°
10.	Takuma Sato	Jordan-Honda EJ12/4	1'18"143	19°	1'15"791	18°	1'14"940	15°	1'19"430	20°
11.	Jacques Villeneuve	BAR-Honda 004/07	1'16"448	9°	1'14"843	9°	1'14"564	9°	1'19"341	19°
12.	Olivier Panis	BAR-Honda 004/08	1'16"333	7°	1'15"057	12°	1'14"713	11°	1'18"206	8°
14.	Jarno Trulli	Renault R202/05	1'18"465	21°	1'15"344	15°	1'14"688	10°	1'18"028	6°
15.	Jenson Button	Renault R202/06	1'17"473	15°	1'15"426	16°	1'14"854	13°	1'18"959	18°
16.	Eddie Irvine	Jaguar R3/05	1'17"765	17°	1'16"267	21°	1'14"882	14°	1'18"483	11°
17.	Pedro de la Rosa	Jaguar R3/04	1'16"801	11°	1'15"208	13°	1'15"089	16°	1'18"151	7°
20.	Heinz-Harald Frentzen	Arrows-Cosworth A23/04	1'16"793	10°	1'15"018	11°	1'15"115	19°	1'18"494	12°
21.	Enrique Bernoldi	Arrows-Cosworth A23/03	1'17"018	13°	1'15"326	14°	1'15"102	17°	1'18"013	5°
22.	Alex Yoong	Minardi-Asiatech PS02/03	1'19"050	22°	1'17"005	22°	1'17"347	22°	1'20"222	22°
23.	Mark Webber	Minardi-Asiatech PS02/04	1'18"034	18°	1'16"143	20°	1'15"508	21°	1'19"696	21°
24.	Mika Salo	Toyota TF102/07	1'16"259	6°	1'15"584	17°	1'15"111	18°	1'18"746	16°
25.	Allan McNish	Toyota TF102/08	1'18"311	20°	1'15"918	19°	1'15"321	20°	1'18"816	17°

Maximum speeds

N°	Driver	P1 Qualifs	Pos.	P1 Race	Pos.	P2 Qualifs	Pos.	P2 Race	Pos.	Finish Qualifs	Pos.	Finish Race	Pos.	Trap Qualifs	Pos.	Trap Race	Pos.
1.	M. Schumacher	277,4	1°	271,8	1°	304,8	1°	298,0	4°	301,4	1°	300,3	4°	334,3	1°	337,2	2°
2.	R. Barrichello	276,9	2°	271,4	2°	300,6	4°	297,8	5°	299,1	3°	300,1	5°	329,5	2°	337,0	3°
3.	D. Coulthard	272,6	6°	271,2	3°	298,7	6°	298,5	2°	296,6	5°	299,9	6°	322,9	6°	334,2	9°
4.	K. Räikkönen	273,2	5°	268,0	5°	298,1	7°	295,4	8°	295,2	7°	298,5	7°	322,1	9°	333,0	11°
5.	R. Schumacher	275,4	4°	265,9	7°	301,6	3°	298,1	3°	298,9	4°	301,8	1°	325,1	4°	336,7	4°
6.	J.P. Montoya	276,0	3°	268,3	4°	301,7	2°	293,4	13°	300,5	2°	298,1	8°	328,6	3°	334,0	10°
7.	N. Heidfeld	267,9	15°	262,3	12°	294,5	16°	291,7	14°	291,9	17°	295,3	14°	319,7	14°	332,2	13°
8.	F. Massa	268,5	14°	260,4	16°	295,0	14°	290,5	16°	292,7	15°	292,9	16°	322,9	7°	328,8	16°
9.	G. Fisichella	270,6	7°	264,0	8°	298,8	5°	293,7	11°	295,3	6°	295,8	13°	323,8	5°	332,3	12°
10.	T. Sato	270,0	9°	266,6	6°	297,2	10°	294,9	10°	293,8	8°	298,0	9°	322,4	8°	337,5	1°
11.	J. Villeneuve	268,7	13°	253,6	22°	294,5	18°	283,7	22°	292,9	13°	284,5	22°	321,1	12°	319,7	21°
12.	O. Panis	267,5	19°	256,3	21°	296,2	11°	289,4	17°	293,2	10°	292,0	17°	320,8	13°	328,1	17°
14.	J. Trulli	267,6	17°	260,3	17°	297,3	9°	293,5	12°	292,7	14°	297,1	11°	321,1	11°	331,4	14°
15.	J. Button	269,0	12°	263,7	10°	295,4	13°	291,5	15°	293,0	12°	293,7	15°	321,2	10°	331,3	15°
16.	E. Irvine	267,5	18°	258,2	20°	294,5	17°	285,4	21°	292,1	16°	288,8	21°	317,0	18°	318,5	22°
17.	P. de la Rosa	270,0	10°	258,8	18°	293,9	20°	286,4	20°	291,4	18°	290,1	19°	316,2	21°	323,1	19°
18.	H-H. Frentzen	267,9	16°	262,1	14°	294,0	19°	295,0	9°	290,9	19°	295,9	12°	318,3	17°	334,8	7°
19.	E. Bernoldi	269,0	11°	258,7	19°	294,7	15°	295,8	7°	290,6	20°	297,7	10°	316,5	19°	334,2	8°
22.	A. Yoong	262,5	22°	263,2	11°	290,6	22°	289,3	18°	287,6	22°	290,5	18°	315,8	22°	326,1	18°
23.	M. Webber	266,1	21°	262,3	13°	291,8	21°	287,3	19°	287,6	21°	289,5	20°	316,4	20°	322,7	20°
24.	M. Salo	266,8	20°	263,9	9°	295,7	12°	299,0	1°	293,0	11°	300,9	2°	319,0	15°	335,6	6°
25.	A. McNish	270,1	8°	260,9	15°	297,6	8°	296,8	6°	293,5	9°	300,4	3°	318,9	16°	335,8	5°

Race

Classification & Retirements

Pos.	Driver	Team	Lap	Time	Average	
1.	M. Schumacher	Ferrari	70	1:33:36.111	195,682 km/h	
2.	D. Coulthard	McLaren Mercedes	70	1.132	195,642 km/h	
3.	R. Barrichello	Ferrari	70	7.082	195,435 km/h	
4.	K. Räikkönen	McLaren Mercedes	70	37.563	194,381 km/h	
5.	G. Fisichella	Jordan Honda	70	42.812	194,201 km/h	
6.	J. Trulli	Renault	70	48.947	193,991 km/h	
7.	R. Schumacher	Williams BMW	70	51.518	193,903 km/h	
8.	O. Panis	BAR Honda	69	1 lap	192,589 km/h	
9.	F. Massa	Sauber Petronas	69	1 lap	192,579 km/h	
10.	T. Sato	Jordan Honda	69	1 lap	192,316 km/h	
11.	M. Webber	Minardi Asiatech	69	1 lap	191,789 km/h	
12.	N. Heidfeld	Sauber Petronas	69	1 lap	191,541 km/h	
13.	H-H. Frentzen	Arrows Cosworth	69	1 lap	190,251 km/h	
14.	A. Yoong	Minardi Asiatech	68	2 laps	188,963 km/h	
15.	J. Button	Renault	65	5 laps	191,951 km/h	Engine overheat

Driver	Team		Reason
J.P. Montoya	Williams BMW	57	Broken engine
A. McNish	Toyota	46	Spin due to a gearbox problem
E. Irvine	Jaguar	42	Engine overheat
M. Salo	Toyota	42	Brake problem created by a puncture
P. de la Rosa	Jaguar	30	Gearbox problem
E. Bernoldi	Arrows Cosworth	17	Worrying vibrations in the right rear
J. Villeneuve	BAR Honda	9	Drop in oil pressure

Fastest laps

	Driver	Time	Lap	Average
1.	J.P. Montoya	1'15"960	50	206,682 km/h
2.	M. Schumacher	1'15"971	37	206,652 km/h
3.	R. Barrichello	1'16"100	21	206,302 km/h
4.	D. Coulthard	1'16"369	69	205,575 km/h
5.	R. Schumacher	1'16"446	57	205,368 km/h
6.	K. Räikkönen	1'16"553	70	205,081 km/h
7.	G. Fisichella	1'16"658	44	204,800 km/h
8.	F. Massa	1'17"017	38	203,845 km/h
9.	J. Trulli	1'17"128	68	203,552 km/h
10.	O. Panis	1'17"202	38	203,357 km/h
11.	N. Heidfeld	1'17"265	68	203,191 km/h
12.	T. Sato	1'17"336	67	203,005 km/h
13.	M. Salo	1'17"539	28	202,473 km/h
14.	J. Button	1'17"747	33	201,931 km/h
15.	M. Webber	1'17"807	67	201,776 km/h
16.	E. Irvine	1'17"813	38	201,760 km/h
17.	H-H. Frentzen	1'17"892	32	201,556 km/h
18.	A. McNish	1'18"263	38	200,600 km/h
19.	A. Yoong	1'18"466	32	200,081 km/h
20.	P. de la Rosa	1'18"964	28	198,819 km/h
21.	E. Bernoldi	1'19"125	13	198,415 km/h
22.	J. Villeneuve	1'20"084	5	196,039 km/h

Pit stops

	Driver	Time	Lap	Stop n°
1.	P. De la Rosa	1'40"403	1	1
2.	J.P. Montoya	31"811	14	1
3.	T. Sato	28"895	14	1
4.	E. Bernoldi	32"384	15	1
5.	E. Bernoldi	1'23"311	16	2
6.	M. Salo	30"706	25	1
7.	R. Barrichello	31"908	26	1
8.	M. Salo	40"734	26	2
9.	H-H. Frentzen	43"377	30	1
10.	M. Salo	18"347	31	3
11.	J. Button	31"658	36	1
12.	N. Heidfeld	32"640	37	1
13.	A. Yoong	33"834	37	1
14.	M. Schumacher	32"636	38	1
15.	M. Webber	35"774	39	1
16.	F. Massa	31"167	40	1
17.	E. Irvine	44"574	40	1
18.	O. Panis	32"791	41	1
19.	A. McNish	2'04"851	41	1
20.	R. Schumacher	41"760	42	1
21.	J. Trulli	30"617	42	1
22.	R. Schumacher	30"451	44	1
23.	N. Heidfeld	17"770	44	2
24.	K. Räikkönen	28"619	45	1
25.	G. Fisichella	32"886	45	1
26.	A. Yoong	33"368	44	2
27.	T. Sato	32"312	46	2
28.	F. Massa	18"442	48	2
29.	D. Coulthard	30"175	49	1
30.	H-H. Frentzen	31"330	49	2
31.	J.P. Montoya	29"183	51	2
32.	N. Heidfeld	33"052	51	3
33.	R. Barrichello	28"602	54	2

Race leaders

Driver	Laps in the lead	Nber of Laps	Kilometers
R. Barrichello	1 > 25	25	109,025 km
M. Schumacher	26 > 37	12	52,332 km
J.P. Montoya	38 > 50	13	56,693 km
M. Schumacher	51 > 70	20	87,220 km

Driver	Nber of Laps	Kilometers
M. Schumacher	32	139,552 km
R. Barrichello	25	109,025 km
J.P. Montoya	13	56,693 km

Lap chart

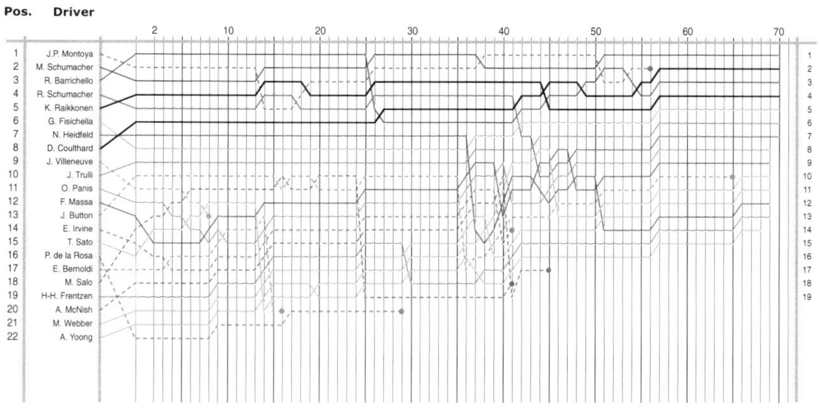

Gaps on the leader board

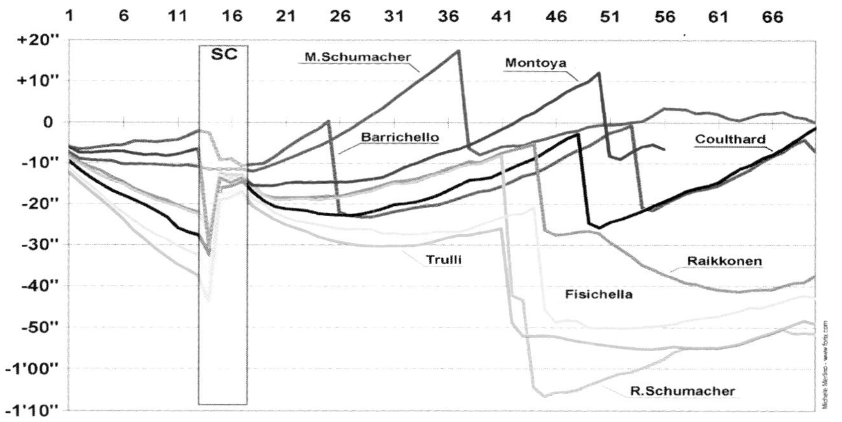

Championship after eight rounds

Drivers

1. M. Schumacher 70
2. R. Schumacher 27
3. J.P. Montoya 27
4. D. Coulthard 26
5. R. Barrichello 16
6. J. Button 8
7. K. Räikkönen 7
8. G. Fisichella 6
9. N. Heidfeld 5
10. J. Trulli 4
11. E. Irvine 3
12. F. Massa 3
13. M. Webber 2
14. M. Salo 2
15. H-H. Frentzen 2
16. J. Villeneuve 0
17. A. McNish 0
18. A. Yoong 0
19. P. de la Rosa 0
20. O. Panis 0
21. T. Sato 0
22. E. Bernoldi 0

Constructors

1. Scuderia Ferrari Marlboro 86
2. BMW WilliamsF1 Team 54
3. West McLaren Mercedes 33
4. Mild Seven Renault F1 Team 12
5. Sauber Petronas 8
6. DHL Jordan Honda 6
7. Jaguar Racing 3
8. KL Minardi Asiatech 2
9. Panasonic Toyota Racing 2
10. Orange Arrows 2
11. Lucky Strike BAR Honda 0

The circuit

Name :	Gilles Villeneuve, Montréal
Date :	June 9, 2002
Length :	4361 meters
Distance :	70 laps, 305,270 km
Temperature :	warm and sunny, 24°c
Track température :	32°c

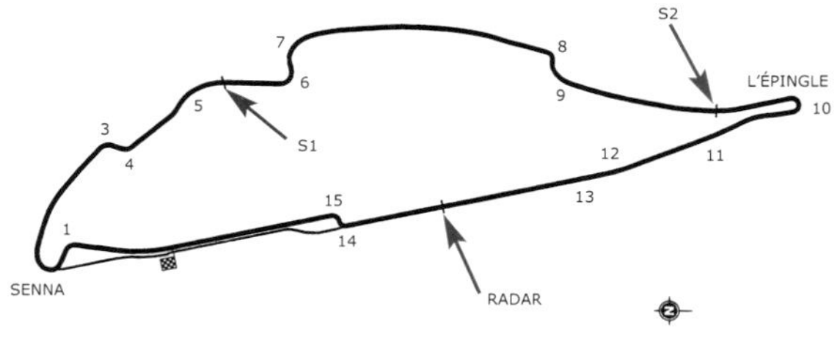

BRIDGESTONE

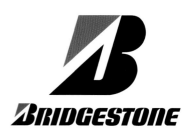

Best result for a driver running Bridgestone tyres:

Michael Schumacher, Ferrari, winner

All results : © 2002 Fédération Internationale de l'Automobile, 2, Ch. Blandonnet, 1215 Geneva 15, Switzerland

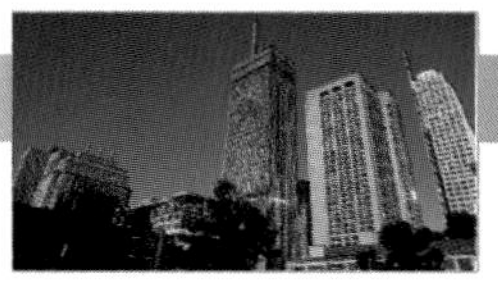

KIMI AND THE FERRARIS

Kimi Räikkönen was once again impressive on his way to third place, adding some spice to the fight for top honours behind the Ferrari.
At the Nürburgring, the Scuderia notched up another one-two finish, the first "*wrong way round*" one, which seemed to please Rubens Barrichello, as he finished ahead of Michael Schumacher.

Yet another pole position for Juan Pablo Montoya, who was beginning to carve out a reputation for himself as the king of the one lap flyer.

That makes four for Juan Pablo

The Williams-BMWs had not been favourite to take pole position. On Saturday, bang on midday, long faces were the order of the day in the team garage. Montoya could not decide which way to go with the settings on his car and the team were expecting a place on the second or maybe even the third row of the grid.

But right from Ralf Schumacher's first lap, it was obvious a little miracle had occurred. The German had no hesitation in plonking himself at the top of the time sheet with a lead made all the more comfortable by the fact that Michael Schumacher had run into transmission problems on his Ferrari and was forced to switch to the spare car.

For his part, Juan Pablo Montoya went off the track on his first flying lap and had to wait for his third run to take pole position. By that stage, the end of the session was too close for Ralf Schumacher to respond and brother Michael made a small mistake on his final lap.

So that was that and Juan Pablo Montoya had just secured the eighth pole position of his career, his fourth of the season. "*I have to admit I'm very happy with the way things went*", commented the Colombian, the moment he stepped from the cockpit. "*After all the problems we had this morning, I really had no worthwhile data for setting up the car. I started qualifying with no idea what would happen. But in fact, the car turned out to get quicker and quicker.*"

The Colombian went on to admit that the 9 thousandths of a second which separated him from Ralf Schumacher was not significant. "*The gap is really nothing*", he said. "*It's just luck, that's all.*"

Michael Schumacher plays to the gallery in parc ferme

BAR and Villeneuve contract wrangles

From the moment he joined the team at the start of the year, David Richards did a double take when he saw how much he was paying Jacques Villeneuve: on a salary of 20 million dollars per year, the Canadian ranks as the best paid F1 driver after Michael Schumacher.

The obscene salary might have been justified if Villeneuve was fighting tooth and nail with the German for the world title, but it seemed completely disproportionate for someone who, so far this year, had failed to score a single point! "*It is a complete waste to spend this sort of money on a driver when our current car is so uncompetitive*", had said David Richards through gritted teeth at the San Marino Grand Prix. "*We would do better investing this money in technology.*"

He went on to add, that spending this sort of money would be out of the question in 2003. "*I refuse to spend 25% of my budget paying Jacques Villeneuve*", concluded Richards, by the time the series had moved on to Monaco.

The Canadian did not take kindly to these remarks. "*Richards gets on my nerves with these remarks*", explained Villeneuve. "*It's easy for him. He has*

only been with the team six months and already he is criticising. Me, I've been fighting for this team for the past four years. Where would it be today without me? It is not right to complain about my salary. As far as I'm aware, David is also paid. I have always worked hard and respected my contract. If my team felt I was worth this money, then it's because I gave something in return."

The impasse stemmed from the fact that the Canadian had negotiated his contract with former BAR boss Craig Pollock, who is of course... Jacques Villeneuve's manager.

Having just got behind his new desk, David Richards had difficulty handling this situation, given that Villeneuve had a cast iron contract for 2003 and there was no way out of it. "*If I could drive for McLaren or Ferrari, then things would be different*", continued Jacques Villeneuve. "*But there is no point in my changing teams just to finish sixth. I will stay at BAR. There is no other choice.*" David Richards unhappy and Jacques Villeneuve hanging on to his steering wheel: the atmosphere would only get more tense as the season drew to a close.

Starting grid

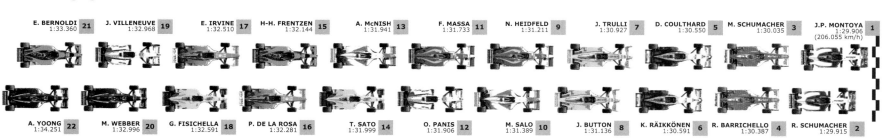

Pos	Driver	Time		Pos	Driver	Time
21	E. BERNOLDI	1:33.360		22	A. YOONG	1:34.251
19	J. VILLENEUVE	1:32.968		20	M. WEBBER	1:32.996
17	E. IRVINE	1:32.510		18	G. FISICHELLA	1:32.591
15	H-H. FRENTZEN	1:32.144		16	P. DE LA ROSA	1:32.281
13	A. McNISH	1:31.941		14	T. SATO	1:31.999
11	F. MASSA	1:31.733		12	O. PANIS	1:31.906
9	N. HEIDFELD	1:31.211		10	M. SALO	1:31.389
7	J. TRULLI	1:30.927		8	J. BUTTON	1:31.136
5	D. COULTHARD	1:30.550		6	K. RÄIKKÖNEN	1:30.591
3	M. SCHUMACHER	1:30.035		4	R. BARRICHELLO	1:30.387
1	J.P. MONTOYA	1:29.906 (206.055 km/h)		2	R. SCHUMACHER	1:29.915

Ferrari on best behaviour

The atmosphere was electric in the closing stages of the European Grand Prix. Rubens Barrichello was slowing lap by lap and stuck behind him, Michael Schumacher looked threatening and was having to restrain himself from not charging past the Brazilian.

The sad scenario at the Austrian Grand Prix, where the Scuderia had made Rubens move over for Michael looked as though it might well be about to happen again. However, to think this was to forget that the FIA World Council was due to meet the following Wednesday to sit in judgement on the Zeltweg debacle. With the potential threat of a double disqualification for its cars, Ferrari was not about to do anything that could be perceived as pure provocation by the governing body.

In a world gone mad, Michael Schumacher effectively restrained himself from taking the lead. *"After the second pit stop, the team decided we had to maintain our current positions"*, explained the four times world champion. *"We were told to back off to spare the cars and that's what we did. I tried everything I could to pass Rubens during the pit stops, but I was stuck in traffic and I could not build up a lead. After that, it was too late."* Thus, having made a phenomenal start, Rubens Barrichello took the second win of his career. *"At the start, I was not sure exactly where to brake for the new first corner"*, recounted the Brazilian, with a sparkle in his eyes. *"I backed off well before the turn and when I saw a gap ahead of me, I accelerated again and went for it. Three corners later, there was a space down the inside of Ralf and I went through. It was good fun."*

The victory was all the more enjoyable, given that the Brazilian's weekend had got off to a bad start. *"Everything went wrong on Friday and Saturday morning"*, he continued. *"My tyres were not working properly and I changed my mind about which ones to use, switching to Michael's choice. It was the right decision. I have to say the team really helped me and but for them, I would not have won today."* After leading from start to

finish, as usual, *"Rubinho"* was in tears on the podium. *"My wife and son are here this weekend, so it's a really fantastic day for me."* Back in the paddock, Jean Todt confirmed that the Brazilian's win was the result of a team decision. *"We knew we would be more competitive in the race than in*

qualifying, partly thanks to the excellent performance of our Bridgestone tyres. This result shows that Ferrari is determined to reach its targets."*

And what if one of those targets was to appease the members of the FIA World Council?

Kimi on the podium

Kimi Räikkönen was proving to be something of a revelation. During his first year in F1, in 2001, he made such a strong impression on Ron Dennis, that the McLaren boss paid Peter Sauber several tens of millions of dollars to bring him into his team.
In Australia, on his McLaren debut, the young Finn finished third. This good start preceded a lean patch, which only ended here at the Nurburgring. Having started sixth, the consistent Räikkönen

ended up third. He had a straightforward race. *"I just made one mistake, under braking"*, he said. *"Jenson Button got past me, but it was not a problem as I knew he was pitting twice, while I was on a one-stop."*
The pit stops also helped the Finn get by Ralf Schumacher's Williams. *"We were not as quick as the Ferraris, but we were better than the Williams, which is some consolation"*, he concluded.

(below)
A brief off-track excursion for Felipe Massa, who managed to catch up with the pack and finish sixth.

(left)
"Things are getting better guys!" Olivier Panis
V

Race summary

> The two Williams cross swords at the start. Barrichello overtakes them on the opening lap **(1)**.

> Behind the leaders, the Jordans tangle and cause havoc in the pack **(2)**.

> Kimi Räikkönen records

his first podium finish since Australia. He does a good job of fighting off the two Renaults **(3)**.

> Felipe Massa continues to impress at the wheel of the Sauber. The young driver takes the liberty of passing his team-mate **(4)**.

> Michael Schumacher makes a rare mistake, sliding briefly off the track. Barrichello clears off **(5)**.

> Despite his mistake, Schumacher manages to catch his team-mate and finishes in his wheel tracks. Ferrari racks up its third one-two finish

of the season **(6)**.

> A jubilant Rubens Barrichello in parc ferme after the race **(7)**.

Good job

Since refuelling was reintroduced into Formula 1, the races have really become a team sport. At the Nurburgring, the Renault mechanics made the difference. Jenson Button finished the Grand Prix in fifth place.

paddock

Un-drive-able

> Early morning in the McLaren pits. Having qualified fifth, David Coulthard would retire after a collision with Juan Pablo Montoya.

"The car was almost undriveable. I had to fight just to keep it on the road." Back in the pits, Juan Pablo Montoya was far from impressed with his Williams FW24. Having started from pole position, the Colombian never looked like a plausible winner. By the end of the opening lap, he had already been overtaken by his team-mate and the two Ferraris. After that, he lost around three second per lap to the red cars. It was terribly disappointing for him. *"It's the third time I've failed to finish a race after starting from pole"*, he complained, sitting outside his motorhome. *"At the first corner, I let Ralf go by, because I did not want to risk colliding with him. After that I had to fight my car like mad. It was impossible to drive and there was nothing I could but wait to change tyres during the pit stop."*
It was on lap 28, that David Coulthard tried to go round the outside of him. *"It was very tight and I could not stop the car from getting sideways. Unfortunately we touched. It was my fault and I went to see David afterwards to apologise."*
For his part, Ralf Schumacher could not even hold onto the lead for a whole lap. He finished fourth, over a minute down on the Ferraris. It had been a disaster. *"I am really disappointed"*, he sighed after the finish. *"We knew this would be a tough race, but not as bad as this. The Ferraris are really very strong and my car was very difficult to drive right from the start."*
The Williams engineers were not happy bunnies. Technical Director Patrick Head had made his excuses and left immediately after the chequered flag, leaving development engineer Sam Michael to face the music and the questions. *"We had a problem with rear tyre wear"*, he admitted. *"It was the same story at Monaco. Our cars destroy the tyres very quickly and then there's no grip. We still have a lot of work to do to sort out this problem, but at least we now have a pretty good idea how to go about it!"*

Peter Sauber got carried away by Brazilian soccer fever on Friday morning. At the end of the match, he even donned a soccer shirt on loan from Felipe Massa.

Weekend gossip

> On Wednesday, Michael Schumacher had been karting at his father's track in Kerpen. There was another family member out on the circuit, the world champion's three year old son Mick. And if Junior was not going fast enough for his father's liking, then he got a nudge from behind to speed him up!

> This year, the Nurburgring had been extended by 588 metres, with the addition of the "Mercedes Arena" section, shortly after the main straight.

The Nurburgring circuit nestles in the Eifel mountains, in the west of Germany, in the Treves region, famous for Moselle wines.
V

Soccer World Cup: Viva Brazil!

The paddock was like a ghost town on Friday morning. Just about everyone working in Formula 1 had downed tools and was sitting in front of super-view plasma TV screens in the motorhomes to watch the Brazil v England World Cup quarter final match. In the McLaren, Williams, Jordan and BAR camps, the English F1 community went from ecstasy to agony and back again several times, as the game went first one way, then the other. In the end, it was the smaller Brazilian paddock community which was able to keep smiling. Many of them were watching at the Sauber encampment, where green and yellow was the dominant colour among the mechanics and journalists surrounding Felipe Massa. The young Brazilian was jumping and dancing on the motorhome tables by the end of the game and even the usually dour Peter Sauber seemed to join in the fun.
Out on track a couple of hours later, the Brazilian had less cause to celebrate. He ended the day in 16th place, five places behind team-mate Nick Heidfeld.

Practice

All the time trials

N°	Driver	Car/Engine/Chassis	Practice friday	Pos.	Practice saturday	Pos.	Qualifying	Pos.	Warm-up	Pos.
1.	Michael Schumacher	Ferrari 2002/221	1'32"041	2°	1'30"658	1°	1'30"035	3°	1'32"987	2°
2.	Rubens Barrichello	Ferrari 2002/220	1'32"969	4°	1'31"332	3°	1'30"387	4°	1'32"671	1°
3.	David Coulthard	McLaren-Mercedes MP4/17/07	1'31"886	1°	1'31"811	7°	1'30"550	5°	1'34"143	3°
4.	Kimi Räikkönen	McLaren-Mercedes MP4/17/06	1'32"298	3°	1'31"176	2°	1'30"591	6°	1'34"324	4°
5.	Ralf Schumacher	Williams-BMW FW24/06	1'33"119	6°	1'31"685	5°	1'29"915	2°	1'35"615	14°
6.	Juan Pablo Montoya	Williams-BMW FW24/05	1'33"122	5°	1'31"833	8°	1'29"906	1°	1'35"978	17°
7.	Nick Heidfeld	Sauber-Petronas C21/06	1'33"963	11°	1'31"422	4°	1'31"211	9°	1'35"550	12°
8.	Felipe Massa	Sauber-Petronas C21/07	1'34"680	16°	1'32"715	11°	1'31"733	11°	1'35"460	10°
9.	Giancarlo Fisichella	Jordan-Honda EJ12/5	1'34"755	17°	1'33"167	16°	1'32"591	18°	1'34"914	7°
10.	Takuma Sato	Jordan-Honda EJ12/4	1'34"136	12°	1'33"017	13°	1'31"999	14°	1'34"804	6°
11.	Jacques Villeneuve	BAR-Honda 004/09	1'34"522	15°	1'33"681	15°	1'32"968	19°	1'34"969	8°
12.	Olivier Panis	BAR-Honda 004/08	1'33"921	10°	1'33"202	17°	1'31"906	12°	1'35"145	9°
14.	Jarno Trulli	Renault R202/05	1'32"526	7°	1'32"412	9°	1'30"927	7°	1'37"370	20°
15.	Jenson Button	Renault R202/06	1'33"708	8°	1'32"698	10°	1'31"136	8°	1'35"749	16°
16.	Eddie Irvine	Jaguar R3/05	1'35"579	21°	1'33"157	15°	1'32"510	17°	1'37"598	21°
17.	Pedro de la Rosa	Jaguar R3/04	1'34"322	14°	1'35"736	22°	1'32"281	16°	1'35"656	15°
20.	Heinz-Harald Frentzen	Arrows-Cosworth A23/01	1'34"315	13°	1'33"668	18°	1'32"144	15°	1'34"461	5°
21.	Enrique Bernoldi	Arrows-Cosworth A23/03	1'35"260	19°	1'33"877	20°	1'33"360	21°	1'35"545	11°
22.	Alex Yoong	Minardi-Asiatech PS02/03	1'37"503	22°	1'35"016	21°	1'34"251	22°	1'38"060	22°
23.	Mark Webber	Minardi-Asiatech PS02/04	1'35"372	20°	1'33"146	14°	1'32"996	20°	1'35"614	13°
24.	Mika Salo	Toyota TF102/07	1'33"715	9°	1'31"803	6°	1'31"389	10°	1'36"146	18°
25.	Allan McNish	Toyota TF102/08	1'34"941	18°	1'32"863	12°	1'31"941	13°	1'36"200	19°

Maximum speeds

N°	Driver	P1 Qualifs	Pos.	P1 Race	Pos.	P2 Qualifs	Pos.	P2 Race	Pos.	Finish Qualifs	Pos.	Finish Race	Pos.	Trap Qualifs	Pos.	Trap Race	Pos.
1.	M. Schumacher	272,6	4°	272,5	7°	232,6	4°	226,6	4°	255,7	4°	254,2	2°	308,9	3°	308,9	6°
2.	R. Barrichello	274,3	3°	273,2	6°	236,0	1°	231,5	1°	256,0	3°	254,7	1°	310,1	1°	306,1	12°
3.	D. Coulthard	271,2	7°	274,1	4°	228,3	15°	225,6	9°	251,6	9°	250,1	10°	304,6	14°	306,1	12°
4.	K. Räikkönen	268,3	20°	271,0	12°	231,2	7°	229,4	2°	251,6	8°	250,8	7°	305,1	22°	307,0	10°
5.	R. Schumacher	275,3	1°	274,5	2°	231,2	7°	225,9	8°	251,6	8°	253,5	4°	309,3	2°	309,9	4°
6.	J.P. Montoya	274,8	2°	274,1	5°	231,1	8°	223,0	17°	256,4	2°	250,8	8°	307,6	4°	308,5	7°
7.	N. Heidfeld	271,2	8°	270,2	14°	228,0	17°	223,1	15°	251,5	10°	248,2	14°	306,8	6°	307,6	6°
8.	F. Massa	269,7	13°	268,1	19°	227,1	18°	223,3	13°	250,6	12°	247,3	17°	307,6	5°	307,6	6°
9.	G. Fisichella	269,3	15°	267,7	19°	229,2	13°	218,6	22°	249,6	16°	244,8	21°	303,0	19°	301,6	22°
10.	T. Sato	270,6	11°	269,7	15°	230,2	10°	224,1	12°	252,0	7°	248,5	13°	305,2	11°	304,3	15°
11.	J. Villeneuve	268,5	19°	267,0	21°	225,1	21°	220,1	20°	247,7	21°	245,6	19°	304,3	16°	303,7	16°
12.	O. Panis	270,0	12°	270,8	13°	226,4	19°	221,9	19°	249,0	19°	247,8	15°	305,0	13°	303,7	16°
14.	J. Trulli	268,6	18°	272,3	9°	229,3	12°	224,2	11°	250,4	13°	249,9	12°	305,5	18°	305,5	13°
15.	J. Button	271,0	10°	274,1	3°	233,6	3°	228,9	3°	250,2	14°	251,9	5°	305,8	10°	308,4	8°
16.	E. Irvine	269,4	14°	267,9	18°	225,9	20°	220,0	21°	249,8	15°	244,1	22°	304,3	15°	303,2	18°
17.	P. de la Rosa	272,0	6°	269,4	16°	229,8	11°	223,2	14°	251,1	11°	247,7	16°	306,4	9°	303,2	18°
18.	H.-H. Frentzen	269,2	16°	272,3	10°	230,6	9°	224,9	10°	247,3	22°	250,0	11°	305,0	11°	303,1	20°
19.	E. Bernoldi	269,0	17°	272,5	8°	228,8	14°	226,2	5°	249,3	18°	246,0	18°	305,0	12°	310,2	2°
22.	A. Yoong	265,9	22°	267,2	20°	224,0	22°	222,3	18°	249,6	17°	245,2	20°	302,4	21°	310,7	1°
23.	M. Webber	266,2	21°	266,5	22°	228,1	16°	223,0	16°	247,7	20°	247,7	20°	302,4	20°	303,2	19°
24.	M. Salo	271,0	9°	272,2	11°	232,1	5°	225,9	7°	252,9	6°	251,2	6°	307,3	7°	309,8	5°
25.	A. McNish	272,5	5°	275,7	1°	231,5	6°	226,0	6°	253,1	5°	253,8	3°	307,7	5°	310,1	3°

Race

Classification & Retirements

Pos.	Driver	Team	Lap	Time	Average
1.	R. Barrichello	Ferrari	60	1:35:07.426	194,741 km/h
2.	M. Schumacher	Ferrari	60	0.294	194,731 km/h
3.	K. Räikkönen	McLaren Mercedes	60	46.435	193,170 km/h
4.	R. Schumacher	Williams BMW	60	1:06.963	192,483 km/h
5.	J. Button	Renault	60	1:16.943	192,151 km/h
6.	F. Massa	Sauber Petronas	59	1 lap	191,133 km/h
7.	N. Heidfeld	Sauber Petronas	59	1 lap	191,102 km/h
8.	J. Trulli	Renault	59	1 lap	191,077 km/h
9.	O. Panis	BAR Honda	59	1 lap	190,334 km/h
10.	E. Bernoldi	Arrows Cosworth	59	1 lap	189,141 km/h
11.	P. de la Rosa	Jaguar	59	1 lap	189,122 km/h
12.	J. Villeneuve	BAR Honda	59	1 lap	189,099 km/h
13.	H-H. Frentzen	Arrows Cosworth	59	1 lap	189,062 km/h
14.	A. McNish	Toyota	59	1 lap	188,744 km/h
15.	M. Webber	Minardi Asiatech	58	2 laps	186,826 km/h
16.	T. Sato	Jordan Honda	58	2 laps	185,505 km/h

Driver	Team	Lap	Reason
M. Salo	Toyota	52	Gearbox problem
A. Yoong	Minardi Asiatech	49	Broken hydraulic pomp
E. Irvine	Jaguar	42	Loss of hydraulic pressure
J.P. Montoya	Williams BMW	28	Spins and hits Coulthard
D. Coulthard	McLaren Mercedes	28	Hit by Montoya
G. Fisichella	Jordan Honda	27	Unstable car after a hit with Sato

Fastest laps

	Driver	Time	Lap	Average
1.	M. Schumacher	1'32"226	26	200,871 km/h
2.	R. Barrichello	1'32"785	44	199,661 km/h
3.	K. Räikkönen	1'33"159	59	198,860 km/h
4.	J. Button	1'33"676	47	197,762 km/h
5.	R. Schumacher	1'33"856	49	197,383 km/h
6.	N. Heidfeld	1'34"224	56	196,612 km/h
7.	J. Trulli	1'34"246	57	196,566 km/h
8.	H-H. Frentzen	1'34"503	47	196,031 km/h
9.	D. Coulthard	1'34"583	21	195,866 km/h
10.	O. Panis	1'34"609	58	195,812 km/h
11.	J.P. Montoya	1'34"635	21	195,758 km/h
12.	F. Massa	1'34"683	57	195,659 km/h
13.	J. Villeneuve	1'34"809	56	195,399 km/h
14.	T. Sato	1'35"029	57	194,946 km/h
15.	M. Salo	1'35"267	39	194,459 km/h
16.	E. Bernoldi	1'35"391	48	194,207 km/h
17.	A. McNish	1'35"503	58	193,979 km/h
18.	P. de la Rosa	1'35"644	52	193,693 km/h
19.	M. Webber	1'35"880	37	193,216 km/h
20.	E. Irvine	1'36"662	19	191,653 km/h
21.	A. Yoong	1'36"932	21	191,119 km/h
22.	G. Fisichella	1'37"011	3	190,963 km/h

Pit stops

	Driver	Time	Lap	Stop n°		Driver	Time	Lap	stop n°
1.	G. Fisichella	35"979	1	1	18.	F. Massa	36"497	31	1
2.	T. Sato	1'23"550	1	1	19.	A. Yoong	52"885	31	2
3.	A. Yoong	22"553	7	1	20.	E. Irvine	48"976	32	1
4.	M. Webber	34"462	19	1	21.	P. de la Rosa	36"520	33	1
5.	J. Villeneuve	35"393	20	1	22.	K. Räikkönen	35"983	35	1
6.	J. Trulli	33"722	21	1	23.	T. Sato	35"618	36	2
7.	A. McNish	38"646	21	1	24.	A. McNish	34"072	39	2
8.	J. Button	33"057	22	1	25.	M. Salo	33"089	41	2
9.	G. Fisichella	33"170	21	2	26.	J. Trulli	32"015	42	2
10.	H-H. Frentzen	48"500	22	1	27.	M. Webber	45"085	41	2
11.	E. Bernoldi	34"517	23	1	28.	M. Schumacher	31"690	43	2
12.	M. Schumacher	32"665	24	1	29.	E. Bernoldi	33"355	42	2
13.	M. Salo	41"573	23	1	30.	J. Button	31"930	44	2
14.	R. Barrichello	32"818	25	1	31.	R. Barrichello	31"580	45	2
15.	O. Panis	38"326	29	1	32.	J. Villeneuve	32"452	44	2
16.	R. Schumacher	35"795	30	1	33.	H-H. Frentzen	34"526	44	2
17.	N. Heidfeld	35"785	30	1					

Race leaders

Driver	Laps in the lead	Nber of Laps	Kilometers	Driver	Nber of Laps	Kilometers
R. Barrichello	1 > 60	60	308,743 km	R. Barrichello	60	308,743 km

Lap chart

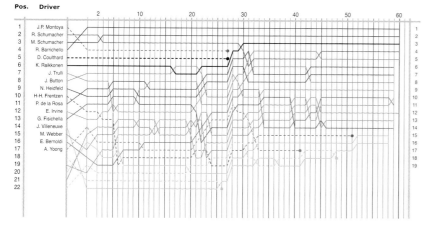

Gaps on the leader board

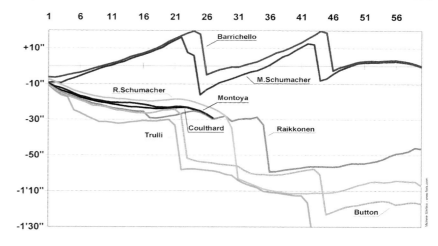

Championship after nine rounds

Drivers

1. M. Schumacher 76
2. R. Schumacher 30
3. J.P. Montoya 27
4. R. Barrichello 26
5. D. Coulthard 26
6. K. Räikkönen 11
7. J. Button 10
8. G. Fisichella 6
9. N. Heidfeld 5
10. J. Trulli 4
11. F. Massa 4
12. E. Irvine 3
13. M. Webber 2
14. M. Salo 2
15. H-H. Frentzen 2
16. J. Villeneuve 0
17. A. McNish 0
18. A. Yoong 0
19. P. de la Rosa 0
20. O. Panis 0
21. T. Sato 0
22. E. Bernoldi 0

Constructors

1. Scuderia Ferrari Marlboro 102
2. BMW WilliamsF1 Team 57
3. West McLaren Mercedes 37
4. Mild Seven Renault F1 Team 14
5. Sauber Petronas 9
6. DHL Jordan Honda 6
7. Jaguar Racing 3
8. KL Minardi Asiatech 2
9. Panasonic Toyota Racing 2
10. Orange Arrows 2
11. Lucky Strike BAR Honda 0

The circuit

Name :	Nürburgring
Date :	June 23, 2002
Length :	5146 meters
Distance :	60 laps, 308,743 km
Temperature :	sunny with cloudy periods, warm, 21°c
Track temperature:	31°c

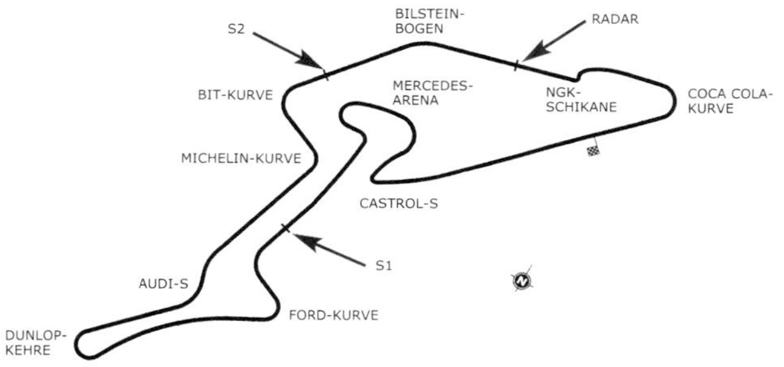

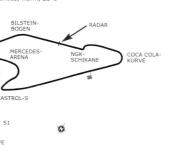

Best result for a driver running Bridgestone tyres:

Rubens Barrichello, Ferrari, winner

SUNSHINE AND SHOWERS

If there had been any doubts about Ferrari's superiority they were washed away at Silverstone. Despite starting from the back of the grid, Barrichello took just 19 laps to overtake the field. On a damp track, Ferrari made use of Bridgestone's excellent intermediate tyres. Looking at the performance of other teams using the same rubber, it was definitely the best solution.

With his seventh win of the season, Michael Schumacher shattered the hopes of any other pretenders to the title.

The Montoya train steams on

At Silverstone, Juan Pablo Montoya racked up his fourth consecutive pole position. After three race retirements, would he finally convert pole into a win? In England, he improved his time on his very last lap. "*We made a lot of changes to the car during practice. In the morning, I only managed one lap in the dry and so we were not very well prepared for qualifying. In the end, we changed three settings at the same time, the car was better balanced and that was it. But I don't know where we found the necessary tenths. And to be honest, I don't care!*" he explained in his own inimitable way.

The Colombian reckoned that the secret to success in the race would all hang on the tyres. "*Michelin has done a lot of work on its tyres and they're better this weekend. A lot better in fact. But, having said that, I don't think they will be quite up to the level of the opposition. Michelin still has a lot of work to do*", he added.

After three retirements on the trot, the Williams driver seemed very impatient to reacquaint himself with the chequered flag, even if he had long since given up any hope of taking the world title. "*It's true I have not scored any points since the Austrian Grand Prix in the middle of May*", he admitted, staring into space. "*Of course I would like to win the race, but the most important thing is to pick up some points. You have to aim for one thing at a time.*"

Ferrari rapped on the knuckes

Cast your minds back to the 12th May and the Austrian Grand Prix. Rubens Barrichello, who had led from the start, slowed down and let team-mate Michael Schumacher take the win.

To show who the "*real*" winner was, the German had pushed the Brazilian to the top step of the podium, while the German National Anthem was being played.

It caused a major scandal, given the high visibility of the sport. In the days following the race, newspapers, television programmes and team bosses – even those who had previously applied similar tactics – decried Ferrari's strategy, claiming it made a mockery of the sport.

This prompted the FIA World Council to punish the team in question. Given that team orders are perfectly legal, all the Council could act on was the podium procedure. That is what they did on 26th

June in Paris, fining the Scuderia, Michael Schumacher and Rubens Barrichello a million dollars. Half of it payable on the spot and the other half suspended for twelve months.

In other words, as long as the Ferrari drivers did not swap podium places during the next year, the fine would only be half a million dollars. A sizeable amount maybe, but it represents just 0.16% of Ferrari's supposed annual budget (302 million dollars in 2002.) The reason given for the fine by the FIA was that "*it is the duty of each team to ensure that its drivers respect the podium procedures*". The world council further "*deplored the way in which the team orders were carried out*". Nevertheless, it recognised that it was common for teams to decide the finishing order of their drivers and decided "*with regret*" that they could not impose any sanctions on Ferrari in respect of this matter.

Starting grid

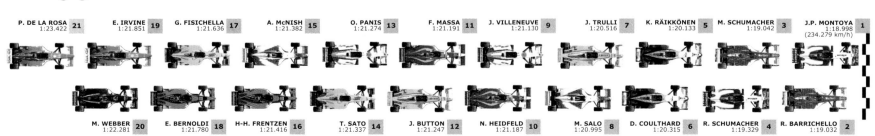

| P. DE LA ROSA 21 1:23.422 | E. IRVINE 19 1:21.851 | G. FISICHELLA 17 1:21.636 | A. McNISH 15 1:21.382 | O. PANIS 13 1:21.274 | F. MASSA 11 1:21.191 | J. VILLENEUVE 9 1:21.130 | J. TRULLI 7 1:20.516 | K. RÄIKKÖNEN 5 1:20.133 | M. SCHUMACHER 3 1:19.042 | J.P. MONTOYA 1 1:18.998 (234.279 km/h) |

| M. WEBBER 20 1:22.281 | E. BERNOLDI 18 1:21.780 | H-H. FRENTZEN 16 1:21.416 | T. SATO 14 1:21.337 | J. BUTTON 12 1:21.247 | N. HEIDFELD 10 1:21.187 | M. SALO 8 1:20.995 | D. COULTHARD 6 1:20.315 | R. SCHUMACHER 4 1:19.329 | R. BARRICHELLO 2 1:19.032 |

Even the heavens are on Michael's side!

For the fourth Grand Prix in a row, Juan Pablo Montoya was starting from pole. However, his hopes of staying ahead of the Ferraris did not even last half an hour in the race. Having made a good start, the Colombian was in the lead until the first drops of rain arrived, around lap 12. After stopping for rain tyres, he emerged from pit lane with an eight second lead. That seemed comfortable enough, but in less than two laps, he was swallowed up by Ferrari's world champion. The Ferrari drivers had opted for intermediate Bridgestones, as it was not raining that heavily, but the Michelin runners went for full wets. This meant they were all praying for a heavier downpour. This resulted in the Ferraris immediately pulling out a four to five second lead over the Michelin users and Montoya was soon caught and passed by Rubens Barrichello. Some feat, as the Brazilian had been forced to start from the back of the grid, after his car stalled at the start of the formation lap. The situation was at its worst on lap 32, by which time the Colombian was trailing more than 50 seconds behind Michael Schumacher. He only made small inroads into that gap by the end of the race. "*There was nothing I could do about the Ferraris today*", regretted Juan Pablo Montoya as he stepped down from the podium. "*I defended myself as best I could, but as soon as it started to rain, the Ferraris literally disappeared. I gave up fighting and, towards the end, I even asked the team if I could drop the engine revs to be sure of finishing.*"

It seemed as though the Michelin engineers still had a lot to do to improve their performance in the rain. That Sunday at Silverstone, the showers and Rubens Barrichello's start line problem had handed the win to Michael Schumacher on a plate. This season, the German could not only count on his talent, he could also rely on luck and the quality of his Bridgestone tyres, which worked particularly well in the Silverstone drizzle.

^
7th win of the season for Michael Schumacher, due in part to the rain and his tyres.

Jacques Villeneuve finished 4th. He would not score points again until the United States.
v

Both BARs in the points

Two cars in the points and just off the podium positions too: the BAR team could not have hoped for more in a race staged in its own back garden, given that the Brackley factory is only about ten kilometres from Silverstone.

Over a hundred members of staff had turned up in the grandstands to cheer home their cars and they could all go home happy. Of course, Jacques Villeneuve still managed to look miserable after finishing fourth, but Olivier Panis was in seventh heaven. The Frenchman finished fifth, also picking up his first points of the season.

With a glass of champagne in his hand at the team motorhome, Olivier was all smiles after the race. "*I am more than happy and it is a fantastic day for the team, especially as so many people are here from the factory. I could almost feel the pressure coming from them in the grandstands.*" Actually, it was down to a particularly well thought out strategy that the two BARs finished in the points. In order to outwit the tricky and very localised weather conditions in the area, BAR had positioned several observers in various villages around the circuit, as well as sending up team boss David Richards' private helicopter.

This complex information system meant that both cars stopped at exactly the right time to change tyres and that did the trick. "*It was a very tough afternoon, but the result makes it worthwhile*", concluded Olivier Panis.

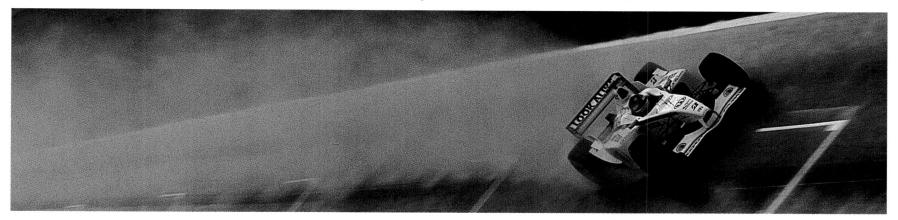

Race summary

> At the start, Barrichello is missing from the front row (1).

> From the back of the grid, Rubens Barrichello

stages a spectacular comeback. He deals with Panis on the way to the podium (2).

> Battle rages behind the

Ferraris for the minor placings (3).

> Suddenly, the BAR cars appear competitive. Villeneuve, from eight

on the grid, makes the most of the misfortunes that befall the McLarens and Williams to score his first points of the

season (4).

> After Montoya's retirement, Michael Schumacher is home free to score his

seventh win of the season (5).

> A champagne shower for Ross Brawn and the Ferrari drivers (6).

> Celebrations in the BAR camp. Panis records his first finish of the season in 5th place (7).

First points

Finally! After ten grands prix, the BAR team saw its efforts rewarded. At Silverstone, both its cars were in the points: Jacques Villeneuve finished fourth and Olivier Panis fifth.

Arrows in torment

Missing a grand prix is a very serious offence for a team to commit, even if the regulations make no mention of an actual penalty. However, if a team fails to show for more than three races, then it risks nothing less than total exclusion from the championship.

The Arrows situation therefore looked fairly serious on Thursday, when the orange cars failed to present themselves for the scrutineering checks. There was a very simple reason for this; namely that the cars were not at the track. The chassis were stuck a few miles down the road in their Leafield base, as there were no Cosworth engines to fit in the back of them. The British race stewards decided to make a special concession, allowing the cars to be scrutineered by 10 o'clock on Friday morning, one hour before the start of free practice. This they managed to do. In order to sort out the situation, Tom Walkinshaw had to put his hand in his pocket and pull out a cheque made out to Ford, who would not release the engines on the grounds of non-payment of outstanding bills. Niki Lauda, the man in overall charge at Cosworth did not mince his words. "*I will be intransigent with Arrows*", he boomed. "*I have given them enough time to pay. From now on, no money, no engines!*" Come Friday, and the electronic control units for the engines had yet to put in an appearance, so the cars were unable to run until the Saturday.

Weekend gossip

> Lisa Dennis, wife of Ron had written a series of five children's books, based on two characters called Mac and Lauren (geddit?) two little Formula 1 cars, featuring eyes as wing mirrors and the front wing drawn as a mouth.

> Felipe Massa changed the artwork on his helmet to celebrate Brazil's five wins in the World Cup.

> Rubens Barrichello turned up at Silverstone wearing a T-shirt bearing the legend "2-0," designed to irritate his team-mate Michael Schumacher, after the Germans were beaten by that score in the World Cup. "*After the match, I kept trying to call Michael everywhere, but he didn't reply on any of his numbers. He seemed to have disappeared*", joked the Brazilian.

> On Thursday, McLaren showed off the new kit which its pit crew would be wearing during the races. Developed with the help of the European Space Agency, the suit featured a built-in cooling system to keep the mechanics chilled during pit stops in hot climates. It involved a network of tubes, containing a refrigerated fluid which passed through several layers of material. Given the cool conditions in Silverstone, it was not used at this grand prix.

> "*Smile, you're on camera!*" The Arrows engineers were not too sure what to do with themselves on Thursday.

> Felipe Massa drove an extraordinary race at Silverstone, given that the Brazilian went off the track at the first corner and was last as the field completed the opening lap. "*It was Villeneuve's fault*", he said. "*He made a very slow start and I had to go on the grass to avoid him.*" Massa then staged a meteoric climb through the field, finding himself sixth by lap 26, having been one of the first to pit for rain tyres. But he dropped to eighth after a spin and never made it back into the points. At the wheel of the other Sauber, Nick Heidfeld finished sixth.

Kimi Räikkönen's efforts would come to nothing, as the Finn's engine let him down.
∨

results

Practice

All the time trials

N°	Driver	Car/Engine/Chassis	Practice friday	Pos.	Practice saturday	Pos.	Qualifying	Pos.	Warm-up	Pos.
1.	Michael Schumacher	Ferrari 2002/221	1'31"881	2°	1'20"428	2°	1'19"042	3°	1'22"815	2°
2.	Rubens Barrichello	Ferrari 2002/220	1'31"457	1°	1'20"230	1°	1'19"032	2°	1'22"371	1°
3.	David Coulthard	McLaren-Mercedes MP4/17/07	1'35"170	12°	1'21"326	5°	1'20"315	6°	1'24"903	9°
4.	Kimi Räikkönen	McLaren-Mercedes MP4/17/06	1'34"473	7°	1'21"768	6°	1'20"133	5°	1'24"214	3°
5.	Ralf Schumacher	Williams-BMW FW24/06	1'34"766	11°	1'20"708	3°	1'19"329	4°	1'25"707	15°
6.	Juan Pablo Montoya	Williams-BMW FW24/05	1'33"842	4°	1'21"076	4°	1'18"998	1°	1'24"439	5°
7.	Nick Heidfeld	Sauber-Petronas C21/06	1'34"752	10°	1'21"769	7°	1'21"187	10°	1'24"723	6°
8.	Felipe Massa	Sauber-Petronas C21/07	1'34"676	8°	1'22"472	12°	1'21"191	11°	1'24"862	8°
9.	Giancarlo Fisichella	Jordan-Honda EJ12/6	1'33"434	3°	1'22"680	16°	1'21"636	17°	1'25"204	12°
10.	Takuma Sato	Jordan-Honda EJ12/4	1'33"901	5°	1'22"812	17°	1'21"337	14°	1'24"224	4°
11.	Jacques Villeneuve	BAR-Honda 004/06	1'34"373	6°	1'22"284	10°	1'21"130	9°	1'24"741	7°
12.	Olivier Panis	BAR-Honda 004/08	1'35"534	14°	1'23"244	20°	1'21"274	13°	1'26"099	18°
14.	Jarno Trulli	Renault R202/05	1'36"244	16°	1'22"466	11°	1'20"516	7°	1'25"074	10°
15.	Jenson Button	Renault R202/06	1'34"744	9°	1'21"998	8°	1'21"247	12°	1'25"959	17°
16.	Eddie Irvine	Jaguar R3/05	1'35"682	15°	1'22"527	13°	1'21"851	19°	1'26"888	21°
17.	Pedro de la Rosa	Jaguar R3/04	1'35"324	13°	1'22"543	14°	1'23"422	21°	1'25"799	16°
20.	Heinz-Harald Frentzen	Arrows-Cosworth A23/01			1'22"174	9°	1'21"416	16°	1'25"160	11°
21.	Enrique Bernoldi	Arrows-Cosworth A23/03			1'22"628	15°	1'21"780	18°	1'26"786	20°
22.	Alex Yoong	Minardi-Asiatech PS02/03	1'37"997	18°	1'25"527	22°	1'24"785	22°		
23.	Mark Webber	Minardi-Asiatech PS02/04	1'37"835	17°	1'23"679	21°	1'22"281	20°	1'26"617	19°
24.	Mika Salo	Toyota TF102/07			1'23"184	19°	1'20"995	8°	1'25"243	13°
25.	Allan McNish	Toyota TF102/08	1'38"477	19°	1'22"845	18°	1'21"382	15°	1'25"461	14°

Maximum speeds

N°	Driver	P1 Qualifs	Pos.	P1 Race	Pos.	P2 Qualifs	Pos.	P2 Race	Pos.	Finish Qualifs	Pos.	Finish Race	Pos.	Trap Qualifs	Pos.	Trap Race	Pos.
1.	M. Schumacher	310,4	2°	306,0	2°	277,3	2°	259,6	3°	299,0	1°	294,6	3°	280,0	8°	255,9	5°
2.	R. Barrichello	311,1	1°	309,1	1°	277,5	1°	260,1	1°	297,1	3°	298,0	1°	272,0	16°	252,5	7°
3.	D. Coulthard	301,9	20°	303,7	8°	275,7	5°	253,8	9°	291,8	13°	289,8	7°	290,7	1°	256,5	4°
4.	K. Räikkönen	303,9	12°	300,9	16°	275,5	6°	250,5	12°	293,7	5°	295,3	2°	280,9	7°	243,1	14°
5.	R. Schumacher	308,9	3°	303,7	7°	272,3	11°	257,2	5°	297,1	2°	291,7	5°	277,7	11°	257,5	1°
6.	J.P. Montoya	308,4	5°	302,7	9°	276,4	4°	258,0	4°	296,8	4°	293,2	4°	282,4	5°	249,5	10°
7.	N. Heidfeld	308,6	4°	301,5	14°	270,8	12°	254,0	7°	293,7	6°	291,4	6°	277,9	10°	255,6	6°
8.	F. Massa	306,0	7°	302,6	10°	274,3	9°	255,3	6°	293,7	7°	289,6	9°	284,6	3°	249,1	11°
9.	G. Fisichella	303,7	15°	304,4	3°	270,1	13°	246,9	16°	291,8	14°	289,0	12°	272,9	15°	239,1	15°
10.	T. Sato	303,9	13°	299,0	18°	273,3	10°	248,9	13°	291,6	15°	288,0	15°	274,1	14°	256,7	3°
11.	J. Villeneuve	300,0	21°	296,9	20°	267,7	18°	247,2	15°	289,3	20°	286,3	19°	271,3	18°	247,4	12°
12.	O. Panis	303,2	18°	304,4	4°	269,7	14°	252,3	11°	289,3	18°	287,4	17°	282,7	4°	251,5	8°
14.	J. Trulli	306,8	6°	302,4	13°	275,0	8°	252,5	10°	292,5	10°	289,2	11°	285,9	2°	249,8	9°
15.	J. Button	303,7	14°	301,2	15°	268,8	16°	253,9	8°	292,6	8°	289,7	8°	275,5	13°	244,5	13°
16.	E. Irvine	305,5	8°	300,6	17°	275,5	7°	247,6	14°	292,6	9°	286,7	18°	281,0	6°	233,6	16°
17.	P. de la Rosa	296,5	22°	302,5	12°	266,9	19°	259,6	2°	289,5	17°	288,0	13°	269,5	19°	257,1	2°
18.	H-H. Frentzen	303,1	19°	303,8	5°	264,8	20°	242,8	18°	289,3	19°	287,5	16°	276,7	12°	226,2	19°
19.	E. Bernoldi	305,0	11°	303,7	6°	268,9	15°	246,1	17°	289,8	16°	288,0	14°	265,7	20°	222,6	20°
22.	A. Yoong	303,3	16°			237,2	22°			286,0	22°			259,6	22°		
23.	M. Webber	303,2	17°	298,5	19°	252,5	21°	237,2	20°	287,6	21°	284,8	20°	260,1	21°	233,6	17°
24.	M. Salo	305,1	10°	302,5	11°	267,9	17°	242,0	19°	292,2	12°	289,4	10°	279,5	9°	231,2	18°
25.	A. McNish	305,2	9°			276,6	3°			292,2	11°			271,6	17°		

Race

Classification & Retirement

Pos.	Driver	Team	Lap	Time	Average	
1.	M. Schumacher	Ferrari	60	1:31:45.015	201,649 km/h	
2.	R. Barrichello	Ferrari	60	14.578	201,116 km/h	
3.	J.P. Montoya	Williams BMW	60	31.661	200,496 km/h	
4.	J. Villeneuve	BAR Honda	59	1 lap	197,891 km/h	
5.	O. Panis	BAR Honda	59	1 lap	197,682 km/h	
6.	N. Heidfeld	Sauber Petronas	59	1 lap	197,612 km/h	
7.	G. Fisichella	Jordan Honda	59	1 lap	197,577 km/h	
8.	R. Schumacher	Williams BMW	59	1 lap	197,390 km/h	
9.	F. Massa	Sauber Petronas	59	1 lap	196,939 km/h	
10.	D. Coulthard	McLaren Mercedes	58	2 laps	193,068 km/h	
11.	P. de la Rosa	Jaguar	58	2 laps	192,521 km/h	
12.	J. Button	Renault	54	6 laps	191,082 km/h	Problem on left front wheel.

Driver	Team		Reason
T. Sato	Jordan Honda	51	Exploded engine
K. Räikkönen	McLaren Mercedes	45	Broken engine
J. Trulli	Renault	30	Electronic problem, gearbox downshifts on its own
E. Bernoldi	Arrows Cosworth	29	Broken transmission shaft
E. Irvine	Jaguar	24	Spin
H-H. Frentzen	Arrows Cosworth	21	Engine trouble
M. Salo	Toyota	16	Broken transmission
M. Webber	Minardi Asiatech	10	Off
A. McNish	Toyota	1	Clutch problem at the start

Fastest Laps

	Driver	Time	Lap	Average
1.	R. Barrichello	1'23"083	58	222,760 km/h
2.	M. Schumacher	1'23"826	52	220,785 km/h
3.	R. Schumacher	1'24"586	58	218,802 km/h
4.	J. Villeneuve	1'24"949	56	217,867 km/h
5.	N. Heidfeld	1'24"996	57	217,746 km/h
6.	F. Massa	1'25"058	57	217,587 km/h
7.	O. Panis	1'25"063	58	217,575 km/h
8.	G. Fisichella	1'25"104	58	217,470 km/h
9.	K. Räikkönen	1'25"409	5	216,693 km/h
10.	J.P. Montoya	1'25"469	50	216,541 km/h
11.	D. Coulthard	1'25"492	56	216,483 km/h
12.	P. de la Rosa	1'25"540	57	216,361 km/h
13.	T. Sato	1'25"804	46	215,696 km/h
14.	J. Button	1'26"074	5	215,019 km/h
15.	J. Trulli	1'26"519	5	213,913 km/h
16.	M. Salo	1'26"723	4	213,410 km/h
17.	E. Bernoldi	1'27"328	5	211,932 km/h
18.	E. Irvine	1'27"781	5	210,838 km/h
19.	H-H. Frentzen	1'28"111	6	210,048 km/h
20.	M. Webber	1'28"321	7	209,549 km/h

Pit stops

	Driver	Time	Lap	Stop n°
1.	H-H. Frentzen	36"915	12	1
2.	F. Massa	33"817	12	1
3.	J.P. Montoya	34"905	13	1
4.	M. Schumacher	35"378	13	1
5.	K. Räikkönen	1'02"575	13	1
6.	R. Schumacher	54"574	13	1
7.	J. Trulli	32"642	13	1
8.	J. Button	48"287	13	1
9.	R. Barrichello	35"531	13	1
10.	J. Villeneuve	34"600	13	1
11.	M. Salo	34"978	13	1
12.	E. Bernoldi	35"199	13	1
13.	E. Irvine	36"381	13	1
14.	O. Panis	38"591	13	1
15.	N. Heidfeld	34"017	13	1
16.	G. Fisichella	33"268	13	1
17.	P. de la Rosa	37"050	14	1
18.	T. Sato	33"364	14	1
19.	D. Coulthard	31"236	15	1
20.	D. Coulthard	53"408	23	2
21.	K. Räikkönen	36"441	24	2
22.	J. Trulli	34"746	25	2
23.	J. Button	48"855	25	2
24.	E. Bernoldi	33"100	26	2
25.	E. Bernoldi	31"468	27	3
26.	J. Button	35"075	27	3
27.	K. Räikkönen	34"167	28	3
28.	J. Trulli	32"211	28	3
29.	D. Coulthard	31"151	28	3
30.	F. Massa	33"283	30	2
31.	R. Schumacher	54"279	31	2
32.	P. de la Rosa	32"730	30	2
33.	M. Schumacher	33"430	33	2
34.	R. Barrichello	32"580	33	2
35.	R. Schumacher	33"398	35	3
36.	J. Button	32"999	36	4
37.	D. Coulthard	51"227	36	4
38.	K. Räikkönen	35"330	37	4
39.	T. Sato	34"574	37	2
40.	N. Heidfeld	32"815	38	2
41.	P. de la Rosa	34"536	37	3
42.	J. Villeneuve	35"332	39	2
43.	G. Fisichella	32"656	39	2
44.	R. Barrichello	31"463	40	3
45.	J.P. Montoya	34"021	40	2
46.	O. Panis	33"228	40	2
47.	F. Massa	31"469	40	3
48.	M. Schumacher	31"909	43	3

Race Leaders

Driver	Laps in the lead	Nber of Laps	Kilometers
J.P. Montoya	1 > 15	15	77,011 km
M. Schumacher	16 > 60	45	231,345 km

Driver	Nber of Laps	Kilometers
M. Schumacher	45	231,345 km
J.P. Montoya	15	77,011 km

Lap chart

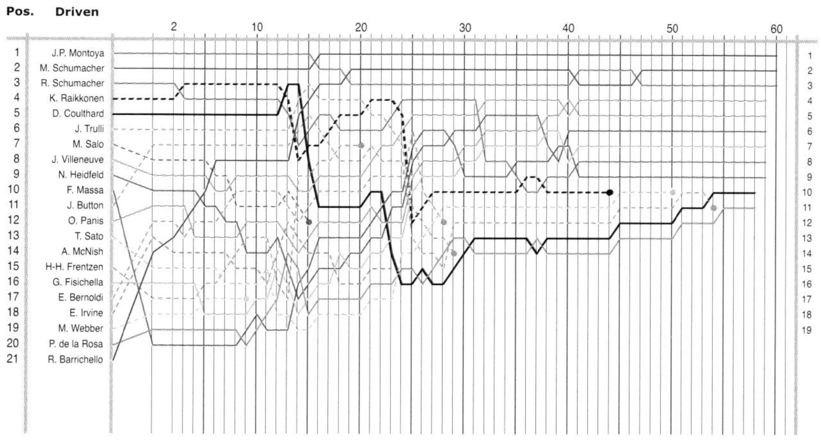

Pos.
Driven
2
10
20
30
40
50
60
1 J.P. Montoya
2 M. Schumacher
3 R. Schumacher
4 K. Raikkonen
5 D. Coulthard
6 J. Trulli
7 M. Salo
8 J. Villeneuve
9 N. Heidfeld
10 F. Massa
11 J. Button
12 O. Panis
13 T. Sato
14 A. McNish
15 H-H. Frentzen
16 G. Fisichella
17 E. Bernoldi
18 E. Irvine
19 M. Webber
20 P. de la Rosa
21 R. Barrichello

Gaps on the leader board

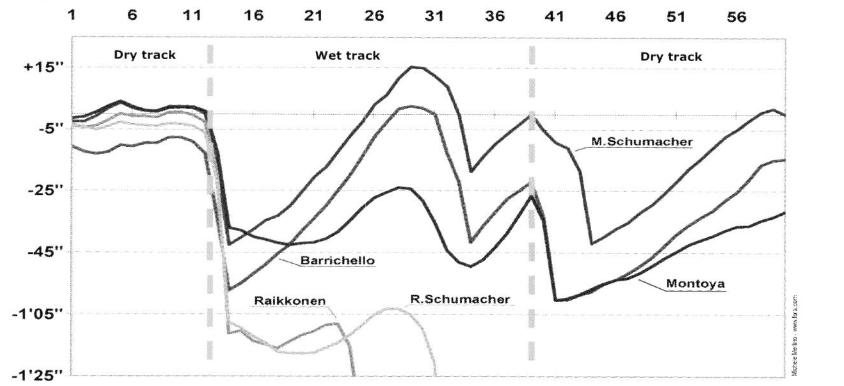

1
6
11
16
21
26
31
36
41
46
51
56
Dry track
Wet track
Dry track
+15"
-5"
-25"
-45"
-1'05"
-1'25"
M.Schumacher
Barrichello
Raikkonen
R.Schumacher
Montoya

Championship after ten rounds

Drivers

1. M. Schumacher 86
2. R. Barrichello 32
3. J.P. Montoya 31
4. R. Schumacher 30
5. D. Coulthard 26
6. K. Räikkönen 11
7. J. Button 10
8. N. Heidfeld 6
9. G. Fisichella...6
10. J. Trulli 4
11. F. Massa 4
12. J. Villeneuve..3
13. E. Irvine 3
14. O. Panis...2
15. M. Webber 2
16. M. Salo..2
17. H-H. Frentzen...2
18. A. McNish...0
19. A. Yoong 0
20. P. de la Rosa..0
21. T. Sato...0
22. E. Bernoldi 0

Constructors

1. Scuderia Ferrari Marlboro 118
2. BMW WilliamsF1 Team 61
3. West McLaren Mercedes 37
4. Mild Seven Renault F1 Team 14
5. Sauber Petronas 10
6. DHL Jordan Honda 6
7. Lucky Strike BAR Honda 5
8. Jaguar Racing...3
9. KL Minardi Asiatech 2
10. Panasonic Toyota Racing 2
11. Orange Arrows 2

The circuit

Nom :	Silverstone
Date :	July 7, 2002
Length :	5141 meters
Distance :	60 laps, 308,356 km
Temperature :	cloudy with showers 16°c
Track temperature :	17°c

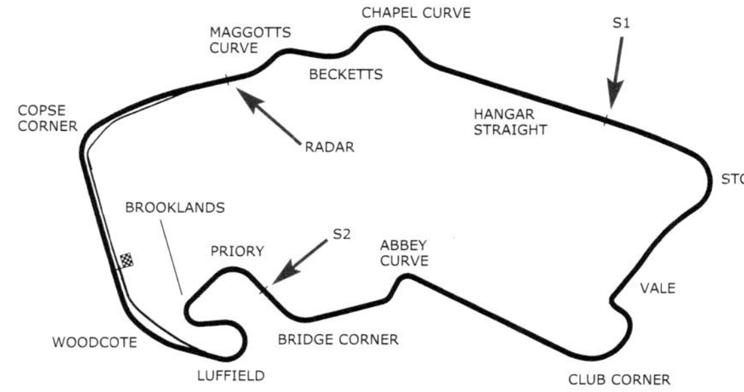

CHAPEL CURVE
MAGGOTTS CURVE
S1
BECKETTS
COPSE CORNER
RADAR
HANGAR STRAIGHT
STOWE
BROOKLANDS
S2
PRIORY
ABBEY CURVE
VALE
WOODCOTE
BRIDGE CORNER
LUFFIELD
CLUB CORNER

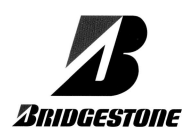

BRIDGESTONE

Best result for a driver running Bridgestone tyres:

Michael Schumacher, Ferrari, winner

All results : © 2002 Fédération Internationale de l'Automobile, 2, Ch. Blandonnet, 1215 Geneva 15, Switzerland

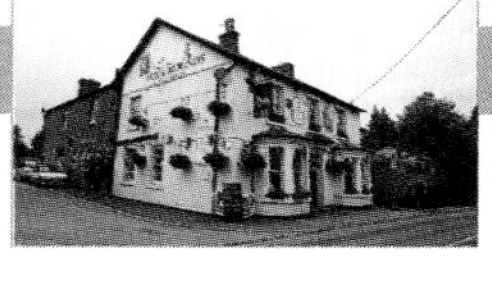

AND THAT MAKES FIVE!

At Magny-Cours, only the eleventh
Grand Prix of the season, Michael
Schumacher secured his fifth world
championship crown.

Statisticians love to classify, archive
and establish hierarchies. They
thrive on absolutes, records,
extremes. They climb the highest
mountains and head for the Pole in
ever more extreme conditions.
In sport, the limits are always being
extended, higher, longer, faster.
Formula 1 is no exception to this
rule and every time a driver proves
he is a special talent, the question is
always posed: is he the greatest?
However, motor racing is not a sport
which lends itself to comparisons of
its greats. How can one say if
Ayrton Senna drove better than
Stirling Moss, or that Juan Manuel
Fangio was more talented than
Michael Schumacher?
Talent in motor racing is a value
seen through a filter, distorted by
the quality of the machinery
involved. With five world titles to his
name, Michael Schumacher is
assured of a place among the gods
of the steering wheel. But is he the
best of all time? We will never
know...

> The Arrows make a one lap appearance on Saturday afternoon. They just cruised round, before heading home again. It made a nonsense of proceedings and it failed to impress Bernie Ecclestone.

> A fifth consecutive pole position for Juan Pablo Montoya. An incredible achievement which was about to come to an end. "*I really did not expect to get pole today*", said a happy Colombian. "*The Ferraris definitely looked stronger.*"

> A big fright for Giancarlo Fisichella on Saturday morning: he went off the track at high speed, ending up in a tyre barrier at the Estoril corner. He had to be taken to Nevers hospital for a complete check-up. He returned to the circuit in the afternoon, apparently uninjured, but chose not to take part in qualifying.

Arrows: the saga continues

A fortnight earlier in Silverstone, the Arrows team had looked on the edge of extinction. It was only in the early hours of Friday morning that the Cosworth engines were delivered so that the mechanics could start bolting them into the chassis. The cars had not even been able to run on Friday, as the engines' electronic control units had not been supplied by Ford, who were waiting for a long overdue payment.

Finally, Arrows boss Tom Walkinshaw had signed a personal cheque to settle matters and it seemed that all was in order again. Indeed, in Magny-Cours, the cars went through scrutineering and were ready to go out on track.

However, come Friday, they spent the entire day in the garage, while Heinz-Harald Frentzen and Enrique Bernoldi never got changed out of their civvies. Officially, it was because the team did not want to risk damaging the cars, given the team had very few spare parts, as they did not have the wherewithal to make them.

In fact, it seemed as though all this manoeuvring was part of a Tom Walkinshaw plan to sell the team. He almost admitted as much: "*I don't have to explain myself about what is going on in the team*", he snapped. "*If I tell you I had forbidden my drivers from running today, because they did better than usual at Silverstone adopting that policy, you wouldn't believe me... So what do you want me to tell you? At the moment, negotiations are taking place with my lawyers in London and they advised me not to run the cars, so as not to compromise their discussions.*"

Rumour had it that there were three potential investors considering buying Arrows: a Canadian consortium led by Craig Pollock, the Vivendi Group and the Red Bull company, currently sponsors of the Sauber team. Of course, only one bid could be successful and apparently the three parties were fighting over it.

Saturday was a farce: the two Arrows went out at the start of qualifying, when no other cars were on the track. They each did just one lap, without any intention of posting a competitive time, came back to the pits, at which point the team packed its bags, neither of the cars having qualified. Their appearance had been purely to collect their share of the television rights money.

Renault fires Button

On Saturday afternoon, Renault Sport President Patrick Faure announced his driver line-up for 2003: Jarno Trulli, already driving for Renault this season and Fernando Alonso, currently the test driver. As for Jenson Button, this year's other driver... nothing. Renault said it would try and help the Englishman find a seat, but there were no guarantees.

Starting grid

Position	Driver	Time
18	M. WEBBER	1:14.800
16	M. SALO	1:13.837
14	T. SATO	1:13.542
12	F. MASSA	1:13.501
10	N. HEIDFELD	1:13.370
8	J. TRULLI	1:13.030
6	D. COULTHARD	1:12.498
4	K. RÄIKKÖNEN	1:12.244
2	M. SCHUMACHER	1:12.008
19	A. YOONG	1:16.798
17	A. McNISH	1:13.949
15	P. DE LA ROSA	1:13.656
13	J. VILLENEUVE	1:13.506
11	O. PANIS	1:13.457
9	E. IRVINE	1:13.188
7	J. BUTTON	1:12.761
5	R. SCHUMACHER	1:12.424
3	R. BARRICHELLO	1:12.197
1	J.P. MONTOYA	1:11.985 (158,224 km/h)

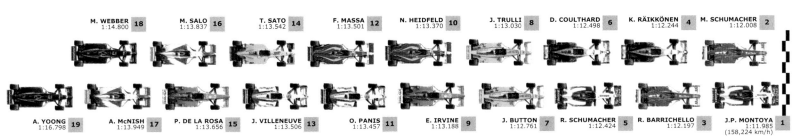

A surprise for Michael Schumacher

He had missed out on pole position by 23 thousandths of a second and, for once, the Williams-BMWs had seemed capable of matching his pace. It seemed therefore that Michael Schumacher's chances of taking the title here were pretty slim and the man himself certainly was not expecting to leave Magny-Cours with the championship in his pocket. In the early part of the race, he had to cope with being held up by Juan Pablo Montoya. The Ferrari was clearly quicker than the Williams, but there was no way to get past.

Schumacher had to wait for the first pit stops to do so, except that he got it wrong leaving the pits, crossing the white line which officially separates the pit lane from the track. "*It was entirely my fault*", he admitted after the race. "*I was looking in my mirrors to see the cars coming on the track and at the same time, I was talking on the radio. I was not paying enough attention. But I don't think I crossed the line by much. It must have been a case of millimetres rather than centimetres!*"

Condemned to a drive-through penalty, the German dropped back to third, behind Juan Pablo Montoya and Kimi Räikkönen. The Williams man was off the pace after his second refuelling stop, while the McLaren driver put up a heck of a fight. Montoya was running fourth and any hopes of a championship title were slipping away with each passing lap.

Then, just five laps from the end, Kimi Räikkönen ran wide on a patch of oil and left the door wide open for Michael Schumacher.

Given that neither Rubens Barrichello nor Juan Pablo Montoya had finished in second place, this win meant that Michael got his hands on his fifth world championship crown. It was more than he had hoped for. "*I've been very relaxed all weekend long. To be honest, I was not even thinking about the title, as it seemed almost impossible for me to get it here. But, in the race, when I saw Rubens retire and how much quicker I was than Juan Pablo, I began to think I might have a chance after all. Later, after my penalty, Kimi was going so quickly that, once again, I thought it would be impossible. When I passed him, suddenly all the weight of the championship seemed to be on my shoulders. It was very hard and they were the worst five laps of my career.*"

Mission accomplished, Michael Schumacher could finally savour the moment. "*It was very, very emotional. I must say there were some tears inside my helmet*", he admitted with embarrassment. "*It is my fifth title and all of them have been a bit special, each in its own way. You never get used to this sort of emotion. Actually, we hadn't planned anything for here* (editor's note: a party had actually been planned for Sunday night in Hockenheim, one week later.) *We will have to see what we can do. At the moment I don't know. Everyone knows that after winning, I like to smoke a good cigar, but as it seems I am some sort of idol for young people, it's best if you do not say that.*" The fact he had also equalled Juan Manuel Fangio's record of five titles, did not seem to mean that much to him. "*People have often mentioned this record to me. Unfortunately, and I apologise for this, I don't feel much about that. You cannot compare what Fangio did with what we do today. Back then, driving involved a lot more effort. These days, there are a lot more people to look after us and it is more of a team sport. I just want to appreciate what I have done for myself, without trying to make comparisons with someone else.*"

<
A brief off-track excursion for Michael Schumacher in qualifying. Come Sunday though and it was another impeccable race. A small mistake from Kimi Räikkönen and the matter was settled. The Schumacher-Ferrari-Bridgestone trio were thus crowned after just 11 of the 17 races.

Race summary

> A scare for Ferrari at the start of the formation lap: Rubens Barrichello's car refuses to fire up. The Brazilian is less than impressed as he watches the others leave the grid **(1)**.

> Starting from pole, Montoya manages to fend off Schumacher and Räikkönen. He would finish 4th **(2)**.

> Kimi Räikkönen finds himself leading, thanks to the run of pit stops **(3)**.

> The battle between Schumacher and Räikkönen is fierce. The German tries every which way to get by **(4)**.

> Sliding off the track on McNish's oil, Räikkönen goes straight on at the Adelaide corner. He gets back on track, but Schumacher is long gone **(5)**.

> Michael Schumacher wins the race and takes his fifth world title at the same time **(6)**.

> Mr. Montezemolo celebrates with his team **(7)**.

Technicolour dream

What could be better than a close up of an F1 car?
Five close ups of course.

The biggest loser

Poor Kimi

There is no doubting that Kimi Räikkönen is a major talent, but the young Finn still lacks experience. Leading with five laps to go, he was preparing to take his first ever grand prix win, when he slid on oil left by Allan McNish's Toyota. Michael Schumacher did not have to be asked twice and slipped by. McLaren reckoned the move took place under the yellow flags and protested the Ferrari driver. However, the Magny-Cours Stewards rejected the protest, confirming the German's fifth world title.

Poor Rubinho

Rubens Barrichello's run of bad luck continued. Because of an electrical problem, his car would not fire up on the grid and the mechanics left it up on jacks. Rubinho was so angry that he actually packed his bags and left the circuit for home. He was sitting in his plane on the runway when he heard that

Michael Schumacher had managed to win and take the championship after all. In a fine example of friendship between team-mates, the Brazilian headed back for the track to offer his congratulations!

Poor Juan Pablo

While Ralf Schumacher finished fifth and was delighted with his brother's achievement, Juan Pablo Montoya was in a filthy mood as he struggled out of his fire suit after the race. This was the fifth consecutive time that he had failed to convert pole position into a win, because of a poor tyre choice. He had been leading up until his second pit stop, but from then on he could not match the pace of the quickest cars. "*I had a big problem with the balance of my car and it was very hard to drive. Our tyre choice was not the right one for the race. As the race went on, I had less and less grip.*"

Jenson Button signs for BAR

In London, on the Monday after the French Grand Prix, the BAR team announced it had signed a long-term contract (two years with a further two year option) with Jenson Button. The English driver had just been dumped by the Renault team, who had announced the previous Saturday that he would be replaced for 2003, by the Spaniard Fernando Alonso.

For Button, it meant yet another change of direction in his career, but given BAR's ambitious plans, under the new leadership of David Richards, it seemed to have some potential. "*Jenson has an*

extraordinary talent and he needs the right environment to bring it out", said Richards. "*I have put in place a long term plan destined to bring success to BAR. It will not happen overnight, but I am convinced that Jenson can win the world championship in the course of the four years he is about to spend with us.*" With Button signed up, a huge question mark was forming over the identity of his team-mate. Who would jump ship? Olivier Panis or Jacques Villeneuve? On race day in France, the rumours were changing by the hour. On the one hand, it seemed that Jacques Villeneuve

had a cast iron contract, drawn up by his manager Craig Pollock, in the days when he in charge at BAR. However, the Canadian admitted he was still negotiating. "*You can always talk, even when a contract is signed*", he commented on the Saturday.

There was always the common sense way of looking at the problem. Why would David Richards want to keep a star driver who cost him more, complained more and was often slower than Olivier Panis? The Frenchman looked like a real asset for the future development of the team and its car.

Practice

All the time trials

N°	Driver	Car/Engine/Chassis	Practice friday	Pos.	Practice saturday	Pos.	Qualifying	Pos.	Warm-up	Pos.
1.	Michael Schumacher	Ferrari 2002/219	1'14"240	3°	1'12"974	1°	1'12"008	2°	1'14"174	1°
2.	Rubens Barrichello	Ferrari 2002/220	1'14"750	4°	1'13"503	4°	1'12"197	3°	1'14"888	2°
3.	David Coulthard	McLaren-Mercedes MP4/17/08	1'14"025	1°	1'13"249	3°	1'12"498	6°	1'15"817	9°
4.	Kimi Räikkönen	McLaren-Mercedes MP4/17/06	1'14"097	2°	1'12"995	2°	1'12"244	4°	1'15"714	7°
5.	Ralf Schumacher	Williams-BMW FW24/06	1'14"970	5°	1'13"728	7°	1'12"424	5°	1'16"184	12°
6.	Juan Pablo Montoya	Williams-BMW FW24/05	1'15"271	10°	1'13"633	6°	1'11"985	1°	1'16"755	14°
7.	Nick Heidfeld	Sauber-Petronas C21/06	1'14"209	16°	1'14"108	9°	1'13"370	10°	1'15"534	5°
8.	Felipe Massa	Sauber-Petronas C21/07	1'16"030	13°	1'14"211	12°	1'13"501	12°	1'15"519	4°
9.	Giancarlo Fisichella	Jordan-Honda EJ12/6	1'15"422	12°	1'14"949	15°	Forfeit		Forfeit	
10.	Takuma Sato	Jordan-Honda EJ12/4	1'16"167	15°	1'14"503	13°	1'13"542	14°	1'16"068	11°
11.	Jacques Villeneuve	BAR-Honda 004/06	1'16"457	17°	1'15"036	16°	1'13"506	13°	1'16"821	15°
12.	Olivier Panis	BAR-Honda 004/08	1'16"163	14°	1'14"557	14°	1'13"457	11°	1'16"058	10°
14.	Jarno Trulli	Renault R202/05	1'16"763	19°	1'14"161	10°	1'13"030	8°	1'15"455	3°
15.	Jenson Button	Renault R202/06	1'15"218	9°	1'13"553	5°	1'12"761	7°	1'15"673	6°
16.	Eddie Irvine	Jaguar R3/05	1'14"983	6°	1'14"018	8°	1'13"188	9°	1'15"804	8°
17.	Pedro de la Rosa	Jaguar R3/04	1'15"179	8°	1'14"211	11°	1'13"656	15°	1'16"612	13°
20.	Heinz-Harald Frentzen	Arrows-Cosworth A23/01					1'18"497	21°		
21.	Enrique Bernoldi	Arrows-Cosworth A23/03					1'19"843	22°		
22.	Alex Yoong	Minardi-Asiatech PS02/03	1'19"015	20°	1'17"207	20°	1'16"798	19°	1'19"045	19°
23.	Mark Webber	Minardi-Asiatech PS02/04	1'16"496	18°	1'15"797	19°	1'14"800	18°	1'17"873	18°
24.	Mika Salo	Toyota-TF102/07	1'15"161	7°	1'15"516	17°	1'13"837	16°	1'16"889	16°
25.	Allan McNish	Toyota-TF102/08	1'15"411	11°	1'15"650	18°	1'13"949	17°	1'17"056	17°

Maximum speeds

N°	Drive	P1 Qualifs	Pos.	P1 Race	Pos.	P2 Qualifs	Pos.	P2 Race	Pos.	Finish Qualifs	Pos.	Finish Race	Pos.	Trap Qualifs	Pos.	Trap Race	Pos.
1.	M. Schumacher	174,3	8°	173,6	8°	281,8	1°	282,5	1°	No data available				306,0	1°	312,5	1°
2.	R. Barrichello	172,5	9°			280,2	4°							304,6	3°		
3.	D. Coulthard	174,5	6°	170,8	9°	277,8	8°	279,7	4°					299,4	12°	304,6	11°
4.	K. Räikkönen	170,8	16°	189,9	2°	279,8	5°	279,2	5°					298,6	15°	308,3	5°
5.	R. Schumacher	176,2	5°	182,2	4°	281,5	3°	282,2	2°					304,2	4°	308,4	4°
6.	J.P. Montoya	182,3	2°	168,8	12°	281,7	2°	281,9	3°					304,6	2°	308,2	7°
7.	N. Heidfeld	171,8	12°	165,8	15°	275,9	14°	276,6	13°					302,0	5°	305,6	10°
8.	F. Massa	186,4	1°	168,3	14°	275,2	17°	276,3	14°					300,2	11°	308,5	3°
9.	G. Fisichella																
10.	T. Sato	162,3	20°	170,8	10°	276,9	9°	275,5	16°					301,6	7°	304,4	12°
11.	J. Villeneuve	179,4	3°	180,3	6°	276,4	11°	275,6	15°					299,1	14°	306,2	9°
12.	O. Panis	172,0	11°	176,0	7°	275,9	15°	276,9	11°					297,0	17°	308,5	2°
14.	J. Trulli	174,5	7°	164,7	16°	276,2	12°	277,7	8°					299,3	13°	304,3	13°
15.	J. Button	172,3	10°	170,4	11°	276,5	10°	276,9	9°					300,7	9°	306,3	8°
16.	E. Irvine	171,6	13°	196,7	1°	275,7	16°	276,9	10°					297,1	16°	302,5	16°
17.	P. de la Rosa	178,8	4°	187,9	3°	275,9	13°	276,9	12°					296,3	18°	303,0	15°
18.	H-H. Frentzen	164,2	19°			274,6	18°							300,6	10°		
19.	E. Bernoldi	158,4	21°			272,7	19°							295,7	19°		
22.	A. Yoong	170,6	17°	180,6	5°	272,7	19°	271,9	17°					293,1	21°	298,6	18°
23.	M. Webber	169,8	18°	168,4	13°	272,5	20°	270,4	18°					295,7	20°	298,7	17°
24.	M. Salo	170,8	15°	158,5	18°	278,4	7°	277,8	7°					301,6	8°	308,2	6°
25.	A. McNish	171,1	14°			278,9	6°							302,0	6°	303,3	14°

Race

Classifications & Retirements

Pos.	Driver	Team	Lap	Time	Average	
1.	M. Schumacher	Ferrari	72	1:32:09.837	199,135 km/h	
2.	K. Räikkönen	McLaren Mercedes	72	1.105	199,096 km/h	
3.	D. Coulthard	McLaren Mercedes	72	31.976	197,991 km/h	
4.	J.P. Montoya	Williams BMW	72	40.676	197,681 km/h	
5.	R. Schumacher	Williams BMW	72	41.773	197,642 km/h	
6.	J. Button	Renault	71	1 lap	195,937 km/h	
7.	N. Heidfeld	Sauber Petronas	71	1 lap	194,357 km/h	
8.	M. Webber	Minardi Asiatech	71	1 lap	193,568 km/h	
9.	P. de la Rosa	Jaguar	70	2 laps	192,971 km/h	
10.	A. Yoong	Minardi Asiatech	68	4 laps	187,593 km/h	
11.	A. McNish	Toyota	65	7 laps	193,516 km/h	Exploded engine

Driver	Team		Reason
E. Irvine	Jaguar	53	Broken rear wing, off
J. Trulli	Renault	50	Exploded engine
F. Massa	Sauber Petronas	49	Mechanical failure
M. Salo	Toyota	49	Exploded engine
J. Villeneuve	BAR Honda	36	Exploded engine
O. Panis	BAR Honda	30	Vibrations due to hit with Sato
T. Sato	Jordan Honda	24	Off at the Lycée corner
R. Barrichello	Ferrari	0	Engine will not start on the dummy grid

Fastest laps

	Driver	Time	Lap	Average
1.	D. Coulthard	1'15"045	62	203,925 km/h
2.	M. Schumacher	1'15"311	25	203,205 km/h
3.	K. Räikkönen	1'15"406	53	202,949 km/h
4.	R. Schumacher	1'15"584	24	202,471 km/h
5.	J.P. Montoya	1'15"697	26	202,169 km/h
6.	J. Button	1'15"957	22	201,477 km/h
7.	O. Panis	1'16"278	4	200,629 km/h
8.	J. Trulli	1'16"300	20	200,571 km/h
9.	E. Irvine	1'16"456	20	200,162 km/h
10.	P. de la Rosa	1'16"515	58	200,007 km/h
11.	J. Villeneuve	1'16"667	23	199,611 km/h
12.	N. Heidfeld	1'16"847	22	199,143 km/h
13.	F. Massa	1'17"029	46	198,673 km/h
14.	M. Webber	1'17"087	26	198,523 km/h
15.	M. Salo	1'17"295	28	197,989 km/h
16.	A. McNish	1'17"304	47	197,966 km/h
17.	T. Sato	1'17"565	6	197,300 km/h
18.	A. Yoong	1'18"998	37	193,721 km/h

Pit stops

	Driver	Time	Lap	Stop n°
1.	O. Panis	1'39"131	1	1
2.	F. Massa	14"368	7	1
3.	F. Massa	14"438	10	2
4.	J. Button	26"501	20	1
5.	J. Villeneuve	24"580	20	1
6.	A. Yoong	25"996	20	1
7.	J. Trulli	25"697	21	1
8.	E. Irvine	26"040	21	1
9.	O. Panis	26"660	20	2
10.	R. Schumacher	24"312	22	1
11.	J.P. Montoya	25"488	24	1
12.	A. McNish	31"549	24	1
13.	M. Webber	25"819	24	1
14.	P. de la Rosa	26"551	24	1
15.	M. Salo	25"795	25	1
16.	M. Schumacher	25"251	26	1
17.	K. Räikkönen	25"121	27	1
18.	F. Massa	25"632	27	3
19.	D. Coulthard	26"795	28	1
20.	N. Heidfeld	25"035	28	1
21.	M. Schumacher	14"415	35	2
22.	P. de la Rosa	26"552	39	2
23.	J.P. Montoya	29"135	43	2
24.	E. Irvine	20"400	43	2
25.	R. Schumacher	26"612	44	2
26.	J. Button	28"103	44	2
27.	M. Salo	26"520	44	2
28.	A. Yoong	27"229	43	2
29.	A. McNish	26"665	45	2
30.	J. Trulli	26"230	46	2
31.	M. Schumacher	25"569	48	3
32.	M. Webber	25"667	47	2
33.	R. Schumacher	14"399	48	3
34.	K. Räikkönen	24"877	49	2
35.	N. Heidfeld	27"059	49	2
36.	D. Coulthard	24"069	54	2
37.	P. de la Rosa	26"908	56	3
38.	D. Coulthard	14"159	59	3
39.	J. Button	24"850	59	3

Race leaders

Driver	Laps in the lead	Nber of Laps	Kilometers
J.P. Montoya	1 > 23	23	97,587 km
M. Schumacher	24 > 25	2	8,502 km
K. Räikkönen	26	1	4,251 km
D. Coulthard	27 > 28	2	8,502 km
M. Schumacher	29 > 35	7	29,757 km
J.P. Montoya	36 > 42	7	29,757 km
K. Räikkönen	43 > 49	7	29,757 km
D. Coulthard	50 > 54	5	21,255 km
K. Räikkönen	55 > 67	13	55,263 km
M. Schumacher	68 > 72	5	21,263 km

Driver	Nber of Laps	Kilometers
J.P. Montoya	30	127,344 km
K. Räikkönen	21	89,271 km
M. Schumacher	14	59,514 km
D. Coulthard	7	29,757 km

Lap chart

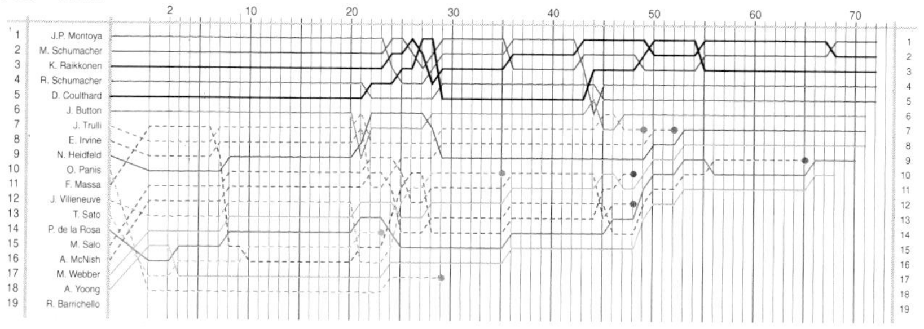

Gaps on the leader board

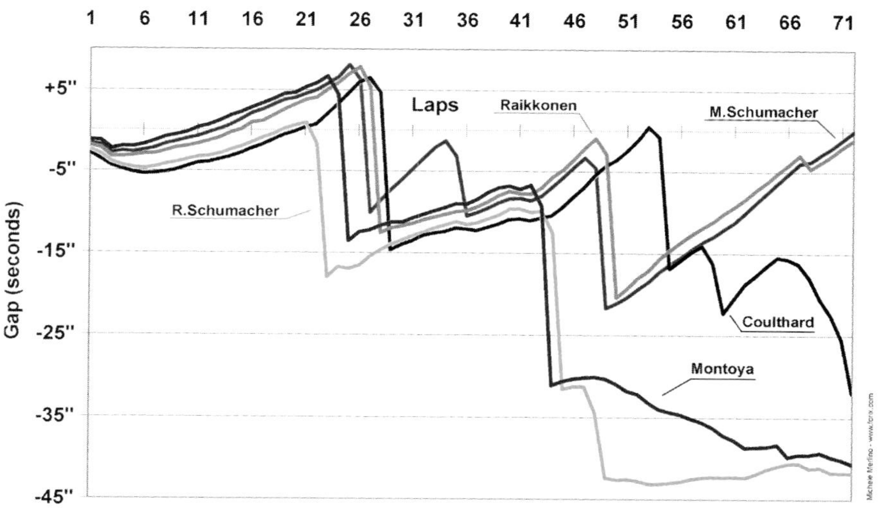

Championship after eleven rounds

Drivers

1. **M. Schumacher 96**
2. J.P. Montoya 34
3. R. Barrichello...32
4. R. Schumacher 32
5. D. Coulthard..30
6. K. Räikkönen 17
7. J. Button 11
8. N. Heidfeld...6
9. G. Fisichella...6
10. J. Trulli 4
11. F. Massa 4
12. J. Villeneuve..3
13. E. Irvine 3
14. O. Panis...2
15. M. Webber 2
16. M. Salo..2
17. H-H. Frentzen...2
18. A. McNish..0
19. A. Yoong 0
20. P. de la Rosa..0
21. T. Sato...0
22. E. Bernoldi 0

Constructors

1. Scuderia Ferrari Marlboro 128
2. BMW WilliamsF1 Team 66
3. West McLaren Mercedes 47
4. Mild Seven Renault F1 Team 15
5. Sauber Petronas 10
6. DHL Jordan Honda 6
7. Lucky Strike BAR Honda 5
8. Jaguar Racing..3
9. KL Minardi Asiatech..................................2
10. Panasonic Toyota Racing 2
11. Orange Arrows 2

All results : © 2002 Fédération Internationale de l'Automobile, 2, Ch. Blandonnet, 1215 Geneva 15, Switzerland

The circuit

Name :	Magny-Cours, Nevers
Date :	July 21, 2002
Length :	4251 meters
Distance :	72 laps, 305,886 km
Temperature :	warm and sunny, 25°c
Track temperature :	35°c

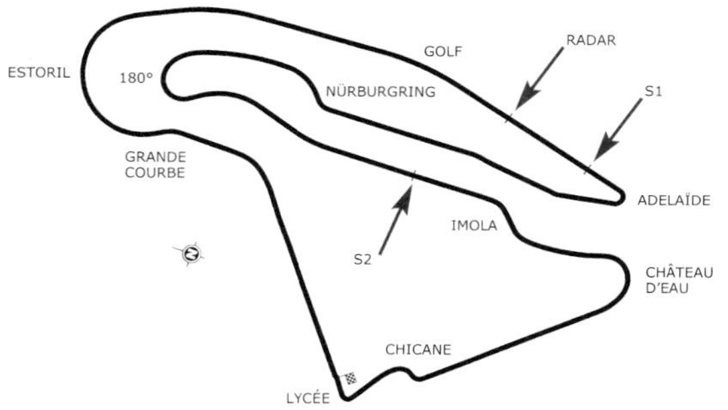

BRIDGESTONE

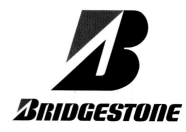

Best result for a driver running Bridgestone tyres:

Michael Schumacher, Ferrari, winner

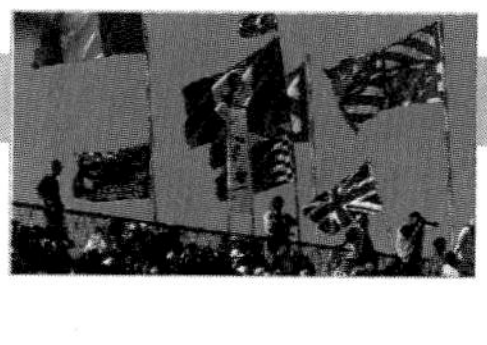

THE FIRST ONE AT HOME

Strange to relate, but Michael Schumacher had never been on pole position at Hockenheim and he had never won there in a Ferrari. This lapse was now corrected, as the newly-crowned world champion, set the fastest lap in qualifying, before going on to win on Sunday.

Constantly on pole position since the Monaco Grand Prix, Juan Pablo Montoya had to settle for fourth place on the grid in Hockenheim.

David Coulthard had good reason to smile in Hockenheim, as he had just been reconfirmed as a McLaren driver.

Michael Schumacher's first Hockenheim pole

In 2001, on the old Hockenheim track layout, Juan Pablo Montoya had taken the first pole position of his Formula 1 career. This year, on a much modified circuit, the Colombian still hoped to repeat the feat, especially after his incredible run of five pole positions which began at the Monaco Grand Prix.

Arrows still there

Max Mosley, President of the International Automobile Federation (FIA) had issued a warning to the Arrows team: if they produced a repeat performance of their nonsense at the French Grand Prix (when the cars only did three laps in qualifying, deliberately slowing down in the last sector of the track) they could be suspended. This penalty could be applied for several races, even to the end of the season, in accordance with article 151c of the sporting code, which relates to "*any action prejudicial to the interests of the sport*".
Sure enough, the two Arrows ran normally at Hockenheim. Heinz-Harald Frentzen qualified 15th and Enrique Bernoldi was 18th. But it was not the on-track performance of the orange cars which set tongues wagging in the paddock, but the behind the scenes goings-on. Craig Pollock was spotted having several lengthy discussions over the weekend. The latest rumours had it that Jacques Villeneuve's manager had finally done a deal to buy the Arrows team, with only details such as whether or not the acquisition of the factory was included, needing to be finalised.

In the end though, it was Michael Schumacher who celebrated his newly acquired world championship title by taking the top slot on the grid, much to the great delight of the spectators. After the German had taken his fifth title a week earlier, the organisers instantly sold the 30,000 grandstand seats which they still had on their hands. That meant an additional 30,000 fans who had come to cheer on their hero. "*It's my first pole at Hockenheim and it is a dream to get it today*", commented Schumi. "*I can really feel the support of the crowd and I would like to offer them a win. It would be my first here in a Ferrari.*" However, the Williams-BMWs were not far behind, as Ralf Schumacher was only beaten by 181 thousandths of a second by his big brother. "*It's one of those weekends where everything is working right from the start*", rejoiced the world champion's little brother. "*I quickly found the right balance on the car and it's super to start "my" Grand Prix from the front row.*" Fourth behind Rubens Barrichello's Ferrari, Juan Pablo Montoya was not too disappointed either. "*I had a lot of understeer on my first run and I made a mistake on my last quick lap. It is a shame, but after five poles in a row, I think I can put up with starting from the second row. Anyway, I'm pretty confident for the race and I think it should go better than usual for us.*"

McLaren announces its driver line-up

The McLaren team's "*Communications Centre*" (how can one describe such a sophisticated structure as a "*motorhome*"?) was jam packed with journalists on Friday to hear team boss Ron Dennis announce his 2003 driver line-up. There were no surprises as the Englishman confirmed that his two current drivers, David Coulthard and Kimi Räikkönen, were being kept on. As was the team's test driver, Alexander Wurz. The Austrian was in Hockenheim and admitted he hoped that the team would run three cars in next year's grands prix, which was another rumour doing the rounds.
Mika Häkkinen, to no one's great surprise, announced that his sabbatical had matured into full time retirement. The Finn was not in Germany and he delivered his news via the medium of a video shown by McLaren. He said he had enjoyed an exceptional career, but now wanted to dedicate his time to his family. Other pieces of the 2003 jigsaw puzzle were also falling into place. On Friday, Peter Sauber announced he was taking up his option to keep Nick Heidfeld. He had nothing to say on the subject of his second driver. In the Toyota camp, team boss Ove Andersson admitted he had not yet made any decisions about the Japanese squad's 2003 drivers. But it was probable he would be looking to replace Allan McNish with a driver who could bring more to the team.

Starting grid

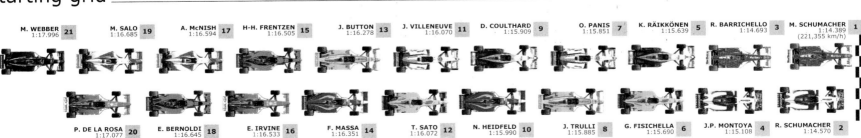

Position	Driver	Time
21	M. WEBBER	1:17.996
20	P. DE LA ROSA	1:17.077
19	M. SALO	1:16.685
18	E. BERNOLDI	1:16.645
17	A. McNISH	1:16.594
16	E. IRVINE	1:16.533
15	H-H. FRENTZEN	1:16.505
14	F. MASSA	1:16.351
13	J. BUTTON	1:16.278
12	T. SATO	1:16.072
11	J. VILLENEUVE	1:16.070
10	N. HEIDFELD	1:15.990
9	D. COULTHARD	1:15.909
8	J. TRULLI	1:15.885
7	O. PANIS	1:15.851
6	G. FISICHELLA	1:15.690
5	K. RÄIKKÖNEN	1:15.639
4	J.P. MONTOYA	1:15.108
3	R. BARRICHELLO	1:14.693
2	R. SCHUMACHER	1:14.570
1	M. SCHUMACHER	1:14.389 (221,355 km/h)

The fight hots up to be "*best of the rest*"

With the world championship wrapped up by Michael Schumacher, the main point of interest for the remaining grands prix would now switch to the purely honorary title of "*runner-up*".

It was currently closely contested with Juan Pablo Montoya, Ralf Schumacher, Rubens Barrichello and David Coulthard all in the running.

In Hockenheim, all four of those drivers finished in the points, one behind the other, but a good way behind Michael Schumacher. Right from the start, Ralf Schumacher conserved his front row advantage to run second, just behind his brother and ahead of Rubens Barrichello.

At first, the gap between the Williams-BMW and the Ferrari increased, eventually settling down at around 2.4 seconds in the run up to the first pit stops. Ralf was then unlucky to be held up by a slowing Jacques Villeneuve. Later on, he even had to make a third visit to the pits, because of a drop in hydraulic pressure in the engine. "*If you look at all the problems I had today, I think I can be happy to finish on the podium*", he commented after the race.

His team-mate Juan Pablo Montoya was the main beneficiary of Ralf's woes, exchanging his long-held fourth place for second at the flag. "*Of course I had not expected to finish second*", admitted the Colombian. "*Naturally, I made the most of Ralf and Rubens having problems, but that's racing. It's my best result in seven grands prix, even though I started from pole in the last five races.*"

During the race, Montoya pulled off a fantastic passing move on Kimi Räikkönen, at the end of a duel that went on for half a lap. It was definitely the most exciting move of the year. "*I made a bit of a mess of the start and so I was stuck behind Kimi*", explained the Colombian. "*He was running much slower than me, but I could not pass him and the*

team used the telemetry to drop my revs a bit to save the engine. After a while, we decided I was losing too much time, so the team increased the revs again and told me to go for it. Even so, it wasn't easy, but Kimi made a small mistake and I was able to overtake him coming into the stadium section. He tried to stay alongside me, but to be honest there is not enough room for two cars at that point!*"

Out in a world of his own at the head of the field, Michael Schumacher took his ninth win of the season. He was definitely not bored by it all and was delighted to take his first German Grand Prix win at the wheel of a Ferrari.

∧
While they fought at the back, it was all quiet up the front end for Michael Schumacher in the German Grand Prix. "*It is the first time I win here in a Ferrari and I thank God for making it possible*", he remarked.

Briefly

> Olivier Panis was running sixth when his BAR got out of shape and stopped on lap 40. It was a big disappointment given his position at the time. "*I'm gutted*", he admitted. "*Everything was going so well. It's a shame.*"

> The BAR and Jordan teams had a new Honda engine. Giancarlo Fisichella qualified sixth for Jordan and Olivier Panis was seventh for BAR. It was their best performance of the season.

> Film director Luc Besson was in Hockenheim as a guest of Jean Todt. It provided him with the opportunity to take a close look at the world of F1, having recently shot a film during the Le Mans 24 Hours race.

> After the race, the German television channel, RTL presented Michael Schumacher with the F3 car he drove to win the 1990 German F3 championship. He tried it in the paddock... and stalled!

Race summary

> In front of an enthusiastic crowd, Michael Schumacher's Ferrari leads from his brother at the first corner (1).

> Behind them, the toughest battle of the season rages between Montoya and Räikkönen. It ends in favour of the Colombian

after they ran shoulder to shoulder for several corners (2).

> Ralf Schumacher was unable to fend off his

team-mate, but he managed to get the better of Rubens Barrichello (3).

> After a puncture on the

straight, Räikkönen's race ends in spectacular fashion (4).

> Thanks to Nick Heidfeld, Germany has three

drivers in the points (5).

> In parc ferme, the two brothers congratulate one another on a job

well done, much to the delight of the fans (6) who invade the track at the end of the race. The party is just beginning (7).

It was not Renault's day in Hockenheim. Having qualified 13th, Jenson Button retired with engine failure.

> While David Coulthard finished fifth, Kimi Räikkönen had to retire after picking up a puncture, which damaged his suspension as he tried to make it back to the pits.

A new layout, a new grandstand: Hockenheim was revitalised

The Hockenheim circuit is a real classic on the Formula 1 calendar. Grands Prix have been staged there regularly since 1977 (with just one exception in 1985) and it was well know for its endless "*autobahn*" straights through the forest. But now these memories were consigned to the past and a rich past at that. The Hockenheim circuit was built in 1932. At first it had a triangular layout with a loose surface which made for much excitement. In 1938, the track was drastically modified, producing its famously fast layout. Shortly after that, during the last war, it was used as a tank testing ground. It was not until 1957 and the laying of a tarmac surface, that international events were held there, starting with a motorcycle grand prix. The famous stadium, with its huge grandstands and 120,000 spectators was built in 1964. However, in 2000, the organisers realised that staging a grand prix was proving too expensive, as they had to pay FOM (Formula One Management, run by Bernie Ecclestone) ten million dollars for the privilege. They could not

fund this sum from ticket sales. They came up with the solution of building additional viewing areas to increase their spectator capacity, but that necessitated a complete redesign of the circuit.
Work began on 2nd January and was completed just in time for the grand prix. The result of all these efforts was a brand new circuit, very modern and featuring overtaking opportunities.

The drivers were unanimous in their praise of the new look, even though Friday saw a glut of slides and off-track excursions as the surface was dirty and dusty.
However, thanks to large run-off areas, many of them with an asphalt surface, there were no serious accidents. "*I love this new circuit*", commented Ralf Schumacher. "*It is great fun and it is one of the best tracks I have driven on.*"

Felipe Massa learns a lesson from Peter Sauber

Felipe Massa made an extraordinary start, whizzing up to 11th place, just ahead of his team-mate.
The two Saubers ran nose to tail up to lap 33, when the team asked the Brazilian to move over and let Nick Heidfeld through. He obeyed and they then stayed in that order after the second run of pit stops, even though the German got carried away and briefly ran across the grass. He got back on track, still ahead of his team-mate and picked up a

point for sixth place.
Massa finished seventh and was deeply unimpressed. The Brazilian did not understand why he had been asked to let Heidfeld pass him and a tense discussion ensued with Peter Sauber. Asked why he had issued team orders, the Swiss boss refused to comment before leaving the circuit by helicopter to appear on a television programme in Zurich.

> The new Hockenheim designed by Hermann Tilke met with unanimous approval from the drivers. It also got an ultra-modern new grandstand.

> Takuma Sato brakes with his carbon discs glowing. The Japanese driver finished eighth.

Practice

All the time trials

N°	Driver	Car/Engine/Chassis	Practice friday	Pos.	Practice saturday	Pos.	Qualifying	Pos.	Warm-up	Pos.
1.	Michael Schumacher	Ferrari 2002/221	1'16"086	1°	1'14"487	1°	1'14"389	1°	1'16"726	1°
2.	Rubens Barrichello	Ferrari 2002/219	1'16"248	2°	1'15"459	3°	1'14"693	3°	1'17"240	2°
3.	David Coulthard	McLaren-Mercedes MP4/17/08	1'16"440	4°	1'16"206	9°	1'15"909	9°	1'17"880	7°
4.	Kimi Räikkönen	McLaren-Mercedes MP4/17/06	1'16"344	3°	1'16"482	12°	1'15"639	5°	1'17"963	9°
5.	Ralf Schumacher	Williams-BMW FW24/06	1'16"934	5°	1'15"154	2°	1'14"570	2°	1'17"893	8°
6.	Juan Pablo Montoya	Williams-BMW FW24/05	1'17"187	7°	1'15"472	4°	1'15"108	4°	1'17"972	10°
7.	Nick Heidfeld	Sauber-Petronas C21/06	1'17"573	13°	1'15"862	5°	1'15"990	10°	1'17"711	6°
8.	Felipe Massa	Sauber-Petronas C21/07	1'17"361	8°	1'15"997	6°	1'16"351	14°	1'18"033	11°
9.	Giancarlo Fisichella	Jordan-Honda EJ12/6	1'17"805	16°	1'16"093	7°	1'15"690	6°	1'17"290	3°
10.	Takuma Sato	Jordan-Honda EJ12/4	1'17"684	14°	1'16"494	13°	1'16"072	12°	1'17"544	5°
11.	Jacques Villeneuve	BAR-Honda 004/06	1'17"954	17°	1'16"938	16°	1'16"070	11°	1'18"765	17°
12.	Olivier Panis	BAR-Honda 004/08	1'17"482	12°	1'16"694	14°	1'15"851	7°	1'17"236	4°
14.	Jarno Trulli	Renault R202/05	1'18"658	20°	1'16"403	11°	1'15"885	8°	1'18"295	13°
15.	Jenson Button	Renault R202/06	1'18"211	19°	1'17"455	20°	1'16"278	13°	1'18"791	18°
16.	Eddie Irvine	Jaguar R3/05	1'17"136	6°	1'16"876	15°	1'16"533	16°	1'18"348	14°
17.	Pedro de la Rosa	Jaguar R3/04	1'17"732	15°	1'17"218	18°	1'17"077	20°	1'18"420	15°
20.	Heinz-Harald Frentzen	Arrows-Cosworth A23/01	1'17"471	10°	1'17"163	17°	1'16"505	15°	1'19"910	20°
21.	Enrique Bernoldi	Arrows-Cosworth A23/03	1'17"481	11°	1'17"258	19°	1'16"645	18°	1'18"226	12°
22.	Alex Yoong	Minardi-Asiatech PS02/03	1'20"164	22°	1'20"314	22°				
23.	Mark Webber	Minardi-Asiatech PS02/04	1'19"594	21°	1'18"291	21°	1'18"158	22°	1'20"158	22°
24.	Mika Salo	Toyota TF102/07	1'18"023	18°	1'16"195	8°	1'16"685	19°	1'18"653	16°
25.	Allan McNish	Toyota TF102/08	1'17"422	9°	1'16"399	10°	1'16"594	17°	1'19"318	19°

Maximum speeds

N°	Driver	P1 Qualifs	Pos.	P1 Race	Pos.	P2 Qualifs	Pos.	P2 Race	Pos.	Finish Qualifs	Pos.	Finish Race	Pos.	Trap Qualifs	Pos.	Trap Race	Pos.
1.	M. Schumacher	223,6	2°	215,7	8°	273,5	3°	268,5	4°	278,4	2°	275,4	1°	326,2	1°	319,8	9°
2.	R. Barrichello	223,3	3°	217,7	4°	274,8	1°	270,2	3°	278,2	3°	273,5	4°	322,3	4°	319,1	10°
3.	D. Coulthard	220,3	7°	217,7	3°	267,0	11°	267,8	6°	274,9	6°	271,8	6°	315,3	10°	316,7	15°
4.	K. Räikkönen	218,7	9°	215,2	10°	267,0	10°	267,1	5°	272,0	11°	269,8	11°	312,1	19°	313,6	18°
5.	R. Schumacher	223,9	1°	219,6	1°	273,7	2°	271,4	1°	278,0	4°	274,6	2°	321,3	7°	319,5	10°
6.	J.P. Montoya	222,4	4°	218,1	2°	270,7	4°	271,4	2°	278,9	1°	274,6	3°	322,3	5°	320,7	6°
7.	N. Heidfeld	217,8	12°	212,2	17°	267,7	9°	263,5	11°	271,8	15°	267,3	17°	315,5	9°	320,0	7°
8.	F. Massa	216,9	15°	213,6	14°	265,1	17°	262,2	16°	271,5	18°	268,7	14°	315,2	11°	318,2	13°
9.	G. Fisichella	221,2	5°	216,4	7°	268,9	6°	264,9	7°	276,4	5°	271,6	7°	324,0	2°	326,8	1°
10.	T. Sato	221,0	6°	216,6	6°	268,7	7°	263,2	12°	273,4	7°	270,3	10°	323,7	3°	322,1	5°
11.	J. Villeneuve	215,7	19°	209,1	20°	269,4	5°	262,4	15°	272,8	10°	268,7	15°	319,8	8°	323,8	3°
12.	O. Panis	217,9	11°	212,6	16°	268,3	8°	262,9	13°	273,2	8°	269,3	12°	321,9	6°	323,0	4°
14.	J. Trulli	217,3	13°	214,4	12°	265,5	15°	261,1	17°	271,7	17°	268,0	16°	314,1	13°	316,5	16°
15.	J. Button	213,3	21°	213,3	15°	266,9	12°	259,1	18°	272,0	12°	266,2	19°	313,6	17°	317,4	14°
16.	E. Irvine	219,6	8°	214,0	13°	266,0	14°	262,5	14°	271,1	19°	268,9	13°	317,4	14°	317,4	14°
17.	P. de la Rosa	216,3	17°	180,4	21°	261,6	20°			273,0	9°			313,0	18°	221,9	21°
18.	H-H. Frentzen	216,3	18°	209,6	19°	263,3	19°	258,3	19°	271,0	20°	266,6	18°	309,8	21°	310,0	20°
19.	E. Bernoldi	216,9	16°	215,4	9°	265,3	16°	263,8	9°	272,0	12°	272,5	5°	313,8	14°	325,7	2°
22.	A. Yoong	212,5	22°			256,1	22°			264,1	22°			307,1	22°		
23.	M. Webber	214,1	20°	210,9	18°	258,6	21°	257,6	20°	268,0	21°	265,4	20°	313,3	16°	310,5	19°
24.	M. Salo	217,2	14°	217,3	5°	266,3	13°	263,9	8°	271,8	16°	271,4	8°	314,2	12°	320,0	8°
25.	A. McNish	218,6	10°	214,8	11°	263,3	18°	263,6	10°	272,0	14°	271,2	9°	311,4	20°	319,1	11°

Race

Classification & Retirements

Pos.	Driver	Team	Lap	Time	Average
1.	M. Schumacher	Ferrari	67	1:27:52.078	209,262 km/h
2.	J.P. Montoya	Williams BMW	67	10,503	208,846 km/h
3.	R. Schumacher	Williams BMW	67	14,466	208,689 km/h
4.	R. Barrichello	Ferrari	67	23,195	208,345 km/h
5.	D. Coulthard	McLaren Mercedes	66	1 lap	206,112 km/h
6.	N. Heidfeld	Sauber Petronas	66	1 lap	204,780 km/h
7.	F. Massa	Sauber Petronas	66	1 lap	204,464 km/h
8.	T. Sato	Jordan Honda	66	1 lap	203,802 km/h
9.	M. Salo	Toyota	66	1 lap	203,613 km/h

Driver	Team	Lap	Reason
G. Fisichella	Jordan Honda	60	Broken engine
K. Räikkönen	McLaren Mercedes	60	Off
E. Irvine	Jaguar	58	Brake fluid leak
E. Bernoldi	Arrows Cosworth	49	Broken engine
O. Panis	BAR Honda	40	Engine problem which resulted in a spin
J. Trulli	Renault	37	Off
J. Villeneuve	BAR Honda	28	Gearbox problem
J. Button	Renault	25	Engine problem
A. McNish	Toyota	24	Hydraulic problem
M. Webber	Minardi Asiatech	24	Loss of hydraulic pressure
H-H. Frentzen	Arrows Cosworth	19	Hydraulic leak
P. de la Rosa	Jaguar	1	Transmission problem

Fastest laps

	Driver	Time	Lap	Average
1.	M. Schumacher	1'16"462	44	215,354 km/h
2.	R. Schumacher	1'16"513	47	215,210 km/h
3.	J.P. Montoya	1'16"693	33	214,705 km/h
4.	R. Barrichello	1'16"845	45	214,280 km/h
5.	D. Coulthard	1'17"530	43	212,387 km/h
6.	K. Räikkönen	1'17"895	24	211,392 km/h
7.	G. Fisichella	1'18"053	44	210,964 km/h
8.	N. Heidfeld	1'18"062	46	210,940 km/h
9.	J. Trulli	1'18"280	35	210,352 km/h
10.	O. Panis	1'18"405	27	210,017 km/h
11.	T. Sato	1'18"448	43	209,902 km/h
12.	M. Salo	1'18"497	45	209,771 km/h
13.	F. Massa	1'18"562	44	209,597 km/h
14.	E. Irvine	1'18"859	16	208,808 km/h
15.	E. Bernoldi	1'19"084	43	208,214 km/h
16.	J. Villeneuve	1'19"400	22	207,385 km/h
17.	M. Webber	1'19"485	22	207,163 km/h
18.	A. McNish	1'19"597	17	206,898 km/h
19.	J. Button	1'19"695	23	206,617 km/h
20.	H-H. Frentzen	1'19"995	16	205,842 km/h

Pit stops

	Driver	Time	Lap	Stop n°		Driver	Time	Lap	Stop n°
1.	J. Trulli	29"293	16	1	17.	J.P. Montoya	28"864	30	1
2.	F. Massa	30"561	20	1	18.	J. Trulli	18"664	33	2
3.	M. Salo	30"599	21	1	19.	K. Räikkönen	45"609	37	2
4.	N. Heidfeld	29"246	22	1	20.	F. Massa	30"403	42	2
5.	A. McNish	31"405	23	1	21.	M. Salo	29"911	43	2
6.	J. Villeneuve	30"671	24	1	22.	N. Heidfeld	30"161	44	2
7.	E. Bernoldi	33"327	24	1	23.	T. Sato	32"221	44	2
8.	O. Panis	31"317	25	1	24.	R. Barrichello	42"445	46	2
9.	E. Irvine	35"546	25	1	25.	G. Fisichella	32"682	45	2
10.	R. Barrichello	29"701	26	1	26.	E. Bernoldi	35"791	45	2
11.	K. Räikkönen	30"535	26	1	27.	M. Schumacher	29"626	47	2
12.	T. Sato	29"075	26	1	28.	R. Schumacher	29"901	48	2
13.	M. Schumacher	29"099	27	1	29.	E. Irvine	28"921	47	2
14.	G. Fisichella	52"911	28	1	30.	J.P. Montoya	28"572	49	2
15.	R. Schumacher	31"191	29	1	31.	D. Coulthard	29"286	49	2
16.	D. Coulthard	28"676	29	1	32.	R. Schumacher	27"917	63	3

Race leaders

Driver	Laps in the lead	Nber of Laps	Kilometers	Driver	Nber of Laps	Kilometers
M. Schumacher	1 > 26	26	118,924 km	M. Schumacher	62	283,458 km
R. Schumacher	27 > 29	3	13,722 km	R. Schumacher	4	18,296 km
J.P. Montoya	30	1	4,574 km	J.P. Montoya	1	4,574 km
M. Schumacher	31 > 47	17	77,758 km			
R. Schumacher	48	1	4,574 km			
M. Schumacher	49 > 67	19	86,906 km			

Lap chart

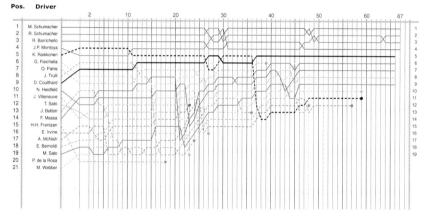

Gaps on the leader board

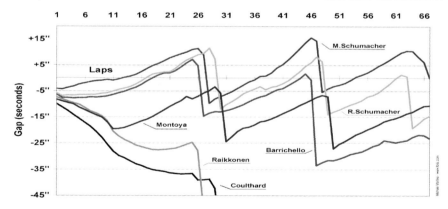

Championship after twelve rounds

Drivers

1. **M. Schumacher** **106**
2. J.P. Montoya 40
3. R. Schumacher 36
4. R. Barrichello 35
5. D. Coulthard 32
6. K. Räikkönen 17
7. J. Button 11
8. N. Heidfeld..7
9. G. Fisichella......................................6
10. J. Trulli 4
11. F. Massa 4
12. J. Villeneuve 3
13. E. Irvine 3
14. O. Panis 2
15. M. Webber 2
16. M. Salo 2
17. H-H. Frentzen...................................2
18. A. McNish...0
19. A. Yoong 0
20. P. de la Rosa 0
21. T. Sato 0
22. E. Bernoldi 0

Constructors

1. Scuderia Ferrari Marlboro 141
2. BMW WilliamsF1 Team 76
3. West McLaren Mercedes 49
4. Mild Seven Renault F1 Team 15
5. Sauber Petronas 11
6. DHL Jordan Honda 6
7. Lucky Strike BAR Honda 5
8. Jaguar Racing 3
9. KL Minardi Asiatech 2
10. Panasonic Toyota Racing 2
11. Orange Arrows 2

The circuit

Name : Hockenheim
Date : July 28, 2002
Length : 4574 meters
Distance : 67 laps, 306,458 km
Temperature : warm and sunny, 31°c
Track Temperature : 38°c

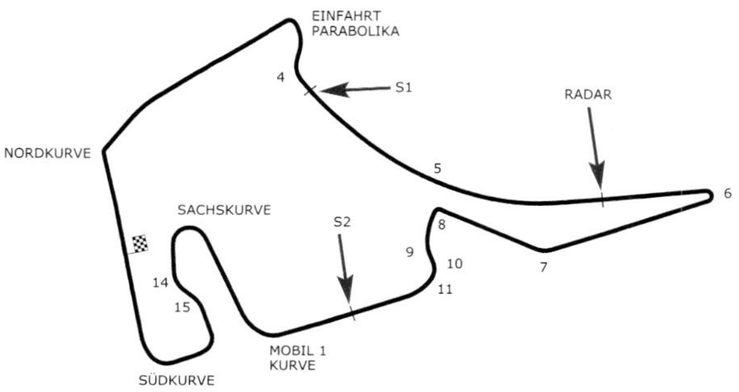

Best result for a driver running Bridgestone tyres:

Michael Schumacher, Ferrari, winner

THE PERFECT DUO

The 2002 vintage of the Hungarian Grand Prix is the undoubted winner of the trophy for the most boring race in recent years.

Absolutely nothing happened during its 77 lap duration and the gaps between the cars gradually expanded as the race went on... and on and on.

It was nothing more than a Sunday procession which ended with a Ferrari one-two; Rubens Barrichello leading home Michael Schumacher, mainly because the German was doing all he could to get the Brazilian to finish as runner-up in the championship. The result also meant that the Ferrari-Bridgestone alliance clinched the constructors' crown.

A dirty track and plenty of cars off it

His mission was to qualify and he did it: newcomer Anthony Davidson succeeded in doing better than Alex Yoong, whom he replaced in the Minardi cockpit. The British driver managed to qualify for the first grand prix of his career.
∨

As the Hungaroring is hardly used in between the grands prix, the Budapest track is always very dusty on the first day of practice. It makes driving trickier than usual and this year, several drivers found themselves spinning off the circuit. However, the two Ferraris still managed to post the quickest times, ahead of Ralf Schumacher's Williams and Kimi Räikkönen's McLaren. Friday practice for the Hungarian Grand Prix turned into something of a RallyCross meeting, with cars cutting the grass, spinning like tops and

bouncing over the kerbs and into the gravel traps. It was enough to move a few centimetres off the racing line to discover a surface that had much in common with black ice. Just about everyone got caught out, including Michael Schumacher and David Coulthard; the McLaren man also suffering a puncture.
But a glance at the time sheet proved it had done little to change the pecking order, with the two Ferraris quickest ahead of Ralf Schumacher in the Williams. "*The day went well, but Friday*

does not mean much, whether you are third or last", explained Ralf. "*I think that in race trim, the Ferraris will be the best, while we will have to keep an eye on the McLarens.*"
These were in fact fourth, with Kimi Räikkönen and seventh, courtesy of David Coulthard. "*The circuit is very slippery, but we have managed to find a good set-up. We will have to see if we can improve it still further tomorrow, when the track will have more grip*", suggested the young Finn.

Ferrari as ever

The qualifying session did not change much, with the two Ferraris monopolising the front row, Barrichello ahead of Michael Schumacher by only 59 thousandths of a second.
Behind them came the two Williams. "*I have to thank the team for all their efforts*", commented Ralf Schumacher, in third place. "*I really did not expect such a good result, given that it had been a very difficult weekend up until then. We completely changed the set-up during the qualifying session. I don't think I have ever made so many changes in one session, in my entire career.*" His Colombian team-mate, one second further back, was not so enthusiastic about his afternoon's performance. "*Of course, the second row is not too bad. But I'm not at all happy. I never found*

the right balance on my car. We tried different settings, but we never found the perfect solution."
The third row was an all-Italian affair: Giancarlo Fisichella in his Jordan and Jarno Trulli, for whom sixth place was his best grid position of the year in his Renault.
Further back came the two McLaren Mercedes. David Coulthard was tenth, just ahead of team-mate Kimi Räikkönen. For the silver arrows, it was their worst qualifying result of the season and the team was lost in conjecture as to the cause of this woeful performance. "*It's a bit like Monaco or Magny-Cours, two circuits with slightly similar characteristics. We don't understand what happened*", lamented team boss Ron Dennis.

Starting grid

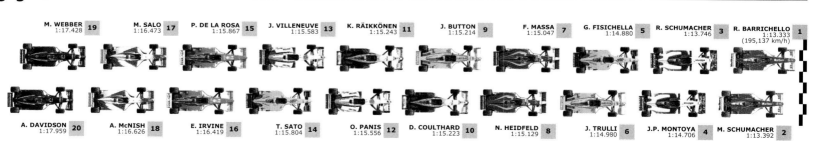

| M. WEBBER 19 1:17.428 | M. SALO 17 1:16.473 | P. DE LA ROSA 15 1:15.867 | J. VILLENEUVE 13 1:15.583 | K. RÄIKKÖNEN 11 1:15.243 | J. BUTTON 9 1:15.214 | F. MASSA 7 1:15.047 | G. FISICHELLA 5 1:14.880 | R. SCHUMACHER 3 1:13.746 | R. BARRICHELLO 1 1:13.333 (195,137 km/h) |
| A. DAVIDSON 20 1:17.959 | A. McNISH 18 1:16.626 | E. IRVINE 16 1:16.419 | T. SATO 14 1:15.804 | O. PANIS 12 1:15.556 | D. COULTHARD 10 1:15.223 | N. HEIDFELD 8 1:15.129 | J. TRULLI 6 1:14.980 | J.P. MONTOYA 4 1:14.706 | M. SCHUMACHER 2 1:13.392 |

Rubens Barrichello's turn

Usually, he bursts into tears the moment he sets foot on the top step of the podium. In Budapest however, his cheeks stayed as dry as a declaration from Jean Todt. It has to be said that Rubens Barrichello did not have much to get excited about: this win, his second of the season owed more to the restraint of Michael Schumacher than to his own talent.
In contrast to the Austrian Grand Prix, where he had to hand the win to his team-mate, it was the German's turn to stay quietly out of the limelight.

A little spurt just for the fun of it

Lap 70. Having been running right up Rubens Barrichello's gearbox, Michael Schumacher suddenly dropped 3.4 seconds behind. But then he charged right back again, after setting the fastest lap of the race. "*I was getting a bit bored*", he said. "*I asked the pits who had the fastest lap and they told me it was Rubens in*

1'16.8. *I told myself it was doable and decided to try and beat it. At least it gave me something to do. As we were running two seconds off our quickest pace, I let him pull away and then went for it. And there you go.*" Indeed, although this statement made Rubinho's performance even more open to ridicule.

"*Obviously, we want Rubens to finish second in the championship*", explained Michael Schumacher after the race. "*It would have been stupid of me to take valuable points off him by finishing in front.*" After the Hungarian Grand Prix, the Brazilian moved into second place in the world championship, with a five point lead over the two BMW-Williams drivers. "*I was fourth in the championship in 2000 and third last year. Why not make it second this time?*" was "*Rubinho's*" justification. The party went on long into the night,

as the Scuderia celebrated winning the Constructors' title that day, thanks to its one-two finish. The result had been a foregone conclusion from the moment the start lights went out. "*When I got to the first corner, I looked in the mirrors and there was no one there!*" recalled Barrichello. "*I didn't even have to bother braking late.*"

∧ Rubens Barrichello leads Michael Schumacher and heads towards a magnificent win!

Start. While Rubens Barrichello is already comfortably in the lead, the two Schumacher brothers are locked in a battle which ended in favour of the elder of the two.
∨

Race summary

> The pack charges down to the first corner. Barrichello has started from pole and stays ahead of the field **(1)**.

> The race is over after the first corner. The positions would not change for 77 laps **(2)**.

> The two McLarens are lagging behind their two principal rivals. But Räikkönen gets the better of Coulthard to finish 4th **(3)**.
> Fisichella v Massa for sixth place. The Jordan is back in the points **(4)**.

> Davidson makes his F1 debut in Hungary **(5)**.
> At the end of an easy race, Rubens

Barrichello celebrates winning. However, lap times show that Schumacher slowed to let his team-mate emerge from the pit stops in the lead **(6)**.

> Ferrari celebrates its 4th consecutive constructors' title **(7)**.

An arranged victory

In Budapest, Rubens Barrichello took his second win of the season. But it was definitely down to the cooperation of his team-mate who chose not to pose any threat.

BMW-Williams: Another failure

The FW 24 was not proving a great success for the Williams team. A simple evolution of the 2001 season FW23, this year's car was not capable of challenging the Ferraris.

In Budapest, Ralf Schumacher finished third at the end of a lonely race. Having lost ground to the Ferraris in the early stages, the German managed to stabilise the gap on around lap 11. "*It was a boring race*", admitted the Williams-BMW driver. "*But I did not expect to finish third, so I am quite* happy from that point of view. It seems I had the only car which was more or less capable of sticking with the pace of the Ferraris. For us, our tyres seem to get better after the first six or seven laps. The opening laps, with new tyres are difficult and then the tyres come good. But it's a bit late by then.*"

Ralf Schumacher's team-mate, Juan Pablo Montoya went through a hellish afternoon and finished eleventh. Having fought off Kimi Räikkönen in the opening laps, the Colombian flew off the road just as the Finn went past him. "*It definitely wasn't my weekend*", he complained. "*I was hit from behind at the start and something came off the car and it then had terrible understeer. I had to correct the steering so much that my left elbow still hurts. There were times when the car was totally impossible to drive. Anyway, I never managed to find the right balance all weekend.*"

Arrows absent and nothing to say

It was the longest running soap opera of the summer. After a farcical and deliberate non-qualification in the French Grand Prix and a normal appearance in the German event, the Arrows team simply failed to turn up this weekend in Budapest. Its trucks had left England the previous week, heading for Hungary, but as soon as they had arrived, they turned around and headed home on orders from team owner Tom Walkinshaw. The man himself was not in Budapest – he was holidaying on his yacht! However, he explained he had withdrawn his team so as not to compromise discussions regarding its sale. It seemed the Scotsman had found an American buyer. The team's no-show meant it risked a fine from FOM, the company run by Bernie Ecclestone which controls the commercial interests of Formula 1. Rumour had it that this severe case of absenteeism, which was deemed bad for the image of the sport and was in breach of contract with race organisers, risked a fine of between 800,000 to a million dollars.

Practice

All the time trials

N°	Driver	Car/Engine/Chassis	Practice friday	Pos.	Practice saturday	Pos.	Qualifying	Pos.	Warm-up	Pos.
1.	Michael Schumacher	Ferrari 2002/221	1'16"346	1°	1'14"308	1°	1'13"392	2°	1'16"864	1°
2.	Rubens Barrichello	Ferrari 2002/220	1'16"952	2°	1'14"469	2°	1'13"333	1°	1'17"000	2°
3.	David Coulthard	McLaren-Mercedes MP4/17/08	1'17"704	7°	1'16"348	11°	1'15"223	10°	1'18"234	8°
4.	Kimi Räikkönen	McLaren-Mercedes MP4/17/06	1'17"298	4°	1'15"746	3°	1'15"243	11°	1'17"659	3°
5.	Ralf Schumacher	Williams-BMW FW24/06	1'17"228	3°	1'16"236	8°	1'13"746	3°	1'18"170	6°
6.	Juan Pablo Montoya	Williams-BMW FW24/05	1'18"961	16°	1'15"912	4°	1'14"706	4°	1'19"152	16°
7.	Nick Heidfeld	Sauber-Petronas C21/06	1'19"051	17°	1'16"300	9°	1'15"129	8°	1'18"182	7°
8.	Felipe Massa	Sauber-Petronas C21/04	1'17"704	8°	1'15"944	5°	1'15"047	7°	1'18"246	9°
9.	Giancarlo Fisichella	Jordan-Honda EJ12/6	1'17"399	5°	1'16"201	7°	1'14"880	5°	1'17"972	4°
10.	Takuma Sato	Jordan-Honda EJ12/4	1'17"598	6°	1'16"844	17°	1'15"804	14°	1'18"132	5°
11.	Jacques Villeneuve	BAR-Honda 004/06	1'18"388	12°	1'16"710	15°	1'15"583	13°	1'19"008	14°
12.	Olivier Panis	BAR-Honda 004/08	1'18"846	14°	1'16"140	6°	1'15"556	12°	1'18"320	11°
14.	Jarno Trulli	Renault R202/05	1'18"360	11°	1'16"311	10°	1'14"980	6°	1'19"138	15°
15.	Jenson Button	Renault R202/06	1'18"250	10°	1'16"790	16°	1'15"214	9°	1'18"284	10°
16.	Eddie Irvine	Jaguar R3/05	1'18"718	13°	1'17"478	18°	1'16"419	16°	1'18"500	12°
17.	Pedro de la Rosa	Jaguar R3/04	1'18"036	9°	1'16"631	13°	1'15"867	15°	1'18"503	13°
22.	Anthony Davidson	Minardi-Asiatech PS02/03	1'19"490	19°	1'18"483	20°	1'17"959	20°	1'20"793	20°
23.	Mark Webber	Minardi-Asiatech PS02/04	1'19"526	20°	1'18"320	19°	1'17"428	19°	1'20"648	19°
24.	Mika Salo	Toyota TF102/07	1'18"890	15°	1'16"515	12°	1'16"473	17°	1'19"313	17°
25.	Allan McNish	Toyota TF102/08	1'19"171	18°	1'16"710	14°	1'16"626	18°	1'19"650	18°

Maximum speeds

N°	Driver	P1 Qualifs	Pos.	P1 Race	Pos.	P2 Qualifs	Pos.	P2 Race	Pos.	Finish Qualifs	Pos.	Finish Race	Pos.	Trap Qualifs	Pos.	Trap Race	Pos.
1.	M. Schumacher	292,0	2°	292,5	1°	247,7	2°	240,3	1°	256,8	4°	254,8	1°	299,6	6°	302,9	2°
2.	R. Barrichello	293,3	1°	288,4	5°	251,2	1°	239,5	3°	258,3	3°	252,2	3°	302,7	1°	301,0	4°
3.	D. Coulthard	287,2	11°	288,0	6°	243,0	5°	237,3	5°	254,4	7°	252,2	4°	299,4	7°	301,0	5°
4.	M. Räikkönen	288,0	9°	287,2	8°	240,6	10°	240,2	2°	255,2	5°	251,7	6°	302,4	2°	301,4	3°
5.	R. Schumacher	291,0	3°	290,1	3°	246,2	4°	238,8	4°	259,1	2°	252,3	2°	301,5	3°	300,7	7°
6.	J.P. Montoya	289,8	4°	291,8	2°	246,4	3°	235,0	9°	259,4	1°	251,8	5°	301,5	4°	303,2	1°
7.	N. Heidfeld	285,6	17°	283,9	14°	242,4	7°	230,2	19°	251,6	14°	245,9	18°	293,8	18°	295,0	16°
8.	F. Massa	284,8	18°	284,2	13°	240,3	12°	232,5	15°	250,7	17°	247,0	16°	295,3	17°	296,7	14°
9.	G. Fisichella	287,1	12°	284,4	12°	240,6	11°	232,8	14°	251,9	13°	247,9	15°	297,0	13°	297,1	13°
10.	T. Sato	286,2	16°	283,4	15°	239,4	14°	235,7	6°	251,1	16°	248,4	13°	296,4	14°	296,0	15°
11.	J. Villeneuve	286,4	14°	279,7	19°	242,5	6°	232,0	17°	250,4	18°	246,0	17°	299,0	8°	298,5	10°
12.	O. Panis	286,3	15°	287,0	9°	241,7	8°	233,1	13°	251,4	15°	249,2	11°	296,1	16°	297,8	11°
14.	J. Trulli	288,1	8°	283,3	16°	237,4	17°	232,2	16°	254,7	6°	248,5	12°	297,8	10°	294,6	18°
15.	J. Button	289,0	6°	282,1	17°	241,0	9°	234,9	10°	254,3	8°	248,3	14°	297,4	12°	294,0	19°
16.	E. Irvine	289,4	5°	286,0	10°	236,3	18°	234,4	11°	253,6	10°	250,2	9°	300,2	5°	298,9	9°
17.	P. de la Rosa	287,9	10°	287,8	7°	239,0	15°	235,6	7°	253,8	9°	251,6	8°	296,2	15°	300,3	8°
22.	A. Davidson	278,9	20°	279,7	18°	231,6	20°	229,8	20°	244,1	20°	243,9	20°	291,1	20°	293,1	20°
23.	M. Webber	280,2	19°	277,7	20°	234,7	19°	230,9	18°	246,4	19°	244,8	19°	292,6	19°	294,6	17°
24.	M. Salo	287,0	13°	286,0	11°	238,8	16°	235,1	8°	253,0	12°	249,8	10°	297,7	11°	297,6	12°
25.	A. McNish	288,5	7°	288,6	4°	239,5	13°	233,2	12°	253,2	11°	251,7	7°	298,6	9°	300,9	6°

Race

Classifications & Retirements

Pos.	Driver	Team	Lap	Time	Average
1.	R. Barrichello	Ferrari	77	1:41:49.001	180,364 km/h
2.	M. Schumacher	Ferrari	77	0.434	180,351 km/h
3.	R. Schumacher	Williams BMW	77	13.355	179,971 km/h
4.	M. Räikkönen	McLaren Mercedes	77	29.479	179,498 km/h
5.	D. Coulthard	McLaren Mercedes	77	37.800	179,255 km/h
6.	G. Fisichella	Jordan Honda	77	1:08.804	178,355 km/h
7.	F. Massa	Sauber Petronas	77	1:13.612	178,217 km/h
8.	J. Trulli	Renault	76	1 lap	177,783 km/h
9.	N. Heidfeld	Sauber Petronas	76	1 lap	177,755 km/h
10.	T. Sato	Jordan Honda	76	1 lap	177,424 km/h
11.	J.P. Montoya	Williams BMW	76	1 lap	177,393 km/h
12.	O. Panis	BAR Honda	76	1 lap	176,184 km/h
13.	P. de la Rosa	Jaguar	75	2 laps	174,430 km/h
14.	A. McNish	Toyota	75	2 laps	174,402 km/h
15.	M. Salo*	Toyota	75	2 laps	173,736 km/h
16.	M. Webber	Minardi Asiatech	75	2 laps	173,628 km/h

Driver	Team		Reason
A. Davidson	Minardi Asiatech	59	Spin
J. Button	Renault	31	Spin
E. Irvine	Jaguar	24	Misfiring problems
J. Villeneuve	BAR Honda	21	Transmission problems

* Mika Salo, originally in 13th place, was given a 25 seconds penalty for cutting in front of Pedro de la Rosa at the pit exit, right after his refuelling stop.

Fastest laps

	Driver	Time	Lap	Average
1.	M. Schumacher	1'16"207	72	187,778 km/h
2.	R. Barrichello	1'16"891	31	186,107 km/h
3.	M. Räikkönen	1'16"926	54	186,022 km/h
4.	D. Coulthard	1'17"290	33	185,146 km/h
5.	R. Schumacher	1'17"783	30	183,973 km/h
6.	O. Panis	1'18"126	28	183,165 km/h
7.	J.P. Montoya	1'18"163	51	183,078 km/h
8.	N. Heidfeld	1'18"185	8	183,027 km/h
9.	T. Sato	1'18"247	46	182,882 km/h
10.	J. Trulli	1'18"438	51	182,437 km/h
11.	F. Massa	1'18"458	52	182,390 km/h
12.	G. Fisichella	1'18"578	12	182,112 km/h
13.	E. Irvine	1'18"889	19	181,394 km/h
14.	A. Davidson	1'19"347	54	180,347 km/h
15.	M. Salo	1'19"408	30	180,208 km/h
16.	J. Button	1'19"455	23	180,101 km/h
17.	M. Webber	1'19"567	30	179,848 km/h
18.	P. de la Rosa	1'19"646	48	179,670 km/h
19.	J. Villeneuve	1'19"861	19	179,186 km/h
20.	A. McNish	1'19"937	28	179,015 km/h

Pit stops

	Driver	Time	Lap	Stop n°
1.	J.P. Montoya	31"914	22	1
2.	A. Davidson	33"352	24	1
3.	A. McNish	31"547	26	1
4.	M. Webber	37"246	26	1
5.	P. de la Rosa	31"996	27	1
6.	M. Salo	30"712	28	1
7.	G. Fisichella	30"208	29	1
8.	T. Sato	30"529	30	1
9.	M. Schumacher	30"568	31	1
10.	F. Massa	29"737	31	1
11.	J. Trulli	30"312	31	1
12.	R. Barrichello	30"974	32	1
13.	N. Heidfeld	29"917	32	1
14.	R. Schumacher	29"751	33	1
15.	O. Panis	31"090	33	1
16.	D. Coulthard	29"613	34	1
17.	M. Räikkönen	31"119	35	1
18.	T. Sato	33"607	49	2
19.	M. Webber	43"122	49	2
20.	A. McNish	35"686	50	2
21.	G. Fisichella	30"351	51	2
22.	M. Salo	30"698	51	2
23.	P. de la Rosa	30"508	51	2
24.	F. Massa	30"303	53	2
25.	R. Schumacher	30"173	54	2
26.	A. Davidson	32"940	52	2
27.	J. Trulli	28"972	54	2
28.	N. Heidfeld	29"836	54	2
29.	M. Schumacher	29"229	55	2
30.	R. Barrichello	29"334	56	2
31.	Montoya	30"096	55	2
32.	O. Panis	31"421	55	2
33.	D. Coulthard	29"695	58	2
34.	M. Räikkönen	29"341	61	2

Race leaders

Driver	Laps in the lead	Nber of Laps	Kilometers
R. Barrichello	1 > 32	32	127,194 km
R. Schumacher	33	1	3,975 km
R. Barrichello	34 > 77	44	174,900 km

Driver	Nber of Laps	Kilometers
R. Barrichello	76	302,094 km
R. Schumacher	1	3,975 km

Lap chart

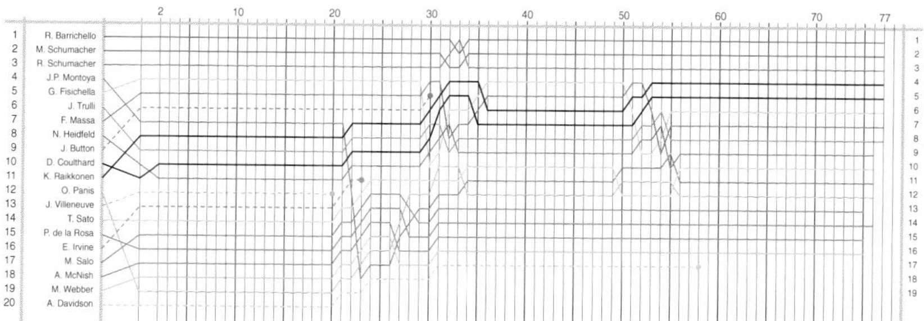

Gaps on the leader board

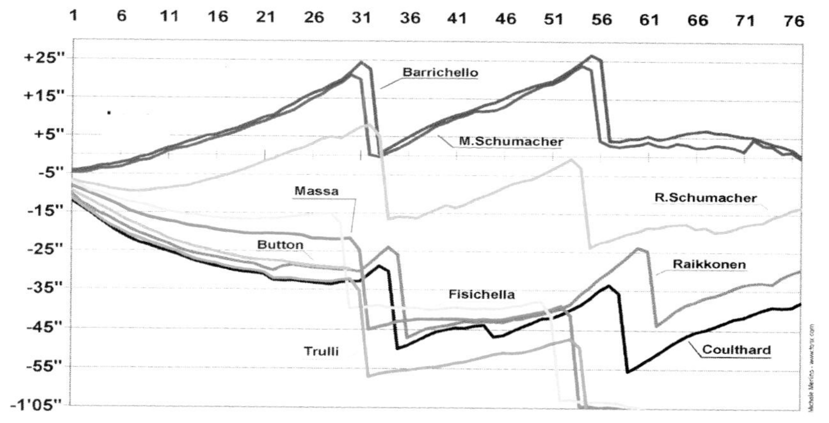

Championship after thirteen rounds

Drivers

1. **M. Schumacher 112**
2. R. Barrichello 45
3. R. Schumacher 40
4. J.P. Montoya 40
5. D. Coulthard 34
6. K. Räikkönen 20
7. J. Button 11
8. N. Heidfeld 7
9. G. Fisichella 7
10. J. Trulli 4
11. F. Massa 4
12. J. Villeneuve 3
13. E. Irvine 3
14. O. Panis 2
15. M. Webber 2
16. M. Salo 2
17. H-H. Frentzen 2
18. A. McNish 0
19. A. Yoong 0
20. P. de la Rosa 0
21. T. Sato 0
22. E. Bernoldi 0
23. A. Davidson 0

Constructors

1. **Scuderia Ferrari Marlboro 157**
2. BMW WilliamsF1 Team 80
3. West McLaren Mercedes 54
4. Mild Seven Renault F1 Team 15
5. Sauber Petronas 11
6. DHL Jordan Honda 7
7. Lucky Strike BAR Honda 5
8. Jaguar Racing 3
9. KL Minardi Asiatech 2
10. Panasonic Toyota Racing 2
11. Orange Arrows 2

The circuit

Name :	Hungaroring, Budapest
Date :	August 18, 2002
Length :	3975 meters
Distance :	77 laps, 306,069 km
Temperature :	warm and sunny, 28°c
Track Temperature :	30°c

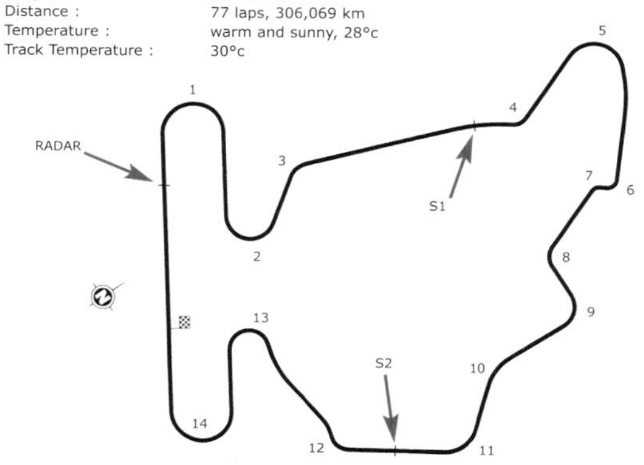

BRIDGESTONE

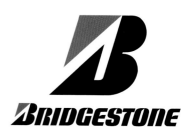

Best result for a driver running Bridgestone tyres:

Rubens Barrichello, Ferrari, winner

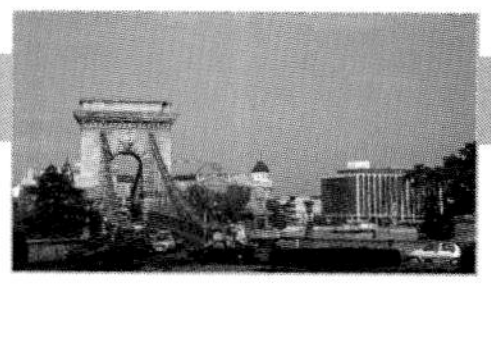

2003 TAKES SHAPE

If you thought the Hungarian Grand Prix was boring, you ain't seen nuthin' yet! The Belgian Grand Prix was even worse. Even down the back of the field, the positions remained unchanged for the whole race. The fact that the Belgian track is considered to be the best of the year made absolutely no difference. If you wanted action, it was to be found in the paddock, round the back of motorhomes where strange deals were struck. That is how Olivier Panis (photo) came to sign a contract with Toyota for 2003. In the Sauber camp, it turned out Heinz-Harald Frentzen would be going back to the future, having spent three years with the Swiss team from 1994 to 1996.

Front row for Kimi Räikkönen, his best qualifying of the season.

Michael Schumacher adds Spa to his collection

Of the 17 circuits visited in 2002, there was only one where Michael Schumacher had never started from pole position and that was Spa.
Surprising really, given that the German loves this roller-coaster track in the Ardennes mountains. He felt at home here and he almost was at home, given that his birthplace of Kerpen is just a few kilometres from the circuit where he made his Formula 1 debut in 1991. Spa was also the scene of the first of his 62 victories, in 1992.
This year, the German filled the gap in his cv. Shortly before the rain arrived, Michael Schumacher secured the 48th pole of his career, his

fifth of the season. "*I am very happy, because it was not until I arrived on Thursday that I realised I had never been on pole here*", he explained. "*I was fairly confident I could do it, as the car was perfectly set-up. In the end, I only managed two clear laps, as I got caught out by the yellow flags. On top of that, at the very end, we miscalculated how much time was left.*"
Kimi Räikkönen was unlucky to run across a patch of sand on his quickest lap. But for that, data from the first and second sectors showed that the Finn was definitely quickest on his fourth and final run. "*I think that if he had not run into trouble, he*

would have taken pole by a few fractions of a second", theorised Pascal Vasselon, the man in charge of Michelin's F1 involvement. While "if" might well spell "F1" backwards, it has no place in the sport, so Räikkönen had to settle for second place, which nevertheless meant his McLaren-Mercedes would start on the front row of the grid. "*It's my best qualifying performance of the season*", remarked the Finn. "*It's good and I'm happy, but it would have been better still to be on pole. Having said that, I think it will be an interesting race as the car is working very well on this circuit.*"

Pollock gives up

Rumour had it that this would be the last Belgian Grand Prix, because of anti-tobacco laws passed by the local government. These laws were out of step with FIA legislation implementing a complete ban on tobacco advertising in the sport as from 2006. When the FIA World Council met at the end of October to discuss proposed new regulations for the sport, the Belgian Grand Prix was indeed removed from the 2003 calendar.

A surprise in the Spa paddock: having failed to show in Budapest, Arrows appeared in the Belgian paddock. On Thursday, the two cars went through scrutineering, although it was unclear who would be driving them. Heinz-Harald Frentzen had resigned from the team and was not even in Spa. On Friday, the cars did not run. That evening, the team put out a press release stating that it was withdrawing from the Belgian Grand Prix "*because of the large amount of paperwork which needed to be examined in order to proceed with the sale of the team*". A sale which Craig Pollock no longer wanted to get involved with. "*I made an offer and was waiting for a contract to arrive in the post*", he said. "*But nothing came.*"

Starting grid

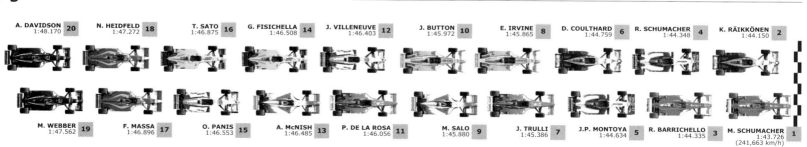

| A. DAVIDSON 1:48.170 20 | N. HEIDFELD 1:47.272 18 | T. SATO 1:46.875 16 | G. FISICHELLA 1:46.508 14 | J. VILLENEUVE 1:46.403 12 | J. BUTTON 1:45.972 10 | E. IRVINE 1:45.865 8 | D. COULTHARD 1:44.759 6 | R. SCHUMACHER 1:44.348 4 | K. RÄIKKÖNEN 1:44.150 2 |
| M. WEBBER 1:47.562 19 | F. MASSA 1:46.896 17 | O. PANIS 1:46.553 15 | A. McNISH 1:46.485 13 | P. DE LA ROSA 1:46.056 11 | M. SALO 1:45.880 9 | J. TRULLI 1:45.386 7 | J.P. MONTOYA 1:44.634 5 | R. BARRICHELLO 1:44.335 3 | M. SCHUMACHER 1:43.726 1 (241,663 km/h) |

And yet another record for Schumi

Nigel Mansell was cruising the Spa paddock. He was there to meet old pals and also to congratulate Michael Schumacher if the German went on to beat his record of the most number of wins in a season, which the Englishman set in 1992, with 9 victories, a feat later equalled by Schumacher in 1995, 2000 and 2001. Having retired from the sport at the start of 1995, Mansell runs various golf businesses and seems to be enjoying life.

He did not make the trip in vain. On Sunday, he appeared delighted to shake Michael Schumacher's hand, after his tenth win of the season, thus erasing his own name from the top of the table. It was also the sixth time the German had won the Belgian Grand Prix and the fiftieth consecutive race which had featured a Ferrari driver on the podium!

It was an easy win for Schumacher. After a tedious race a fortnight earlier in Hungary, the Belgian event was even duller. On paper, the Ardennes track had promised an exciting race, but the 2002 edition was a processional affair, with only a few retirements changing the running order. "*Yes, it was a perfect race*", admitted Michael Schumacher as he stepped off the podium. To be honest, we had not expected it to be that easy. "*Things had gone well all weekend, but you never know what can happen in the race, especially with the uncertainty about the weather. But I made a good start ahead of Rubens and that was it basically. As we were in the lead, we could run at our own pace to the finish. The car was simply perfect. It is ideally suited for this type of circuit, with its high speed corners and it was great fun to drive. I really enjoyed myself.*"

Behind the two red cars, Kimi Räikkönen having started from the front row, ran third at the first corner, before having to give best to Juan Pablo Montoya. "*My car was much better in the race than during the rest of the weekend*", rejoiced the Colombian. "*I was not expecting such a good surprise and I had not expected to match Kimi's pace. But actually, he was trying to stick with Rubens and sliding all over the place. He made a mistake and I managed to get past.*"

It was just about the only overtaking move of the 44 racing laps. The season could not end soon enough.

Juan Pablo keeps the faith

The battle for the rather meaningless title of runner-up in the championship was gradually turning more and more in Rubens Barrichello's favour. With a second place in Spa, the Brazilian had pulled out a bit more of a lead over his closest pursuer, Juan Pablo Montoya. The Brazilian now had a seven point advantage over the Colombian, with three grands prix to go. But the Williams man was not losing heart. "*You never know. If Rubens fails to finish a*

race, the situation could change in a moment. We will see what happens. If everything goes to plan, we should be fairly competitive in the races that are left. For example, this year, we were quite quick in Canada, the only track other than Monza and Indianapolis where you

don't run much downforce. That means I'm still hopeful of finishing second." Practically all the teams would be running at the Monza track the day after Spa for a long test session in preparation for the forthcoming Italian Grand Prix.

< Another one-two for Scuderia Ferrari

^ Michael Schumacher was not in the mood to dish out favours in Spa, so Rubens Barrichello finished second, a long way off his team-mate.

Race summary

> Just a few hundred metres after the start, the field tackles La Source. Michael Schumacher keeps the lead (**1**).

> Trulli made a good start and moved up the outside. Unfortunately, he never made the corner and dropped several places (**2**).

> Villeneuve-Fisichella and Panis-Sato: the four Honda-powered cars fought hard (**3**).

> Ralf Schumacher had a bad start to the race. Having lost 2 places on the opening lap, he never moved up the order (**4**).

> Juan Pablo Montoya drove an aggressive race trying to catch the Ferraris. He would finish third, once again out-performing his team-mate (**5**).

> Jaguar got its second wind after a difficult season. It was the first time Irvine had scored points since Australia (**6**).

> Even on the podium, he's the strongest (**7**).

Olivier Panis to Toyota, Mika Salo heads off to retirement

Spa is tough on engines, as the teams discovered on Sunday afternoon: two Hondas (Fisichella and Panis,) two Renaults (Button and Trulli,) one Mercedes (Räikkönen) and one Ferrari (Massa) did not go the distance on the Spa switchback. Usually, so many engine failures are only seen in the early part of the season, when cars are not yet fully sorted.

The atmosphere was tense at Toyota on Thursday night. The Japanese team had invited hundreds of the world's media to a gala evening at the prestigious Spa Casino, which it had taken over for the evening. It was supposed to be a party to celebrate its first season, at this the race nearest to its headquarters in a suburb to the west of Cologne.

They could have picked a better time. Because it was only the day before that the team announced it was taking on Olivier Panis for the 2003 and 2004 seasons, replacing its current Number 1 driver, Mika Salo. The team went on to say it was also dumping its second driver, Allan McNish, without actually naming his replacement. The press release added that it would not be commenting further. No surprise then that sulking was the order of the day for the drivers on Thursday. Mika Salo hardly said a word, except that he had decided to quit the sport for good at the end of the season.

It was hardly the moment to suggest he join the party with a light heart and a smile on his lips. The Finn had worked with Toyota since 2000, developing the car during a year of private testing. Being sent packing was not quite the reward he had been expecting, even if his performance this season was generally mediocre. Especially when compared with those of McNish, who was not really considered up to the task of driving a Formula 1 car. After 106 grands prix and no wins,

Blink and you miss it: Juan Pablo Montoya's overtaking move on Kimi Räikkönen was about the only one of the whole grand prix.

Mika Salo was surely the only man alive who believed he was quicker than Michael Schumacher; a claim he had often made, based on their performances back in their F3 days. Olivier Panis was not at the party – he was still under contract to BAR until the end of the season of course. His new Toyota contract meant he would continue an F1 career which dated back to his debut with Ligier in 1994. "*It's a really super opportunity for me*", admitted the Frenchman,

who had lost his BAR drive to Englishman Jenson Button. "*Two years on a good salary is a good thing, as I have the possibility of going back to McLaren as a test driver after that.*" Olivier Panis was thus going to be the lead driver for a team with plenty of ambition and the third biggest budget in F1 after Ferrari and McLaren. After a learning year in 2002, Toyota was planning to tackle its second season having told its engineers to build a car which was "*less conservative and more daring.*"

Sauber signs up "HH" once again

At his team's 2002 launch, Peter Sauber admitted he was taking another risk by employing Felipe Massa. Having discovered Kimi Räikkönen the previous year, then "selling" him to McLaren for 30 million Swiss francs, Peter Sauber was once again going the "youth" route with the very young Brazilian. The expectations were not met. During the first half of the season, apart from the Australian and Monaco Grands Prix, Nick Heidfeld always out-qualified Felipe Massa. While the German had picked up seven points, the Brazilian only had four. And points are all that matter to Peter Sauber. He knew his cars could not win and so his goal was to do as well as possible in the Constructors' Championship.

Just 21, Felipe Massa pretty much proved he

deserved his place in Formula 1 and he struggled to understand why the team was getting rid of him. Sauber offered him the role of test driver, but naturally enough, Felipe wants to race. "*We really had no problem with Felipe*", explained Peter Sauber. "*The decision to let him go was taken a long time ago, at Silverstone in fact. We have decided that we need two drivers capable of bringing home more points. But I have to admit that since we took this decision, Felipe has progressed. Today, we might have reached a different decision. But it's too late.*"

Having held talks with Giancarlo Fisichella, Jenson Button and Olivier Panis, he settled on Heinz-Harald Frentzen, who already drove for the team from 1994 to 1996.

Practice

All the time trials

N°	Driver	Car/Engine/Chassis	Practice friday	Pos.	Practice saturday	Pos.	Qualifying	Pos.	Warm-up	Pos.
1.	Michael Schumacher	Ferrari 2002/221	1'47"403	3°	1'44"951	2°	1'43"726	1°	1'48"044	1°
2.	Rubens Barrichello	Ferrari 2002/219	1'48"321	4°	1'45"451	4°	1'44"335	3°	1'49"403	5°
3.	David Coulthard	McLaren-Mercedes MP4/17/07	1'47"356	2°	1'45"407	3°	1'44"759	6°	1'49"104	3°
4.	Kimi Räikkönen	McLaren-Mercedes MP4/17/03	1'47"196	1°	1'44"870	1°	1'44"150	2°	1'49"033	2°
5.	Ralf Schumacher	Williams-BMW FW24/06	1'48"435	5°	1'45"696	6°	1'44"348	4°	1'50"086	8°
6.	Juan Pablo Montoya	Williams-BMW FW24/04	1'48"969	8°	1'45"620	5°	1'44"634	5°	1'50"364	11°
7.	Nick Heidfeld	Sauber-Petronas C21/06	1'51"355	19°	1'47"387	17°	1'47"272	18°	1'50"155	10°
8.	Felipe Massa	Sauber-Petronas C21/04	1'51"068	17°	1'47"092	14°	1'46"896	17°	1'50"896	15°
9.	Giancarlo Fisichella	Jordan-Honda EJ12/6	1'50"144	14°	1'46"866	11°	1'46"508	14°	1'50"941	16°
10.	Takuma Sato	Jordan-Honda EJ12/4	1'50"357	15°	1'47"376	16°	1'46"875	16°	2'07"290	20°
11.	Jacques Villeneuve	BAR-Honda 004/06	1'49"897	13°	1'47"087	13°	1'46"403	12°	1'50"151	9°
12.	Olivier Panis	BAR-Honda 004/08	1'50"392	16°	1'46"628	8°	1'46"553	15°	1'49"806	7°
14.	Jarno Trulli	Renault R202/05	1'49"603	12°	1'47"292	15°	1'45"386	7°	1'49"463	6°
15.	Jenson Button	Renault R202/06	1'48"778	6°	1'46"820	10°	1'45"972	10°	1'50"610	13°
16.	Eddie Irvine	Jaguar R3/05	1'49"222	9°	1'46"873	12°	1'45"865	8°	1'51"500	17°
17.	Pedro de la Rosa	Jaguar R3/03	1'48"902	7°	1'46"759	9°	1'46"056	11°	1'49"107	4°
22.	Anthony Davidson	Minardi-Asiatech PS02/03	1'51"270	18°	1'49"386	20°	1'48"170	20°	1'52"292	18°
23.	Mark Webber	Minardi-Asiatech PS02/04	1'52"343	20°	1'48"735	19°	1'47"562	19°	1'52"653	19°
24.	Mika Salo	Toyota TF102/07	1'49"260	10°	1'46"324	7°	1'45"880	9°	1'50"466	12°
25.	Allan McNish	Toyota TF102/08	1'49"560	11°	1'47"670	18°	1'46"485	13°	1'50"757	14°

Maximum speeds

N°	Driver	P1 Qualifs	Pos.	P1 Race	Pos.	P2 Qualifs	Pos.	P2 race	Pos.	Finish Qualifs	Pos.	Finish Race	Pos.	Trap Qualifs	Pos.	Trap Race	Pos.
1.	M. Schumacher	332,0	2°	328,2	13°	197,0	11°	188,5	11°	280,5	1°	279,5	1°	321,2	1°	319,4	1°
2.	R. Barrichello	332,3	1°	328,9	11°	198,1	7°	193,7	2°	280,5	2°	277,7	5°	315,6	6°	310,7	7°
3.	D. Coulthard	328,2	4°	333,7	3°	197,6	9°	190,6	5°	278,4	6°	277,0	6°	317,0	5°	316,9	3°
4.	K. Räikkönen	327,4	6°	330,4	8°	199,6	5°	187,6	16°	279,6	4°	276,0	9°	318,1	2°	316,9	2°
5.	R. Schumacher	326,6	9°	330,8	7°	199,7	4°	192,9	3°	279,4	5°	278,2	4°	313,8	10°	312,6	6°
6.	J.P. Montoya	327,5	5°	328,7	12°	198,0	8°	188,3	13°	280,0	3°	278,4	3°	317,5	4°	313,4	5°
7.	N. Heidfeld	321,5	18°	335,5	1°	196,5	13°	188,4	12°	272,7	18°	274,2	15°	304,9	17°	307,0	16°
8.	F. Massa	321,8	16°	334,9	2°	196,4	14°	188,9	10°	273,9	16°	275,3	11°	304,3	18°	307,7	14°
9.	G. Fisichella	322,0	15°	327,1	15°	199,9	3°	187,2	19°	274,4	14°	274,3	14°	308,4	16°	308,5	13°
10.	T. Sato	323,6	13°	330,3	9°	193,9	20°	188,3	14°	273,6	17°	278,7	2°	309,9	13°	310,0	10°
11.	J. Villeneuve	328,5	3°	332,5	4°	195,2	15°	187,7	15°	274,4	13°	276,0	8°	309,1	15°	310,7	8°
12.	O. Panis	326,4	10°	330,0	10°	195,0	16°	187,6	17°	274,8	11°	272,1	16°	309,4	14°	309,2	12°
14.	J. Trulli	321,5	17°	323,4	17°	195,0	17°	187,5	18°	274,1	15°	271,9	17°	315,0	8°	310,2	9°
15.	J. Button	327,0	7°	323,3	18°	202,3	1°	194,4	1°	275,6	9°	270,9	18°	317,9	3°	304,7	17°
16.	E. Irvine	322,3	14°	326,6	16°	200,0	2°	189,8	6°	277,2	7°	276,1	7°	310,1	12°	303,2	18°
17.	P. de la Rosa	320,5	19°	327,6	14°	198,9	6°	191,3	4°	274,8	12°	275,9	10°	310,7	11°	309,7	11°
22.	A. Davidson	319,9	20°	319,7	20°	194,6	18°	189,2	8°	269,6	20°	267,6	20°	300,6	20°	291,4	19°
23.	M. Webber	324,3	12°	319,8	19°	194,5	19°	188,9	9°	272,0	19°	267,8	19°	304,0	19°	289,5	20°
24.	M. Salo	325,3	11°	331,6	6°	197,3	10°	189,4	7°	275,9	8°	274,8	13°	314,6	9°	314,3	4°
25.	A. McNish	327,0	8°	332,4	5°	196,7	12°	186,3	20°	275,3	10°	275,2	12°	315,2	7°	307,4	15°

Race

Classifications & Retirements

Pos.	Driver	Team	Lap	Time	Average	
1.	M. Schumacher	Ferrari	44	1:21:20.634	225,970 km/h	
2.	R. Barrichello	Ferrari	44	1.977	225,878 km/h	
3.	J.P. Montoya	Williams BMW	44	18.445	225,119 km/h	
4.	D. Coulthard	McLaren Mercedes	44	19.357	225,077 km/h	
5.	R. Schumacher	Williams BMW	44	56.440	223,386 km/h	
6.	E. Irvine	Jaguar	44	1:17.370	222,443 km/h	
7.	M. Salo	Toyota	44	1:17.809	222,424 km/h	
8.	J. Villeneuve	BAR Honda	44	1:19.855	222,332 km/h	
9.	A. McNish	Toyota	43	1 lap	220,723 km/h	
10.	N. Heidfeld	Sauber Petronas	43	1 lap	220,689 km/h	
11.	T. Sato	Jordan Honda	43	1 lap	220,340 km/h	
12.	O. Panis	BAR Honda	39	5 laps	220,450 km/h	Exploded engine

Driver	Team		Reason
G. Fisichella	Jordan Honda	39	Exploded engine
P. de la Rosa	Jaguar	38	Broken rear suspension, off
F. Massa	Sauber Petronas	38	Broken engine
K. Räikkönen	McLaren Mercedes	36	Broken engine
J. Trulli	Renault	36	Broken engine
A. Davidson	Minardi Asiatech	18	Spin
J. Button	Renault	11	Loss of engine power
M. Webber	Minardi Asiatech	5	Gearbox problems

Fastest Laps

	Driver	Time	Lap	Average
1.	M. Schumacher	1'47"176	15	233,884 km/h
2.	R. Barrichello	1'48"196	16	231,680 km/h
3.	J.P. Montoya	1'49"293	44	229,354 km/h
4.	D. Coulthard	1'49"398	43	229,134 km/h
5.	R. Schumacher	1'49"681	15	228,543 km/h
6.	K. Räikkönen	1'49"764	31	228,370 km/h
7.	J. Villeneuve	1'49"787	43	228,322 km/h
8.	P. de la Rosa	1'50"221	14	227,423 km/h
9.	J. Trulli	1'50"235	15	227,394 km/h
10.	O. Panis	1'50"275	34	227,312 km/h
11.	F. Massa	1'50"595	30	226,654 km/h
12.	E. Irvine	1'50"829	13	226,175 km/h
13.	M. Salo	1'50"832	18	226,169 km/h
14.	T. Sato	1'50"886	26	226,059 km/h
15.	G Fisichella	1'50"969	17	225,890 km/h
16.	N. Heidfeld	1'51"013	19	225,801 km/h
17.	J. Button	1'51"223	6	225,374 km/h
18.	A. McNish	1'51"479	17	224,857 km/h
19.	A. Davidson	1'51"878	12	224,055 km/h
20.	M. Webber	1'52"469	3	222,877 km/h

Pit stops

	Driver	Time	Lap	Stop n°
1.	F. Massa	30"886	14	1
2.	T. Sato	39"049	14	1
3.	E. Irvine	33"349	15	1
4.	J. Villeneuve	31"702	15	1
5.	A. McNish	30"316	15	1
6.	A. Davidson	35"399	15	1
7.	M. Schumacher	30"376	16	1
8.	M. Salo	29"711	16	1
9.	P. de la Rosa	32"363	16	1
10.	R. Barrichello	31"951	17	1
11.	J. Trulli	28"974	17	1
12.	R. Schumacher	30"326	17	1
13.	N. Heidfeld	30"352	17	1
14.	J.P. Montoya	30"057	18	1
15.	K. Räikkönen	30"928	18	1
16.	O. Panis	30"611	18	1
17.	D. Coulthard	30"095	19	1
18.	G. Fisichella	34"154	21	1
19.	T. Sato	31"692	27	2
20.	F. Massa	30"219	28	2
21.	J. Trulli	30"283	29	2
22.	M. Schumacher	30"876	30	2
23.	A. McNish	30"068	29	2
24.	N. Heidfeld	30"090	29	2
25.	E. Irvine	30"018	30	2
26.	M. Salo	29"252	30	2
27.	R. Barrichello	30"370	31	2
28.	R. Schumacher	34"412	31	2
29.	P. de la Rosa	30"001	32	2
30.	O. Panis	28"723	32	2
31.	J.P. Montoya	29"026	33	2
32.	J. Villeneuve	29"456	33	2
33.	K. Räikkönen	29"918	34	2
34.	D. Coulthard	27"451	35	2

Race leaders

Driver	Laps in the lead	Nber of Laps	Kilometers
M. Schumacher	1 > 16	16	111,391 km
R. Barrichello	17	1	6,963 km
M. Schumacher	18 > 44	27	188,001 km

Driver	Nber of Laps	Kilometers
M. Schumacher	43	299,392 km
R. Barrichello	1	6,963 km

Lap chart

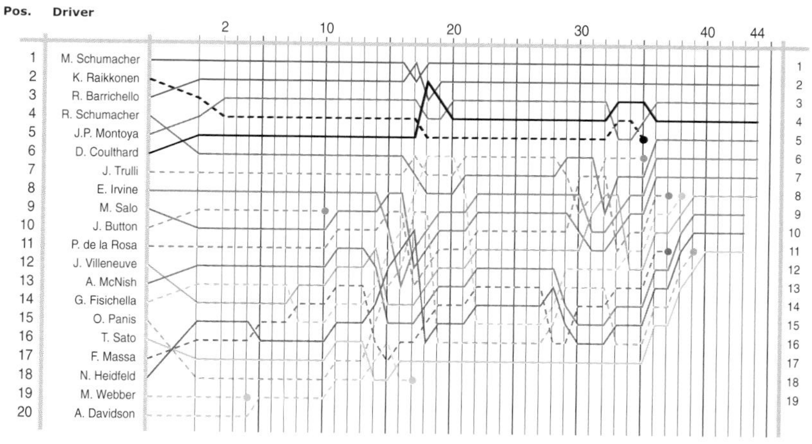

Gaps on the leader board

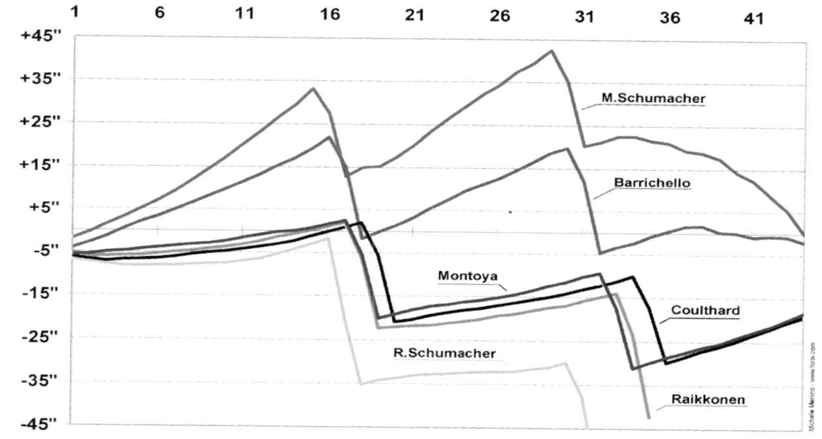

Championship after fourteen rounds

Drivers

1. **M. Schumacher 122**
2. R. Barrichello.......................................51
3. J.P. Montoya 44
4. R. Schumacher 42
5. D. Coulthard..37
6. K. Räikkönen 20
7. J. Button 11
8. N. Heidfeld...7
9. G. Fisichella...7
10. J. Trulli 4
11. F. Massa 4
12. E. Irvine 4
13. J. Villeneuve..3
14. O. Panis...2
15. M. Webber 2
16. M. Salo..2
17. H-H. Frentzen..2
18. A. McNish..0
19. A. Yoong 0
20. P. de la Rosa..0
21. T. Sato...0
22. E. Bernoldi 0
23. A. Davidson..0

Constructors

1. **Scuderia Ferrari Marlboro 173**
2. BMW WilliamsF1 Team 86
3. West McLaren Mercedes..........................57
4. Mild Seven Renault F1 Team 15
5. Sauber Petronas 11
6. DHL Jordan Honda 7
7. Lucky Strike BAR Honda 5
8. Jaguar Racing...4
9. KL Minardi Asiatech.................................2
10. Panasonic Toyota Racing 2
11. Orange Arrows 2

The circuit

Name :	Spa-Francorchamps
Date :	September 1, 2002
Length :	6963 meters
Distance :	44 laps, 306,355 km
Temperature:	cloudy, 15°c
Track température :	18°c

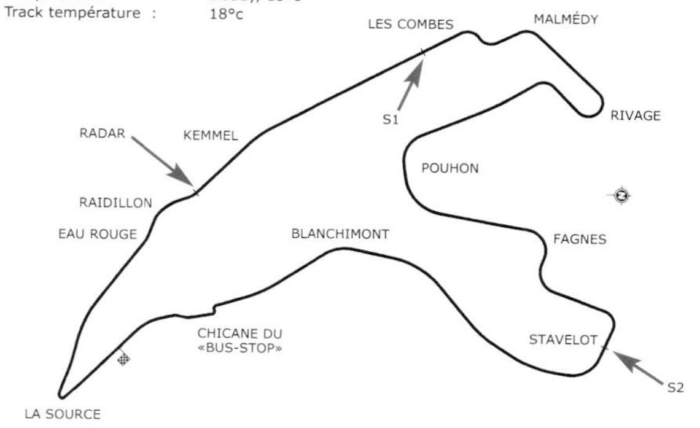

BRIDGESTONE

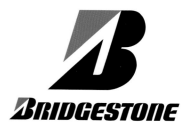

Best result from a driver running Bridgestone tyres:

Michael Schumacher, Ferrari, winner

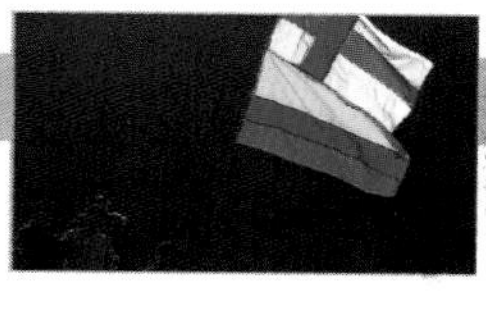

JAGUAR ON THE PROWL AGAIN

No surprise in the Italian Grand Prix. In front of its home crowd, Scuderia Ferrari secured another one-two finish, with Michael Schumacher apparently letting team-mate Rubens Barrichello take the win, to secure second place in the Drivers' Championship. However, behind them, there was no sign of the usual Williams or McLarens, those regular visitors to the podium. No, in third place came a very big surprise in the shape of Eddie Irvine. After being lost in the jungle since the start of the season, the Big Cat Jaguar was back on the prowl again.

The remaining points positions went to the two Renaults and Olivier Panis.

Seventh pole position: Juan Pablo is back on top

Mark Webber qualified 19th in Monza, as he had done in Hungary and Germany. It's a hard life at the back of the pack.
∨

Finally, a closely contested qualifying session! Ralf Schumacher, brother Michael and Juan Pablo Montoya fought it out to the hundredth of a second, as they strived for the perfect lap. On the Monza circuit, built for speed, it was the powerful BMW engine which helped the Colombian driver and his Williams to come out on top, taking his seventh pole position of the season, the tenth of his still short F1 career.

Further satisfaction came from beating the record for the quickest lap in the history of Formula 1 at a stupefying average speed of 259.827 km/h. Up until then the record was held by Keke Rosberg and it dated back to 1985. Montoya did not seem that impressed after the session. "*I talked about this record on Thursday with my engineers*", he explained. "*OK, so I've beaten it, but it does not mean much. We have found two seconds compared with last year and if there are no changes to the track, next year we will go even quicker. This record won't last long.*"
But the Colombian was happy with his day's work.

"*The car worked really well from an aerodynamic point of view*", he continued. "*It is very efficient. On the circuits which need more downforce, we are a bit behind the Ferraris, but here it went well. The tyres were very consistent, which was a big help in balancing the car. It's good to be back on pole, but now we have to finish the job for once!*"
His team-mate Ralf Schumacher finished third, after making a mistake on his third fast lap. He would thus line up behind his brother Michael, who was on the front row. "*I am not surprised to be second as this circuit suits the Williams*", was the world champion's analysis. "*We should be pretty competitive tomorrow in race trim.*"

Schumacher – Villeneuve to Ferrari?

As everywhere else, the superiority of the Italian cars continued to kill any interest in the championship and it looked like being a case of more of the same in 2003.
This prompted Bernie Ecclestone to put on his thinking cap. His idea? To put Jacques Villeneuve in a Ferrari, to give the Scuderia two champion drivers capable of fighting one another; a bit like the days of Alain Prost and Ayrton Senna at

McLaren at the end of the Eighties.
Apparently, in Monza, Ecclestone had several meetings with Jean Todt, as well as the Scuderia's sponsors. For his part, Villeneuve said he was ready to drive for the Maranello team "*from tomorrow morning.*" "*The Ferrari is so perfect that it is the only car in which I could win races*", he admitted, obviously fired up at the challenge of rubbing shoulders with Michael Schumacher.

Starting grid

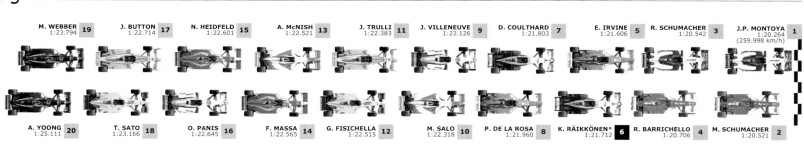

■ * Räikkönen: had his fastest lap disallowed for causing the qualifying accident with Sato. Moved from 5th to 6th place.

M. WEBBER 19 1:23.794	J. BUTTON 17 1:22.714	N. HEIDFELD 15 1:22.601	A. McNISH 13 1:22.521	J. TRULLI 11 1:22.383	J. VILLENEUVE 9 1:22.126	D. COULTHARD 7 1:21.803	E. IRVINE 5 1:21.606	R. SCHUMACHER 3 1:20.542	J.P. MONTOYA 1 1:20.264 (259.998 km/h)
A. YOONG 20 1:25.111	T. SATO 18 1:23.166	O. PANIS 16 1:22.645	F. MASSA 14 1:22.565	G. FISICHELLA 12 1:22.515	M. SALO 10 1:22.318	P. DE LA ROSA 8 1:21.960	K. RÄIKKÖNEN* 6 1:21.712	R. BARRICHELLO 4 1:20.706	M. SCHUMACHER 2 1:20.521

Barrichello makes sure

For once, Ferrari were not sure of winning as they formed up on the grid. Pole position had escaped them and the Williams-BMWs had been devilishly quick during the morning warm-up. On top of that, the tyres were an unknown quantity, especially as the previous week's test had not gone that well for Bridgestone and Ferrari. In the end, all these unknowns delivered the same answer as usual. For the third consecutive race, Scuderia Ferrari finished first and second, Rubens Barrichello ahead of Michael Schumacher this time. It was not even a battle between the two of them, as the team chose to favour the Brazilian to ensure he finished as runner up in the series and with a 17 point lead over Juan Pablo Montoya, it would be resolved in Indianapolis a fortnight later. Once again, Michael Schumacher had to throttle back to leave the top slot to Rubens.

Underneath the podium, the crowd did not care. They came to see a Ferrari one-two and they did. *"It was crazy"*, said Barrichello. *"Michael pointed it out to me, it was incredible. As far as you could see, people were running from every direction. It was a very emotional moment."*

According to the Brazilian, the Scuderia's dominant performance owed much to new Bridgestone tyres, which had only been made the previous weekend. *"The tyres we had today were the right ones. They were extraordinary."* Celebrations were even more joyous at Jaguar. Eddie Irvine finally made it back to third place on the podium, for the first time this season. After the point scored in Belgium, the green team had now pulled off a fantastic reversal of fortune. *"Yes, we have turned it around"*, confirmed the Irishman. *"But actually, the car*

we have today is completely different to the one we had at the start of the year. To be honest, the R3 was born bad and since then, we have changed the rear suspension, then the front suspension, the wings, the radiators, the nose, the gearbox...I'd do better to tell you what hasn't changed: me!"
Naturally, Eddie Irvine was delighted to be back on the podium. *"For a long time I was fourth and I thought that wasn't bad for the team. Then, I was third which is good for the team, but it's also good for me!"*

Massa has de la Rosa off and pays dear

Lap 16. Pedro de la Rosa's Jaguar has just passed Felipe Massa's Sauber which does not seem to go down well with him. The little Brazilian decides to counter-attack, under braking for the Ascari chicane. He moves over to the inside, and gives the Jaguar a serious nudge, sending it into the gravel where its race is over. With broken suspension, Felipe Massa does not go much further. *"De la Rosa passed me by cutting the first chicane"*, explained the

Brazilian. *"So he should have let me pass him. But instead of that, he was slowing me down. I decided to pass him and I was ahead when he ran into me."* The Italian Stewards took a different view and penalised the Sauber driver: he was going to have to drop ten places on the grid for the start of the next race in the United States. Peter Sauber immediately decided to replace him for that event with Heinz-Harald Frentzen.

Race summary

> The Monza chicane. Ralf Schumacher goes straight on, trying to fight off Montoya **(1)**.

> The rest of the pack

muddles through as best it can **(2)**.

> Having qualified 5th, Eddie Irvine ends up on the podium in 3rd

place. It is the high point of Jaguar's season **(3)**.

> Jarno Trulli scores his first points since

Canada. Coming through from the depths of the pack, he finishes a brilliant fourth **(4)**.

> Panis picks up a meagre point. Running well at the halfway mark, he was unable to fight off a charging Button **(5)**.

> Rubens Barrichello takes an easy win for Ferrari, bringing him closer to second place in the championship **(6)**.

> The new podium means spectators can get close and personal with their heroes. Ferrari enjoys the feeling of winning at home **(7)**.

In the spotlight

Winning was still a long way off, but the two Renaults seemed to have shrugged off their poor performances of the summer. In Monza, they both finished in the points.

A fantastic day for the Jaguar team, with third place for Eddie Irvine.

The two Williams get it wrong

The Italian Grand Prix had got off to a good start for Williams. Surging forward from third place on the grid, Ralf Schumacher managed to take the lead at the first corner, ahead of team-mate Juan Pablo Montoya, who had started on pole and the two Ferraris.

While the blue and white cars led the field for the opening three laps, Ralf Schumacher's engine let go on lap four in a cloud of smoke, just after he had let Juan Pablo Montoya through. "*Juan had a problem at the start and I made the most of it to overtake him at the first corner*", explained Ralf. "*But the FIA asked the team to swap places, so I slowed to let Juan get by me again and then the engine went.*"

Montoya only led for a brief moment, before letting the two-stopping Rubens Barrichello slip by into the lead. The Colombian then retired on lap 34 with broken suspension.

New engines for Ferrari and BMW

There was not much of a crowd worshipping at Italy's temple of motor sport. On Thursday, Grand Prix fever had yet to grip the Monza autodrome. In fact, the grandstands were not that packed on Sunday either. It was a symbol of the malaise affecting Formula 1 which had often played to less than full houses in 2002. According to Roberto, business had never been as bad. Sitting at the terrace of a café in Biassono, a little village near the circuit, this specialist in "parallel" ticket sales was experiencing his worst season in five years. If the grandstands were not full, there was no need for spectators to pay inflated prices on the black market.

However, this Italian Grand Prix should have been more interesting than the F1 processions we had witnessed in Hungary and Belgium, because Ferrari's rivals appeared to be joining ranks. It was too late to do anything about this year, but it was soon enough to prepare for 2003.

The first example of this was McLaren's offer of a non-aggression pact with Williams, which would see the two teams pool information, which might help them speed up development of their Michelin tyres. At the same time, BMW had brought out a new engine for Monza. It's power output was reckoned to approach the 900 horsepower mark. This was a good time to bring it along, given that the Italian track features long straights.

However, no one was panicking at Ferrari. The Scuderia had also come up with a new, supposedly more powerful, engine. "*I hope we can score another one-two here*", said Michael Schumacher on Thursday. "*It would be arrogant to say we will, but we will do our best. It will definitely be harder than in Belgium.*" The previous week, at a test session attended by all the teams, the Ferraris were well off the pace. But come the race and they were back to their old habits.

Kimi Räikkönen and Takuma Sato had a very bad crash on Saturday. While the McLaren escaped almost intact, the Jordan was much more seriously damaged.

>

Action! Watched by the two Saubers, Jacques Villeneuve tries to overtake David Coulthard in the braking area at the Ascari chicane.

v

Finnish-Nippon fracas

Saturday's qualifying session had to be interrupted two minutes from the end, after a serious accident involving the McLaren of Kimi Räikkönen and the Jordan of Takuma Sato. The Finn did not see the Japanese driver coming up behind him, moved over and sent the Jordan off the track. The yellow car shot across the gravel trap and slammed into the tyre barriers at the second chicane.

"*It was just a racing accident*", justified Räikkönen. "*Takuma was on his fifth fast lap in a row and the team came on the radio and told me he was* probably coming into the pits and therefore going slowly. I did not see him in my mirrors, I moved across and that was it.*" Naturally, the Japanese driver had a different slant on things. "*This has been the hardest qualifying session of my career*", he commented. "*The car was far from perfect and I also made a few mistakes. But Kimi was cruising and by the way he moved over, he had obviously not seen me. It was lucky that my car was slowed by the gravel trap before hitting the barrier.*" The two men had a face-to-face after the session.

Weekend gossip

> Several models made the most of the Italian sun to show off their charms in the Monza paddock: amongst them, Megan Gale, the official "face" of Vodafone, sponsors to Scuderia Ferrari.

> The Prince of Bahrain, HH Shaikh Salman bin Hamed Al Khalifa announced in Monza that he had just signed a deal with Bernie Ecclestone to host a Grand Prix in 2004.

> The two Saubers turned up in Monza with the HANS system fitted, developed by FIA to give better protection to a driver's head and neck in the case of an accident. Next year, the system will be compulsory in F1, even though many drivers are against it.

> Alex Yoong was back in a Minardi, after his place had been taken, brilliantly for the past two races, by the young British driver Anthony Davidson. Yoong was soon back in his usual groove, qualifying last. But at least he got on the grid and went on to finish 13th.

> No sign of the Arrows team in Monza. For the third consecutive time, the team had failed to show up, which seemed to sign its death knell. Apparently, negotiations regarding its sale to an American group were stagnating. But who would buy a team which had just lost its share of the TV rights money, because of repeated no-shows?

> For a while, the race results were only provisional on Sunday. The scrutineers decided to have a good look at the engine in Ferrari number 1. Its V10 was sealed and routine controls (capacity, electronics and so on) were carried out the next day.

> A sad weekend for McLaren. Kimi Räikkönen was running fourth when his engine let go on lap 30. David Coulthard finished 7th, just outside the points.

Practice

All the time trials

N°	Driver	Car/Engine/Chassis	Practice friday	Pos.	Practice saturday	Pos.	Qualifying	Pos.	Warm-up	Pos.
1.	Michael Schumacher	Ferrari 2002/223	1'22"433	1°	1'21"754	2°	1'20"521	2°	1'25"137	4°
2.	Rubens Barrichello	Ferrari 2002/224	1'22"658	2°	1'21"754	3°	1'20"706	1°	1'24"636	2°
3.	David Coulthard	McLaren-Mercedes MP4/17/08	1'25"044	16°	1'22"522	6°	1'21"803	7°	1'25"547	8°
4.	Kimi Räikkönen	McLaren-Mercedes MP4/17/07	1'23"016	3°	1'22"200	5°	1'21"712	6°	1'25"350	5°
5.	Ralf Schumacher	Williams-BMW FW24/06	1'24"115	7°	1'21"764	4°	1'20"542	3°	1'24"480	1°
6.	Juan Pablo Montoya	Williams-BMW FW24/05	1'23"584	5°	1'21"319	1°	1'20"264	1°	1'24"738	3°
7.	Nick Heidfeld	Sauber-Petronas C21/04	1'25"541	17°	1'23"235	12°	1'22"601	15°	1'25"785	10°
8.	Felipe Massa	Sauber-Petronas C21/07	1'24"929	13°	1'23"206	11°	1'22"565	14°	1'25"428	7°
9.	Giancarlo Fisichella	Jordan-Honda EJ12/6	1'24"629	11°	1'23"375	13°	1'22"515	12°	1'26"556	15°
10.	Takuma Sato	Jordan-Honda EJ12/4	1'24"990	14°	1'23"453	15°	1'23"166	18°	1'26"201	13°
11.	Jacques Villeneuve	BAR-Honda 004/06	1'24"833	12°	1'23"142	10°	1'22"126	10°	1'26"464	14°
12.	Olivier Panis	BAR-Honda 004/08	1'25"027	15°	1'23"501	16°	1'22"645	16°	1'25"394	6°
14.	Jarno Trulli	Renault R202/05	1'24"538	9°	1'23"712	17°	1'22"383	11°	1'26"705	16°
15.	Jenson Button	Renault R202/06	1'24"396	10°	1'24"204	18°	1'22"714	17°	1'27"198	17°
16.	Eddie Irvine	Jaguar R3/05	1'23"460	4°	1'22"697	8°	1'21"606	5°	1'25"899	11°
17.	Pedro de la Rosa	Jaguar R3/03	1'24"183	8°	1'22"642	7°	1'21"960	8°	1'30"192	20°
22.	Alex Yoong	Minardi-Asiatech PS02/03	1'26"365	20°	1'24"744	19°	1'25"111	20°	1'28"408	19°
23.	Mark Webber	Minardi-Asiatech PS02/04	1'26"162	19°	1'25"169	20°	1'23"794	19°	1'27"596	18°
24.	Mika Salo	Toyota TF102/07	1'23"925	6°	1'23"442	14°	1'22"318	10°	1'25"751	9°
25.	Allan McNish	Toyota TF102/08	1'25"546	18°	1'22"967	9°	1'22"521	13°	1'26"081	12°

Maximum speeds

N°	Driver	P1 Qualifs	Pos.	P1 Race	Pos.	P2 Qualifs	Pos.	P2 Race	Pos.	Finish Qualifs	Pos.	Finish Race	Pos.	Trap Qualifs	Pos.	Trap Race	Pos.
1.	M. Schumacher	344,6	3°	344,2	4°	346,5	3°	346,7	2°	330,2	2°	324,3	3°	358,8	3°	359,0	4°
2.	R. Barrichello	341,8	6°	346,7	1°	345,0	4°	346,8	1°	329,0	4°	328,3	1°	357,3	4°	357,0	5°
3.	D. Coulthard	343,6	5°	345,6	2°	344,6	7°	345,0	3°	325,7	10°	323,1	5°	356,2	8°	363,0	1°
4.	M. Räikkönen	344,7	2°	341,3	6°	344,7	5°	339,5	5°	327,2	5°	319,8	8°	354,2	12°	354,2	11°
5.	R. Schumacher	341,2	10°	332,7	17°	342,8	14°	333,2	18°	329,3	3°	316,9	15°	352,9	13°	346,2	19°
6.	J.P. Montoya	341,7	7°	343,9	5°	343,1	12°	341,9	7°	331,1	1°	327,0	2°	352,7	15°	354,6	8°
7.	N. Heidfeld	341,1	9°	340,1	11°	344,4	8°	341,3	8°	325,6	11°	317,6	12°	357,1	6°	354,2	10°
8.	F. Massa	340,6	15°	335,1	15°	343,6	9°	336,2	14°	324,3	15°	314,4	17°	356,2	7°	351,3	15°
9.	G. Fisichella	344,2	4°	344,4	3°	346,8	2°	344,6	4°	326,3	8°	323,4	4°	360,3	1°	362,2	2°
10.	T. Sato	339,7	15°	340,9	9°	340,8	17°	338,5	12°	318,1	10°	355,9	10°	355,9	10°	354,2	9°
11.	J. Villeneuve	341,7	8°	332,5	18°	343,5	11°	335,0	16°	326,6	6°	314,2	18°	357,2	5°	347,4	18°
14.	J. Trulli	338,6	16°	341,2	7°	344,7	6°	344,0	5°	326,5	7°	321,7	6°	355,0	11°	355,1	7°
15.	J. Button	345,1	1°	337,1	13°	347,7	1°	336,2	15°	326,1	9°	317,3	13°	360,2	2°	352,7	12°
16.	E. Irvine	338,5	17°	337,3	12°	341,7	16°	339,5	10°	323,1	17°	318,1	11°	346,5	18°	350,8	16°
17.	P. de la Rosa	335,8	18°	337,1	14°	338,7	18°	338,7	11°	316,6	16°	316,6	14°	352,9	16°	352,9	13°
22.	A. Yoong	330,3	20°	328,3	20°	330,7	20°	328,8	20°	315,4	20°	309,2	20°	343,9	19°	345,6	17°
23.	M. Webber	333,5	19°	330,5	19°	331,2	19°	330,9	19°	330,9	19°	311,0	19°	348,9	17°	345,6	19°
24.	M. Salo	341,0	11°	341,0	8°	342,3	15°	341,0	9°	324,7	13°	319,5	9°	352,8	14°	356,2	6°
25.	A. McNish	341,0	12°	340,1	10°	343,5	10°	343,0	6°	324,5	14°	320,0	7°	352,0	16°	361,5	3°

Race

Classifications & Retirements

Pos.	Driver	Team	Lap	Time	Average
1.	R. Barrichello	Ferrari	53	1:16:19.982	241,090 km/h
2.	M. Schumacher	Ferrari	53	0.255	241,076 km/h
3.	E. Irvine	Jaguar	53	52.579	238,353 km/h
4.	J. Trulli	Renault	53	58.219	238,063 km/h
5.	J. Button	Renault	53	1:07.770	237,574 km/h
6.	O. Panis	BAR Honda	53	1:08.491	237,537 km/h
7.	D. Coulthard	McLaren Mercedes	53	1:09.047	237,509 km/h
8.	G. Fisichella	Jordan Honda	53	1:10.891	237,415 km/h
9.	J. Villeneuve	BAR Honda	53	1:21.068	236,896 km/h
10.	N. Heidfeld	Sauber Petronas	53	1:22.046	236,847 km/h
11.	M. Salo	Toyota	52	1 lap	236,311 km/h
12.	T. Sato	Jordan Honda	52	1 lap	235,188 km/h
13.	A. Yoong	Minardi Asiatech	47	6 laps	211,987 km/h

Driver	Team	Lap	Reason
J.P. Montoya	Williams BMW	34	Broken chassis
M. Räikkönen	McLaren Mercedes	30	Broken engine
M. Webber	Minardi Asiatech	21	Electronic problems
F. Massa	Sauber Petronas	17	Hit with de la Rosa, broken suspension and right rear wheel
P. de la Rosa	Jaguar	16	Hit by Massa
A. McNish	Toyota	14	Broken front suspension
R. Schumacher	Williams BMW	5	Exploded engine due to loss of pneumatic distribution system

Fastest laps

	Driver	Time	Lap	Average
1.	R. Barrichello	1'23"657	15	249,289 km/h
2.	M. Schumacher	1'24"242	25	247,558 km/h
3.	D. Coulthard	1'24"962	52	245,460 km/h
4.	J.P. Montoya	1'25"094	25	245,079 km/h
5.	G. Fisichella	1'25"215	53	244,731 km/h
6.	M. Räikkönen	1'25"219	29	244,720 km/h
7.	O. Panis	1'25"335	15	244,387 km/h
8.	J. Trulli	1'25"368	48	244,292 km/h
9.	T. Sato	1'25"392	52	244,224 km/h
10.	E. Irvine	1'25"579	48	243,690 km/h
11.	R. Schumacher	1'25"717	3	243,298 km/h
12.	J. Button	1'25"849	49	242,924 km/h
13.	N. Heidfeld	1'25"867	44	242,873 km/h
14.	J. Villeneuve	1'25"883	46	242,828 km/h
15.	M. Salo	1'25"971	45	242,579 km/h
16.	M. Webber	1'27"104	19	239,424 km/h
17.	A. McNish	1'27"230	6	239,078 km/h
18.	A. Yoong	1'27"401	42	238,610 km/h
19.	P. de la Rosa	1'27"600	15	238,068 km/h
20.	F. Massa	1'27"770	12	237,607 km/h

Pit stops

	Driver	Time	Lap	Stop n°		Driver	Time	Lap	Stop n°
1.	D. Coulthard	36"835	1	1	11.	J.P. Montoya	29"426	30	1
2.	A. McNish	44"962	12	1	12.	M. Salo	27"989	30	1
3.	N. Heidfeld	25"963	18	1	13.	M. Salo	15"611	33	2
4.	R. Barrichello	27"334	19	1	14.	J. Villeneuve	27"945	34	1
5.	O. Panis	27"979	19	1	15.	T. Sato	26"927	35	1
6.	J. Trulli	27"661	22	1	16.	R. Barrichello	26"426	37	2
7.	J. Button	27"710	24	1	17.	N. Heidfeld	26"009	36	2
8.	M. Schumacher	29"188	28	1	18.	G. Fisichella	26"140	37	1
9.	E. Irvine	30"196	28	1	19.	D. Coulthard	25"968	37	2
10.	A. Yoong	7'02"916	28	1	20.	O. Panis	24"952	41	2

Race leaders

Driver	Laps in the lead	Nber of Laps	Kilometers	Driver	Nber of Laps	Kilometers
R. Schumacher	1 > 3	3	17,069 km	R. Barrichello	40	231,720 km
J.P. Montoya	4	1	5,793 km	M. Schumacher	9	52,137 km
R. Barrichello	5 > 19	15	86,895 km	R. Schumacher	3	17,069 km
M. Schumacher	20 > 28	9	52,137 km	J.P. Montoya	1	5,793 km
R. Barrichello	29 > 53	25	144,825 km			

Lap chart

Pos.	Driver
1	J.P. Montoya
2	M. Schumacher
3	R. Schumacher
4	R. Barrichello
5	E. Irvine
6	K. Raikkonen
7	D. Coulthard
8	P. de la Rosa
9	J. Villeneuve
10	M. Salo
11	G. Fisichella
12	A. McNish
13	F. Massa
14	N. Heidfeld
15	O. Panis
16	J. Button
17	T. Sato
18	M. Webber
19	A. Yoong
20	J. Trulli

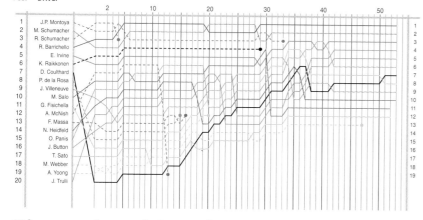

Gaps on the leader board

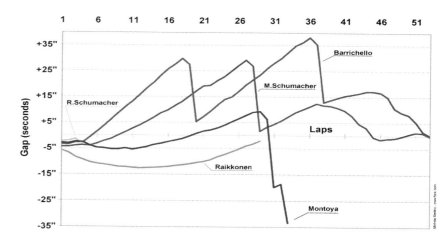

Championship after fifteen rounds

Drivers

1. **M. Schumacher** **128**
2. R. Barrichello 61
3. J.P. Montoya 44
4. R. Schumacher 42
5. D. Coulthard 37
6. K. Räikkönen 20
7. J. Button 13
8. E. Irvine 8
9. J. Trulli 7
10. N. Heidfeld 7
11. G. Fisichella 7
12. F. Massa 4
13. J. Villeneuve 3
14. O. Panis 3
15. M. Webber 2
16. M. Salo 2
17. H-H. Frentzen 2
18. A. McNish 0
19. A. Yoong 0
20. P. de la Rosa 0
21. T. Sato 0
22. E. Bernoldi 0
23. A. Davidson 0

Constructors

1. **Scuderia Ferrari Marlboro** **189**
2. BMW WilliamsF1 Team 86
3. West McLaren Mercedes 57
4. Mild Seven Renault F1 Team 20
5. Sauber Petronas 11
6. Jaguar Racing 8
7. DHL Jordan Honda 7
8. Lucky Strike BAR Honda 6
9. KL Minardi Asiatech 2
10. Panasonic Toyota Racing 2
11. Orange Arrows 2

The circuit

Name : Autodromo nazionale di Monza
Date : September 15, 2002
Length : 5793 meters
Distance : 53 laps, 306,719 km
Temperature : warm and sunny, 23°c
Track temperature : 33°c

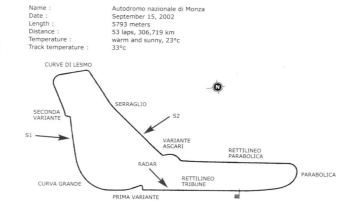

Best result for a driver running Bridgestone tyres:

Rubens Barrichello, Ferrari, winner

MORE CONTROVERSY

After the scandal of the Austrian Grand Prix, where Rubens Barrichello was made to hand the win to Michael Schumacher within sight of the flag, the reverse happened at Indianapolis. Having totally dominated the race, Michael Schumacher slowed in the last corner allowing Rubens Barrichello to close on him, to finish in parade order. It all went pear shaped. In the ensuing confusion, it was Rubens Barrichello who was first across the line, just 11 thousandths of a second ahead of the world champion!

The spectators and the American media were not impressed. This time it was not deliberate, but Ferrari had brewed up yet another storm.

> Michael Schumacher tackles the famous banking section on the part of the track which uses the Speedway oval at Indianapolis. Pole position awaits.

Yet another pole for Schumacher

Qualifying is one thing, the race another. That seemed to be the view of several drivers at the end of the qualifying session at the Indianapolis circuit. A more conservative tyre choice on Saturday afternoon ought to pay dividends in the race. David Coulthard was definitely banking on this theory, having qualified his McLaren-Mercedes in third place. "*Tyres will play a very important role tomorrow*", analysed the Scotsman. "*I think we can go very well in the race and I hope we can maintain our qualifying pace.*"

His team-mate Kimi Räikkönen was only sixth on the grid, just two tenths of a second slower. In Indianapolis, the lap times were all very close as the track layout demands less from the chassis than others such as Spa or Barcelona. "*I am a bit disappointed to be only sixth of course, but the fact I had to take the spare car did not help*", explained the Finn. Meanwhile, Scuderia Ferrari had both its cars on the front row, while the best performance for a Williams-BMW was Juan Pablo Montoya's fourth place. "*I am disappointed and frustrated*", snapped the Colombian. "*This was not the result I was expecting and it's a shame to lose a place to David (Coulthard) for just one thousandth of a second. I will be starting the race from the dirty side of the track, which won't help either.*"

Heinz-Harald Frentzen back in an F1 car for one race. Until 2003 that is.
∨

"HH" comes home

14h00, Friday afternoon. The first day of free practice was over. Looking relaxed in shiny new Sauber overalls, Heinz-Harald Frentzen took off his helmet and a small smile creased his lips which proved he was happy to be back behind the wheel of a Formula 1 car.

With Felipe Massa penalised at the previous round in Italy – he would have had to start ten places back from his qualifying position on the grid this weekend – Peter Sauber did not hesitate to spot a loophole in the rules and replace him for this race with Heinz-Harald Frentzen, who would in any case be driving for the team in 2003.

For the German, this United States Grand Prix was therefore something of a dress rehearsal. "*Everything went well*", he observed. "*I immediately got my bearings, even though I had only tried the car at a Silverstone test. The C21 is an excellent car.*"

With South America not far away, hordes of Colombians had arrived in Indianapolis to cheer on their idol, Juan Pablo Montoya.
∨

Starting grid

Row (odd)	Driver	Time		Driver	Time
19	M. SALO	1:13.213			
17	P. DE LA ROSA	1:12.739			
15	T. SATO	1:12.647			
13	E. IRVINE	1:12.282			
11	H-H. FRENTZEN	1:12.083			
9	G. FISICHELLA	1:11.902			
7	J. VILLENEUVE	1:11.738			
5	R. SCHUMACHER	1:11.587			
3	D. COULTHARD	1:11.413			
1	M. SCHUMACHER	1:10.790 (213.182 km/h)			

Row (even)	Driver	Time
20	A. YOONG	1:13.809
18	M. WEBBER	1:13.128
16	A. McNISH	1:12.723
14	J. BUTTON	1:12.401
12	O. PANIS	1:12.161
10	N. HEIDFELD	1:11.953
8	J. TRULLI	1:11.888
6	K. RÄIKKÖNEN	1:11.633
4	J.P. MONTOYA	1:11.414
2	R. BARRICHELLO	1:11.058

Barrichello by a hundredth

The two Ferrari drivers had run out of ideas for spicing up the races! While Michael Schumacher had shown he was the master of the United States Grand Prix and was about to take the chequered flag, he slowed at the very last corner to let his team-mate close up going down the finish straight. The two men crossed the line side by side, at least to the naked eye and neither man knew which of them had been designated the winner by the timing beam. On the screens, it was the name of Rubens Barrichello which appeared at the top of the order; at first with a lead of 0.0 seconds over Michael Schumacher and then, when the figures were taken to the nearest thousandth of a second by the TAG Heuer timing system, the gap was revealed as 11 thousandths of a second in favour of the Brazilian. At the end of a 306 kilometre race, that represented a distance of just …62 centimetres!

It had not been planned that way by the two drivers concerned. *"Our team has been fantastic this season with everyone working well together"*, explained Michael Schumacher. *"At the last corner, I slowed to try and arrange a dead heat with*

Rubens. But we got it a bit wrong! But anyway, Rubens deserved this win for everything he has done for the team this season. There was nothing planned, but in one way, I have paid him back for what he did in Austria."

For his part, the Brazilian seemed a bit embarrassed to have taken a win which was not his. Michael Schumacher had led for 73 laps, apart from a brief moment during the pit stops and the final 300 metres! *"To be honest, I wasn't really sure what to do"*, mumbled Barrichello. *"We had good fun in the race and we were flat out from start to finish, then when I saw Michael slow in the last corner, I hesitated. We had not talked about it before the race. I wanted to make a dead heat, but I ended up in front. What can I say?"*

On the pit wall, Scuderia boss Jean Todt seemed to find the situation amusing. Whatever the outcome, Ferrari had achieved its goal for the weekend, as Rubens Barrichello had now secured second place in the championship. It was the perfect place for a one-two finish, given that the United States is the biggest market in the world for the Prancing Horse marque.

^
"So that's how you steal my win is it?" It was all smiles on the podium and the two Ferrari men seemed pleased with their efforts at surprising the crowd.

Technical Director Patrick Head and team principal Frank Williams could not calm down after the race: their two drivers had collided on the second lap, costing Ralf Schumacher one place and some points. Given the shunt was his fault and that he also nearly wiped out his team-mate in Monza, the German could expect a serious dressing down from his masters.
v

Negative reaction and lively discussion

It seemed that Scuderia Ferrari could not bring itself to win the world championship in the quiet understated style of great champions.

After the infamous inversion of the finishing order in the Austrian Grand Prix and the manipulated outcome to the Grands Prix in Europe, Hungary and Italy, where Michael Schumacher meekly held station behind Rubens Barrichello, the final bouquet to a controversial season was thrown on stage in the United States Grand Prix.

However, this time, no pre-planned strategy was involved. Michael Schumacher had simply wanted both Ferraris to cross the line side by side *"to make it look nicer!"*

Problem was, Rubens Barrichello had no way of knowing and ended up winning the race.

In the hours after the race, the two drivers spent ages justifying their actions with varying degrees of success. Michael Schumacher began by invoking a problem of coordination, before claiming it was a payback for what had happened in Austria, even though one could take the view he had done this at least three times already.

On Sunday in the paddock, the reactions were mainly negative. *"It would have been better for the sport if the race had not ended this way"*, maintained David Coulthard, one of the few who dared express any opinion. After the storm of protest following the Austrian Grand Prix, FIA President Max Mosley had warned the Scuderia not to do it again.

At that time, Ferrari, Michael Schumacher and Rubens Barrichello had been censured by the FIA World Council, but their offence was simply to have swapped places on the podium and had nothing to do with what happened on the track.

The day after this latest episode, the American press did not hold back. *"Ferrari sparks controversy"* was the Indianapolis Star headline on Monday. *"In America, we race to the last corner, without taking points or strategy into account"*, said the TV sports presenter on Sunday night on Channel 13. In the United States, victory is all that matters and gifted wins are not part of the scene, hence the general incomprehension of what occurred at Indy.

Race summary

> Start (1).

> The pack threads its way through the first chicane. Schumacher is long gone, so

Barrichello leads the way (2).

> Start of lap 2. Montoya jinks outside Ralf Schumacher at

the end of the straight. The German brakes late and rams his team-mate (3). Schumacher has to pit for a new rear

wing (4).

> Starting 7th, Villeneuve finishes in the points once again; the first time since

Silverstone (5).

> After Italy, Jarno Trulli is in the points again. He holds off Villeneuve to take 5th

place (6).

> The famous Indianapolis podium. The winning car is raised in front of

Barrichello's eyes, still incredulous at having won (7).

Gentlemen, start your engines!

Set inside the famous IMS (Indianapolis Motor Speedway) the Formula 1 circuit makes the most of the gigantic setting of the American oval.

Sarah Fisher drives a McLaren: the feminine touch comes to F1

Fourth in qualifying, Juan Pablo Montoya finished fourth at the end of a lonely race.

Sarah Fisher got to drive her three laps thanks to Bernie Ecclestone, who agreed to change the day's timetable to fit in her run.

She is just 1 metre 58 tall and is only 21 years old. But that does not stop her. Sarah Fisher raced this season in IRL, a single seater formula with very powerful cars running only on oval circuits. It is the sort of racing that requires a big heart and according to some, some other large organs, located between the legs of the male of the species.

That at least was the perceived wisdom, until little Sarah Fisher took pole position at the Kentucky Speedway oval on 11th August 2002. She also finished fourth at Nazareth and has taken part several times in the daunting Indy 500.

On Friday, after the Formula 1 practice, Sarah Fisher also did three laps of the grand prix track at Indianapolis, at the wheel of a McLaren Formula 1 car. The drive was organised by sponsor TAG Heuer. After a slow first sighting lap, she lapped in 1:32.651. It was nothing special, but no one had asked her to go for pole.

She was all smiles as she stepped from the cockpit. "Every racer in the world, including Americans, wants to try a Formula 1 car, as it is so extreme. The acceleration and braking are fantastic. The first time I hit the throttle, I said *"Whoa, my God, thank goodness these cars have traction control to deal with so much power!"* It was a very short run, as she only completed one quick lap. *"It was super and great fun. I was just thinking about taking Turn 4 flat out, when they called me on the radio and told me to come in."*

Fisher did not find the drive physically demanding. *"I can't see any reason why there aren't more lady racing drivers. I was lucky to have parents who started me racing when I was five. That means I've been racing for 17 years and the problem is that a lot of women start late, in their thirties. That's too late."*

Sarah Fisher would have fond memories of her experience. *"I don't know how fast I was going, as I did not have time to look at the dashboard! And these F1 steering wheels are too complicated with too many buttons! That's F1, it's high tech."*

As an Indianapolis resident, Sarah Fisher was a spectator for the grand prix. No doubt the thought crossed her mind that she would like to be on the grid one day.

results

Practice

All the time trials

N°	Driver	Car/Engine/Chassis	Practice friday	Pos.	Practice saturday	Pos.	Qualifying	Pos.	Warm-up	Pos.
1.	Michael Schumacher	Ferrari 2002/223	1'13"548	1°	1'11"158	1°	1'10"790	1°	1'13"183	1°
2.	Rubens Barrichello	Ferrari 2002/222			1'11"394	2°	1'11"058	2°	1'13"321	2°
3.	David Coulthard	McLaren-Mercedes MP4/17/06	1'14"919	3°	1'11"909	5°	1'11"413	3°	1'13"930	8°
4.	Kimi Räikkönen	McLaren-Mercedes MP4/17/07	1'14"986	4°	1'12"162	8°	1'11"633	6°	1'13"765	5°
5.	Ralf Schumacher	Williams-BMW FW24/06	1'15"291	10°	1'11"849	4°	1'11"587	5°	1'14"650	16°
6.	Juan Pablo Montoya	Williams-BMW FW24/04	1'15"632	16°	1'11"992	7°	1'11"414	4°	1'14"223	11°
7.	Nick Heidfeld	Sauber-Petronas C21/01	1'15"260	9°	1'11"910	6°	1'11"953	10°	1'14"603	15°
8.	Heinz-Harald Frentzen	Sauber-Petronas C21/02			1'12"589	10°	1'12"083	11°	1'14"236	12°
9.	Giancarlo Fisichella	Jordan-Honda EJ12/6	1'15"209	7°	1'12"220	9°	1'11"902	9°	1'14"154	10°
10.	Takuma Sato	Jordan-Honda EJ12/4	1'15"659	17°	1'12"826	16°	1'12"647	15°	1'13"718	4°
11.	Jacques Villeneuve	BAR-Honda 004/04	1'15"035	5°	1'12"726	13°	1'11"738	7°	1'14"377	14°
12.	Olivier Panis	BAR-Honda 004/08	1'15"941	18°	1'12"746	14°	1'12"161	12°	1'13"471	3°
14.	Jarno Trulli	Renault R202/05	1'15"256	8°	1'12"756	15°	1'11"888	8°	1'14"254	13°
15.	Jenson Button	Renault R202/06	1'15"548	13°	1'12"878	17°	1'12"401	14°	1'14"074	9°
16.	Eddie Irvine	Jaguar R3/05	1'14"123	2°	1'11"688	3°	1'12"282	13°	1'13"898	7°
17.	Pedro de la Rosa	Jaguar R3/06	1'15"304	11°	1'12"679	12°	1'12"739	17°	1'14"844	17°
22.	Alex Yoong	Minardi-Asiatech PS02/03	1'16"138	19°	1'13"562	20°	1'13"809	20°	1'15"522	20°
23.	Mark Webber	Minardi-Asiatech PS02/04	1'15"629	15°	1'13"547	19°	1'13"128	18°	1'15"257	19°
24.	Mika Salo	Toyota TF102/07	1'15"421	12°	1'12"656	11°	1'13"213	19°	1'13"867	6°
25.	Allan McNish	Toyota TF102/08	1'15"589	14°	1'13"204	18°	1'12"723	16°	1'15"220	18°

Maximum speeds

N°	Driver	P1 Qualifs	Pos.	P1 Race	Pos.	P2 Qualifs	Pos.	P2 Race	Pos.	Finish Qualifs	Pos.	Finish Race	Pos.	Trap Qualifs	Pos.	Trap Race	Pos.
1.	M.Schumacher	268,1	5°	263,4	1°	173,7	12°	174,6	1°	340,3	1°	344,3	3°	341,1	3°	345,0	13°
2.	R. Barrichello	268,8	3°	261,8	2°	174,5	8°	173,9	2°	339,0	2°	345,7	2°	343,7	1°	347,2	5°
3.	D. Coulthard	269,1	2°	260,9	4°	173,7	14°	168,1	13°	329,1	14°	342,3	6°	334,9	14°	340,9	16°
4.	K. Räikkönen	268,5	4°	254,1	12°	173,9	10°	165,2	19°	329,2	13°	329,6	20°	333,7	16°	339,4	19°
5.	R.Schumacher	267,1	6°	260,2	5°	178,3	2°	164,5	20°	329,7	11°	345,8	1°	336,6	10°	347,3	4°
6.	J.P. Montoya	269,8	1°	261,8	3°	178,3	3°	165,7	17°	329,5	12°	338,7	12°	337,2	9°	346,0	10°
7.	N. Heidfeld	261,3	15°	247,6	19°	171,8	18°	168,7	10°	331,5	8°	335,9	14°	336,5	11°	346,9	8°
8.	H-H. Frentzen	258,9	19°	246,1	20°	175,0	6°	165,2	18°	333,3	5°	335,1	15°	338,6	5°	345,8	11°
9.	G. Fisichella	266,7	7°	253,9	13°	174,1	9°	171,1	4°	333,5	4°	333,7	19°	339,5	4°	343,8	14°
10.	T. Sato	261,1	16°	252,5	15°	173,7	13°	169,0	9°	331,1	9°	338,8	11°	337,6	7°	350,1	1°
11.	J. Villeneuve	263,8	11°	254,8	11°	173,2	15°	167,3	14°	334,8	3°	339,5	10°	341,9	2°	347,0	6°
12.	O. Panis	262,0	14°	256,7	8°	173,9	11°	168,6	11°	331,5	7°	342,6	5°	337,7	6°	347,4	3°
14.	J. Trulli			256,0	9°			169,3	7°			336,0	13°			340,8	18°
15.	J. Button	263,4	13°	255,3	10°	174,5	7°	169,2	8°	332,1	6°	339,5	9°	337,5	8°	348,0	2°
16.	E. Irvine	266,6	8°	259,8	6°	175,8	5°	170,1	6°	328,2	15°	343,0	4°	332,9	18°	346,9	7°
17.	P. de la Rosa	264,9	9°	252,2	16°	172,5	16°	166,5	15°	327,6	17°	340,1	8°	330,6	19°	346,1	9°
22.	A. Yoong	260,3	17°	251,2	18°	171,2	19°	168,3	12°	327,9	16°	334,3	16°	334,9	13°	340,8	17°
23.	M. Webber	260,0	18°	251,6	17°	171,9	17°	166,1	16°	330,0	10°	333,7	18°	335,2	12°	338,6	20°
24.	M. Salo	264,5	10°	257,8	7°	176,0	4°	170,6	5°	326,5	19°	341,4	7°	332,9	17°	345,2	12°
25.	A. McNish	263,6	12°	252,6	14°	179,6	1°	171,2	3°	326,9	18°	334,3	17°	334,0	15°	343,1	15°

Race

Classifications & Retirements

Pos.	Driver	Team	Lap	Time	Average
1.	R. Barrichello	Ferrari	73	1:31:07.934	201,475 km/h
2.	M. Schumacher	Ferrari	73	0.011	201,475 km/h
3.	D. Coulthard	McLaren Mercedes	73	7.799	201,189 km/h
4.	J.P. Montoya	Williams BMW	73	9.911	201,111 km/h
5.	J. Trulli	Renault	73	56.847	199,402 km/h
6.	J. Villeneuve	BAR Honda	73	58.211	199,353 km/h
7.	G. Fisichella	Jordan Honda	72	1 lap	198,309 km/h
8.	J. Button	Renault	72	1 lap	197,818 km/h
9.	N. Heidfeld	Sauber Petronas	72	1 lap	197,532 km/h
10.	E. Irvine	Jaguar	72	1 lap	196,986 km/h
11.	T. Sato	Jordan Honda	72	1 lap	196,915 km/h
12.	O. Panis	BAR Honda	72	1 lap	196,339 km/h
13.	H-H. Frentzen	Sauber Petronas	71	2 laps	195,847 km/h
14.	M. Salo	Toyota	71	2 laps	195,756 km/h
15.	A. McNish	Toyota	71	2 laps	195,240 km/h
16.	R. Schumacher	Williams BMW	71	2 laps	194,642 km/h

Driver	Team		Reason
K. Räikkönen	McLaren Mercedes	51	Broken engine
A. Yoong	Minardi Asiatech	47	Exploded engine
M. Webber	Minardi Asiatech	39	Loss of power steering
P. de la Rosa	Jaguar	28	Gearbox stuck in fifth gear and broken transmission

Fastest laps

	Driver	Time	Lap	Average
1.	R. Barrichello	1'12"738	27	207,473 km/h
2.	M. Schumacher	1'12"754	26	207,427 km/h
3.	J.P. Montoya	1'12"798	72	207,302 km/h
4.	R. Schumacher	1'13"260	71	205,995 km/h
5.	D. Coulthard	1'13"481	41	205,375 km/h
6.	K. Räikkönen	1'13"819	42	204,435 km/h
7.	J. Villeneuve	1'13"848	48	204,354 km/h
8.	G. Fisichella	1'14"025	34	203,866 km/h
9.	J. Trulli	1'14"026	27	203,863 km/h
10.	E. Irvine	1'14"190	41	203,412 km/h
11.	O. Panis	1'14"263	47	203,212 km/h
12.	J. Button	1'14"265	71	203,207 km/h
13.	T. Sato	1'14"556	47	202,414 km/h
14.	N. Heidfeld	1'14"557	27	202,411 km/h
15.	M. Salo	1'14"672	54	202,099 km/h
16.	H-H. Frentzen	1'14"796	64	201,764 km/h
17.	A. McNish	1'14"882	40	201,533 km/h
18.	A. Yoong	1'15"347	38	200,289 km/h
19.	M. Webber	1'15"367	29	200,236 km/h
20.	P. de la Rosa	1'15"498	25	199,888 km/h

Pit stops

	Driver	Time	Lap	Stop n°
1.	R. Schumacher	1'31"121	2	1
2.	O. Panis	28"955	21	1
3.	J. Villeneuve	29"847	25	1
4.	T. Sato	28"423	26	1
5.	M. Salo	29"830	26	1
6.	M. Schumacher	28"653	27	1
7.	R. Barrichello	28"205	28	1
8.	N. Heidfeld	28"543	28	1
9.	J. Trulli	32"174	29	1
10.	J. Button	32"311	30	1
11.	H-H. Frentzen	28"361	30	1
12.	J.P. Montoya	31"743	32	1
13.	G. Fisichella	31"985	37	1
14.	A. Yoong	31"446	40	1
15.	D. Coulthard	30"912	42	1
16.	A. McNish	45"106	41	1
17.	K. Raïkkönen	32"883	43	1
18.	E. Irvine	30"247	43	1
19.	R. Schumacher	30"832	43	2
20.	M. Schumacher	28"275	49	2
21.	N. Heidfeld	27"979	48	2
22.	R. Barrichello	27"784	50	2
23.	H-H. Frentzen	27"887	49	2
24.	O. Panis	28"956	49	2
25.	T. Sato	29"264	50	2
26.	J. Villeneuve	28"590	51	2
27.	M. Salo	32"642	51	2

Race leaders

Driver	Laps in the lead	Nber of Laps	Kilometers
M. Schumacher	1 > 26	26	108,992 km
R. Barrichello	27 > 28	2	8,384 km
M. Schumacher	29 > 48	20	83,840 km
R. Barrichello	49 > 50	2	8,384 km
M. Schumacher	51 > 72	22	92,224 km
R. Barrichello	73	1	4,192 km

Driver	Nber of Laps	Kilometers
M. Schumacher	68	285,056 km
R. Barrichello	5	20,960 km

Lap chart

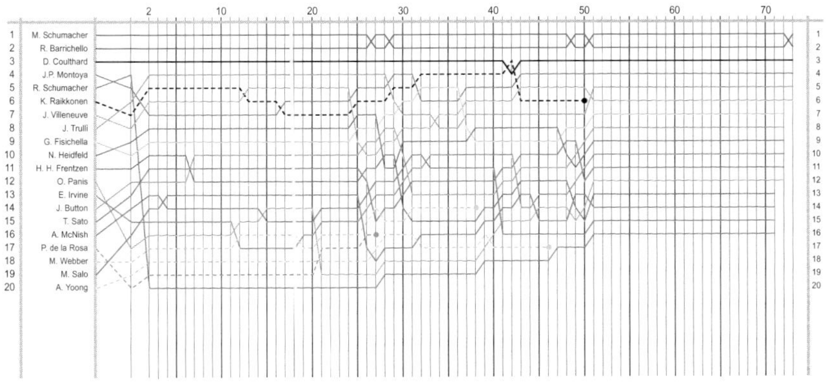

Gaps on the leader board

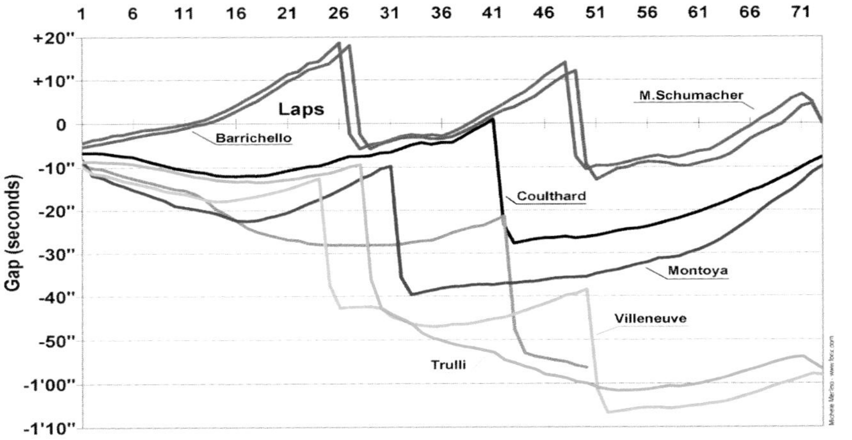

Championship after sixteen rounds

Drivers

1. **M. Schumacher 134**
2. R. Barrichello 71
3. J.P. Montoya 47
4. R. Schumacher 42
5. D. Coulthard 41
6. K. Räikkönen 20
7. J. Button 13
8. J. Trulli 9
9. E. Irvine 8
10. N. Heidfeld 7
11. G. Fisichella 7
12. J. Villeneuve 4
13. F. Massa 4
14. O. Panis 3
15. M. Webber 2
16. M. Salo 2
17. H-H. Frentzen 2
18. A. McNish 0
19. A. Yoong 0
20. P. de la Rosa 0
21. T. Sato 0
22. E. Bernoldi 0
23. A. Davidson 0

Constructors

1. **Scuderia Ferrari Marlboro 205**
2. BMW WilliamsF1 Team 89
3. West McLaren Mercedes 61
4. Mild Seven Renault F1 Team 22
5. Sauber Petronas 11
6. Jaguar Racing..8
7. Lucky Strike BAR Honda 7
8. DHL Jordan Honda 7
9. KL Minardi Asiatech..................................2
10. Panasonic Toyota Racing 2
11. Orange Arrows 2

All results : © 2002 Fédération Internationale de l'Automobile, 2, Ch. Blandonnet, 1215 Geneva 15, Switzerland

The circuit

Name :	Indianapolis
Date :	September 29, 2002
Length :	4192 meters
Distance :	73 laps, 306,016 km
Temperature :	warm and sunny, 26°c
Track Temperature :	34°c

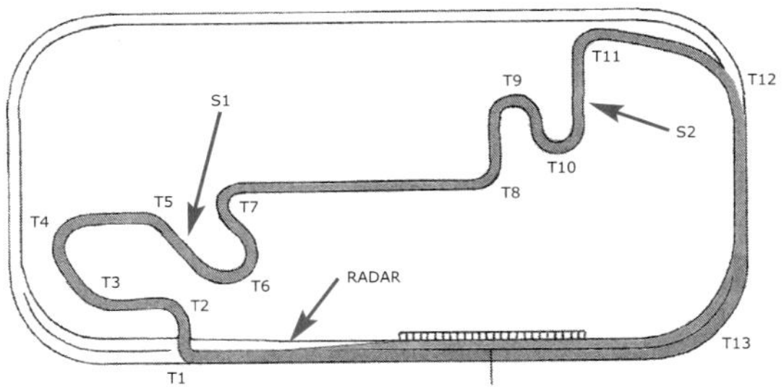

BRIDGESTONE

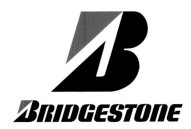

Best result for a driver running Bridgestone tyres:

Rubens Barrichello, Ferrari, winner

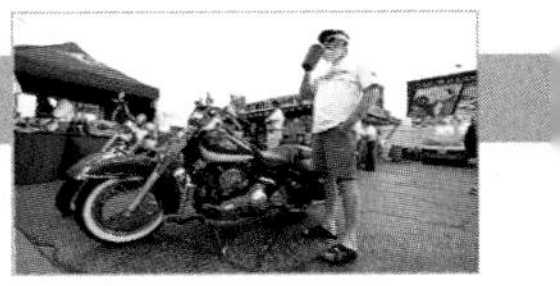

A PROPHET IN HIS OWN LAND

It was the perfect end to the season for Ferrari, with another one-two finish; its ninth of the season and the fourth in a row!
But the year also had a dream ending for Japanese driver Takuma Sato, who chose his home race to bring his Jordan home in the points for the first time this year.
The spectators were delighted and treated him like a hero after the race.

Seventh pole position for Michael Schumacher

Qualifying ended in favour of the two Ferraris yet again. For Michael Schumacher, it was his seventh pole of the season. In third place, David Coulthard was the best of the rest, just under eight tenths slower than the pole time. "*I am reasonably happy with our performance*", said the Scotsman. "*We made progress throughout the season and even if we should be aiming higher, our immediate goal is to get ahead of the Williams, which we managed today. We could not do better this season, but at least we have proved we are no longer that far behind the Ferraris. Next season could be closer.*" In the other McLaren, Kimi Raikkonen was fourth. He would have been quicker if had not run wide at the first corner on his best lap. He was nevertheless ahead of both Williams; Ralf Schumacher beating

Juan Pablo Montoya by 63 thousandths of a second. "*It's always nice to qualify ahead of your team-mate, even if the gap, as usual, is very small*",

underlined Ralf. "*We are not very happy to see the McLarens ahead of us, but I am sure we will give them a hard time in the race.*"

A terrible accident for Allan McNish

Saturday afternoon in the decisive phase of the qualifying session, with a quarter of an hour to go. Allan McNish's Toyota got out of shape in the terrifyingly quick 130R corner, reckoned by many to be the most challenging corner of the whole year, harder still than the famous Eau Rouge at Spa. The Scotsman's car went into a slide, before suddenly correcting and snapping violently the other way and hitting the barrier without really slowing down at all. Fortunately, it went in backwards.

The red and white car was completely pulverised. But somehow the driver climbed out unaided, before having to lie down on the grass bank at the side of the track. He was taken to the circuit medical centre, where a close inspection revealed just a few bruises and pains in his right knee. "*I'm alright*", said Allan a bit later. "*I am going to see the doctors tomorrow morning to decide what to do, but I hope to race.*" The next day, he took part in the warm-up, but his knee was hurting badly and the doctors decided he could not race.

Starting grid

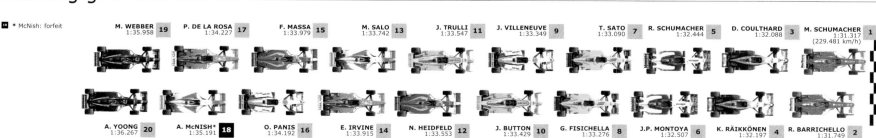

M. WEBBER 19 — 1:35.958	F. MASSA 15 — 1:33.979	J. TRULLI 11 — 1:33.547	T. SATO 7 — 1:33.090	D. COULTHARD 3 — 1:32.088
P. DE LA ROSA 17 — 1:34.227	M. SALO 13 — 1:33.742	J. VILLENEUVE 9 — 1:33.349	R. SCHUMACHER 5 — 1:32.444	M. SCHUMACHER 1 — 1:31.317 (229.481 km/h)

A. YOONG 20 — 1:36.267	O. PANIS 16 — 1:34.192	N. HEIDFELD 12 — 1:33.553	J. BUTTON 10 — 1:33.429	J.P. MONTOYA 6 — 1:32.507	R. BARRICHELLO 2 — 1:31.749
A. McNISH* 18 — 1:35.191	E. IRVINE 14 — 1:33.915	G. FISICHELLA 8 — 1:33.276	K. RÄIKKÖNEN 4 — 1:32.197

A record breaking year for Ferrari

"Nobody had expected it at the start of the season. Normally, to do something like this is impossible." As he got off the podium, Michael Schumacher was forced to admit that the 2002 season, just ended with another Ferrari one-two, had really been exceptional, possibly unique in the history of motor sport.
In Suzuka, the five times world champion recorded his eleventh win of the season (a record), scoring a total of 144 points (another record) and finishing every single race on the podium (a third record). In fact, apart from the Malaysian Grand Prix, where he damaged his car and had to come into the pits, going on to finish third, Michael Schumacher never finished lower than second.
He had not retired from a race since the 2001 German Grand Prix; a reliability record never witnessed before in the history of the sport. On top of that, the car was clearly superior to any others on the grid. After such a season, it is hard to see how Ferrari can make their usual claim of hoping to do better next year!
"It's true", admitted Michael Schumacher. *"Our results this year present us with a* challenge for 2003. To be honest, I think we will win races next year, but I don't know if we will win the championship. In fact, you don't need to win all the time like we did this year to take the title. I will settle for winning enough to get the championship."*
Now the work was over, it was party time. *"We will all be at the Misano circuit next weekend for a big celebration. After that, I will go on holiday, but I am not going to say where. I will rest until the new car is ready."*
As the team left Suzuka that night, Ferrari could congratulate itself on a job well done.

∧
Speedy refuelling stop for Michael Schumacher. Another job done another win.

The end of the season could not come too soon for Williams, whose performance was unravelling with every passing grand prix. In Suzuka, Juan Pablo Montoya finished fourth.
∨

Felipe Massa back behind the wheel for one last time

Shadowed by the imposing figure of his manager Ricardo Tedeschi, Felipe Massa was all smiles in the Suzuka paddock. He was back in the Sauber C21 cockpit this weekend and, for the time being, that was all that mattered. The penalty imposed on him in Monza, for having caused an accident involving Pedro de la Rosa (moving back ten places on the grid in the United States) had meant he missed the race in Indianapolis, replaced by Heinz-Harald Frentzen.
But the penalty was long forgotten and the Brazilian was back in harness and happy again. *"Of course I am delighted to be back racing again"*, he said. *"And I love this circuit. It's my first time here, but it is even better than I expected. It's even better than Spa."*
However, it seemed that this Japanese Grand Prix would be the last of his short career in Formula 1. A career that began in March with the Australian Grand Prix and in the course of which, Massa proved he was a worthy contender. Two sixth places and a fifth meant he was 13th in the drivers' championship and five times he proved to be quicker than his more experienced team-mate Nick Heidfeld, three of them in the last three grands prix.
Despite this solid performance, Peter Sauber had decided to replace him with the veteran Heinz-Harald Frentzen for 2003. Felipe Massa was thus without a drive.
Toyota was apparently looking for a Brazilian driver to second Olivier Panis in its F1 team next year, but the Japanese were apparently angling for Christiano de Matta, currently racing in the States.

Therefore the Japanese Grand Prix might be the end of the F1 road for Massa, but maybe that would only be a temporary state of affairs, given that his undoubted talent deserved better than retirement at the age of 22, or an anonymous job as a test driver.

Race summary

> Once again, Michael Schumacher and his Ferrari started from the top slot on the grid and they soon disappeared into the distance **(1)**.

> Behind the lead group, there was a great battle between Irvine, Massa and Villeneuve. Irvine would finish 9th **(2)**.

> Montoya and Räikkönen would start the race together. The Colombian will try and get past and finishes fourth **(3)**.

> Qualified ahead of his team-mate, Sato made the most of the retirements to haul his Jordan home fifth. It was big moment for the

lad **(4)**.
> Salo was the only driver flying Toyota colours as McNish did not start. The Finn fought hard in the

pack all race long **(5)**.
> Last podium of the season. For Räikkönen it was his first appearance since France **(6)**.

> No wonder Takuma Sato is delighted, as he celebrates 5th place and his first points with his mechanics and his home crowd **(7)**.

The sun sets on 2002

The Williams team in silhouette. A disappointing season for a team which had thought it could be in the running for the world title.

>^
The magnificent Takuma Sato. Fifth and in the points for the first time this season, the Japanese driver was treated like a hero and better than a winner at Suzuka

Weekend gossip

"I wasn't going to dye it red just when Toyota have fired me." Mika Salo was enjoying his last Grand Prix at Suzuka.
v

Champagne flowed everywhere in Suzuka. Bridgestone celebrated its 100th grand prix and its 70th F1 win.
v

> Soccer King Pele was in Suzuka. The Brazilian champion loves Formula 1 and often turns out for the Sao Paulo race. In Japan on business, he did not want to miss Suzuka.

> Asiatech's future seemed uncertain. The Asian consortium who ran ex-Peugeot engines in the Minardis had said in Monza that it planned to come into F1 with its own team, building chassis and engine. But there was no sign of where the finances would come from. A few weeks after the grand prix, Asiatech announced it was quitting F1.

> 100: that's the number of grand prix starts Ralf Schumacher celebrated in Suzuka, as did Bridgestone and the West partnership with McLaren-Mercedes. Effectively, this race represented a century for all those whose F1 careers kicked off at the start of the 1997 Grand Prix season. Bridgestone has done incredibly well in those 100 starts, winning 70 races, including the last one at Suzuka, with a brand new tyre designed especially for the occasion.

> 18h30 Sunday night. As the paddock was in the throes of packing up for the journey home, the Minardi engineers were having fun. They had programme their computers linked to the cars to make the engines rev to the tune of *"When The Saints Go Marching In."* Laughter all round. A few moments later, these same engineers then deliberately over-revved the engine until it blew up. Deafness all round!

> Dr. Werner Laurenz had just left BMW to join the ranks of Mercedes. Managing Director of the F1 engine development programme, he had already been replaced by Heinz Paschen, the engine's designer.

> Was Jacques Villeneuve really going to drive for BAR in 2003? This had generally been believed to be the case, until rumours of a return to racing in the States began gathering momentum over the summer. *"As far as I'm concerned, Jacques has a contract with us for 2003 and he will drive for us"*, insisted BAR boss David Richards.

Practice

All the time trials

N°	Driver	Car/Engine/Chassis	Practice friday	Pos.	Practice saturday	Pos.	Qualifying	Pos.	Warm-up	Pos.
1.	Michael Schumacher	Ferrari 2002/222	1'36"109	6°	1'32"978	1°	1'31"317	1°	1'36"249	1°
2.	Rubens Barrichello	Ferrari 2002/223	1'35"402	3°	1'33"688	6°	3'13"749	2°	1'36"650	2°
3.	David Coulthard	McLaren-Mercedes MP4/17/06	1'34"730	2°	1'33"636	5°	1'32"088	3°	1'36"930	4°
4.	Kimi Räikkönen	McLaren-Mercedes MP4/17/09	1'34"232	1°	1'33"290	3°	1'32"197	4°	1'36"652	3°
5.	Ralf Schumacher	Williams-BMW FW24/06	1'35"995	5°	1'33"233	2°	1'32"444	5°	1'37"167	5°
6.	Juan Pablo Montoya	Williams-BMW FW24/04	1'35"742	4°	1'33"525	4°	1'32"507	6°	1'38"226	15°
7.	Nick Heidfeld	Sauber-Petronas C21/01	1'37"781	16°	1'34"933	12°	1'33"553	12°	1'37"685	11°
8.	Felipe Massa	Sauber-Petronas C21/02	1'37"492	15°	1'34"743	10°	1'33"979	15°	1'37"533	7°
9.	Giancarlo Fisichella	Jordan-Honda EJ12/6	1'36"744	10°	1'34"879	11°	1'33"276	8°	1'37"601	8°
10.	Takuma Sato	Jordan-Honda EJ12/4	1'37"196	13°	1'34"657	8°	1'33"090	7°	1'37"709	12°
11.	Jacques Villeneuve	BAR-Honda 004/04	1'38"138	19°	1'35"107	13°	1'33"349	9°	1'37"628	10°
12.	Olivier Panis	BAR-Honda 004/08	1'37"927	17°	1'35"538	15°	1'34"192	16°	1'38"344	17°
14.	Jarno Trulli	Renault R202/05	1'36"529	9°	1'35"330	14°	1'33"547	11°	1'37"281	6°
15.	Jenson Button	Renault R202/06	1'37"014	12°	1'34"723	9°	1'33"429	10°	1'37"775	14°
16.	Eddie Irvine	Jaguar R3/05	1'36"190	7°	1'34"544	7°	1'33"915	14°	1'38"284	16°
17.	Pedro de la Rosa	Jaguar R3/06	1'36"490	8°	1'35"567	16°	1'34"227	17°	1'38"358	18°
22.	Alex Yoong	Minardi-Asiatech PS02/03	1'39"142	20°	1'37"972	20°	1'36"267	20°	1'41"132	20°
23.	Mark Webber	Minardi-Asiatech PS02/04	1'37"997	18°	1'36"585	18°	1'35"958	19°	1'39"208	19°
24.	Mika Salo	Toyota TF102/07	1'36"893	11°	1'36"265	21°	1'33"742	13°	1'37"612	9°
25.	Allan McNish	Toyota TF102/08	1'37"384	14°	1'36"640	19°	1'35"191	18°	1'37"734	13°

Maximum speeds

N°	Driver	P1 Qualifs	Pos.	P1 Race	Pos.	P2 Qualifs	Pos.	P2 Race	Pos.	Finish Qualifs	Pos.	Finish Race	Pos.	Trap Qualifs	Pos.	Trap Race	Pos.
1.	M.Schumacher	293,9	5°	288,0	4°	313,8	2°	313,5	4°	289,6	1°	283,4	12°	306,9	1°	294,1	1°
2.	R. Barrichello	295,5	2°	289,6	2°	313,6	3°	315,3	2°	288,2	5°	287,4	2°	298,7	6°	286,1	4°
3.	D. Coulthard	296,5	1°	281,8	15°	311,4	8°	309,4	15°	288,2	4°	281,9	15°	300,7	2°	273,7	13°
4.	K. Räikkönen	294,8	3°	289,4	3°	312,3	6°	312,5	8°	287,5	6°	285,9	5°	297,1	7°	284,1	7°
5.	R.Schumacher	293,5	6°	287,6	5°	311,5	7°	312,8	7°	289,0	3°	287,6	1°	299,5	5°	288,0	2°
6.	J.P. Montoya	294,2	4°	287,4	6°	312,3	5°	313,6	3°	289,1	2°	286,0	4°	300,4	4°	285,1	6°
7.	N. Heidfeld	286,3	17°	282,1	14°	306,0	17°	307,9	16°	281,7	17°	281,3	16°	288,4	15°	276,4	11°
8.	F. Massa	285,6	18°	280,4	16°	302,8	18°	306,7	17°	281,3	18°	277,7	18°	291,0	13°	267,5	16°
9.	G. Fisichella	291,1	12°	285,3	9°	309,6	10°	311,6	9°	286,0	10°	283,5	11°	294,7	10°	282,2	8°
10.	T. Sato	291,7	8°	285,1	10°	309,8	9°	311,2	12°	287,3	7°	284,7	8°	300,5	3°	285,5	5°
11.	J. Villeneuve	292,5	7°	291,4	1°	312,9	4°	318,7	1°	286,2	8°	286,8	3°	296,1	8°	286,5	3°
12.	O. Panis	291,3	10°	274,2	19°	314,0	1°	311,1	13°	286,2	9°	282,6	14°	290,0	14°	255,5	19°
14.	J. Trulli	288,6	15°	282,5	13°	309,4	11°	310,7	14°	285,1	12°	283,2	13°	294,8	9°	275,3	12°
15.	J. Button	289,2	13°	283,7	12°	308,9	12°	312,9	5°	284,5	14°	283,5	10°	292,6	12°	276,6	10°
16.	E. Irvine	291,2	11°	286,0	8°	307,3	15°	311,4	10°	285,5	11°	284,5	9°	286,0	18°	270,8	14°
17.	P. de la Rosa	291,3	9°	287,0	7°	308,4	13°	311,4	11°	285,0	13°	285,5	6°	287,0	16°	270,8	15°
22.	A. Yoong	284,2	19°	278,0	17°	301,8	20°	306,2	18°	279,5	19°	277,7	17°	267,9	20°	262,4	18°
23.	M. Webber	283,3	20°	277,8	18°	302,1	19°	305,6	19°	278,9	20°	277,7	19°	278,3	19°	266,4	17°
24.	M. Salo	289,2	14°	284,8	11°	308,3	14°	312,9	6°	283,8	15°	284,9	7°	293,9	11°	277,2	9°
25.	A. McNish	287,0	16°			306,1	16°			283,6	16°			286,7	17°		

Race

Classifications & Retirements

Pos.	Driver	Team	Lap	Time	Average	
1.	M. Schumacher	Ferrari	53	1:26:59.698	212,644 km/h	
2.	R. Barrichello	Ferrari	53	0.506	212,624 km/h	
3.	K. Räikkönen	McLaren Mercedes	53	23.292	211,700 km/h	
4.	J.P. Montoya	Williams BMW	53	36.275	211,177 km/h	
5.	T. Sato	Jordan Honda	53	1:22.694	209,328 km/h	
6.	J. Button	Renault	52	1 tour	208,591 km/h	
7.	N. Heidfeld	Sauber Petronas	52	1 tour	208,505 km/h	
8.	M. Salo	Toyota	52	1 tour	208,070 km/h	
9.	E. Irvine	Jaguar	52	1 tour	207,296 km/h	
10.	M. Webber	Minardi Asiatech	51	2 tours	203,761 km/h	
11.	R. Schumacher	Williams BMW	48	5 tours	212,015 km/h	Moteur explosé

Driver	Team	Lap	Reason
P. de la Rosa	Jaguar	40	Transmission problem
G. Fisichella	Jordan Honda	38	Exploded engine
J. Trulli	Renault	33	Mecanical problems
J. Villeneuve	BAR Honda	28	Exploded engine
A. Yoong	Minardi Asiatech	15	off
O. Panis	BAR Honda	9	Accelerator problem
D. Coulthard	McLaren Mercedes	8	Electrical problem affecting the accelerator
F. Massa	Sauber Petronas	4	Off

Fastest laps

	Driver	Time	Lap	Average
1.	M. Schumacher	1'36"125	15	218,003 km/h
2.	R. Barrichello	1'36"345	23	217,505 km/h
3.	R. Schumacher	1'36"590	26	216,954 km/h
4.	J.P. Montoya	1'36"757	38	216,579 km/h
5.	K. Räikkönen	1'36"848	46	216,376 km/h
6.	M. Salo	1'37"761	20	214,355 km/h
7.	T. Sato	1'37"840	35	214,182 km/h
8.	J. Trulli	1'38"000	30	213,832 km/h
9.	J. Button	1'38"046	31	213,732 km/h
10.	J. Villeneuve	1'38"058	24	213,706 km/h
11.	G. Fisichella	1'38"217	23	213,360 km/h
12.	D. Coulthard	1'38"251	6	213,286 km/h
13.	N. Heidfeld	1'38"534	21	212,673 km/h
14.	E. Irvine	1'38"647	40	212,430 km/h
15.	P. de la Rosa	1'38"836	35	212,023 km/h
16.	F. Massa	1'39"954	3	209,652 km/h
17.	M. Webber	1'40"232	51	209,070 km/h
18.	A. Yoong	1'40"937	6	207,610 km/h
19.	O. Panis	1'42"082	4	205,282 km/h

Pit stops

	Driver	Time	Lap	Stop n°
1.	O. Panis	56"848	6	1
2.	O. Panis	6'23"085	7	2
3.	J. Trulli	28"687	15	1
4.	J. Button	29"270	16	1
5.	M. Salo	29"912	18	1
6.	N. Heidfeld	30"713	19	1
7.	J. Villeneuve	29"868	19	1
8.	M. Schumacher	30"576	20	1
9.	G. Fisichella	30"856	20	1
10.	R. Barrichello	30"594	21	1
11.	T. Sato	28"925	21	1
12.	P. de la Rosa	29"885	21	1
13.	K. Räikkönen	30"853	22	1
14.	E. Irvine	29"171	22	1
15.	M. Webber	30"523	22	1
16.	R. Schumacher	29"748	24	1
17.	J.P. Montoya	29"197	25	1
18.	J. Button	32"430	32	2
19.	M. Salo	30"270	34	2
20.	N. Heidfeld	31"161	35	2
21.	G. Fisichella	29"896	35	2
22.	T. Sato	31"196	36	2
23.	R. Barrichello	29"585	37	2
24.	M. Schumacher	29"534	38	2
25.	P. de la Rosa	28"667	37	2
26.	E. Irvine	28"580	38	2
27.	R. Schumacher	27"910	39	2
28.	J.P. Montoya	28"381	40	2
29.	M. Webber	29"060	39	2
30.	K. Räikkönen	28"256	41	2

Race leaders

Driver	Laps in the lead	Nber of Laps	Kilometers
M. Schumacher	1 > 20	20	116,224 km
R. Barrichello	21	1	5,821 km
M. Schumacher	22 > 53	32	186,272 km

Driver	Nber of Laps	Kilometers
M. Schumacher	52	302,496 km
R. Barrichello	1	5,821 km

Lap chart

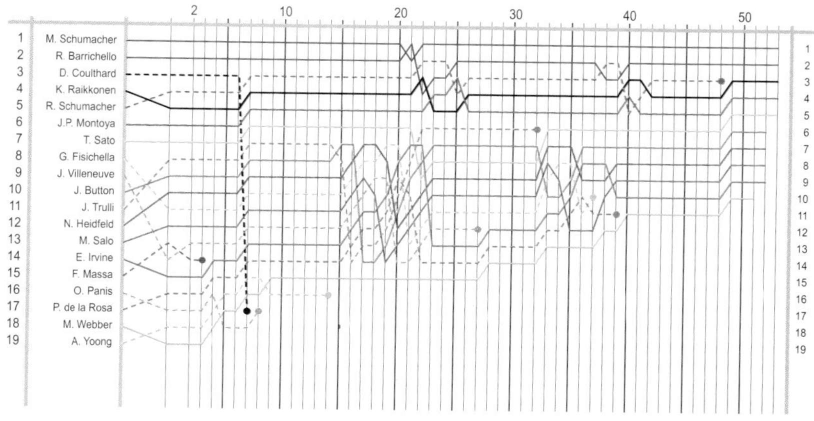

Gaps on the leader board

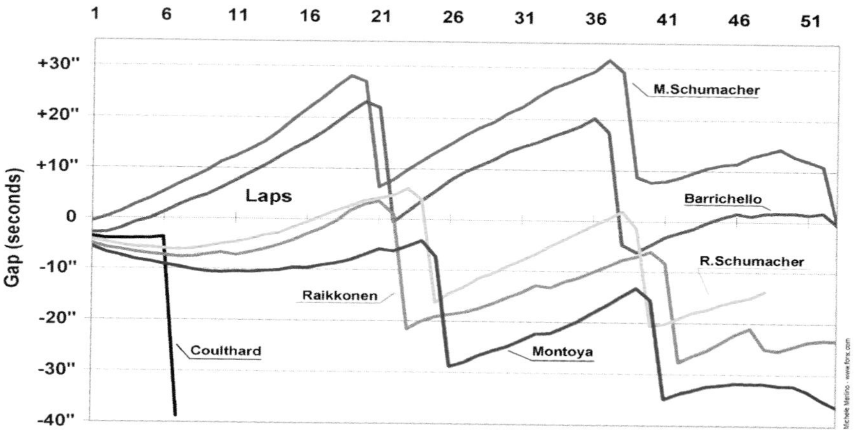

Championship after seventeen rounds

Drivers

1. **M. Schumacher 144**
2. R. Barrichello..77
3. J.P. Montoya 50
4. R. Schumacher 42
5. D. Coulthard..41
6. K. Räikkönen 24
7. J. Button 14
8. J. Trulli 9
9. E. Irvine 8
10. N. Heidfeld...7
11. G. Fisichella...7
12. J. Villeneuve...4
13. F. Massa 4
14. O. Panis..3
15. T. Sato..2
16. M. Webber 2
17. M. Salo...2
18. H-H. Frentzen..2
19. A. McNish..0
20. A. Yoong 0
21. P. de la Rosa...0
22. E. Bernoldi 0
23. A. Davidson...0

Constructors

1. **Scuderia Ferrari Marlboro 221**
2. BMW WilliamsF1 Team 92
3. West McLaren Mercedes 65
4. Mild Seven Renault F1 Team 23
5. Sauber Petronas 11
6. DHL Jordan Honda 9
7. Jaguar Racing...8
8. Lucky Strike BAR Honda 7
9. KL Minardi Asiatech.................................2
10. Panasonic Toyota Racing 2
11. Orange Arrows 2

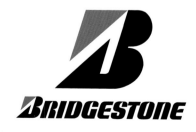

All results : © 2002 Fédération Internationale de l'Automobile, 2, Ch. Blandonnet,
1215 Geneva 15, Switzerland

The circuit

Name :	Suzuka circuit
Date :	October 13, 2002
Length :	5821 meters
Distance :	53 laps, 308,317 km
Temperature :	warm and sunny, 27°c
Track temperature :	30°c

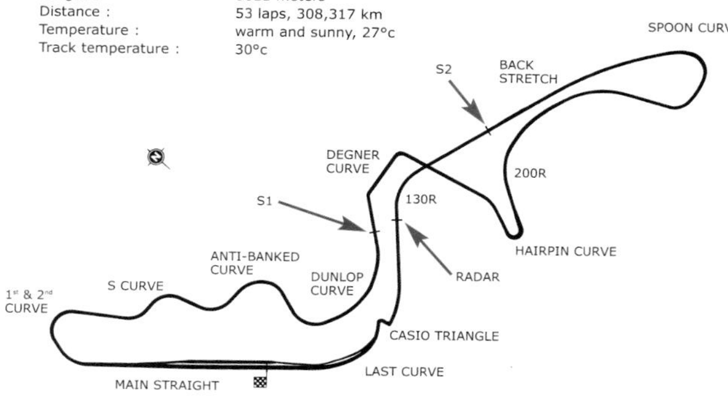

BRIDGESTONE

Best result for a driver running Bridgestone tyres:

Michael Schumacher, Ferrari, winner

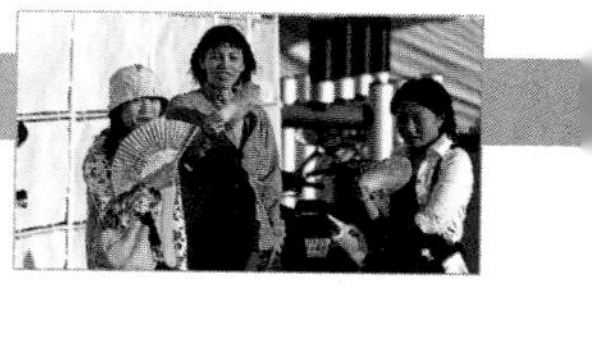

Räikkönen, a strange phenomenon

Ron Dennis has seen a fair few complicated characters pass though his doors and into his cars, especially in the days of Honda power and the turbulent pairing of Alain Prost and Ayrton Senna. This season, he found himself dealing with Räikkönen, the "*Iceman*". "*He is even less emotional than Häkkinen*", states the McLaren boss in a non-judgemental way. So the team has gone from Mika to Kimi, plunging ever deeper into a silent world.

His double world champion had taken a dubious sabbatical, eventually transformed into a more plausible and permanent retirement. Dennis now had to rely on another young Finn and of course, the immovable David Coulthard, to represent McLaren-Mercedes, as it faced up to the inexorable rise of Ferrari and tried to revive its fortunes. "*Wait and see*", was all Räikkönen would say on the subject, be it in Melbourne at the start of the year for his McLaren-Mercedes debut, or in Suzuka at season's end. In fact, even as a little lad he expressed himself with actions rather than words. "*At home, Kimi said nothing*", recalls his mother. "*He was shy, but one day, his desire to race was so strong that he left.*"

At the end of 1997, while Michael Schumacher and Jacques Villeneuve were colliding in Jerez, today's Silver Arrows driver left his home in Lappenranta, near Espoo. He had never travelled, he was eighteen years old and he was heading off to Holland to go kart racing with the Peter De Bruin team, having spent his youth messing around in Helsinki.

"*I was living with a family, but I only understood Finnish*", he says. "*It wasn't a problem. I had nothing to say, I was there to race.*" He started to learn the official language of F1, staying with an English family. "*In 1999, when I started car racing in Formula Renault, I went to live in England. The people who looked after me had children. I spoke with them.*"

However, he did not speak with the Sauber people when his meteoric rise saw him arrive in F1 last year. "*I had bought a big house near Zurich, because I don't like Monaco where most of the other drivers live. I need space and I hate feeling enclosed and it also meant I was near the factory. But when I went there in between the races, everyone spoke Swiss-German, so I kept quiet.*

"*Hello," "goodbye," "yes," "no" and "OK," that was my lot, but it worked very well.*"

This year, having been bought from Peter Sauber by McLaren-Mercedes, Räikkönen acquired a pied-a-terre in the London suburb of Chigwell, while keeping his Swiss home, where along with trainer Mark Arnall, he spends a lot of time cycling around the Zurich Lake: eighty kilometres at a time to strengthen mind and body.

"*Over time, we saw Kimi open up*", reveals Mercedes press man Wolfgang Schattling. "*It was not always easy. At first we were faced with some difficult media situations, but he gradually got more comfortable with it. When he feels confident, he can be funny.*"

That does not apply when faced with an opponent, especially one as diametrically opposed as the total extrovert South American, Juan Pablo Montoya. Over thirty four race weekends since the start of 2001, he has never managed to say more than "hello" to the Colombian. The other impediment to speech is the clock.

"*I am not a morning person*", admits Räikkönen. "*When I was ten, I loved ice hockey. I wanted to be a professional, but I gave up because training started too early. These days, when I have a day off during the season, I go skating or snowboarding, but more than anything I sleep to the max!*"

A champion yawner, he hates Saturday mornings at the grands prix, when he has to head for his car like a zombie for the nine o'clock start to free practice. But by qualifying time in the afternoon, he is bright eyed and bushy tailed. From seventeen sessions this year, he beat David Coulthard, who has been with the team since 1996, ten to seven! He looked on course to claim his first win on 21st July at Magny-Cours, but with five laps to go, he cracked under pressure from Michael Schumacher, going off on a patch of oil, which the track marshals had not yet flagged up. He also made his first visit to the front row of the grid at Spa on 31st August.

Kimi Räikkönen would never have made it to the English or European Formula Renault series, where he was discovered by Sauber, if it had not been for his mother's sister. She was married to the man whose family owned the Rapala company, famous around the world for making fishing lures. "*I come from a middle class background*", he declares. His father was a bulldozer driver, who had to pack in work because of back problems, while his mother worked for a pensions firm. Kimi, like elder brother Rami, who is trying to make a career for himself in rallying with the family benefactor in the co-driver's seat, would not have made it into F1 without the financial help of Rapala.

"*It would be cool to become the youngest ever world champion*", he reckons, at the end of the 2002 season, without sounding as though he is bragging. Born on 17th October 1979, this young man is in a hurry, so much so that last year, FIA insisted his Superlicense was only provisional, until he proved himself, given his major lack of experience. He has until 15th July 2005, or more realistically, until the end of the 2004 season, to achieve his ambition. He will have to do better than Emerson Fittipaldi, who won the 1972 title at the age of 25 years and 272 days. He will also have to put an end to Ferrari's charge.

Although he has yet to win a grand prix, he can look at Mika Häkkinen to see that his dream is entirely feasible. His predecessor at McLaren-Mercedes became world champion in 1998 and again in 1999, having only won his first race at the final round of the 1997 season.

"*What's important in life is to have fun and to do things that are fun*", philosophises Räikkönen, struggling to elaborate his argument. "*And to be healthy of course, because...it would be much harder to do things that are fun if you are not!*" The problem is that, when he pulls out all the stops behind the wheel, his team-mate has no fun at all.

McLaren team veteran David Coulthard can probably feel the ground slipping away from under his feet: after Mika Häkkinen's retirement, he thought he would definitely be McLaren's number 1. But this season, he was outqualified 10 to 7 by Kimi Räikkönen. It must have been a blow to his confidence!
<

Youth: a fad going out of fashion

Frank Williams attracted a lot of attention when he fished Jenson Button out of the British F3 series to put him in a grand prix cockpit in 2000. Despite his lack of experience, the young Englishman had a promising season. But, as the team needed to find room for Montoya, he fronted up at Benetton, renamed Renault the following year. However, he is on the move again and will line up for a restructured BAR next year.

The first to latch onto the idea behind Buttonmania was Peter Sauber. By spreading his net over the Formula Renault series to catch Kimi Räikkönen for the 2001 season, he was looking even further down the lower formulae. But his gamble paid off, as proved by the fact McLaren snaffled the young Finn away from him for this year. Sauber reacted by playing the youth card once again, in the shape of Felipe Massa. The advantage of these "baby drivers" is that they are malleable and compliant and do not require the huge salaries paid out to the super stars. It seemed like the perfect formula for cutting costs and modelling a driver to suit a team's own image, while benefiting from their natural talent and youth which could provide instant results. But it didn't quite work out that way with Massa, who came to F1 from the Italian F3000 series. The young Brazilian was quick, but the team was disappointed with his overall performance. "He is very quick, but young guys like him, capable of fighting it out in the pack behind Schumacher are two a penny," was Sauber's final conclusion.

With Massa sacked, the youth policy suddenly seemed old hat. In fact the Swiss team has taken a step in the opposite direction, taking Frentzen back into the fold, after he was an emblematic character in their early days from 1994 to 1996.

With Panis enthroned at Toyota and Irvine's return to form at the end of the season, once his Jaguar took on a new lease of life, F1 recruitment policy seems to be back on track. In F1 as in life, experience cannot be gained overnight.

Give up this seat for an elderly person! The "baby drivers" are no longer fashionable with the top teams.

(below)
PIn 2003, Toyota is putting its faith in Olivier Panis, who made his F1 debut in 1994.

(opposite)
Jacques Villeneuve, Juan Pablo Montoya and Allan McNish are not in the first flush of youth. Only the Scotsman will be not be driving in F1 next season.
>

The Asiatech mystery

It arrived, it raced, it went, but no one ever knew what it was. The Asiatech group, run by the very strange John Gano, with Enrique Scalabrone as its technical director announced in Suzuka, to no one's great surprise that, *"problems with a previously firm financial agreement prevent us from moving on to the second stage of the programme."*
In 2000, Asiatech had taken over the intellectual property rights to Peugeot Sport's F1 activities, as well as its staff and its Velizy headquarters. In 2001, it supplied Arrows with engines only barely developed from those which the Prost team had used the previous year. In 2002, the V10s went to Minardi. Yet, only four weeks before throwing in the towel in Suzuka, Gano and Scalabroni had held a surreal and rambling press conference in the Monza paddock, outlining Asiatech's plans to run its own F1 team as from 2004, based out of a former Williams property in Didcot. With whom? How? And above all, where was the money coming from to buy an existing team or to set one up from scratch, especially when this route requires paying the FIA a 48 million dollar deposit? *"That's not your problem, it's ours"*, barked the deeply unpleasant Gano. He mentioned *"some rich Asian families"*, coming from *"various countries."* Indeed, when the project first started, the name of Hideo Morita, son of the late founder of the Sony empire was sited as the principal backer. So the operation has ground to a halt and all the former Peugeot employees are now out of work. Will we ever find out the truth behind this strange tale?

< Financed by a mysterious Japanese consortium, the Asiatech marque will disappear from the grids next season. However, that other Japanese company, Toyota, is here for the long term.

Ford, the eternal comeback

Life is not easy when you are pulling F1 strings from America, where the arcane rituals of the sport remain a mystery and you want to appear politically coherent. From its base in Detroit, Ford continues to seem naïve and surprised at the goings-on in the paddock.
It was Ford which was behind Jackie Stewart's team in 1997, providing engines, before deciding to buy the team outright after three years, to turn it into Jaguar Racing. So, instead of finally racing under its own name, with "real" Fords on the grid, as is the case in the World Rally Championship and was in the past in the Le Mans 24 Hours, it chose to promote one of its prestige brands. And why Jaguar rather than Aston Martin? Why continue with it, given that since its launch in 2000, it has failed to win a race. The questions were asked and the board decided to stick with Jaguar for 2003 and beyond, although it is making sure not all its eggs are in the one basket. Having supplied Arrows with customer Cosworth engines, as used by Jaguar in 2001, it is now Jordan's turn to have the benefit of Detroit backing, with one major difference. Its V10, based on the 2002 Jaguar units, will not be a Cosworth, but a Ford Cosworth RS! For almost a quarter of a century, Formula 1 was pretty much Formula Ford, as the grids were full of the company's V8 engines. Back then, Cosworth was a separate entity but it was bought out by Ford, allowing the American giant to compete in F1 without really doing so at first hand.
When things go wrong, Ford is quick to wash its hands of the affair, but when it is winning, squeezing any publicity value out of the achievement has proved difficult. Between 1967 and 1999, engines badged "Cosworth", "Ford-Cosworth" or "Ford" have won 175 grands prix, a record which Ferrari will have trouble matching before 2004. Is anyone aware of this?

Niki Lauda is all powerful within Ford's "Premier Performance Division." This year he embarked on a spectacular programme to transform the Big Cat team.
<

Recap of the 2002 season

Position in the Championship	Driver	Team	1. Australian Grand Prix	2. Malaysian Grand Prix	3. Brazilian Grand Prix	4. San Marino Grand Prix	5. Spanish Grand Prix	6. Austrian Grand Prix	7. Monaco Grand Prix	8. Canadian Grand Prix	9. European Grand Prix	10. British Grand Prix	11. French Grand Prix	12. German Grand Prix	13. Hungarian Grand Prix	14. Belgian Grand Prix	15. Italian Grand Prix	16. United States Grand Prix	17. Japanese Grand Prix	Number of pole positions	Number of victories	Number of fastest laps	Number of laps in the lead	Number of kilometers in the lead	Number of points
1	Michael SCHUMACHER	Ferrari	1	3	1	1	1	1	2	1	2	1	1	1	2	1	2	2	1	7	11	7	558	2764,268	144
2	Rubens BARRICHELLO	Ferrari	A	A	A	2	A	2	7	3	1	2	A	4	1	2	1	1	2	3	4	5	307	1445,188	77
3	Juan Pablo MONTOYA	Williams BMW	2	2	5	4	2	3	A	A	A	3	4	2	11	3	A	4	4	7	-	3	65	297,930	50
4	Ralf SCHUMACHER	Williams BMW	A	1	2	3	(11)	4	3	7	4	8	5	3	3	5	A	16	(11)	-	1	-	44	232,718	42
5	David COULTHARD	McLaren Mercedes	A	A	3	6	3	6	1	2	A	10	3	5	5	4	7	3	A	-	1	1	95	345,647	41
6	Kimi RÄIKKÖNEN	McLaren Mercedes	3	A	(12)	A	A	A	A	4	3	A	2	A	4	A	A	A	3	-	-	1	21	89,271	24
7	Jenson BUTTON	Renault	A	4	4	5	(12)	7	A	(15)	5	(12)	6	A	A	A	5	8	6	-	-	-	-	-	14
8	Jarno TRULLI	Renault	A	A	A	9	(10)	A	4	6	8	A	A	A	8	A	4	5	A	-	-	-	-	-	9
9	Eddie IRVINE	Jaguar	4	A	7	A	A	A	9	A	A	A	A	A	A	6	3	10	9	-	-	-	-	-	8
10	Nick HEIDFELD	Sauber Petronas	A	5	A	10	4	A	8	12	7	6	7	6	9	10	10	9	7	-	-	-	-	-	7
11	Giancarlo FISICHELLA	Jordan Honda	A	13	A	A	A	5	5	5	A	7	DNS	A	6	A	8	7	A	-	-	-	-	-	7
12	Jacques VILLENEUVE	BAR Honda	A	8	(10)	7	7	(10)	A	A	12	4	A	A	A	8	9	6	A	-	-	-	-	-	4
13	Felipe MASSA	Sauber Petronas	A	6	A	8	5	A	A	9	6	9	A	7	7	A	A	-	A	-	-	-	-	-	4
14	Olivier PANIS	BAR Honda	A	A	A	A	A	A	A	8	9	5	A	A	12	(12)	6	12	A	-	-	-	-	-	3
15	Takuma SATO	Jordan Honda	A	9	9	A	A	A	A	10	16	A	A	8	10	11	12	11	5	-	-	-	-	-	2
16	Mark WEBBER	Minardi Asiatech	5	A	11	11	DNS	12	11	11	15	A	8	A	16	A	A	A	10	-	-	-	-	-	2
17	Mika SALO	Toyota	6	12	6	A	9	8	A	A	A	A	A	9	15	7	11	14	8	-	-	-	-	-	2
18	Heinz-Harald FRENTZEN	Arrows Cosworth /	A	11	A	A	6	11	6	13	A	A	DNQ	-	-	-	-	13	-	-	-	-	-	-	2
		Sauber Petronas																					-	-	-
	Then:																			-	-	-	-	-	-
19	Allan McNISH	Toyota	A	7	A	A	8	9	A	A	14	A	(11)	A	14	9	A	15	DNS	-	-	-	-	-	-
20	Alex YOONG	Minardi Asiatech	7	A	13	DNQ	DNS	A	A	14	A	DNQ	10	DNQ	-	-	13	A	A	-	-	-	-	-	-
21	Pedro de la ROSA	Jaguar	8	10	8	A	A	A	10	A	11	11	9	A	13	A	A	A	A	-	-	-	-	-	-
22	Enrique BERNOLDI	Arrows Cosworth	A	A	A	A	A	A	12	A	10	A	DNQ	A	-	-	-	-	-	-	-	-	-	-	-
23	Anthony DAVIDSON	Minardi Asiatech	-	-	-	-	-	-	-	-	-	-	-	-	A	A	-	-	-	-	-	-	-	-	-

Number of laps and kms completed in 2002

Driver	Maximum 1090 laps	Maximum 5175,022 kms	GP finished / GP contested
1. M. Schumacher	1090	5175,022	17/17
2. Montoya	990	4716,475	13/17
3. Heidfeld	965	4572,374	14/17
4. R. Schumacher	973	4531,501	13/17
5. Salo	924	4396,465	11/17
6. Coulthard	941	4357,811	13/17
7. Button	862	4065,644	9/17
8. Barrichello	822	3919,639	12/17
9. Irvine	815	3904,530	7/17
10. Trulli	834	3874,420	7/17
11. Villeneuve	794	3864,753	8/17
12. Räikkönen	792	3775,917	6/17
13. Sato	760	3686,800	10/17
14. Webber	781	3578,606	11/16
15. Massa	726	3418,894	8/16
16. Fisichella	722	3391,756	8/16
17. de la Rosa	694	3303,040	9/17
18. Panis	697	3282,455	6/17
19. McNish	639	2988,803	7/16
20. Frentzen	568	2567,450	7/12
21. Yoong	513	2399,019	5/11
22. Bernoldi	373	1709,277	2/11
23. Davidson	75	348,898	0/2

Number of pole positions

A. Senna	65	J. Laffite	7
M. Schumacher	50	R. Barrichello	6
J. Clark	33	E. Fittipaldi	6
A. Prost	33	P. Hill	6
N. Mansell	32	J.P. Jabouille	6
J.M. Fangio	29	A. Jones	6
M. Häkkinen	26	C. Reutemann	6
N. Lauda	24	C. Amon	5
N. Piquet	24	G. Farina	5
D. Hill	20	C. Regazzoni	5
Ma. Andretti	18	K. Rosberg	5
R. Arnoux	18	P. Tambay	5
J. Stewart	17	M. Hawthorn	4
S. Moss	16	D. Pironi	4
A. Ascari	14	T. Brooks	3
J. Hunt	14	E. De Angelis	3
R. Peterson	14	T. Fabi	3
J. Brabham	13	J-F. Gonzales	3
G. Hill	13	D. Gurney	3
J. Ickx	13	J-P. Jarier	3
J. Villeneuve	13	J. Scheckter	3
G. Berger	12		
D. Coulthard	12		
J. Rindt	10	**Then:**	
J.P. Montoya	10	H-H. Frentzen	2
J. Surtees	8	G. Fisichella	1
R. Patrese	8	R. Schumacher	1

Number of fastest laps

M. Schumacher	51	R. Barrichello	8
A. Prost	41	J. Hunt	8
N. Mansell	30	G. Villeneuve	8
J. Clark	28	E. Fittipaldi	6
M. Häkkinen	25	H-H. Frentzen	6
N. Lauda	24	J-F. Gonzalez	6
J.M. Fangio	23	D. Gurney	6
N. Piquet	23	M. Hawthorn	6
G. Berger	21	P. Hill	6
D. Hill	19	J. Laffite	6
S. Moss	19	J.P. Montoya	6
A. Senna	19	C. Reutemann	6
D. Coulthard	18	R. Schumacher	6
C. Regazzoni	15	M. Alboreto	5
J. Stewart	15	G. Farina	5
J. Ickx	14	C. Pace	5
A. Jones	13	D. Pironi	5
R. Patrese	13	J. Scheckter	5
R. Arnoux	12	J. Watson	5
J. Brabham	12	J. Alesi	4
A. Ascari	11	J.P. Beltoise	4
J. Surtees	11	P. Depailler	4
Ma. Andretti	10	J. Siffert	4
G. Hill	10	**Then:**	
D. Hulme	9	G. Fisichella	1
R. Peterson	9	E. Irvine	1
J. Villeneuve	9	K. Räikkönen	1

Number of Grand Prix contested

R. Patrese	256	E. Cheever	132	J. Trulli	97	S. Moss	66
G. Berger	210	C. Regazzoni	132	C. Amon	96	T. Fabi	64
A. De Cesaris	208	Ma. Andretti	128	P. Depailler	95	A. Suzuki	64
N. Piquet	204	J. Brabham	126	U. Katayama	95	J-J. Letho	62
J. Alesi	201	O. Panis	125	I. Capelli	94	M. Blundell	61
A. Prost	199	R. Peterson	123	J. Hunt	92	J. Rindt	60
M. Alboreto	194	P. Martini	119	J. Verstappen	91	E. Comas	59
N. Mansell	187	J. Ickx	116	J.P. Beltoise	86	A. Merzario	57
M.Schumacher	179	A. Jones	116	D. Gurney	86	H. Pescarolo	57
G. Hill	176	D. Hill	116	J. Palmer	84	A. Caffi	56
J. Laffite	176	J.Villeneuve	116	M. Surer	82	R. Rodriguez	55
N. Lauda	171	K. Rosberg	114	M. Trintignant	82	H. Schell	55
R. Barrichello	164	P. Tambay	114	S. Johansson	79	R. Stommelen	54
T. Boutsen	163	D. Hulme	112	A. Nannini	77	P. Streiff	54
M. Häkkinen	162	J. Scheckter	112	P. Ghinzani	76	J. Behra	52
J. Herbert	162	J. Surtees	111	V. Brambilla	74	**Then:**	
A. Senna	161	M. Salo	110	M. Gugelmin	74	J. Button	51
M. Brundle	158	E. De Angelis	108	S. Nakajima	74	N. Heidfeld	50
J. Watson	152	P. Alliot	107	H. Stuck	74	J.P. Montoya	34
R. Arnoux	149	G. Fisichella	107	J. Clark	72	K. Räikkönen	34
E. Irvine	147	J. Mass	105	C. Pace	72	E. Bernoldi	28
D. Warwick	147	J. Bonnier	102	A. Modena	70	T. Sato	17
C. Reutemann	146	B. McLaren	101	D. Pironi	70	F. Massa	16
E. Fittipaldi	144	R.Schumacher	100	P. de la Rosa	70	A. McNish	16
H-H. Frentzen	141	J. Stewart	99	B. Giacomelli	69	M. Webber	16
D. Coulthard	141	P. Diniz	98	G. Morbidelli	67	A. Yoong	14
J.P. Jarier	135	J. Siffert	97	G. Villeneuve	67	A. Davidson	2

Number of victories

M. Schumacher	64	R. Arnoux	7
A. Prost	51	T. Brooks	6
A. Senna	41	J. Laffite	6
N. Mansell	31	R. Patrese	6
J. Stewart	27	J. Rindt	6
J. Clark	25	J. Surtees	6
N. Lauda	25	G. Villeneuve	6
J.M. Fangio	24	M. Alboreto	5
N. Piquet	23	R. Barrichello	5
D. Hill	22	G. Farina	5
M. Häkkinen	20	C. Regazzoni	5
S. Moss	16	K. Rosberg	5
J. Brabham	14	J. Watson	5
E. Fittipaldi	14	P. Collins	4
G. Hill	14	D. Gurney	4
A. Ascari	13	E. Irvine	4
Ma. Andretti	12	B. McLaren	4
D. Coulthard	12	R. Schumacher	4
A. Jones	12	T. Boutsen	3
C. Reutemann	12	H-H. Frentzen	3
J. Villeneuve	11	J. Herbert	3
G. Berger	10	P. Hill	3
J. Hunt	10	M. Hawthorn	3
R. Peterson	10	D. Pironi	3
J. Scheckter	10	**Then:**	
D. Hulme	8	J.P. Montoya	1
J. Ickx	8	O. Panis	1

Total number of points scored

M. Schumacher	945	B. McLaren	196.5
A. Prost	798.5	E. Irvine	191
A. Senna	614	M. Alboreto	186.6
N. Piquet	485.5	S. Moss	186.5
N. Mansell	482	R. Arnoux	181
N. Lauda	420.1	J. Ickx	181
M. Häkkinen	420	Ma. Andretti	180
D. Coulthard	400	J. Surtees	180
G. Berger	386	J. Hunt	179
J. Stewart	360	R. Schumacher	177
D. Hill	360	J. Watson	169
C. Reutemann	310	H-H. Frentzen	161
G. Hill	289	K. Rosberg	159,5
E. Fittipaldi	281		
R. Patrese	281	**Then:**	
J.M. Fangio	277.5	G. Fisichella	82
J. Clark	274	J.P. Montoya	81
R. Barrichello	272	O. Panis	64
J. Brabham	255	J. Trulli	37
J. Scheckter	259	K. Räikkönen	33
D. Hulme	248	M. Salo	33
J. Alesi	241	J. Button	28
J. Laffite	228	N. Heidfeld	19
J. Villeneuve	213	P. de la Rosa	6
Regazzoni	212	F. Massa	4
Jones	206	M. Webber	2
Peterson	206	T. Sato	2

Number of laps in the lead

M. Schumacher	3'656	R. Barrichello	517
A. Senna	2'931	R. Arnoux	507
A. Prost	2'683	K. Rosberg	512
N. Mansell	2'058	E. Fittipaldi	478
J. Clark	1'940	D. Hulme	449
J. Stewart	1'918	J. Rindt	387
N. Piquet	1'633	C. Regazzoni	360
N. Lauda	1'590	J. Surtees	307
M. Häkkinen	1'490	D. Pironi	295
D. Hill	1'363	J. Watson	287
J.M. Fangio	1'347	J. Laffite	283
S. Moss	1'164	J-F. Gonzalez	272
G. Hill	1'106	J. Alesi	265
A. Ascari	927	M. Hawthorn	225
D. Coulthard	855	M. Alboreto	218
J Brabham	825	D. Gurney	204
Ma. Andretti	799	P. Tambay	197
G. Berger	754	**Then:**	
R. Peterson	694	R. Schumacher	192
J. Scheckter	674	J.P. Montoya	187
J. Hunt	666	E. Irvine	156
C. Reutemann	650	H-H. Frentzen	149
J. Villeneuve	634	J. Trulli	38
A. Jones	589	G. Fisichella	35
R. Patrese	565	K. Räikkönen	21
G. Villeneuve	534	O. Panis	16
J. Ickx	528	M. Salo	2

Number of kilometers in the lead

M. Schumacher	17'090	G. Villeneuve	2'251
A. Senna	13'430	E. Fittipaldi	2'235
A. Prost	12'474	K. Rosberg	2'165
J. Clark	10'110	J. Surtees	2'117
N. Mansell	9'503	D. Hulme	1'971
J.M. Fangio	9'316	J. Rindt	1'898
J. Stewart	9'160	C. Regazzoni	1'851
N. Piquet	7'756	M. Hawthorn	1'635
M. Häkkinen	7'201	D. Gurney	1'612
N. Lauda	7'058	P. Hill	1'528
D. Hill	6'339	J. Laffite	1'519
G. Hill	4'767	J. Alesi	1'285
J. Brabham	4'540	T. Brooks	1'268
D. Coulthard	4'015	D. Pironi	1'240
G. Berger	3'718	J. Watson	1'238
Ma. Andretti	3'577	R. Schumacher	984
J. Hunt	3'363	P. Tambay	974
R. Peterson	3'262	P. Collins	946
C. Reutemann	3'255	**Then:**	
J. Ickx	3'119	J.P. Montoya	932
J. Villeneuve	2'970	E. Irvine	838
J. Scheckter	2'851	H-H. Frentzen	746
A. Jones	2'847	G. Fisichella	172
G. Farina	2'651	J. Trulli	165
R. Arnoux	2'571	K. Räikkönen	89
R. Patrese	2'553	O. Panis	53
R. Barrichello	2'424	M. Salo	13

The super starting grid

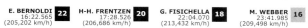

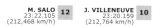

A. YOONG 21 – 20:59.124 (205,322 km/h)
F. MASSA 19 – 22:06.702 (213,169 km/h)
T. SATO 17 – 23:48.831 (208,494 km/h)
P. DE LA ROSA 15 – 23:29.470 (211,358 km/h)
E. IRVINE 13 – 23:27.060 (211,720 km/h)
O. PANIS 11 – 23:21.498 (212,560 km/h)
N. HEIDFELD 9 – 23:15.316 (213,502 km/h)
J. TRULLI 7 – 23:10.923 (214,176 km/h)
K. RÄIKKÖNEN 5 – 23:01.101 (215,700 km/h)
R. SCHUMACHER 3 – 22:52.229 (217,094 km/h)
M. SCHUMACHER 1 – 22:45.865 (218,106 km/h)

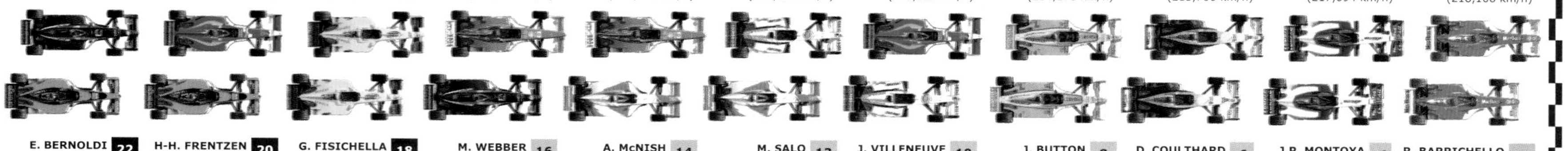

E. BERNOLDI 22 – 16:22.565 (205,202 km/h)
H-H. FRENTZEN 20 – 17:28.526 (206,686 km/h)
G. FISICHELLA 18 – 22:04.070 (213,432 km/h)
M. WEBBER 16 – 23:41.985 (209,498 km/h)
A. McNISH 14 – 23:27.784 (211,611 km/h)
M. SALO 12 – 23:22.105 (212,468 km/h)
J. VILLENEUVE 10 – 23:20.159 (212,764 km/h)
J. BUTTON 8 – 23:13.684 (213,752 km/h)
D. COULTHARD 6 – 23:01.986 (215,561 km/h)
J.P. MONTOYA 4 – 22:53.042 (216,966 km/h)
R. BARRICHELLO 2 – 22:49.723 (217,492 km/h)

The 53 World Champions

Year	Driver	Country	Team	Number of races	Number of poles	Number of victories	Number of fastest laps
1950	Giuseppe Farina	ITA	Alfa Roméo	7	2	3	3
1951	Juan Manuel Fangio	ARG	Alfa Roméo	8	4	3	5
1952	Alberto Ascari	ITA	Ferrari	8	5	6	5
1953	Alberto Ascari	ITA	Ferrari	9	6	5	4
1954	Juan Manuel Fangio	ARG	Mercedes/Maserati	9	5	6	3
1955	Juan Manuel Fangio	ARG	Mercedes	7	3	4	3
1956	Juan Manuel Fangio	ARG	Lancia/Ferrari	8	5	3	3
1957	Juan Manuel Fangio	ARG	Maserati	8	4	4	2
1958	Mike Hawthorn	GB	Ferrari	11	4	1	5
1959	Jack Brabham	AUS	Cooper Climax	9	1	2	1
1960	Jack Brabham	AUS	Cooper Climax	10	3	5	3
1961	Phil Hill	USA	Ferrari	8	5	2	2
1962	Graham Hill	GB	BRM	9	1	4	3
1963	Jim Clark	GB	Lotus Climax	10	7	7	6
1964	John Surtees	GB	Ferrari	10	2	2	2
1965	Jim Clark	GB	Lotus Climax	10	6	6	6
1966	Jack Brabham	AUS	Brabham Repco	9	3	4	1
1967	Denny Hulme	NZ	Brabham Repco	11	0	2	2
1968	Graham Hill	GB	Lotus Ford	12	2	3	0
1969	Jackie Stewart	GB	Matra Ford	11	2	6	5
1970	Jochen Rindt	AUT	Lotus Ford	13	3	5	1
1971	Jackie Stewart	GB	Matra Ford	11	6	6	3
1972	Emerson Fittipaldi	BRE	Lotus Ford	12	3	5	0
1973	Jackie Stewart	GB	Tyrrell Ford	15	3	5	1
1974	Emerson Fittipaldi	BRE	McLaren Ford	15	2	3	0
1975	Niki Lauda	AUT	Ferrari	14	9	5	2
1976	James Hunt	GB	McLaren Ford	16	8	6	2
1977	Niki Lauda	AUT	Ferrari	17	2	3	3
1978	Mario Andretti	USA	Lotus Ford	16	8	6	3
1979	Jody Scheckter	SA	Ferrari	15	1	3	1
1980	Alan Jones	AUS	Williams Ford	14	3	5	5
1981	Nelson Piquet	BRE	Brabham Ford	15	4	3	1
1982	Keke Rosberg	FIN	Williams Ford	16	1	1	0
1983	Nelson Piquet	BRE	Brabham BMW Turbo	15	1	3	4
1984	Niki Lauda	AUT	McLaren TAG Porsche Turbo	16	0	5	5
1985	Alain Prost	FRA	McLaren TAG Porsche Turbo	16	2	5	5
1986	Alain Prost	FRA	McLaren TAG Porsche Turbo	16	1	4	2
1987	Nelson Piquet	BRE	Williams Honda Turbo	16	4	3	4
1988	Ayrton Senna	BRE	McLaren Honda Turbo	16	13	8	3
1989	Alain Prost	FRA	McLaren Honda	16	2	4	5
1990	Ayrton Senna	BRE	McLaren Honda	16	10	6	2
1991	Ayrton Senna	BRE	McLaren Honda	16	8	7	2
1992	Nigel Mansell	GB	Williams Renault	16	14	9	8
1993	Alain Prost	FRA	Williams Renault	16	13	7	6
1994	Michael Schumacher	GER	Benetton Ford	14	6	8	9
1995	Michael Schumacher	GER	Benetton Renault	17	4	9	7
1996	Damon Hill	GB	Williams Renault	16	9	8	5
1997	Jacques Villeneuve	CAN	Williams Renault	17	10	7	3
1998	Mika Häkkinen	FIN	McLaren Mercedes	16	9	8	6
1999	Mika Häkkinen	FIN	McLaren Mercedes	16	11	5	6
2000	Michael Schumacher	GER	Ferrari	17	9	9	2
2001	Michael Schumacher	GER	Ferrari	17	11	9	3
2002	Michael Schumacher	GER	Ferrari	17	7	11	7

Constructors Championship 2002

Position	Team	Number of points	Number of poles	Number of victories	Number of fastest laps	Number of laps in the lead	Number of kms in the lead
1.	Ferrari	221	10	15	12	865	4209,456
2.	Williams BMW	92	7	1	3	109	530,648
3.	McLaren Mercedes	65	0	1	2	116	434,918
4.	Renault	23	-	-	-	-	-
5.	Sauber Petronas	11	-	-	-	-	-
6.	Jordan Honda	9	-	-	-	-	-
7.	Jaguar	8	-	-	-	-	-
8.	BAR Honda	7	-	-	-	-	-
9.	Minardi Asiatech	2	-	-	-	-	-
10.	Toyota	2	-	-	-	-	-
11.	Arrows Cosworth	2	-	-	-	-	-

Number of Constructors Championship
(existing since 1958)

12: Ferrari
  1961 - 64 - 75 - 76 - 77 - 79 - 82 - 83 - 99 - 2000 - 2001-2002

9: Williams
  1980 - 81 - 86 - 87 -92 - 93 - 94 - 96 - 97

8: McLaren
  1974 - 84 - 85 - 88 - 89 - 90 - 91 -98

7: Lotus
  1963 - 65 - 68 - 70 -72 - 73 - 78

2: Cooper 1959 - 60
   Brabham 1966 - 67

1: Vanwall 1958
   BRM 1962
   Matra 1969
   Tyrrell 1971
   Benetton 1995

Number of pole positions per make

Ferrari	158
Williams	119
McLaren	112
Lotus	107
Brabham	39
Renault	31
Benetton	15
Tyrrell	14
Alfa Roméo	12
BRM	11
Cooper	11
Maserati	10
Ligier	9
Mercedes	8
Vanwall	7
March	5
Matra	4
Shadow	3
Lancia	2
Jordan	2
Arrows	1
Honda	1
Lola	1
Porsche	1
Stewart	1
Toleman	1
Wolf	1

Number of victories per make

Ferrari	159
McLaren	135
Williams	108
Lotus	79
Brabham	35
Benetton	26
Tyrrell	23
BRM	17
Cooper	16
Renault	15
Alfa Roméo	10
Ligier	9
Maserati	9
Matra	9
Mercedes	9
Vanwall	9
March	3
Wolf	3
Jordan	3
Honda	2
Eagle	1
Hesketh	1
Penske	1
Porsche	1
Shadow	1
Stewart	1

Number of fastest laps per make

Ferrari	159
Williams	121
McLaren	109
Lotus	70
Brabham	41
Benetton	36
Tyrrell	20
Renault	18
BRM	15
Maserati	15
Alfa Roméo	14
Cooper	13
Matra	12
Ligier	11
Mercedes	9
March	7
Vanwall	6
Surtees	4
Eagle	2
Honda	2
Jordan	2
Shadow	2
Wolf	2
Ensign	1
Gordini	1
Hesketh	1
Lancia	1
Parnelli	1

Family picture of the 2002 Championship. From left to right. Back row: Mark Webber, Alex Yoong, Jacques Villeneuve, Olivier Panis, Giancarlo Fisichella, Takuma Sato, Heinz-Harald Frentzen, Enrique Bernoldi. Second row: Jarno Trulli, Jenson Button, Allan McNish, Mika Salo, Eddie Irvine, Pedro de la Rosa. Front row: Kimi Räikkönen, David Coulthard, Michael Schumacher, Rubens Barrichello, Juan Pablo Montoya, Ralf Schumacher, Nick Heidfeld, Felipe Massa.

Sporting regulations

The FIA will organise the FIA Formula One World Championship (the Championship) which is the property of the FIA and comprises two titles of World Champion, one for drivers and one for constructors. It consists of the Formula One Grand Prix races which are included in the Formula One calendar and in respect of which the ASNs and organisers have signed the organisation agreement provided for in the 1998 Concorde Agreement (...)

LICENCES

10. All drivers, competitors and officials participating in the Championship must hold a FIA Super Licence. Applications for Super Licences must be made to the FIA through the applicant's ASN.

CHAMPIONSHIP EVENTS

11. Events are reserved for Formula One cars as defined in the Technical Regulations.

12. Each Event will have the status of an international restricted competition.

13. The distance of all races, from the start signal referred to in Article 141 to the chequered flag, shall be equal to the least number of complete laps which exceed a distance of 305 km. However, should two hours elapse before the scheduled race distance is completed, the leader will be shown the chequered flag when he crosses the control line (the Line) at the end of the lap during which the two hour period ended. The Line is a single line which crosses both the track and the pit lane.

14. The maximum number of Events in the Championship is 17, the minimum is 8.

16. An Event which is cancelled with less than three months written notice to the FIA will not be considered for inclusion in the following year's Championship unless the FIA judges the cancellation to have been due to force majeure.

17. An Event may be cancelled if fewer than 12 cars are available for it.

WORLD CHAMPIONSHIP

18. The Formula One World Championship driver's title will be awarded to the driver who has scored the highest number of points, taking into consideration all the results obtained during the Events which have actually taken place.

19. Points will not be awarded for the Championship unless the driver has driven the same car throughout the race in the Event in question.

20. The title of Formula One World Champion for Constructors will be awarded to the make which has scored the highest number of points, taking into account all the results obtained by a maximum of 2 cars per make.

21. The constructor of an engine or rolling chassis is the person (including any corporate or unincorporated body) which owns the intellectual property rights to such engine or chassis. The make of an engine or chassis is the name attributed to it by its constructor. If the make of the chassis is not the same as that of the engine, the title will be awarded to the former which shall always precede the latter in the name of the car.

22. Points for both titles will be awarded at each Event according to the following scale :

1st : 10 points; 2nd : 6 points; 3rd : 4 points; 4th : 3 points; 5th : 2 points; 6th : 1 point.

23. If a race is stopped under Articles 155 and 156, and cannot be restarted, no points will be awarded in case A, half points will be awarded in case B and full points will be awarded in case C.

24. Drivers finishing first, second and third in the Championship must be present at the annual FIA Prize Giving ceremony. Any such driver who is absent will be liable to a maximum fine of US $ 50,000.00. All competitors shall use their best endeavours to ensure that their drivers attend as aforesaid.

DEAD HEAT

25. Prizes and points awarded for all the positions of competitors who tie, will be added together and shared equally.

26. If two or more constructors or drivers finish the season with the same number of points, the higher place in the Championship (in either case) shall be awarded to :

a) the holder of the greatest number of first places,

b) if the number of first places is the same, the holder of the greatest number of second places,

c) if the number of second places is the same, the holder of the greatest number of third places and so on until a winner emerges.

d) if this procedure fails to produce a result, the FIA will nominate the winner according to such criteria as it thinks fit.

COMPETITORS APPLICATIONS

42. Applications to compete in the Championship may be submitted to the FIA at any time between 1 November and 15 November each year, on an entry form as set out in Appendix 2 hereto accompanied by the entry fee provided for in the Agreement. Entry forms will be made available by FIA who will notify the applicant of the result of the application no later than 1 December. Successful applicants are automatically entered in all Events of the Championship and will be the only competitors at Events.

44. A competitor may change the make and/or type of engine at any time during the Championship. All points scored with an engine of different make to that which was first entered in the Championship will count (and will be aggregated) for the assessment of Benefits and for determining team positions for pre-qualifying purposes, however such points will not count towards (nor be aggregated for) the FIA Formula One Constructors Championship.

45. With the exception of those whose cars have scored points in the Championship of the previous year, applicants must supply information about the size of their company, their financial position and their ability to meet their prescribed obligations. All applicants who did not take part in the entire Championship for the previous year must also deposit US$500,000.00 with the FIA when submitting their application. This sum will be returned to them forthwith if their application is refused or at the end of their first Championship season provided they have met all the requirements of the Agreement and its schedules.

46. All applications will be studied by the FIA which will publish the list of cars and drivers accepted together with their race numbers on 1 December (or the following Monday if 1 December falls on a week-end), having first notified unsuccessful applicants as set out in article 42.

47. No more than 24 will be accepted from any one competitor.

INCIDENTS

53. Incident means any occurrence or series of occurrences involving one or more drivers, or any action by any driver, which is reported to the stewards by the race director (or noted by the stewards and referred to the race director for investigation) which :

- necessitated the stopping of a race under Article 155;

- constituted a breach of these Sporting Regulations or the Code;

- caused a false start by one or more cars;

- caused an avoidable collision;

- forced a driver off the track;

- illegitimately prevented a legitimate overtaking manoeuvre by a driver;

- illegitimately impeded another driver during overtaking.

54. a) It shall be at the discretion of the stewards to decide, upon a report or a request by the race director, if a driver or drivers involved in an incident shall be penalised.

b) If an incident is under investigation by the stewards, a message informing all Teams of this will be displayed on the timing monitors.

c) If a driver is involved in a collision or Incident (see Article 53), he must not leave the circuit without the consent of the stewards.

55. The stewards may impose a 10 second time penalty on any driver involved in an Incident. However, should such penalty be imposed during the last five laps, or after the end of a race, Artice 56b) below will not apply and 25 seconds will be added to the elapsed race time of the driver concerned.

56. Should the stewards decide to impose a time penalty, the following procedure will be followed :

a) The stewards will give written notification of the time penalty which has been imposed to an official of the team concerned and will ensure that this information is also displayed on the timing monitors.

b) From the time the steward's decision is notified on the timing monitors the relevant driver may cover no more than three complete laps before entering the pits and proceeding to his pit where he shall remain for the period of the time penalty. During the time the car is stationary for the time penalty it may not be worked on. However, if the engine stops, it may be started after the time penalty period has elapsed.

c) When the time penalty period has elapsed the driver may rejoin the race.

d) Any breach or failure to comply with Articles 56 b) or 56 c) may result in the car being excluded.

57. Any determination made or any penalty imposed pursuant to Article 55 shall be without prejudice to the operation of Articles 160 or 161 of the Code.

PROTESTS

58. Protests shall be made in accordance with the Code and accompanied by a fee of 2500.00 Swiss Francs or its equivalent in US Dollars or local currency.

SANCTIONS

59. The stewards may inflict the penalties specifically set out in these Sporting Regulations in addition to or instead of any other penalties available to them under the Code.

CHANGES OF DRIVER

60. During a season, each team will be permitted one driver change for their first car and will be permitted to have three drivers for their second car who may be changed at any time provided that any driver change is made in accordance with the Code and before the start of qualifying practice. After 18.00 on the day of scrutineering, a driver change may only take place with the consent of the stewards. In all other circumstances, competitors will be obliged to use the drivers they nominated at the time of entering the Championship except in cases of force majeure which will be considered separately. Any new driver may score points in the Championship.

PIT LANE

66. a) For the avoidance of doubt and for description purposes, the pit lane shall be divided into two lanes. The lane closest to the pit wall is designated the "fast lane", and the lane closest to the garages is designated the "inner lane", and is the only area where any work can be carried out on a car.

b) Competitors must not paint lines on any part of the pit lane.

c) No equipment may be left in the fast lane. A car may enter or remain in the fast lane only with the driver sitting in the car behind the steering wheel in his normal position, even when the car is being pushed.

d) Team personnel are only allowed in the pit lane immediately before they are required to work on a car and must withdraw as soon as the work is complete.

e) It is the responsibility of the Competitor to release his car after a pit stop only when it is safe to do so.

SPORTING CHECKS

67. Each competitor must have all relevant Super Licences available for inspection at any time during the Event.

SCRUTINEERING

70. Initial scrutineering of the car will take place three days (Monaco : four days) before the race between 10.00 and 16.00 in the garage assigned to each team.

71. Unless a waiver is granted by the stewards, competitors who do not keep to these time limits will not be allowed to take part in the Event.

72. No car may take part in the Event until it has been passed by the scrutineers.

73. The scrutineers may :

a) check the eligibility of a car or of a competitor at any time during an Event,

b) require a car to be dismantled by the competitor to make sure that the conditions of eligibility or conformity are fully satisfied,

c) require a competitor to pay the reasonable expenses which exercise of the powers mentioned in this Article may entail,

d) require a competitor to supply them with such parts or samples as they may deem necessary.

74. Any car which, after being passed by the scrutineers, is dismantled or modified in a way which might affect its safety or call into question its eligibility, or which is involved in an accident with similar consequences, must be re-presented for scrutineering approval.

75. The race director or the clerk of the course may require that any car involved in an accident be stopped and checked.

77. The stewards will publish the findings of the scrutineers each time cars are checked during the Event. These results will not include any specific figure except when a car is found to be in breach of the Technical Regulations.

SUPPLY OF TYRES IN THE CHAMPIONSHIP AND TYRE LIMITATION DURING THE EVENT

78. Supply of tyres : No tyre may be used in the Championship unless the company supplying such tyre accepts and adheres to the following conditions :

- one tyre supplier present in the Championship: this company must equip 100% of the entered teams on ordinary commercial terms.

- two tyre suppliers present : each of them must, if called upon to do so, be prepared to equip up to 60% of the entered teams on ordinary commercial terms.

- three or more tyre suppliers present : each of them must, if called upon to do so, be prepared to equip up to 40% of the entered teams on ordinary commercial terms.

- each tyre supplier must undertake to provide only two specifications of dry-weather tyre and three specifications of wet-weather tyre at each Event, each of which must be of one homogeneous compound only;(...)

79. Quantity and type of tyres :

a) The same driver may not use more than a total of thirty two dry-weather tyres and twenty eight wet-weather tyres throughout the entire duration of the Event. Prior to the qualifying practice each driver may use two specifications of dry-weather tyres but must, before qualifying practice begins, nominate which specification of tyre he will use for the remainder of the Event. For qualifying practice, warm up and the race each driver may use no more than twenty eight tyres (fourteen front and fourteen rear).

b) All dry-weather tyres must incorporate circumferential grooves square to the wheel axis and around the entire circumference of the contact surface of each tyre.

c) Each front dry-weather tyre, when new, must incorporate 4 grooves which are :

- arranged symmetrically about the centre of the tyre tread ;

- at least 14 mm wide at the contact surface and which taper uniformly to a minimum of 10 mm at the lower surface ;

- at least 2.5 mm deep across the whole lower surface ;

- 50 mm (+/- 1.0 mm) between centres.

Furthermore, the tread width of the front tyres must not exceed 270 mm.

d) Each rear dry-weather tyre, when new, must incorporate 4 grooves which are:

- arranged symmetrically about the centre of the tyre tread ;

- at least 14 mm wide at the contact surface and which taper uniformly to a minimum of 10 mm at the lower surface ;

- at least 2.5 mm deep across the whole lower surface ; - 50 mm (+/- 1.0 mm) between centres.

The measurements referred to in c) and d) above will be taken when the tyre is fitted to a wheel and inflated to 20 psi.

e) A wet-weather tyre is one which has been designed for use on a wet or damp track.

All wet-weather tyres must, when new, have a contact area which does not exceed 300 cm² when fitted to the front of the car and 475 cm² when fitted to the rear. Contact areas will be measured over any square section of the tyre which is normal to and symmetrical about the tyre centre line and which measures 200 mm x 200 mm when fitted to the front of the car and 250 mm x 250 mm when fitted to the rear. For the purposes of establishing conformity, only void areas which are greater than 2.5 mm in depth will be considered.

Prior to use at an Event, each tyre manufacturer must provide the technical delegate with a full scale drawing of each type of wet-weather tyre intended for use. With the exception of race day, wet-weather tyres may only be used after the track has been declared wet by the race director and, during the remainder of the relevant session, the choice of tyres is free.

80. Control of tyres :

a) All tyres which are to be used at an Event will be marked with a unique identification.

b) At any time during an Event, and at his absolute discretion, the FIA technical delegate may select the dry-weather tyres to be used by any Team from among the total stock of tyres which such Team's designated supplier has present at the Event.

c) During initial scrutineering, each competitor may have up to forty four dry-weather tyres and thirty six wet-weather tyres for each of his drivers ready for marking in his garage. Tyres not marked during initial scrutineering can be marked at other times by arrangement with the FIA technical delegate.

d) From among the twenty-eight dry-weather tyres chosen for each car for qualifying practice, warm up and the race, the FIA technical delegate will choose at random sixteen tyres (eight front and eight rear) which are the only dry-weather tyres which such car may use in qualifying practice.

e) A competitor wishing to replace an already marked unused tyre by another unused one must present both tyres to the FIA technical delegate.

f) The use of tyres without appropriate identification is strictly forbidden.

81. Wear of tyres :
The Championship will be contested on grooved tyres. The FIA reserve the right to introduce at any time a method of measuring remaining groove depth if performance appears to be enhanced by high wear or by the use of tyres which are worn so that the grooves are no longer visible.

WEIGHING

82. The weight of any car may be checked during the Event as follows :

a) all drivers entered in the Championship will be weighed, wearing their complete racing apparel, at the first Event of the season. If a driver is entered later in the season he will be weighed at his first Event.

b) During qualifying practice :

1) the FIA will install weighing equipment in an area as close to the first pit as possible, this area will be used for the weighing procedure.

2) cars will be selected at random to undergo the weighing procedure. The FIA technical delegate will inform the driver by means of a red light at the pit entrance that his car has been selected for weighing

3) having been signalled (by means of a red light), that his car has been selected for weighing, the driver will proceed directly to the weighing area and stop his engine ;

4) the car will then be weighed and the result given to the driver in writing ;

5) if the car is unable to reach the weighing area under its own power it will be placed under the exclusive control of the marshals who will take the car to be weighed ;

6) a car or driver may not leave the weighing area without the consent of the FIA technical delegate.

c) After the race :

Each car crossing the Line will be weighed. If a car is weighed without the driver, the weight determined under a) above will be added to give the total weight required under Article 4.1 of the Technical Regulations.

d) Should the weight of the car be less than that specified in Article 4.1 of the Technical Regulations when weighed under b) or c) above, the car and the driver will be excluded from the Event save where the deficiency in weight results from the accidental loss of a component of the car due to force majeure.

e) No solid, liquid, gas or other substance or matter of whatsoever nature may be added to, placed on, or removed from a car after it has been selected for weighing or has finished the race or during the weighing procedure. (...)

f) Only scrutineers and officials may enter the weighing area. No intervention of any kind is allowed there unless authorised by such officials.

83. Any breach of these provisions for the weighing of cars may result in the exclusion of the relevant car.

SPARE CAR

86. A competitor may use several cars for practice and the race provided that :

a) he uses no more than two cars (one car for a one car Team) for free practice sessions on each of the two practice days held under Article 115 a) and b) ;

b) he uses no more than three cars (two cars for a one car Team) during qualifying practice;

c) they are all of the same make and were entered in the Championship by the same competitor,

d) they have been scrutineered in accordance with these Sporting Regulations,

e) each car carries its driver's race number.

87. Changes of car may only take place in the pits under supervision of the marshals.

88. No change of car will be allowed after the green light (see Article 139) provided always that if a race has to be restarted under Article 157 Case A, the moment after which no car change will be allowed shall be when the green light for the subsequent start is shown.

GENERAL SAFETY

90. Drivers are strictly forbidden to drive their car in the opposite direction to the race unless this is absolutely necessary in order to move the car from a dangerous position. A car may only be pushed to remove it from a dangerous position as directed by the marshals.

91. Any driver intending to leave the track or to go to his pit or the paddock area must signal his intention to do so in good time making sure that he can do this without danger.

93. A driver who abandons a car must leave it in neutral or with the clutch disengaged and with the steering wheel in place.

94. Repairs to a car may be carried out only in the paddock, pits and on the grid.

96. Save as provided in Article 138, refuelling is allowed only in the pits.

99. Save as specifically authorised by the Code or these Sporting Regulations, no one except the driver may touch a stopped car unless it is in the pits or on the starting circuit.

101. During the periods commencing 15 minutes prior to and ending 5 minutes after every practice session and the period between the green lights being illuminated (Article 139) and the time when the last car enters the parc fermé, no one is allowed on the track with the exception of :

a) marshals or other authorised personnel in the execution of their duty ;

b) drivers when driving or under the direction of the marshals ;

c) mechanics under Article 140 only.

102. During a race, the engine may only be started with the starter except in the pit lane where the use of an external starting device is allowed (...)

104. A speed limit of 80 km/h in practice and 120 km/h during the warm up and the race, or such other speed limits as the Permanent Bureau of the Formula One Commission may decide, will be enforced in the pit lane. Except in the race, any driver who exceeds the limit will be fined US$250 for each km/h above the limit (this may be increased in the case of a second offence in the same Championship season). During the race, the stewards may impose a time penalty on any driver who exceeds the limit.

105. If a driver has serious mechanical difficulties during practice or the race he must leave the track as soon as it is safe to do so.

106. The car's rear light must be illuminated at all times when it is running on wet-weather tyres.

107. Only six team members per participating car (all of whom shall have been issued with and wearing special identification) are allowed in the signalling area during practice and the race.

109. The race director, the clerk of the course or the FIA medical delegate can require a driver to have a medical examination at any time during an Event.

110. Failure to comply with the general safety requirements of the Code or these Sporting Regulations may result in the exclusion of the car and driver concerned from the Event.

FREE PRACTICE, QUALIFYING PRACTICE AND WARM UP

112. No driver may start in the race without taking part in qualifying practice.

113. During all practices there will be a green and a red light at the pit exit. Cars may only leave the pit lane when the green light is on (...)

115. Free practice sessions will take place :

a) Two days (Monaco : three days) before the race from 11.00 to 12.00 and from 13.00 to 14.00.

b) The day before the race from 09.00 to 09.45 and from 10.15 to 11.00.

116. Qualifying practice will take place :

a) The day before the race from 13.00 to 14.00.

b) Each driver is allowed a maximum of 12 laps qualifying practice. Should a driver complete more than 12 laps all times recorded by the driver will be cancelled.

117. Warm up : a free practice session will take place on race day; it will last 30 minutes and start 4 hours and 30 minutes before the starting time of the race.

118. The interval between the free and qualifying practice session may never be less than 1 hour and 30 minutes. Only in the most exceptional circumstances can a delay in free practice or other difficulty on race morning result in a change to the starting time of the race.

119. If a car stops during practice it must be removed from the track as quickly as possible so that its presence does not constitute a danger or hinder other competitors. If the driver is unable to drive the car from a dangerous position, it shall be the duty of the marshals to assist him. If any such assistance results in the car being driven or pushed back to the